Pelican Books
African Affairs
Editor: Ronald Segal

Crisis in Africa

Arthur Gavshon has been writing about international affairs for the
world's biggest news agency since serving with South Africa's
volunteer army during the 1939–45 war. As diplomatic correspondent
he has attended most post-war summit conferences. Working in
Washington, Moscow, Peking, Paris and London, his main base, has
enabled him to build up a wide network of diplomatic and political
friends and sources. Often on personal terms with politicians before
they rose to high office as presidents, premiers or foreign ministers, he
has interviewed and talked informally with successive heads of
government in Europe, the United States, Africa and Asia. With other
members of Washington's corps of diplomatic writers he was aboard
former US Secretary of State Henry Kissinger's 1976 air shuttle – a
mission that aimed but failed to secure a settlement of the Rhodesian
guerrilla war. That was only one among many extensive journeys the
author has made through Africa. His widely published book, *The Last
Days of Dag Hammarskjold*, became a standard work of reference for
its reconstruction of the strange circumstances that led the former
secretary-general of the United Nations to his death in a 1961 air
crash.

ARTHUR GAVSHON

Crisis in Africa

Battleground of East and West

PENGUIN BOOKS

Penguin Books Ltd, Harmondsworth, Middlesex, England
Penguin Books, 625 Madison Avenue, New York, New York 10022, U.S.A.
Penguin Books Australia Ltd, Ringwood, Victoria, Australia
Penguin Books Canada Ltd, 2801 John Street, Markham, Ontario, Canada L3R 1B4
Penguin Books (N.Z.) Ltd, 182–190 Wairau Road, Auckland 10, New Zealand

First published 1981

Copyright © Arthur Gavshon, 1981
All rights reserved

Made and printed in Great Britain by
Richard Clay (The Chaucer Press) Ltd, Bungay, Suffolk
Set in Monophoto Plantin

Except in the United States of America, this book is sold subject
to the condition that it shall not, by way of trade or otherwise, be lent,
re-sold, hired out, or otherwise circulated without
the publisher's prior consent in any form of binding or cover other than
that in which it is published and without a similar condition
including this condition being imposed on the subsequent purchaser

For Laura, Helena and Evelyn
who accepted everything with patience

Contents

List of Figures and Tables

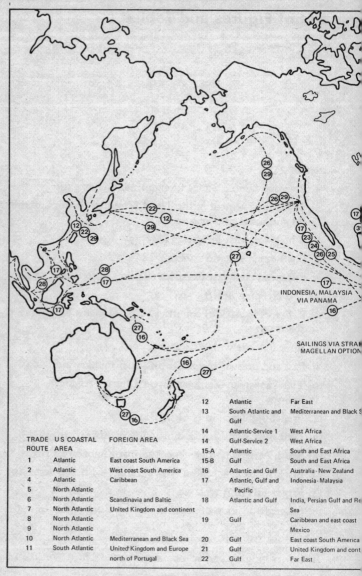

INDONESIA, MALAYSIA
VIA PANAMA

SAILINGS VIA STRA■
MAGELLAN OPTION■

TRADE ROUTE	US COASTAL AREA	FOREIGN AREA			
			12	Atlantic	Far East
			13	South Atlantic and Gulf	Mediterranean and Black S■
			14	Atlantic-Service 1	West Africa
			14	Gulf-Service 2	West Africa
			15-A	Atlantic	South and East Africa
1	Atlantic	East coast South America	15-B	Gulf	South and East Africa
2	Atlantic	West coast South America	16	Atlantic and Gulf	Australia - New Zealand
4	Atlantic	Caribbean	17	Atlantic, Gulf and Pacific	Indonesia - Malaysia
5	North Atlantic				
6	North Atlantic	Scandinavia and Baltic	18	Atlantic and Gulf	India, Persian Gulf and Re■ Sea
7	North Atlantic	United Kingdom and continent			
8	North Atlantic		19	Gulf	Caribbean and east coast Mexico
9	North Atlantic				
10	North Atlantic	Mediterranean and Black Sea	20	Gulf	East coast South America
11	South Atlantic	United Kingdom and Europe north of Portugal	21	Gulf	United Kingdom and cont■
			22	Gulf	Far East

Fig. 1: Essential United States foreign trade routes

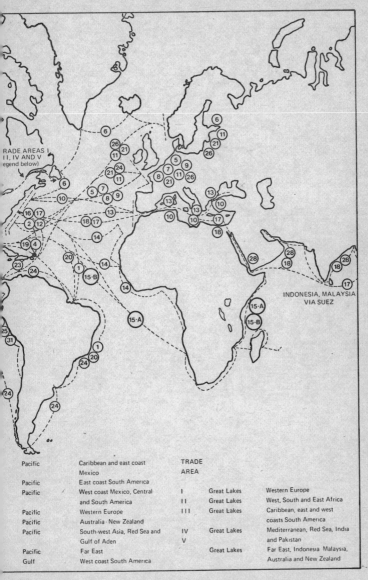

INDONESIA, MALAYSIA
VIA SUEZ

		TRADE AREA		
Pacific	Caribbean and east coast Mexico			
Pacific	East coast South America			
Pacific	West coast Mexico, Central and South America	I	Great Lakes	Western Europe
Pacific	Western Europe	II	Great Lakes	West, South and East Africa
Pacific	Australia-New Zealand	III	Great Lakes	Caribbean, east and west coasts South America
Pacific	South-west Asia, Red Sea and Gulf of Aden	IV	Great Lakes	Mediterranean, Red Sea, India and Pakistan
Pacific	Far East	V	Great Lakes	Far East, Indonesia, Malaysia, Australia and New Zealand
Gulf	West coast South America			

SOURCE: *The Soviet Union and the Third World: A Watershed in Great Power Policy?*, a report to the Committee on International Relations, US House of Representatives, by the Senior Specialists' Division of the Congressional Research Service, 8 May 1977.

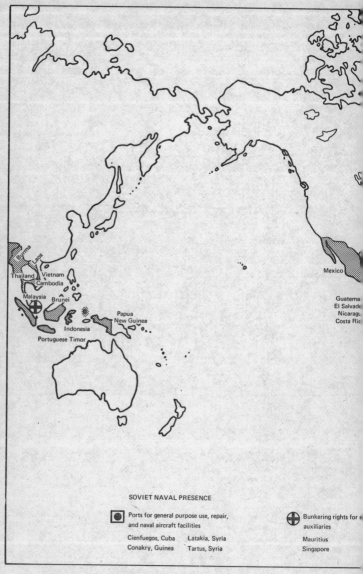

Mexico

Guatema
El Salvade
Nicaragu
Costa Ric

Byrma
Laos
Thailand Vietnam
Cambodia
Malaysia Brunei
Papua
New Guinea
Indonesia
Portuguese Timor

SOVIET NAVAL PRESENCE

Ports for general purpose use, repair,
and naval aircraft facilities

Cienfuegos, Cuba   Latakia, Syria
Conakry, Guinea   Tartus, Syria

Bunkering rights for
auxiliaries

Mauritius
Singapore

Fig. 2: Soviet involvement in the Third World: economic and military
(shaded area – see also Table 1, page 14) and naval presence

Anchorages in international waters

Mediterranean	Gulf of Sollum	Indian Ocean	Socotra Island
	Gulf of Hamamet		Comoro Islands
	Alboran Basin		Chagos Archipelago
	Kithira		Cargados Carajos Shoals

RCE: *The Soviet Union and the Third World: A Watershed in Great Power Policy?*, a
rt to the Committee on International Relations, U S House of Representatives, by the
or Specialists' Division of the Congressional Research Service, 8 May 1977.

Table 1: Soviet military aid (1955–74) and economic aid (1954–76) to the Third World (in million $)

Recipient Countries		Military Aid, 1955–74	Economic Aid, 1954–76	Total Military and Economic Aid
Asia	Afghanistan	490	1,251	1,741
	Bangladesh	35	300	335
	Burma	negl.	16	16
	Cambodia	10	25	35
	Cyprus	25	—	25
	India	1,400	1,943	3,343
	Indonesia	1,095	114	1,209
	Iran	850	750	1,600
	Iraq	1,600	699	2,299
	Laos	5	1	6
	Lebanon	3	—	3
	Maldives	negl.	—	negl.
	Nepal	—	20	20
	Pakistan	60	652	712
	Sri Lanka	10	95	105
	Syria	2,100	417	2,517
	Turkey	—	1,180	1,180
	Yemen (Aden)	80	39	119
	Yemen (Sana)	80	98	178
Africa	Algeria	350	715	1,065
	Angola	—	10 [a]	10 [a]
	Benin	—	5	5
	Cameroon	—	8	8
	Cape Verde	—	b	b
	Central African Republic	—	2	2
	Chad	—	10	10
	Congo	15	14	29
	Egypt	3,450	1,300	4,750
	Equatorial Guinea	2	1	3
	Ethiopia	—	105	105
	Ghana	10	93	103
	Guinea	35	201	236
	Guinea-Bissau	—	14	14
	Kenya	—	48	48
	Mali	10	86	96
	Mauritania	—	5	5
	Morocco	45	98	143
	Mozambique	—	2	2
	Niger	—	2	2
	Nigeria	10	7	17
	Rwanda	—	1	1
	São Tomé and Principe	—	b	b
	Senegal	—	9	9
	Sierra Leone	negl.	28	28
	Somalia	115	154	269
	Sudan	65	64	129
	Tanzania	5	20	25
	Tunisia	—	82	82
	Uganda	20	16	36
	Upper Volta	—	1	1
	Zambia	—	6	6
Latin America	Argentina	—	245	245
	Bolivia	—	31	31
	Brazil	—	83	83
	Chile	—	238	238
	Colombia	—	10	10
	Mexico	—	b	b
	Peru	35	28	63
	Uruguay	—	20	20
Total Aid		12,010	11,362	23,372

[a] estimate [b] agreement signed, but information on amount of aid extended not available.

SOURCES: *Military aid 1955–74*: US Department of State, *Communist Aid to Less Developed Countries in 1974*. *Economic aid, 1954–76*: Material provided by the US Central Intelligence Agency.

Preface

Great-power rivalry in Africa is among the legacies left by European statesmen who, a century ago in Berlin, carved up the continent and whole nations within it into tidy colonial compartments, several with frontiers still in dispute. Russians and Americans attended that inglorious conference but stayed out of the scramble for territories that followed. It is one of history's ironies that Moscow and Washington emerged, with proxies to help them, as leading contestants in the contemporary struggle for position, presence and power in Africa.

This book deals with some of the causes and effects of the east–west confrontation in lands and among people deprived too long of their resources and rights. The process of study has resembled a safari in search of realities through the jungles and swamps of deceptive rhetoric. The search has gone far beyond libraries and files. It has involved visits to key African capitals where national leaders have been interviewed; it incorporates personal reporting of many conferences on African affairs, as well as discussions with politicians, diplomats and academics in Washington, London, Paris, Brussels, Moscow, Peking, Pretoria and elsewhere, over a period of years; it includes on-record and off-record correspondence and conversation with some of the principal players in the drama of east–west tussling in Africa's zones of conflict.

In a situation concerning the two great power blocs and their proclivities in a continent embracing more than fifty states, the ideal of a comprehensive, country-by-country study has proved impossible for reasons of time, space and constant change. Documented vignettes describing historic turning-points have supplanted statistical data on occasions when mood and personalities seemed to reveal more than the dry accounts of bureaucrats. Policies of major world powers in the African setting have been analysed for their geopolitical content; the high price of western associations with the *apartheid* (racial separation) Republic of South Africa has been assessed; and events in Angola and Ethiopia have been detailed for the light they shed on the misconceptions of Washington and its partners and for the way those misconceptions provided the socialist bloc with opportunities they were quick to exploit. Omissions, simplifications or superficialities have, where possible, been balanced by extensive references for readers wanting to know more about specific episodes. The focus, overall, has been less on the state of African countries than on the tactics and techniques used by east and west to advance their competing economic, ideological and strategic interests. The work is offered, therefore, as an introduction to a subject which seems certain to preoccupy powers, pundits and scholars for an indefinite time to come.

Two realities central to the evolving east–west contest have emerged – one with continental, the other with global, implications. In the continental context, the reality is that Africans will ultimately find their own solutions for the daunting problems inherited from their former colonial rulers and for those imposed upon them by their contemporary economic masters in a divided, recessionary world clouded by dangers of war. In the global context, the truth seems to be that a catalogue of western misjudgements, beginning with the American–British refusal to finance the Aswan High Dam in Egypt in 1955, gave the Russians chances to establish an impressive presence throughout Africa.

'African solutions for African problems' may possess the ring of a slogan but the logic of the concept, if fulfilled, could have profound implications. Leaders of the Organization of African Unity (OAU) were aware of the issues when (in Lagos, Nigeria, 28–29 April 1980) they adopted their own plan of action for the economic development of the continent by the year 2000; and committed themselves to set up an 'African Economic Community'. The idea of 'Africa for the Africans' would, again, cast doubt on European–American assumptions that the continent, particularly in the light of past bitterness and present discontents, could be preserved as a primarily western sphere of influence. It would, equally, foreshadow Africa's rejection of capitalist as well as communist intervention in future conflict.

It follows, therefore, that east and west will need to reappraise their approaches to the troubled continent, particularly if turbulence persists and spreads. The Russians will risk losing all credibility if they continue denouncing what they call western 'imperialism' without doing more to help its suffering victims. Tanks, missiles and Kalashnikovs have been, and still are, welcome to liberation movements and beleaguered governments but they hardly raise living standards. The Americans have provided more economic aid but when that support resembles rewards for often-corrupt regimes assuming pro-western stances, the net effect can be counter-productive. Furthermore, if assistance is seen to be related either to the strategic interests or mineral needs of the United States, it can generate jealousies and resentment

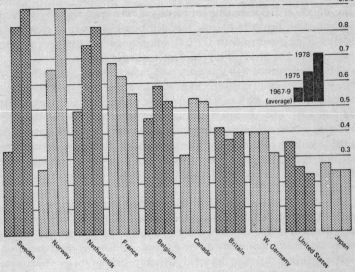

Fig. 3: Who gives what in foreign aid (percentage of donor's gross national product, 1980)
SOURCE: Organization for Economic Cooperation and Development, Paris, 1980.

among non-recipients as has happened, for instance, in the case of President Sese Seko Mobutu's Zaire.

For a majority of African countries the decade of the 1980s began with growing mistrust of all the great powers; with deepening disenchantment over failure by Arab and other oil producers to make more of their huge petrodollar earnings available to the near-bankrupt economies of their continental neighbours; and with brooding bitterness towards the International Monetary Fund (IMF) for imposing harsh, austere terms on borrowers and for what Tanzanian President Julius Nyerere termed its 'meddling' in the affairs of Third World countries generally. Ten of the world's wealthiest non-communist countries control 56 per cent of the IMF vote, which means that directors representing developing countries find themselves consistently outvoted and outmanoeuvred on lending policies; and in 1980 IMF assets exceeded $60 thousand million.* For 1981 alone, the petrodollar surplus of the Organization of Petroleum Exporting Countries (OPEC) was estimated at around $87 thousand million, most of it earning high rates of interest in the western banking system. It was bad enough for Africa's needy, non-oil-producing nations which were receiving few, if

*All money totals, for the sake of convenience, are given in dollars with reminders that the pound sterling was devalued by about 30 per cent to $2·80 in 1949, by a further 14 per cent to $2·40 in 1967, and since then has fluctuated between $1·55 and about $2·45.

any, direct OPEC loans or grants; it was worse having virtually to plead with western banks to borrow recycled petrodollars at interest rates higher than those paid to OPEC whose total external assets were expected by the IMF to exceed $400 thousand million.

The consequence was that each post-independence year, especially since the 1973-4 oil crisis, brought a widening of the gap between the standards of most African states and those of America, Europe and the Middle East. The Africans could not – and never tried to – conceal their reliance on non-African countries for aid to develop, to modernize, to establish their own national identities and a distinctive continental destiny. But by the end of the 1970s most of their export earnings were being used to service debts, mounting steadily because of the ever-rising costs of fuel.

It was a vicious circle. Help that reached the Africans enhanced, rather than reduced, their reliance on outsiders. Among other reasons this was because the aid was usually qualified by hidden political conditions which did not merely divert African inclinations from preferred non-alignment; they also thwarted African yearnings for true economic and political independence. Out of these circumstances flowed new frustrations, aborting high expectations of better times, complicating the business of government in a swiftly changing world. Except for some carefully chosen elitist groups, most leaders of Africa's former colonies were as ill-prepared for the rigours of sovereign independence as the development of their countries had been stunted. It should have come as no surprise when constitutions, nicely drafted in the corridors of West European power, went through window after window. One-party political systems arose. Adventurous soldiers from generals to master-sergeants ousted civilian leaders, at times with the help of still-influential metropolitan conspirators.

The period of transition was one of violence and pain for the fledge-ling nations, and southern protagonists of white supremacy enjoyed a golden summer of propaganda asserting that blacks were not yet fit to govern. Yet troubles attend most processes of political transition and by the 1980s there were several signs that Africans were collecting themselves together for a long march along the winding, rocky trail towards stability.

It was one thing for Africans unsophisticated in the arts of government to make their mistakes. It was quite another thing for the experienced, well-travelled politicians and diplomats of west and east to display as much ignorance as they did about a continent that was not so much dark as darkened. Most of the major powers – and the South Africans who claimed to know their continent best – blundered in their concern to outmanoeuvre one another.

American involvements wavered between benign neglect and romantic embrace – corresponding with the range of Soviet inaction or action. A major Washington misjudgement was for years to arm and fund Portugal, fellow-member of the North Atlantic Alliance (NATO), during the wars of liberation in the Lusitanian empire in Africa. This left the resistance movements with little option but to lean more and more on the east for help. Until Lisbon's authority collapsed, the Kissinger thesis that 'the whites are here to stay' in southern Africa remained accepted wisdom in Washington. It was a basic blunder that contributed to the transformation of the political map of sub-Saharan Africa.

The French invariably marched to their own drums in Africa and elsewhere. For years military actions in francophone countries kept pace with sales of arms and nuclear equipment to South Africa in defiance of United Nations resolutions. By 1981 interventions in and around countries like Tunisia, Chad and the dismantled Central African Empire had become subjects of international controversy, with Paris assailed for maintaining military and civilian personnel in Africa far in excess of the Russians, Cubans and East Germans combined. Between 10,000 and 15,000 French troops were garrisoned in countries sprawling from East to West Africa and more than 320,000 French civilians, settled in the continent, were spreading French culture, commerce, language and tied aid.

British interests, implicitly and often explicitly, were identified with stability in the white supremacist south. Publicly professing abhorrence for *apartheid*, the British nevertheless effectively supported the *status quo* through business dealings, massive investment and a protective diplomacy that staved off extreme international action envisaging trade boycotts and oil embargoes. Britain, with its allies, argued for a non-violent resolution of the black–white struggle in which the blacks vowed to settle for no less than political equality. However, Africans regarded the British position as specious, if not hypocritical, because they said it ignored the violence and force used by South Africa's own troops and police against blacks for the purpose of safeguarding the structure and philosophy of white privilege.

South Africa's white tribe went into an April 1981 election politically traumatized by the pace of change in neighbouring lands which had long cushioned the Republic against pressures from the black North. 'We must adapt or die!' Prime Minister P. W. Botha exhorted his countrymen. But then Ronald Reagan swept into office, vowing to confront the Soviet Union almost everywhere and signalling friendship to the South Africans. For Botha's government this was more of a stimulant than a tranquillizer, and so there were more black deaths than white adaptation as his well-oiled war machine thrust deeply into

Angola (via Namibia), into Mozambique and, covertly, into Zimbabwe. Internally, despite official talk about constitutional change, the screws of *apartheid* tightened on black lives and hopes in order to consolidate the quasi-military regime's grip on power. Botha's National Party won the election, yet not without yielding ground to opponents on the far right and, in white South African terms, the liberal left.

Moscow's miscalculations included failure to persuade Africans to assume socialist forms remotely resembling the Soviet brand. Russians shared some of the economic deficiencies experienced by Africans, yet displayed impatience when their protégés encountered difficulties in advancing from traditional social structures and cultural values towards late-twentieth-century systems of scientific, technical, industrial and political organization. Consequently some of their most important relationships turned out to be alliances of convenience, transient, costly, unfulfilled and disintegrating finally into mutual hostility as in the cases of Egypt, President Sékóu Touré's Guinea, and Somalia.

China's obsessive concern with what it termed Soviet efforts to establish its own 'social imperial system' in Africa and other Third World regions led Peking into strange company. The ideological dispute between the giant communist neighbours brought China into working relations with the Americans, Botswanans, Zaireans and Zimbabweans. There were other occasions when Peking, before and after the Angolan episode, collaborated with groups and movements backed by Pretoria. Many African governments, resenting the transplantation of the Sino–Soviet conflict into their backyards, found this hard to accept.

As this book went to press, Ronald Reagan took over from Jimmy Carter as American president with an electoral commitment radically to revise what he had earlier described as the 'incoherence' of his predecessor's foreign policy. In the African context, specifically, Reagan and his advisers, before and during the campaign for the presidency, criticized Carter's responses to Soviet and Cuban activities, calling them 'confused and misguided'. 'I don't know about you, but I'm concerned – scared is the proper word – about what is going on in Africa,' Reagan told a radio audience soon after Carter's 1976 election. 'Many Americans have interpreted our interest in Africa as an extension of our own desire to achieve racial equality and elimination of injustice based on race. I'm afraid that is a naive over-simplification of what really is at issue.' As he saw it, the basic issue was the power struggle between the United States and the Soviet Union. He suggested that the Russians had the advantage because democracy was rare in most African countries where the people believed in 'one man, one vote, *once*'. He added: 'Whoever gets in power cancels out the opposition.' That led him to the conclusion that 'the African problem is a Russian weapon aimed at us'.

The rhetoric of candidates in American and most other western electoral contests is rarely matched by their performance in office. Therefore in Africa, and elsewhere, governments adopted a wait-and-see attitude before pronouncing any judgements on what they believed might lie ahead for them if a Reagan administration were to give global geopolitical considerations priority over regional realities or if the Americans were to seek somehow to unify both approaches. Nevertheless, few in African and other world capitals doubted that Reagan would be driven by the desire to limit the spread of Moscow's influence through the continent; and that this desire would result in a softer, friendlier stance in relation to South Africa's white minority rulers, committed as they were to the anti-communist crusade.

Reagan himself had helped to spread that impression, notably when he observed during the campaign that South Africans 'certainly don't need us to tell them how to solve their race problems'. And although he maintained he was against the *apartheid* system, he and his aides frequently stressed the importance of South Africa's strategic position and its mineral resources. The new president, at the same time, had to recognize that certain constraints on his administration's freedom of action were implied by, for example, Nigeria's emergence as the second biggest supplier of oil to the United States. Little of all this, however, had the immediate effect of tempering the gleeful expectations of South African leaders who perceived that the rise of Ronald Reagan heralded for them an era of greater comprehension and collaboration with the nations of the west. White South Africa's wish for an alliance was understandable in a continent committed to destroy racism. Yet for the west even economic links with the *apartheid* state posed political and moral problems. Influential African leaders, including Nigerian President Alhaji Shehu Shagari and Zimbabwean Prime Minister Robert Mugabe, sombrely warned outsiders to choose between friendship with black Africa and white South Africa.

In the final two decades of the century, whoever occupies the White House or the Kremlin, it seems certain that a new phase of interdependence faces the nations. Pressures are building up on east and west alike to contribute substantially towards evolving a new international economic order that would make that concept of interdependence a reality. East and west have the choice between controlling, if not abandoning, their rivalries in Africa and elsewhere or risking the breakdown of national and international systems.

Acknowledgements

Secrets are the currency of modern diplomatic exchange. Confidence is its goodwill. Representatives of many nations have helped in the writing of this book. They include presidents, premiers and foreign ministers, past and present, together with ambassadors and high commissioners and their aides in Washington, London and key African capitals. Most asked not to be identified. Their cooperation can be acknowledged but to name them would be to debase both the currency and the goodwill.

My thanks go out, nevertheless, to others whose advice or writings have been enlightening. In alphabetical order: Dr Gordon Adams, assistant professor of political science, Rutgers University, Newark; Alcides Albertiris Pérez, Cuban Embassy, London; Dr Pauline H. Baker, professional staff member, U S Senate Committee on Foreign Relations, Washington; Professor Jerry Bender, Center for International and Strategic Affairs, University of California; Ambassador Nathaniel Davis, formerly assistant secretary of state for African affairs in the State Department; Michael Goldsmith, Paris-based correspondent of the Associated Press who specializes in African affairs; Lewis Gulick, senior staff consultant, House Foreign Affairs Committee; Ambassador Fred C. Hadsel, director of the George C. Marshall Research Foundation in Lexington, Virginia; General Alexander Haig, U S secretary of state, formerly supreme commander, allied forces, Europe; Herbert E. Hetu, director of Public Affairs, Central Intelligence Agency; Colin Legum, editor of *Africa Contemporary Record*; Bernard Rivers who, with Martin Bailey, helped expose the breach of sanctions against Rhodesia by major British and other oil companies; Raul Roa-Kouri, Cuban ambassador to the United Nations; George Ivan Smith, former director of the United Nations Centre in London; Senator John Sparkman, chairman of the U S Senate Committee on Foreign Relations; Cyrus R. Vance, former U S secretary of state; and Andrew Young, former U S ambassador to the United Nations. Talks and correspondence with most of the foregoing, as well as studies of their writings and speeches, were invaluable.

My indebtedness goes also to Michael Dover, Ronald Segal and Mary Omond of Penguin Books, who spurred me on; and I am particularly grateful for the assistance which Peter Phillips provided.

I have made use both of original research and of many U S congressional reports, especially hearings of Senate and House Committees on African Affairs. The personal accounts and memoirs of administration officials relating to specific African episodes have also been used. Background, non-attributable talks with senior American, British, French and African officials have been drawn upon. Explanations of Soviet, Cuban and South African policies have come from officials of those countries on the understanding that their names would not be disclosed.

Ruth Vaughan, whose research, indexing and general secretarial help turned near-chaos into calm order, earned my special gratitude. Her political grasp and knowledge of Africa matched her splendid typing.

Most of all I thank my wife, Audrey, whose perceptive comments and criticisms were never welcome but always valid. Without her understanding, command of language and involvement, the project might never have seen the light of day.

London, May 1981   Arthur Gavshon

Part One

East–West Confrontation in Africa

1. Overview

The grass grows tall from May to October in much of Africa south of the Sahara. And this is the time when tribesmen feed the sour soil as their fathers used to do, by burning the grass. So huge fires race across the savannas and turn whole forests into walls of flame. Then the game runs free and good hunting follows and fine feeding, too.

There were other fires in black Africa beginning in the 1960s and smouldering or blazing on into the 1980s. They swept from Nigeria in the west to Ethiopia in the east, from Sharpeville and Soweto in South Africa to the Mountains of the Moon in Uganda, northwards. But the hunters searched for different prey. Insurrections, wars of independence and black–white conflict scorched the earth and threatened new dangers as the great outside powers intervened, bringing their ideologies and high-grade weaponry with them.

Beyond the ravages of war, famine, poverty and disease racked whole nations. There were numerous inherited border conflicts to be settled. Profound social injustices, some with political or racial origins, split black- as well as white-ruled societies. East and west had long since been competing for facilities and raw materials, not for Africa's sake but in their own global interests. The problems bequeathed by colonialism, which for centuries had darkened the continent and dispossessed its millions, remained to be resolved.

The Soviet Union and the United States, trailed by China and ambitious Islamic countries, led the quest for influence among young states still searching for stability and security. Europe's former colonizing powers, with their huge investments intact even after the dismantling of their imperial systems, went on making and breaking governments. If certain African countries happened to benefit, that was something for the outsiders to shout about. But if Africans were hurt as a result of some foreign squeeze-play, it was usual for either protagonist to blame the other.

Turbulence attended most of Africa's fifty-two countries from the time they achieved an independence that was – and for years remained – more shadowy than substantial. Until the downfall of Portugal's

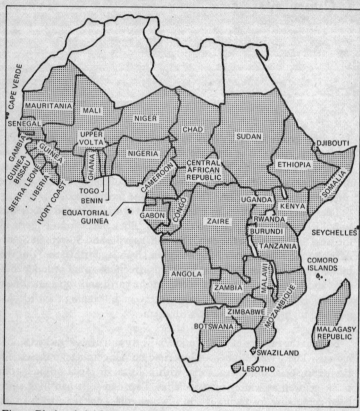

Fig. 4: Black-ruled African nations

dictatorship in 1974 and, with it, Portugal's empire in Africa, American –
and West European – policy had rested on the Henry Kissinger thesis
for southern Africa that 'white rule is here to stay'. White rule not only
collapsed in Mozambique and Angola, pulling down with it the structure of a European state system in Portugal, but it also hurried Rhodesia's reincarnation as Zimbabwe, shook the *apartheid* Republic of South
Africa, and transformed the entire continent into a theatre of superpower competition. Ever since, Soviet–American rivalries in Africa
have intensified, either directly or indirectly, via 'surrogates' – modern
diplomacy's new catch-all phrase for the other side. An ally of the
Soviet Union was invariably branded a 'surrogate'. An ally or friend of
the United States was invariably described as 'ally' or 'friend'.

Since the break-up of the Portuguese empire in Africa, the world
has watched direct French, Moroccan, South African, Cuban,

Somalian, Ugandan and Libyan intervention across borders. The Russians and Americans also have intervened, overtly or covertly, in areas of conflict. French and Cubans alike maintained and used thousands of well-armed air and land strike-forces in support of countries willing to be their hosts. In the northern half of the continent there were wars in the Western Sahara, Chad and, of course, in the Horn itself.

There were also clashes between Arab states; Islamic penetration into black Africa; invasion and counter-invasion by African neighbours; and South African air and land assaults on Angola and Mozambique. The conflict in Western Sahara, suspected depository for a trove of strategic minerals, at times brought Algeria near to war with Morocco, which sought to annex the former Spanish territory. Libya intervened, mostly without success, in Egypt, Sudan, Niger, Uganda, Tunisia, the Central African Republic and the Western Sahara before announcing a 'fusion' with Chad – a conquest that took resurgent Islamic teachings and Soviet and French weapons towards equatorial Africa. Ethiopia, backed by Cuba and the Soviet Union, struggled to suppress Eritrean and Somalian separatism that had the support of anti-communist powers. Uganda under Idi Amin invaded its Tanzanian neighbour, to be met with a counter-offensive that led to the downfall of the dictator. White-ruled South Africa, possessing the most sophisticated war machine on the continent, devastated the military installations of Angola and sent a land force into the Mozambican capital of Maputo to blow up the supposed hide-outs of anti-*apartheid* guerrillas. From the Cape to Cairo, from the Atlantic to the Indian Ocean, years of civil and transborder strife took a countless toll of lives. In most situations an east–west element was discernible.

But the main focus of danger had begun moving inexorably southwards, where the white minority rulers of South Africa vowed to preserve their system of *apartheid* to the bitter end. They sought to reinforce themselves through informal, sometimes secret, alliances with protégés in Namibia, Zimbabwe, Angola and other lands to the north.

It took a British master-politician with a sense of history – and a Conservative one at that – to warn the white South Africans against themselves. Sir Harold Macmillan, prime minister in 1960 which has been designated the 'Year of Africa', travelled through the continent and, in a famous speech to the South African parliament in Cape Town, urged his listeners to reappraise their supremacist racial philosophy: 'The wind of change is blowing through this continent and whether we like it or not this growth of national consciousness is a political fact.' Unless the force of black nationalism was recognized, he went on, the precarious east–west balance might be imperilled, with Africa's emerging new states drawn into the communist camp. As if to emphasize his own country's readiness to practise what it preached, Britain the same year began hurrying the process of decolonization throughout Africa.[1]

White South African lawmakers, led at the time by Prime Minister Hendrik Verwoerd, heard Macmillan out in silence but then proceeded along their own chosen course; rather than come to terms with black nationalism they resolved to resist it. And so began South Africa's programme of massive armament which, by the 1980s, had given the country the immediate capacity to build nuclear weapons, if not the actual weapons themselves.

After Verwoerd, South Africa's incumbent prime minister, B. J. Vorster, since disgraced, borrowed from Macmillan's imagery to tell his *volk* (nation) in a 1977 New Year's Day broadcast: 'The storm has not struck yet. We are only experiencing the whirlwinds that go before it.'

His judgement appeared to be confirmed in the report of a specialist study group to the Committee on International Relations of the US House of Representatives. One of its major conclusions said in part that southern Africa 'seems to be the new troublespot of the world . . . the Angolan civil war may well have opened up an era of acute instability that could threaten regional peace and produce superpower confrontation'.[2]

Here then were some of the objective conditions making for a new-style power scramble in Africa. A century earlier the rape of Africa had been formalized when Europe's imperial powers divided the continent into 'spheres of influence', so creating an international framework for the systematic exploitation of the continent and its people. The mapmakers ruled straight lines on school atlases, carving up huge chunks of Africa into neat colonial compartments. In effect, this division set the illogical frontiers that now demarcate the states of post-colonial Africa. There were no defined boundaries in pre-colonial Africa. But today approximately one-third of the continent's frontiers are the straight lines drawn arbitrarily at the Berlin Conference of 1884–5.

The Conference of Berlin was historic not only for the cynicism displayed by its participants but also for their lack of foresight. Repeatedly, decisions taken at Berlin brought the great powers of Europe to gunpoint. Germany's drive for colonies formed part of the chain of circumstances that led to the outbreak of the First World War. Britain and France – old rivals who were to become close friends – nearly found themselves in a shooting match over the Fashoda incident.[3] And Britain lost friends around the world because of what was taken to be its perfidy in going to war against the Boers of South Africa from 1899 to 1902.

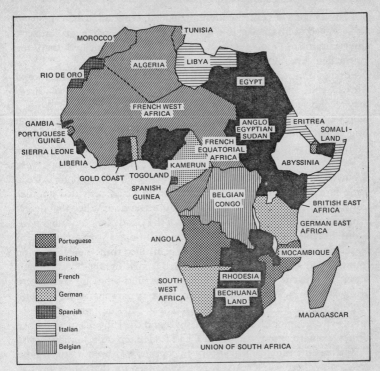

Fig. 5: European conquest of Africa (Berlin Conference, 1884–5)

The Superpowers Move In

There were essential differences between the manipulating and manoeuvring by the great powers over Africa before and after decolonization. Since the break-up of the European empires in Asia and
Africa – initiated by the British in the early days of the east–west cold
war – stronger players arrived on the African scene. In a nuclear world
grown politically more complex, the newly liberated countries drew
gradually together to form a power centre in their own right, aligned
neither to east nor west. This did not prevent Moscow or Washington
from making the countries of the Third World targets of their atten-
tions. Some of these fledgeling states had debts to repay to the Russians,
for instance, because in their independence struggles they had been
helped with arms and money by Moscow. Other Third World countries
felt that they had scores to settle with their old imperialist masters who,
before yielding independence, believed that they could count on American backing through the 1970s.

Thus dangers of confrontation intensified, especially when the Russians moved to fill the vacuum left behind by the departing colonizers. Interventionism, too, assumed forms more sophisticated than the vulgar land-grabbing solemnly sanctified in Berlin.

Foreign forces, for example, determined the outcome of several African civil and transnational conflicts at the 'invitation' of forces they recognized. The Central Intelligence Agency (C I A) of the United States estimated that more than 40,000 Cuban combatants served in Angola and Ethiopia using arms supplied by the Russians. Fidel Castro would later say that the C I A figure was an underestimate. Authorities in Paris reported that between 15,000 and 20,000 French troops were deployed at times through twenty-two states of francophone Africa, some in a combatant role. The situation in Chad provided another ironic pointer to the changing pattern of intervention. When that desert insurrection first began in 1965, rebels of the Chad National Liberation Front fought on camels. Later, with up-to-date Soviet equipment placed at their disposal by Libya, they controlled three-quarters of the country; and in 1978 the French ordered Jaguar fighter-bombers into action to prevent the total victory of guerrillas who, by then, were using tanks, missiles and other modern military paraphernalia. By mid–1980 France withdrew, leaving its parastatal, Elf-Aquitaine, to acquire extensive oil exploration rights in Libya; and the Libyans to announce a 'merger' with a now-compliant Chad leadership on 6 January 1981.

Whereas the nineteenth-century Europeans had been motivated by greed, now there was a scarcely concealed need for their successors to expand their neo-imperial interests. Africa possessed in immeasurable quantities about all of the thirteen basic industrial raw materials needed by a modern economy. No jet airplane, for instance, can be built without cobalt. The United States produces no cobalt but Zaire and Zambia do. The Americans are 88 per cent dependent on imported bauxite, 95 per cent on imported manganese ore, 90 per cent on nickel, 100 per cent on tin – and the relative figures for West Europe show an even greater dependency. The reliance of the west on Africa's strategic materials extends also to aluminium, zinc, chromium, iron, lead and tungsten.[4] These illustrations, of course, leave such energy-yielding commodities as oil and uranium out of account. Africa has deposits of both.

Moscow and Washington consistently acted as though successive crises in Africa were simple extensions of their global geopolitical struggle. Both tended to regard the contest in zero-sum terms with a gain for one perceived automatically as a loss for the other. Captives of their ideologies, each perpetrated a series of resounding blunders in their efforts to win the support of the 440 million Africans.

Ideologues of the Kremlin, convinced that history had a red tie around its neck, favoured the judicious injection of guns, and sometimes combatants, into Africa's flashpoint regions when that seemed likely to make life harder for, or hasten the exit of, the capitalist west. This was one way of giving practical expression to Lenin's concept that revolution and wars of liberation against 'the imperialist west' would, in time, flare in the colonial empires of Asia, Africa and South America. Thus the power of the imperialist nations would be eroded and could be sustained only by force. The colonies, Lenin wrote in a 1917 pamphlet entitled *Imperialism, the Highest Stage of Capitalism*, would thus emerge as the west's 'weakest link'. He who holds Africa, he went on to suggest, holds Europe. After the establishment of the Soviet state he persisted in pressing this theme, with special emphasis on the potential for revolution in the lands of Asia.[5] This provided the Russians with a theoretical basis for attempting to develop a functional and symbiotic relationship between their own Marxist revolutionary aims and those of the nationalist-minded people of Africa, Asia and South America seeking true independence. Moscow was assailed constantly in the west for the sparing, even miserly, amounts of economic aid and trade it made available to friendly African states.

Occupants of the White House, guilt-ridden by association with the west's colonial past and neo-colonial present, preferred to seek out African governments ready to live behind the shield of American security. Later they would provide them with more worldly goods including arms, liberally laced with dashes of anti-communism. It was an approach that followed rather than preceded Moscow's penetration of the continent. The Americans had stumbled from the neglect of the immediate post-war years by way of John F. Kennedy's idealistic do-goodism to a late appreciation of Africa's geostrategic potential. In between, Washington had looked upon black Africa as no more than an extension of US security arrangements in allied Europe and the Middle East, with former colonial powers like France, Britain, Belgium and Portugal exercising first responsibility for keeping the continent stable. The Europeans signally failed in that task.

By the 1980s it had become clear that both the Soviet and American attitudes, fashioned in the decade of the cold war, were obsolete. They had to recognize that hungry Africans could no more easily eat bullets than they could cure their rampant diseases with doses of anti-communist or anti-capitalist medicine. Specialists of various United Nations agencies called attention to some of Africa's other more pressing realities. More than four million black refugees or displaced persons were moving across the continent in waves of misery. Five Africans out of six lacked access to safe water supplies. Life expectancy at birth was twenty-five years less in Africa than the European average. In rural areas near rivers where blackflies breed, one in ten Africans went blind in the prime of life.[6]

The dry statistics of major international organs disclosed even greater tragedies for Africans, which shamed some big powers.

From 1968 to 1974 the most devastating drought for sixty years spread famine and death among up to 200,000 people and more than 3·5 million cattle in a region south of the Sahara, comprising six countries of the Sahel (shoreland). Neighbouring areas also were seriously affected. Yet it took four years to get a coherent programme of international relief going with emergency US grain shipments moving for the first time in November 1972. The United States, France, Canada and the West European states joined the mercy programme, working alongside several African and other governments which pooled their resources and aid plans. But the initial lack of coordination was unwittingly revealed by the nearby Sudanese who, in the early stage of the disaster, exported food supplies to Japan at low world prices and then, weeks later, found themselves importing grain at great expense because they, too, were affected by the drought. The World Bank in its first development report noted that in 1978 the wheat needs of the Sahelians could have been met by *one-twentieth* of the wheat that Europeans feed annually to their cattle.[7]

From 1973 to 1975 famine also struck in Ethiopia but the aged Emperor Haile Selassie for long denied that starvation was rampant. And the international community in Addis Ababa, including officials of relief agencies, diplomats and others, colluded in the monarch's cover-up, in order not to embarrass a regime already being assailed for its corruption, incompetence and lack of care for the condition of its people. It took Haile Selassie eight months, under pressure by demonstrators, to acknowledge with shock that the crisis had become a catastrophe, with an estimated 100,000 Ethiopians already starving to death and with countless thousands emaciated, diseased, and weak with hunger. The nakedness of the emperor's policies had been exposed. His fifty-year regime could 'boast' fewer than 110 doctors for its thirty-one million people; a 5 per cent literacy rate; and a 2 per cent growth rate. More than half of America's programmes of economic and military aid over a twenty-year period had gone to buy modern tanks, supersonic jet fighters and other weapons needed to crush Eritrean separatism in the north and Somalian expansionism in the south. The conspiracy of silence by international observers, far from protecting the imperial Ethiopian government, in fact hastened its downfall 'in the sense that the inevitable revelation of the coverup was perhaps the principal event triggering the military revolt against the Emperor'.[8]

From 1960 to 1975 the Economic Commission for Africa (ECA), also a UN agency, reported that there had been no marked improvement in most African economies. In an even gloomier projection of the continent's prospects, ECA suggested that if past trends continued, and if no changes were to occur in the international economic system, Africa by the end of the century would be worse off, compared with the rest of the world, than it had been in 1960.[9]

The nineteenth-century colonizers bequeathed another explosive legacy. Europe's arbitrary, often illogical partition of Africa split whole peoples and concentrated diverse and often hostile tribal groups into territories which ultimately became sovereign states, so making internal and transborder strife inevitable. It also had the spin-off – could this have been the motive? – drawn from the classical imperial technique of divide and rule. Any map showing the major ethnic, language and kinship groupings of Africa today illustrates the insensitivities and absurdities displayed by the colonizers who, beyond the rhetoric of their 'civilizing missions', in reality made sure that twentieth-century Africa would become a setting for conflict. The contrasts shouted their messages of inequity and iniquity alike.

The vast Zairean land mass in the continental heartland, for instance, is bounded by nine national frontiers. The mosaic of mini-states around the West African bulge, from Senegal to Benin, is its own monument to the rivalries of the nineteenth-century British and French empire-builders. The nicely drawn administrative units within francophone Africa, from Mauritania and Algeria south-eastwards to Chad and the Central African Republic, have been swept, since independence, by gusts of war and civil unrest. In a Scandinavian study, *African Boundary Problems*, edited by Carl Gosta Eifdytsnf, thirty-two frontier disputes in the continent were listed as unresolved in 1970. Chester A. Crocker, an academic chosen by Reagan as assistant secretary of state for foreign affairs, wrote that the Scandinavian catalogue 'represents only a fraction of the potential for conflict'. He observed: 'Nearly half of Africa's international frontiers, as of 1967, had not been physically demarcated, suggesting the scope for argument over essentially territorial questions.'[10] The scope for international exploitation of those arguments also was implicit.

The territorial and personal security of African states and their leaders predictably emerged as a paramount issue in the development of the continent since the early 1950s. They transcended, in many cases, the pressing problems of economic and social advancement. Ambitious outside powers with arms for sale, or to give away, over the years found ready takers.

Nearly sixty successful *coups* took place against established African governments from the early 1950s, with the pace quickening in the late 1970s. There were, in addition, an undisclosed number of failed attempts to seize power. These upheavals were quite apart from wars of secession, cross-border incursions, full-scale invasions, wars of conquest and the interventions of foreign forces requested or invited by beleaguered governments or liberation movements.

To recognize these realities of regional and continental life was not to reflect upon the competence or the wishes of Africans to resolve their own problems in their own ways. Early in its formation the OAU set forth as cardinal articles of faith the precepts that member-nations should respect the sanctity of existing frontiers and refrain from interfering in the internal affairs of fellow members. But they were precepts foredoomed to failure in the conditions bequeathed by the colonial powers and given the deliberation with which the superpowers pursued their global, or geopolitical, designs at the expense of regional realities. Nor, in fact, was this a phenomenon confined to Africa. Virtually every major conflict that flared in the aftermath of the Second World War was in or over a former imperial territory (Indonesia, Palestine, Malaya, the Indian subcontinent and Indo-China, among non-African states or regions).

Conflicts, perhaps, would have been easier to resolve if Africans had been left to themselves to seek their own solutions. They were not. Nor were the sophisticated political structures imposed upon them either relevant to their experience or conducive to their need for stability and security. A majority, therefore, moved into a phase of authoritarianism. As the 1980s began, just fifteen of Africa's fifty-two territories had plural-party systems; twenty-one were under one-party regimes; and sixteen military or civilianized-military governments held office.[11] Namibia, awaiting independence, was under South African control.

It should have been no surprise that independent Africans would want their political institutions to evolve in ways related to systems they knew. What, in fact, was their experience of government in the immediate past? The European-structured colonial systems in fact embodied single-party arrangements. The French, British and Belgian colonial administrations never implanted the refined democratic subtleties of their Parisian, London and Brussels parliaments in the colonial administration of Africa. Instead they imposed rigid frameworks which permitted political opposition only within clear-cut guidelines drawn by the metropolitan power. The radicals of Africa's colonies – who gave voice to their nationalism – risked imprisonment. In time it became almost a precondition for any aspiring nationalist leader to spend part of his apprenticeship behind bars or in banishment. Ben

Bella of Algeria, Habib Bourguiba of Tunisia and Morocco's Sultan Mohammed V were among leaders locked up or exiled by the French. The British did the same with Ghana's Kwame Nkrumah, Jomo Kenyatta of Kenya and Zambia's Kenneth Kaunda before each became president of his state. Patrice Lumumba, first prime minister of the Congo, was released from prison in order to attend the constitutional conference that preceded independence in 1960. All wore those distinctions like badges of courage.

The late twentieth century faced Africans with the challenges of three simultaneous revolutionary situations. First, the revolution of national liberation after centuries of underdevelopment. This involved, primarily, problems of personal and general internal security for leaders in what, for them, was a volatile world. Next, the revolution of science and technology faced new states with the need somehow to overcome their instilled backwardness and to adjust their societies to contemporary demands. All needed communications, power, mobility, education, health, housing and the profoundly complicated infrastructure of a modern economy.

Finally, there was the ideological revolution, imposing on African leaders a choice of competing political systems, cultures, organization and alliances. Concepts of 'pro-communism' or 'anti-communism', of 'western orientation' or 'moderation', were irrelevant to the immediate, workaday needs of peoples yearning for enough food and safe water, more schools and better shelter, hospitals and roads and a coherent agricultural and industrial system that could give them the necessary skills and a bigger share in the resources that their lands could yield.

Governments outside Africa knew what urgent requirements Africans had. But they paid attention to those needs invariably by playing to the gallery of nations. This attitude did not pass unnoticed by the more shrewd leaders of Africa who were well aware of the shifts and swerves in the policies and relationships of some of their own continental partners. They took due note of the manner in which outsiders accommodated themselves to those changes. They became resolved, therefore, to seek 'African solutions for African problems'. They did not intend to sit idly by and wait for a changing of the foreign guards in their own lands.

For the Soviet and American superpowers, able with their nuclear arsenals to destroy every city in the world, life in the days of the cold war had been much simpler.[12] Nations then were neatly divided between east and west, communism and anti-communism. Indeed, the late John Foster Dulles, when he was US secretary of state, found it possible once to denounce countries which took a neutral or non-aligned stance in the cold war as 'immoral'.[13] If this were so, most late-twentieth-century African governments would have to confess to that kind of sin.

The Third World Takes Shape

The iron laws of history were, however, at work in the 1950s. A phase of straightforward adversary politics came to an end in the aftermath of Joseph Stalin's death in 1953. The superpowers had lost the capacity to make any political use of their destructive capabilities, thereby losing their commanding roles. A bipolar world had gone multipolar.

If a single event appears to change the affairs of men and nations, it can fairly be seen as a watershed. Between the 1950s and 1970s three such events were identifiable, each with its own momentum, yet all interacting and developing a collective logic.

The British–French invasion of Egypt in 1956 led the Americans to dispel any assumptions that still lingered among the European colonial powers that they could rely on their major ally for help to preserve their empires. Then there was the Soviet–Chinese ideological feud which festered for years before erupting into a conflict of global dimensions and with Africa a major testing-ground. It was a happening that also began the process of loosening Moscow's tight leadership of the world-wide communist movement. Finally came the 1973 Arab–Israeli war and the fivefold increase in oil prices by the Arab producers.

In the background, perhaps even promoting this pattern of shifting alignments, the dispossessed nations of South America, Africa and Asia were moving slowly closer into a grouping which became known as the Third World. In the late fifties and sixties they had begun establishing a basis of cooperation. The principal factor unifying them was a demand for a fairer share of the earth's wealth and a bigger say in the management of the world's affairs. The less developed countries (LDCs) were beginning to pit themselves against the industrialized consumer societies of the northern hemisphere, communist and capitalist alike, and to assume all the characteristics of a new centre of power.

More than one hundred countries belong to the Third World, half of them African. Together they make up two-thirds of the membership of the United Nations. The Afro–Asian bloc could vote embarrassingly at the UN General Assembly but without compelling the big powers to deviate much from their chosen policies. The outcome invariably was stalemate.

Third World countries cover more than twenty million square miles of the earth's land area of fifty-one million square miles, with Antarctica excepted. They command most of the world's oceanic passageways or straits. Africa, over three times bigger in area than the United States, is at the centre of the system despite its economic impoverishment. Nearly half the world's four thousand million people live in the Third World, including one thousand million mainland Chinese. These people are at varying stages of development, practising some of the world's oldest religions, loyal to certain ancient creeds, different in colour, a few with civilizations pre-dating the Christian era.

Shared experiences and aspirations bind them. Almost all endured centuries of European – or Arab – colonial exploitation. Although a majority graduated to political independence after the Second World War, they remained dominated economically and financially by their former rulers.

The struggle of African countries, among others in the Third World, for true and total independence was the thread that ran constantly through the pattern of the post-decolonization years. It became a central source of accord with the east, and of discord with the west. 'Neo-colonialism', meaning a reassertion of control by the colonial powers and their allies, became a dirty political word in Soviet and Third World lexicons. Independence had ushered in false expectations for the people of the newly freed colonies. In addition, the former European colonial powers were unwilling to surrender control of their protected markets, their access to prized raw materials and the infrastructure of their investments. They were grudging in transferring their expertise and jealously preserved their mastery of international commodity buying and selling.

Summing up the general beliefs of fellow Africans and other Third World delegates, President Kenneth Kaunda of Zambia, a middle-of-the-road leader, told a conference of non-aligned states in Colombo, Sri Lanka, in 1976: 'We are opposed to the present system whereby the wealthier and industrialized countries retain the monopoly of making decisions affecting all other states. We believe in power-sharing as an important guarantee for peace within the international community.'[14]

Emerging as it did from the dangerous bitterness of the east–west cold war, the Third World owed its latter-day influence to European–American, Soviet–Chinese and Islamic–Christian rivalries.

The Transatlantic Front

The watershed in European relations with the Americans came in the mid-1950s. The late Gamal Abdel Nasser, then president of Egypt, accepted a Soviet offer of arms at a time when the British were still occupying the Suez Canal zone. This led the Americans and British to decline what they had long been pondering – the financing of Nasser's multimillion-dollar dream project for a high dam at Aswan that would irrigate a large part of the Nile valley. Moscow consequently volunteered to take on the commitment and, in a single gesture, leapfrogged Soviet influence across the lands of Araby into Africa for the first time on any grand scale. That act gave Nasser the confidence to nationalize the Suez Canal, then operated by a British–French controlling company. In retaliation and in collusion with Israel, the British and French thereupon invaded the Suez zone in October 1956, hoping thus to oust Nasser and regain control of the international waterway that linked them with their colonial bases in the Indian and Pacific Oceans. Washington opposed the venture and the west was split. At one point the US Sixth Fleet, permanently patrolling the Mediterranean, sailed right through the British armada carrying part of the invasion force to its destination.

Under ever-stiffening US pressure, first the British and then the French abandoned the venture, leaving a trail of bitterness and suspicion that took years to eliminate. It turned out also to be the last occasion on which the British, at least, felt they could act militarily without prior American consent.

The Soviet–Chinese Front

Chairman Mao Tse-tung in the 1950s first challenged the assumption of the Soviet leadership that they alone had the right to interpret Marxist–Leninist ideology. Peking criticized Moscow's 1956 invasion of Hungary and its 1968 attack on Czechoslovakia as acts of imperialism. The Chinese also resented the refusal of the Kremlin to share its nuclear weapon secrets with its major ideological ally. There were, in addition, clashes of state interests, notably over Soviet occupation of Chinese territories seized in the nineteenth century. On one level the quarrel between the giant communist neighbours was manifested in their contest for the support and sympathy of Third World nations, particularly in Africa. Each sought to check the spread of the other's influence in a game of far-reaching geopolitical importance.

In Africa, Peking could not match Moscow's free-wheeling sale of modern weapons, often made available to handpicked clients at bargain-basement prices. The Chinese accordingly set out to win friends through functional aid projects, maintaining as they did so a low profile that contrasted with the flamboyant Soviet undertakings. They also took good care to make the most of the fact that they too, like the Africans, were not white.

Mao's boldest achievement, perhaps, was to construct what became known as the Great Uhuru (freedom) Railway, linking Dar es Salaam in

Tanzania with Lusaka in landlocked Zambia, 1,200 miles away. The $500-million project was undertaken after the United States, Britain and Canada disputed its value or relevance to the needs of the two countries. Even when whispers of Chinese interest began filtering through, the western powers dithered and dissembled. British authorities expressed doubts over whether Peking would pick up so costly a commitment and indeed whether, having picked it up, they could ever fulfil it. Pessimistic feasibility studies by World Bank and United Nations teams, led variously by American and British specialists, dampened interest in Washington and Ottawa, too. It was Aswan revisited.

After careful preparation Peking finally took on the task in 1969. More than 20,000 Chinese and 50,000 African workers were thrown into the enterprise which was completed in 1975-6, ahead of schedule. The railroad climbs from Tanzania's coast into the savanna where lions and elephants roam, then 10,000 feet into the mountains before running down to the Congo–Zambezi basin. It became a symbol of China's identification with Africa and its people; a symbol designed also to outshine the Soviet showpiece on the Nile and to demonstrate to the west the depth of Chinese determination to re-enter the world community with a contribution of a very special kind. In that sense it was judged by key African leaders as a triumph for their own diplomacy and for the capacity of poor, developing countries to collaborate in their shared interests.

The Arab–African Front

Some leading Arab oil producers, with thousands of millions of petro-dollars to spend, teamed up with key African leaders not only to advance Islam as a spiritual, political and social force but also to counter the influence of western capitalism and Soviet communism. On the face of things nothing seemed more natural. Two-thirds of all Arabs live in Africa. Within the framework of Third World cooperation, Arabs and Africans share the aim of seeking a new international economic order that will end the dominance exercised so long by the industrialized nations of the northern hemisphere. The Arabs have pushed and prodded the Africans to follow their lead by vastly increasing prices of Africa's scarce raw materials as a means of winning the bigger returns needed for the development of their lands. In the process, too, the Arabs have used the weapon of oil in order to ensure African backing for their anti-Israeli policies. In the aftermath of the 1973 oil crisis they demanded, and got, African acquiescence for a rupture of relations with Israel and, in return, agreed first to guarantee African fuel supplies and then to consider expanding investment and trade with African countries.

Against that, the Africans urged Arab governments to adopt a more activist policy to help them in their own priority objective of liberating southern Africa from white minority rule. On paper both sides agreed to work towards these aims. But, under cover, some key African countries still continued dealing informally with the Israelis, just as some Islamic states kept on doing business with the South Africans. Yet nothing the Arabs said or did ever succeeded in eliminating an African awareness that the Arabs in bygone centuries were as active as the Europeans, perhaps even more active, in the nightmarish traffic in black slavery.

Edgar Snow, the famous American foreign correspondent and author, during a long interview once asked Mao Tse-tung for his appraisal of the implications of the French Revolution. Mao reflected a while and then mused: 'I would think it's a little too early to tell.' By that somewhat cautious token, contemporary historians certainly would insist that a time-span of two or three decades is too brief to permit anything but the most provisional judgements on the evolution of international policies towards independent Africa. With governments, people and problems in a state of constant change, it would indeed be hazardous to predict future trends in superpower attitudes towards the vast and disparate continent. Distance lends haziness to the view of Africa whether from Moscow or Washington. Russians and Americans, like modern Vasco da Gamas, discovered the place for its political and strategic pickings almost by accident, in the course of their global meanderings.

In the case of the former European colonizers, likely policy trends seemed easier to foretell. After all, they had been around the continent for centuries, knowing what it offered and, anyway, apparently able to continue old practices in new forms. It was possible to assume, therefore, that they and the Arab states, too, would go on trying to extract from Africa as much in the future as they had done in the past.

Significantly France provided a symbolic signal that old imperialists never really die. On the eve of independence in Zaire (the former Belgian Congo) in 1960, the Paris government sought to invoke an old preferential claim to take over the country. It cited an 1884 promise by King Leopold II of Belgium that France would have preferential rights to the Congo if, for any unforeseen reasons, the Belgians themselves could no longer exercise control over it.[15]

In responding, the astonished Belgians offered France an answer as dusty as the nineteenth-century pledge. 'In 1884 it was possible to envisage cessions which were either gratuitous or at a heavy cost,' Prime Minister Eyskens said. 'Today territories and peoples are no longer property which may be a matter for international commerce!'

Paris dropped the matter of cession like a hot brick – but without abandoning its ambitions for a stake in the resources of the country's south-eastern province of Katanga.

In the first, full, fine flush of independence men like Kwame Nkrumah, Sékou Touré, Julius Nyerere, and the leaders of francophone countries to the north and west fired their followers with the spirit of Pan-African unity. But it was a spirit that evaporated quickly in the jungle and desert air as soon as the initial generation of elitist rulers began fashioning their nation-states in images inherited from their colonial past. Inevitably, the interests, rivalries and jealousies were transplanted into the OAU from the day of its founding in 1963. The governments of Africa began behaving just like those in Europe.

Yet conditions in the African continent were different. The challenge of shared disease brought together seven governments in the basin of the Upper Volta in a common programme of functional cooperation. Famine forced the formation of the Club du Sahel. The high cost of oil and credit deepened African poverty. In the subcontinent, South Africa's deliberate disruption of landlocked Zambia's outlets to the oceans compelled nine countries of the region to plan a $2,000-million system of road, rail and port development which could provide a basis for a broader economic constellation.

The contemporary African experience therefore suggests that the only certain thing in a changing continent is uncertainty; and, paradoxically, that true progress depends on the degree to which its people face up jointly to adversity. For the superpowers, bracing for a new phase of confrontation in the 1980s, that could be a reminder and a warning.

2. Realities

Blindness opened the eyes of seven West African governments to the need for united action in the basin of the Upper Volta a decade or so after colonial power had taken a formal departure.

They surrendered normal control of their frontiers in a fight to conquer a disease that over generations had robbed many millions of their sight. Since 1974 official cars and trucks, with *oncho* on their windscreens as their password, have been allowed to roll freely across international borders.

Oncho is an abbreviation for *onchocerciasis* or river blindness. It is carried by tiny blackflies which lay their eggs in fast-flowing, well-oxygenated rivers and streams. The carrier lives on human blood and, as it bites, it deposits a threadlike worm under the skin of its victims. The bites cause great itchiness. The worms multiply and their larvae spread through the host body. When they reach the eye they cause lesions which, unless swiftly treated, lead to part or total blindness.

The Upper Volta basin has been perhaps the worst affected but the scourge afflicts Africans in many other parts of the continent.

With so many sufferers, the governments of Ghana, Upper Volta, Benin, Mali, Niger, Togo and the Ivory Coast joined in a $120-million, twenty-year control programme, backed mainly by the former colonial powers and by international agencies, to combat the disease and to restore the once-productive Volta valleys to their old fertility. It was a challenging enterprise. Blackflies have a flight-range of 100 miles and respect no man-made borders. Only cooperative international action could deal with the problem in a systematic way. Several hundred communities had been forced to leave their waterside settlements for safer but harsher and less yielding pastures because of the scourge. Aerial spraying of the breeding grounds began in 1974 with an American product (Abate), proven non-lethal to other freshwater organisms. Monitors moved freely along and across the nearly 300,000-square-mile region in backing-up exercises and their assessments showed positive results emerging in test areas: almost a halving of the proportion of *oncho* victims.

The political by-product of the control programme has been almost as significant as its health gains. The seven concerned governments began extending cooperation into other areas.

Africans are becoming aware that they have far more to share than to quarrel over. In 1978 an official of the United Nations World Health Organization (WHO), Dr David Rowe, illuminated the point for people elsewhere around the world, when he wrote:

If you happen to be born and grow up in rural Africa you are liable to harbour four or more different disease-producing organisms simultaneously. And yet, as a parent you must be fit enough to work, or your family will starve. In your village every child at times suffers the paroxysms of malaria fever, and you and your wife will mourn the death of one or two children from this disease. The snails in the village pond carry *schistosomiasis*, and you do not consider it unusual when your children pass blood in their urine. You take for granted the disfigured faces and fingerless hands of the beggars in the village street suffering from leprosy. If you live near a river where blackflies breed, one in ten of your friends and neighbours will be blind in the prime of life. You know that waves of killing disease such as measles and meningitis and perhaps sleeping sickness are liable to strike your village. But lacking effective remedies, you tend to philosophize in the face of sickness. You make the effort to walk the ten miles to the nearest dispensary when you or your child is ill, but there may be no remedies and it may be too late.

Africans have come to realize as well their need jointly to fight diseases not mentioned by Dr Rowe: diseases of malnutrition, such as rickets and pellagra. Food insufficiencies resulting in general from poor or exhausted soil conditions, a lack of animal protein, of mineral salts, of vitamins, have all contributed to the weakening of a continental stock already decimated by the disasters of nature and men alike.

With the dawn of political freedom, Africans yearned for the knowledge, techniques, effective transportation, agricultural and communication systems that had been denied them so long. They wanted safe water, better housing and funds to exploit their own resources which they then could use for their own purposes and for downstream development. They asked for peace, stability, and the chance to share in the technology of the twentieth century, hoping that somehow these things would enable them to achieve the most basic human right of all: the right to eat.

The Sahelian Disaster

For the twenty-three million people of the Sahelian zone of West Africa, the right to eat was endangered from 1968 to 1974, when the worst and longest drought of the century descended upon them. Famine killed an estimated 200,000 people. Up to six million more were in the grip of malnutrition, reducing their already-limited life expectancy. More than 3·5 million cattle died, by UN counts. The environment and economies of the six worst affected countries – Mauritania, Senegal, Mali, Niger, Upper Volta and Chad – stretching nearly 2,500 miles along the southern edge of the Sahara Desert, were damaged, perhaps permanently.

An international relief operation was launched four years *after* hunger had begun leaving its deadly imprint. Appeals for help from the Sahelians and warnings from independent authorities had arrived too late – or so UN specialized agencies later claimed – for emergency help to have been provided in good time to head off tragedy.[1]

In the catastrophic case history of the Sahel there was much to criticize in the failed organization of relief. 'Taken singly none of the failures in the international relief effort in the Sahel seemed at the time irreparable,' averred Hal Sheets and Roger Morris, who analysed the situation on behalf of the Carnegie Endowment for International Peace. 'None alone seemed decisive. Together, however, they formed a pattern of neglect and inertia that made the rescue operation far less effective than it might have been. An administrative and bureaucratic disaster was added to the natural calamity – inevitably at a higher cost in human lives and suffering.'[2]

Political factors lay behind this major failure of the international rescue effort. Because of Parisian dominance in these stricken countries of francophone Africa, several governments provided only the minimum help needed to restore control of the situation. In the east, the communist states apparently saw little benefit to themselves in offending French susceptibilities at a time when the late President Charles de Gaulle was disengaging militarily from NATO. And besides, there were easier political options available elsewhere in Africa. In the west, the allied powers left it to the French, if not to the Africans, to take the lead in initiating and then packaging a rescue operation.

The Soviet Union looked on inscrutably as the tragedy unfolded. Faced with world-wide appeal by the Food and Agriculture Organization (FAO) of the United Nations for at least fifty-one air transports to deliver food supplies to the disaster zone, Moscow made a single Antonov aircraft available.[3] Three years later, when Somalia invaded Ethiopia, the Russians in a crash programme delivered more than 200 planeloads of arms to their new allies in Addis Ababa, in addition to an even bigger sealift. A senior Soviet diplomat was questioned about Moscow's inactivity at the time of the Sahelian disaster. 'What makes you think the French would have welcomed our planes flying around their new francophone "empire"?' he replied. 'What leads you to believe they wanted unlimited help even from the Americans, their allies?' He was asked if Moscow, nevertheless, had *offered* more help, given the dimensions of the tragedy and Moscow's professed concern for the Africans. 'The Soviet Union', he replied, 'is not in the business of public relations.'[4]

The performance of the United States and other non-communist powers was considerably better than Moscow's effort in the Sahelian saga, despite a sadly slow start. In the midst of the disaster a short-term relief programme was launched, primarily to stave off starvation through emergency deliveries of food, seed-corn for future planting and medicines. Between 1973 and 1976 the cost of this aid totalled $2·4 thousand million. In the 1976–82 period a longer-term programme was inaugurated by the Club du Sahel in an attempt permanently to solve the chronic food deficiencies of the region, and overall commitments amounted to approximately $7·6 thousand million.

A curious assortment of contributors went to the aid of the Sahelians. The French and Americans were the major donors; the West Germans, Dutch, Canadians and Swiss helped, too. Iraq and Israel, Vietnam and Zaire, Argentina and Yugoslavia, Britain and Pakistan, backed up by some other African states, joined the operations. There were some ironies. China, like the Soviet Union, loaned a single aircraft. Iraq was the only one among the money-spinning states of the Arab oil-producers which felt moved to assist.[5]

There is little doubt that Sahel provided both symbol and opportunity for disinterested collaboration between the superpowers; a collaboration that could have fulfilled the double purpose of alleviating African distress and advancing east–west *détente*; perhaps even of transforming that continent into a zone of peace and neutrality. The chance was missed.[6]

A high Senegalese official observed that all nations able to help should have helped; while those who did should have done more and done it more quickly. He went on to make these main points:

1. The communist powers did almost nothing to help in the crisis. They allowed themselves an easy conscience by saying that the western powers, and not they, were responsible for what were the results of colonialism.

2. The Americans initially gave just enough to escape criticism. 'The United States is a very generous country that knows the art of stopping at a symbolic level of aid except when they have a strategic interest,' he continued. 'They had an interest in Asia and put everything in it, bombs and all. Presidents Nguyen Van Thieu and Lon Nol received millions of dollars. The rest of the Third World got crumbs.'

3. Well-off countries of the Third World, able to assist, had not reached the stage of international humanitarianism that would have impelled them to act. 'Assistance from the Arab countries was infinitesimal compared to the needs of our countries and compared to the extra costs imposed on us by the increase in their price of oil.'[7]

An equally bitter complaint against the scale of US help came from a sociologist writing in *Jeune Afrique*. Jean-Pierre N'Diaye wondered if the outside world really cared about the Sahel tragedy:

After the animals, men. Millions of animals are dead. Will millions of men, women and children follow them? The only possible solution to this holocaust is the rapid establishment of airlifts . . . Will international solidarity be fully realized? In the modern world there is no shortage of either aircraft or of pilots. Airlifts and airfields were able to be established in Southeast Asia in record time when it was a question of defeating North Vietnam. Flying Fortresses were able to saturate the Vietnamese countryside with millions of tons of bombs. Would they not now saturate other countrysides with millions of tons of food . . .?[8]

Food scarcity is not a problem confined to Africa. But if anything focused the attention of world governments on its far-reaching implications, it was the Sahelian disaster. An FAO conference in Rome in 1974 considered ways of increasing output. In mid-1979 another parley of 150 states agreed upon a programme of action directed at transforming rural society to meet the needs of the late twentieth century. But the programme stopped short of actually binding governments to carry out the recommendations of the conference.

This first world conference on agrarian reform and rural development set out to define the sort of structural changes needed to eliminate rural poverty nationally and internationally. Underlying the discussions were issues of profound and immediate relevance to the global pretensions of the superpowers, especially in relation to Africa. The experts produced a mass of statistics which suggested that the world may well face frightening new food deficits by the end of the 1980s, unless concerted corrective action is taken. In particular two factors were stressed:

1. In mid-1979 nearly 1·5 thousand million people in the rural areas of the developing world were living in conditions of appalling poverty and food deficiency. Without swift remedial action their numbers would increase by about two-thirds, or a further one thousand million, by the year 2000.

2. In Africa 254 million people were classified among the rural hungry. They were mostly smallholders, working plots under two hectares in area and their output was trailing population growth (currently estimated at an annual 2·9 per cent).

Two options faced the powers, according to John Malecela, Tanzanian minister for agriculture: to implement the recommendations of the conference or to ignore them. The consequence, he warned, of the second option would be the likelihood of 'revolution and world-wide instability'. A more subjective submission came from Morena Leorthi, representing Lesotho, who branded the entire conference as 'a huge and expensive hoax to hoodwink the rural masses and those whose power has been usurped by the élite'.

The conference in Rome succeeded, at least, in identifying the priority tasks facing the world – and not only the developing nations – and there was consensus on the need for a unified attempt to resolve the problem of rural poverty by the provision of more fertilizer, improved irrigation and agricultural equipment, and larger supplies of pesticide. Most important, it was agreed that peasants had to be assured access to land that they could cultivate, and this recommendation carried with it the explicit proposal that national governments should adopt radical programmes for the redistribution of land to those who did not then possess it.

On the multilateral level there was agreement – at least on paper – that bilateral as well as international aid should be directed towards the goal of reducing if not eliminating rural poverty. Industrialized countries of the rich north were urged again and again by Third World delegates to avoid any form of protectionism against the raw and processed agricultural products of the developing nations.

Whether or not, in the coming decade or so, participating countries – especially richer ones lamenting the onset of a deep recession – would set out to implement the adopted action programme was another matter. The poor and hungry of the world had little option but to wait and see.

Struggle for Survival

There is more myth than mystery over why Africans so long suffered disease, poverty and underdevelopment. Part of the explanation for their suffering lies in accidents of geography, vagaries of climate, and natural disasters. Part is rooted, too, in the mistakes of men.

An astronaut looking down would see the African plateau as a vast sheet of rock, shielded from oceanic influences by mountain ranges and sheer cliffs rimming the narrow Atlantic and Indian Ocean coastlines. Over 11 million square miles in area, it covers more than a fifth of the earth's land surface. Great basins rather than folded mountains characterize the plateau and from some flow the continent's five great rivers.

The Congo, Nile, Volta, Niger and Zambezi tumble down to the sea, mostly over steep ledges and through ravines, making navigation into

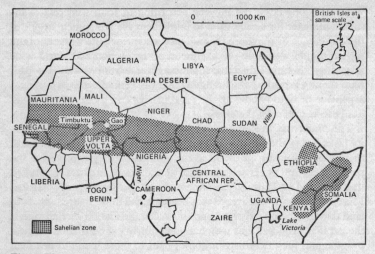

Fig. 6: The creeping desert
SOURCE: *The Economist*, 17 May 1980.

the deep interior impossible. For millennia, inner Africa was isolated from the outside world, meaning mainly Europe and West Asia.

A continent locked up from the seas for 500 million years was bad enough. Even worse was that it should straddle the steaming, humid, cruel equator, lined with forests along the Congo basin and in the heavily watered regions along the West African coast. Where rivers run, forests often turn into jungles. Where jungles spread, swamps form. Forest, jungle and swamp become breeding grounds for killer-pests.

Beyond the equatorial zone, to the north and south, roll the grass-lands, bush-country and savanna. The topsoil, baked on ancient rock by the sun of endless summers, is poor. Rainfalls over the centuries became more erratic, ranging from virtually none at all in the Sahara Desert to 170 inches a year in western coastal states like Sierra Leone.

With eroded expanses the desert advanced, parching people, plant life and cattle, forcing Africans to search for game and to scratch for crops. To escape the encroaching sands, to cheat the carriers of disease, to seek new pastures, tribes or nations moved with their herds in some of Africa's great, unrecorded migrations. Migrations often caused con-flict.

The Sahara – Arabic for 'wilderness' – split Africa in two more than 5,000 years ago. The sea of sand, covering more than three million square miles, is nearly as big as the United States. Some widely quoted estimates have suggested that it is creeping southwards at the rate of thirty miles a year – or 18 feet each hour – not only because of diminishing rainfall but also because of ill-managed human and animal occupation and activity. Planless over-grazing, dating back to the late nineteenth century, has been suggested as a major cause. 'The physical destruction of the Sahel was not an overnight process,' Nicholas Wade wrote in the journal *Science* in 1974. 'Its beginnings can be traced back to the French colonization of the late nineteenth century when the Sahelian people lost, with their political power, the control over their range and wells which was vital to the proper management of their resources.'[9]

North of the Sahara, along the Mediterranean littoral, the people were exposed variously to Phoenician, Greek, Roman and other European influences, as well as those of Islam. Below the Sahara lay what is now called black Africa, with its vast variety of clans and tribes, national entities. They are categorized by some ethnologists – arguably – into three main groups: Bantu, Negroes and Hamites. But from the Atlantic to the Indian Ocean, from Timbuktu to Pretoria, they are as different from each other culturally, often physically, in historical experience and politically, as Sicilians are distinct from Scandinavians or Slavs.

Civilizations existed in the continent long before the coming of the white man. Around the life and times of Christ the blacksmiths of Benin (in what is now Nigeria) were producing their bronzes, smelting and designing copper ornaments and utensils, putting iron to workaday use, mining and fashioning gold for a variety of purposes. Wheeled carts were being used in Nigeria and horses were put to work, while later, in the Congo, elephants were tamed to meet the needs of men for moving huge loads.[10]

In what was Rhodesia, once the land of Ophir and reputedly the site of the legendary King Solomon's mines, the mysterious Zimbabwe ruins are located. The origins of the huge stone monuments have for centuries been a subject of speculation. They may have been built more than a thousand years ago by either the Bantu-speaking peoples or, as some have suggested, invaders from the Arab north.

One of the sad realities for Africans was that the Arab traders who crossed the Sahara in their caravans, back and forth regularly over the centuries, usually left their tools behind. They needed to travel light. So the implements the Arabs had made or acquired from contacts with Europeans, their wheels and advanced instruments which could have helped so much to develop Africa's agricultural and manufacturing processes, simply were not available to be exchanged for the metal and leatherwork, the carvings and ivory and other products they sought from the sub-Saharan peoples. Here, then, was another factor arresting African development.

If the interior of the continent was sealed off from the overseas world since, and even before, the Middle Ages, it did not mean coastal Africans waited idly by for traders to come to them. In fact they were in vigorous commerce with countries across the Indian Ocean and on the Arabian Peninsula from at least the eleventh century onwards. Sub-Saharan leather and iron products found their way to Europe by way of the trans-Saharan caravan trails. Paul Bohannan noted in his study, *African Outline*, that 'there are portrait busts of Negroes in Roman art. Europe must recognize the fact that it was *Europe* that woke up only in the fifteenth century.' [11]

Deep inside the continent, though, the pressures of their hostile environment impelled Africans to share their way of life in tightly disciplined systems of social organization described by outsiders as 'tribalism'. The concept of 'tribalism' had, of course, no less validity for Europeans, whether they were the Welsh, Scots or Irish of the British Isles or the Bretons, Corsicans, or Basques of France and Spain. It meant that people huddled together beneath a collective social umbrella for their own well-being. Livingstone reported finding communities in nineteenth-century Africa that did not know their neighbours, or the names of hills, twenty miles away. But Livingstone, if he had travelled through Europe or Asia, might have encountered exactly the same sort of thing, especially where the people of a region spoke their special language or dialect and lacked transport. Tribal or community codes protected and promoted conformism in the general interest. There was no time, no place, no need for egocentric individualism.

By sharing adversities – the merciless elements and disease – Africans were able to survive. The sense of community they evolved was reflected not only in the cohesiveness of their social systems but also in their approach to religion. With impeccable logic they concluded from their own experience that forces of evil, rather than of good, surrounded them. The jungle had its beasts of prey and reptiles. Rivers, lakes and swamps spawned their flying, stinging disease-carriers. Deserts sent forth messages of thirst and hunger. If a beneficent Creator happened to be presiding over the earthly order he did so, at least to Africans, in ways beyond their understanding. All available evidence provided by the rites, prayers and traditions that have survived the centuries suggests that Africans devoted themselves, as a result, to the appeasement of a divinity of devils.

For any people, in such circumstances, that was a reasonable deduction. Not surprisingly Africans wanted to live, to strive for happiness and health. How then to achieve these things? Not, surely, by defying the evils which menaced them. Perhaps, instead, by appeasing the forces at source and then by rooting out their causes. These deductions provided the basis for the system of sacrifice: sacrifice by offering scarce food, the blood of chickens and goats, the wearing of tokens, talismans and charms. But that was not all. Like Christians, many Africans did not accept that the dead are truly dead. They believed their ancestors lived on, sometimes in earthly forms as animals or trees, and able to wreak belated vengeance on luckless victims. Hence the worship of ancestral spirits and the attempts by charlatans, posing as witch doctors, to claim contact with the dead.

These, on the whole, were disintegrating beliefs. They were always transcended by an acknowledgement, grudging and tacit perhaps, among the diverse religions of the continent, of some higher deity who, having created the universe, withdrew leaving the world to its own devices. Some people found themselves more fortunate than others, not necessarily by accident. Herein lay the 'moral' content of their approach. Beyond an inevitable tendency towards fatalism, there seemed to be a recognition that there was scope – perhaps even ultimate salvation – for those who practised goodness, generosity and devotion in the quest to fulfil their instant needs.

The Dark Years

Africans had human foes to fight, too.

The fifteenth-century voyages of discovery by the Portuguese brought rival nations to the fringes of the continent in search of riches. No understanding of black attitudes towards whites today is possible without awareness of what turned out to be one of the darkest, most inglorious periods in history. This centred on the organized traffic in African slaves which, starting in the early sixteenth century, lasted for more than three hundred years. Its toll was immeasurable. Its psychological and political effects on Africans still persist.

Africans became victims of three different kinds of slavery, according to most authorities.

Within the continent rulers often enslaved prisoners of war. But Africans treated their own slaves more humanely than did Arab, European or American owners. Their invariable purpose was not commercial but to enhance either their prestige or power. The slaves could be assimilated into their new social group, acquire rights and even rise to positions above those of free men. The African slave therefore assumed a form of kinship status and could count upon treatment that was generally benign.[12]

Arab marauders worked the north and east coasts of the continent for slaves that they then sold to dealers in the Arabian peninsula, Turkey and the Middle East. Their system was to employ Swahili middlemen to round up the victims. This was done by the dispatch of raiding and negotiating parties into the interior in quest of 'bodies' – men, women and children – who, chained together, carrying ivory and other local products in their hands or on their backs, were marched to coastal trading centres. From there they were dispatched in tightly crammed dhows to the market-places of the Middle East. No one now-adays could know just how many thousands, or tens of thousands, of the captives perished either on the overland or during the sea journeys.

Befitting their commercial sophistication, the major powers of Europe organized their slave-trading practices on a cost-effective basis. They concentrated their activities mainly up and down Africa's west coast, from Cape Verde to Angola; and, conforming to the rules of the game, channelled their 'buying' arrangements through kings and other rulers who in those days held sway along the West African coast. They focused on the North and South American and Caribbean markets where there was high demand for efficient plantation workers able, unlike Indian or other bondmen, to survive the rigours of the tropics.

In time the Portuguese, Spanish, British, French, Dutch, Scandinavians and Germans rationalized their operations in a neat trian-gular pattern. Ships brought European goods for 'sale' (exchange) to loyal rulers along the West African coast. These 'importers' paid for the goods with slaves. The human cargo then was shipped across the Atlantic for disposal to Caribbean and American dealers. Using the proceeds, the shipowners then loaded up with sugar or other products for delivery to Europe. Each leg of the three-way journey yielded its particular profit.

By the twentieth century, according to the conventionally conser-vative estimate of Charlotte and Denis Plimmer, 'some 11,000,000 Negroes had been sold ... and transported by whites in the stinking holds of slaveships, to be marketed in scores of American and West Indian ports'.[13] Other writers have offered far higher estimates (up to 150 million), taking into account the numbers of victims who, seeking to evade capture, perished in the wars caused within Africa by the trade or along the routes to servitude. The figure of eleven million relates to those who actually landed alive at their destinations, but leaves out of account those who died in resisting capture, or from exhaustion, dis-ease, displaying defiance and a variety of other factors.[13]

Nor was this all. To compensate local rulers and dealers for the victims they had captured, and for the palm oil, gum, gold and ivory they also provided, the Europeans 'paid' with outdated rifles, bullets, gunpowder, vivid clothing and alcohol – rum, wines and liqueurs.[14]

There were other brutalities, too numerous to cite, yet enough to have aroused the consciences of Europeans for a considerable time.

Thus wrote General H. Meynier, a Frenchman, in 1911:

From the first day of their encounter Europeans affirmed the principle of their superiority over the black race. They have forced Africans into slavery, justifying it on the basis of superior strength. To open markets for their trade in Africa, they have stamped out the last vestiges of African civilization. If one compares their methods with those of the Berbers and even the Arabs, the parallel to this day does not favour the Europeans.[15]

W. W. Howith, a Briton, seventy-three years earlier, had written with even greater bitterness in *Colonization and Christianity*:

The barbarisms and atrocities perpetrated by the so-called Christians in every area of the world and on all the peoples they have been able to subjugate have no parallel in any other era of world history, in any other race, however savage, coarse, pitiless or shameless it may have been.

A modern African leader has offered a contemporary judgement. 'Africa remains marked by the crimes of the slave traders,' President Ahmed Sékou Touré of Guinea said in 1962. 'Up to now her potentialities are restricted by underpopulation.'

To illustrate the extent of that underpopulation, in relative terms, a Guyanan professor of history, the late Dr Walter Rodney, cited the following, necessarily imprecise, estimates of continental populations from 1650 to 1900:

Table 2: Estimates of continental populations (in millions)

	1650	1750	1850	1900
Africa	100	100	100	120
Europe	103	144	274	423
Asia	257	437	656	837

'They indicate a consensus among researchers on population that the huge African continent has an abnormal record of stagnation,' Rodney wrote. 'There is no causative factor other than the trade in slaves to which attention can be drawn.'[16]

The wealth of a nation is ultimately vested in its human resources. To the extent to which those resources are reduced, so a nation's, or a continent's, capacity to develop is lessened. Even worse, to the extent that Africans contributed to the development of American and Caribbean output, Africa shouldered part of the burden of European–American–Caribbean development. The shrewd slave-dealers, after all, hand-picked only the healthiest, most virile and youngest among the human specimens lined up before them in the melancholy market-places. They would always command the highest prices.

Profits from the triangular trade – with slaving as its base – helped finance Britain's Industrial Revolution and launch some of its best-known commercial institutions, which were still flourishing in the late twentieth century. It was Lord North who, as prime minister in 1783, reminded Quaker proponents of abolition that the slave trade was essential not only for Britain but for almost all the nations of Europe.[17]

In his book *Capitalism and Slavery* – written originally as a doctoral dissertation – Eric Williams, sometime prime minister of Trinidad and Tobago, documented with muted sarcasm how some of Britain's great families and firms defended or benefited from the slave system. David and Alexander Barclay, members of a Quaker family, who in 1756 were engaged in the slave trade, made fortunes that enabled them to marry into wealthy banking families. It was from these beginnings that the Barclays Bank of today emerged, with some of its key international interests still centred in Africa. Lloyd's of London, the world-wide insurance and underwriting institution, also owed its origins to the slave trade. James Watt's steam engine was developed with funds provided by the slave-owners of the West Indies. Williams observed, too, that Gladstone, Disraeli, Burke, Coleridge and Carlyle – prime ministers, poets, writers – were among the supporters of or apologists for the system. 'It was in vain for moralists to point out that every brick of the great warehouses of Bristol and Liverpool was cemented in Negro blood,' Professor D. W. Brogan reflected in an introduction to Williams's work.[18]

Nineteenth-century Britain, transformed by the Industrial Revolution, began first slowly, then more swiftly, to take advantage of the fact that there were more lucrative alternatives to the widely condemned trade in African slaves. The rising manufacturing and merchant classes discovered that Africa was in need of all the products a newly industrialized society had to offer. Conversely, Africa itself, as slaving declined, was able to provide a cornucopia of palm oil, timber, rubber, cotton and the other raw materials needed to keep the ever-expanding industries of Britain going. It was a recognition as timely as it was expedient for the campaign first to abolish slavery, later properly to emancipate the Africans in bondage in the New World, Europe, southern Africa and elsewhere.

Formal abolition came first in 1808, when British colonies were well supplied with slaves. It was enacted in the name of 'justice, humanity and sound policy'. Emancipation followed later on grounds of a more genuine humanitarianism evoked by campaigners like Thomas Clarkson, James Stephen and his son, and James Ramsay. The role played by William Wilberforce, according to the study by Williams, was exaggerated by historians. In Williams's view, Wilberforce explicitly disavowed 'any intention of emancipating the slaves'.[18]

Self-interest, coupled with a belated humanitarian concern, effectively ended organized slavery by the late nineteenth century.

But bondage took other forms.[19]

Collapse of Colonialism

The structure of colonialism ensured for the next seventy years that the underdevelopment of Africans would be perpetuated, so that white men would benefit from Africa's valuable resources, from black labour and from sales to a black captive market.

An attempt to justify the white man's mission was offered by a man reputed to have been one of Britain's most successful governors. Sir Philip Mitchell, representative of the late King George VI in Uganda and Kenya from 1948 to 1954, described the condition of the East African people as he said the British found them in 1890:

They [the blacks] had no wheeled transport and no animal transport either. They had no roads nor towns; no tools except small hand hoes, axes, wooden digging sticks and the like; no manufactures and no industrial products except the simplest domestic handiwork; no commerce as we understand it and no currency, although in some places barter of produce was facilitated by the use of small shells; they had never heard of working for wages. They went stark naked or clad in the bark of trees or the skins of animals; and they had no means of writing, even by hieroglyphics, nor of numbering except by their fingers or making notches in a stick or knots in a piece of grass or fibre; they had no weights or measures of general use. Perhaps most astonishing of all to the modern European mind they had no calendar nor notation of time. Before European occupation there was no way of saying '1st January, 1890' or '2.30 p.m.' or their equivalents in any language . . . They were pagan, spirit or ancestor propitiators in the grip of magic or witchcraft, their minds cribbed and confined by superstition . . . They are a people who in 1890 were in a more primitive condition than anything of which there is any record in pre-Roman Britain.[20]

In the Belgian Congo (Zaire) bordering Uganda, then the personal property of Leopold II of Belgium, much else was going on at the time that Mitchell was describing. Africans were being hunted down in the forests, forced to work on the big estates, organized into chain gangs, flogged and manhandled. Leopold was fulfilling his pledge at the Berlin Conference to bring civilization, Christianity and uplift to the unfortunates whom he referred to as 'savages'. Workers on his estates who failed to fulfil required quotas of production, or otherwise satisfy their white masters, had a hand or foot, or sometimes both, amputated. The system of forced labour – and it persisted until the Second World War – was the rule and took the place of taxes. Periodically, entire tribes which rebelled were massacred. On the evidence of diplomats, writers, politicians, historians and missionaries (Belgians among them) up to five *million* Congolese died in the period between the mid-1880s and 1910. Among the protesters were men like Sir Winston Churchill, Theodore Roosevelt, Mark Twain, Sir Arthur Conan Doyle, E. D. Morel, sometime British foreign secretary Sir Edward Grey, and Roger Casement (the Irishman working as a British diplomat who was later to be executed during the First World War on treason charges). The international hue and cry that followed the revelations compelled Leopold by 1908 to begin yielding to the pressures for reform.

The ravages wrought by some of Europe's colonizers so scarred African minds and memories with bitterness and hostility that they sealed the fate of colonialism. Realities for Africans, as servants or bondmen to their European masters, inexorably led to the struggles and wars of independence which would involve the superpowers of the future.

Apart from the historic inevitability, colonialism collapsed because of the avarice of its practitioners. Certainly the colonial powers had brought some administrative coherence to parts of the continent. They had introduced machines, equipment, techniques, even certain social values, universally valid, to Africa. But essentially it was a coherence for the purpose of profit.

It advanced, at least temporarily, the interests of the metropolitan power and the white settler communities. Any overspill benefits derived by the African were largely fortuitous, despite what was called 'the paramountcy of native interests'. A glance at some aspects of colonial activity in Africa tells its own story of the profit factor in the underdevelopment of the continent.

Railroads, highways, schools, hospitals, agricultural techniques and various socio-economic services were indeed introduced. By the 1950s, however, when it had become clear that the days of Europe's empires were numbered, communications generally within and between French, Belgian, British, Portuguese and other African territories were abysmal. As one example, to make a telephone call from Nairobi in the east to Dakar in the west, it was necessary to get through to London, and then Paris, before reaching Africa again. Illiteracy in most of Africa levelled out at around 85–90 per cent at the time of decolonization. Disease continued to take its unrecorded toll. Drug-making firms offloaded in Africa dubious products and techniques which were banned in their home societies. They were still doing so in the 1980s.

The industrial development of most colonies was ignored. Instead, the focus was on agricultural practices geared to yield quick profits rather than to serve local needs. Production of crops for export took precedence over those needed for home consumption. Cotton and coffee, for example, were cultivated for export to overseas factories where big profits lay in the refining processes. Dairy products and meat, which could have supplied hungry, underfed Africans, were accorded secondary if not tertiary importance.

These were among the factors which contributed to the poverty and backwardness of Africans in the days of colonialism. During the 1950s in parts of rural Africa, average *annual* cash earnings were less than £12 (or about $34 at the prevailing exchange rate). Whites viewed Africans in general as backward and ignorant, unfit for any but the most menial or repetitive and unskilled jobs. This, though, did not preclude blacks, when called upon to do so, from driving locomotives in the former Belgian Congo, serving as bank clerks, carrying out the most perilous functions in the gold, copper, uranium and other mines of Southern and Central Africa. Yet illiteracy is not a phenomenon confined to Africa. In the United States, for example, 1·5 million American boys were rejected as unfit for service in the Second World War on grounds of illiteracy. Throughout imperial Africa, the need for coherently planned programmes of education and training was either ignored or set aside for real or imagined lack of funds even while whites complained constantly at what they saw as African inefficiency and inferiority. When Britain transferred power to Zambia (formerly the protectorate of Northern Rhodesia) in October 1964, the country, with a population of nearly four million, had precisely twenty-four black university graduates.

The political reality for some 200 million Africans in the mid-1950s was that their continent – excluding the independent states of South Africa, Egypt, Liberia, Libya and Ethiopia – was being ruled by *five million* whites. Some British, French and other colonies were granted limited measures of self-rule, theoretically to prepare local populations for the sort of refined systems of parliamentary democracy developed over centuries in Europe. Time would show that political institutions imported from the Old World had little in common with African experience, custom or culture. The essential need of the overwhelming majority of blacks was for the staple things of life so long denied them: enough food, safe water, effective medical services, land to work, productive jobs, clothing, proper shelter, reasonable education and the right to manage their own affairs in their own way. The nice paper subtleties of constitutions fashioned by the cool, constitutional lawyers of London, Paris and elsewhere that would enshrine the privileges of well-groomed élites were acceptable only to those who would inherit the authority once exercised by their former rulers, but to the mass of

Africans they were meaningless. It should have surprised no one in touch with Africa's realities when African parliaments, one after another, tossed those constitutions out of the window.

Freedom Deferred

Decolonization, it became clear, hardly heralded a brave new world of true independence. Fresh challenges had to be faced and once the euphoria of freedom celebrations evaporated the high aspirations of expectant peoples had somehow to be contained. Africa's formal political emancipation since the 1960s proved, in fact, to be only the beginning of a new struggle for total independence because few, if any, of the metropoles surrendered their investments, transferred their expertise, or loosened their control of the commanding heights of the national economies. The departing colonial powers preserved their ability to make and break governments, help or hurt incumbent rulers, manoeuvre or manipulate to protect their interests.

Africans themselves contributed to their own difficulties. In a succession of cases, élite groups of Africans simply moved in to assume the roles of the former European rulers, as if that constituted their interpretation of true independence. They behaved as if they were rightful heirs to the privileges they had previously assailed, privileges that included the splendid residences, high salaries, lavish living standards and unnumbered domestic and personal staffs of their former rulers. President Félix Houphouët-Boigny of the Ivory Coast built an air-conditioned palace and park for himself costing millions of dollars, with materials flown in from the Soviet Union, pulling down perfectly good buildings to make the necessary space, and dressing his courtiers in French-styled costumes while tens of thousands of his people, notably the Senoufo, went hungry.

Erstwhile Emperor Bokassa I of the Central African Empire, one of the world's poorest countries, set up nine palaces for himself, one for each of his nine wives, bought mansions and properties in France and had France pay for his $22-million coronation in 1978. The French, who acquired coveted rights to mine uranium after setting up Bokassa in office, duly unseated him in 1979 for his role in shooting and killing defiant schoolchildren protesting against his edicts. President Sese Seko Mobutu of bankrupt Zaire stopped over in Nairobi in September 1977 with a seventy-strong entourage which included two doctors, two head waiters, a chef and dozens of lovely young women. He had, with the aid of money from the American taxpayer, made himself reportedly one of the world's ten richest men. Gabon's President El Hadi Omar Bongo treated himself to a 'little Versailles' costing an estimated $700 million when his country began producing oil. It was a palace complete with push-button contraptions that made walls vanish at a touch, revolving doors, and a variety of other symbols of a white potentate's 'civilization'.

There were other excesses. The repression, political murders and injustices of ousted Presidents Idi Amin of Uganda (after eight years) and Francisco Macías Nguema of Equatorial Guinea (after eleven years), both deposed in 1979, foreshadowed a house-cleaning in Africa.

Meanwhile cases of corruption, nepotism and dictatorial whimsy formed a catalogue too long to cite. But it was significant that the widely publicized infamies of these dictators did nothing to prevent east and west alike from doing business with them. The Russians sent arms and instructors to Amin and, for a time, with the Cubans were helping Equatorial Guinea economically and with education. Post-Franco Spain, France, Switzerland and, until 1976, the United States were assisting the Macías regime. U S companies were mining diamonds in Bokassa's empire and obtained a five-year concession to explore for oil.

Men like Amin, Bokassa and Macías were the products, generally, of British, French and Spanish colonial policies. Amin's *coup*, which toppled the radically oriented President Milton Obote in 1971, neither surprised nor displeased the British government of Prime Minister Edward Heath. London had advance information of the event, yet refrained from warning Obote, who might have been able to take preventive action.[21]

Obote had offended the British with his outspoken onslaught on the Heath government's proposed sale of arms to South Africa and with his nationalization of British firms in Uganda. Bokassa's personal relations with Valéry Giscard d'Estaing preceded Giscard's rise to the French presidency and went to the point of shared hunting expeditions, gifts of diamonds and implied endorsement by Paris of the emperor's policies. But when Bokassa stood accused of involvement in the mass execution of children, the French had little option but to abandon Giscard's friend. The Spanish authorities dropped Macías only when his nephew led a bloodless *coup* against him. By then, conscious of their across-the-board economic involvement with their former colony, the Spanish had connived at Macías's use of torture, murder and forced labour in the cocoa plantations. Until 1976, at least, they had banned media coverage of all this.[22]

After his downfall, Amin first took refuge in Libya, vowing one day to reconquer Uganda; Bokassa received sanctuary in the Ivory Coast, thanks to Giscard's intervention with the aged Houphoüet-Boigny; and Macías was executed in September 1979. Each had left his country in ruins, blood-soaked, stricken economically, fearful, ethnically torn. There was a prolonged tussle for the succession in Uganda. In what had now become the Central African Republic Bokassa's French-installed replacement relied on Paris for his security. President Teodor Obiang Nguema Mbasogo, who took over from Macías, reverted to reliance on the west after years of collaboration with the communist powers. All needed outside aid urgently. All had to wait . . .

The Politics of Aid

In a world in recession Africa's growing needs were for survival and subsistence. 'It is a matter of humanity to conquer hunger and disease,' said former West German Chancellor Willy Brandt's Commission in offering its 'Programme for (North–South) Survival' in 1980. For 'humanity' to win the war on want and sickness Africa, in particular, needed help. But international aid, like truth, comes in many colours. And a new reality had transcended early African fantasies of what post-colonial freedom might bring. East and west were using aid to advance or preserve their own interests and to score national or ideological gains. 'Food is now the greatest weapon we have for keeping the peace of the world . . . as other countries become more reluctant to upset us,' declaimed US Secretary for Agriculture John Block shortly before President Reagan's inauguration. Leaders of the Soviet Union preferred to use more conventional weapons as instruments of aid.

France, though, already had provided a classic illustration of the politics of aid. With the wary agreement of five partners in 1978–9 it launched the Association Concertée pour le Développement de l'Afrique to rationalize their varied aid programmes, and so to enhance their cost-effectiveness. In a style reminiscent of nineteenth-century diplomacy each was allocated a special sphere of responsibility coinciding with its influence and talents. By May 1980 the five countries had agreed France would undertake rural development in the Senegal and Niger river basins; Britain could improve road and railroad links in the Sudan and between Zimbabwe and Mozambique; West Germany should do the same in eastern and southern Africa; while Belgium and Canada took on other specified works. The United States, long excluded from old colonial preserves, volunteered for a public-health programme of almost transcontinental proportions and embracing millions of people.

By early 1981, with a $35-million congressional grant, the Americans had launched pilot schemes in eleven countries for a five-year drive to eradicate child diseases. Regional vaccination centres were planned, 4,000 Africans were to be trained, coordination with WHO was agreed.

Revelation of the secretly negotiated arrangements in March 1981, however, brought angry protests from French medical, research, and pharmaceutical institutions and from politicians. They complained that the door had been opened for US firms to capture Africa's expanding pharmaceutical market; that France's pioneering scientific activities in African public health would suffer; and above all that the Americans would reap a golden political harvest for their highly visible humanitarian activities. As the controversy rumbled on the health of Africa's people was hardly remembered.

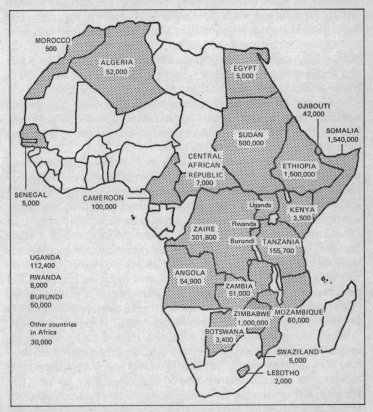

Fig. 7: Refugees in African countries (UN estimates November 1980)
SOURCE: *US News & World Report* map; basic data: UN High Commissioner for Refugees.

3. The Arms Race

For Africa's three most notorious dictators, Idi Amin, Francisco Macías Nguema and Salah Ad-din Ahmed Bokassa I, 1979 was a bad year. But although fourteen million Ugandans, Equatorial Guineans and Central Africans were suddenly freed from tyranny, fresh uncertainties beset them. Internally, there were rivals who plotted for power and vengeance-seekers with scores to settle. Externally, foreign governments jostled to gain new influence or recover old privileges.

It was, on the other hand, a vintage period for those military and political elitists – Frantz Fanon's 'spoilt children of yesterday's colonialism' and their challengers – who inherited power or seized it, sometimes with the help of their former rulers.

The American ambassador to the United Nations, Andrew Young, observed: 'Of forty-eight African nations to have achieved independence at least forty of those achieved independence without violence.'[1] But continuous conflict came in the aftermath of orderly transition. Up to sixty successful *coups* took place plus an unrecorded number of failed attempts to topple incumbent leaders. More than half Africa's fifty-two countries were affected by the forty civil or trans-border wars. By the 1980s, of the twenty-nine leaders who signed the charter setting up the OAU in 1963 five were still in office, seventeen had been deposed, three killed in *coups* and four had died of natural causes.

The reason why violence followed relatively peaceful power transfers in British and French Africa (Zimbabwe and Algeria excepted) was clear.

Weakened by war, unable to push back tides of nationalism rising around the world, Britain and France put away their nineteenth-century presumptions that direct political control was needed to preserve access to the resources and markets of their colonial territories. They felt able to abandon what they recognized to be an obsolete framework of thought because they had groomed heirs to take over, heirs ready and willing to settle for the shadow rather than the substance of true independence. Foreign economic dominance in key areas was perpetuated by indirect means.

The succession therefore passed generally to leaders more concerned with achieving authority than fundamental change, despite their radical rhetoric. Their social standards, political judgements and moral values had been moulded in the universities, polytechnics, military colleges, cafés and salons of London, Paris and their environs.

The influences they absorbed often had greater relevance to maintaining the old order than to fulfilling the new expectations of their countrymen. Ultimately, on assuming office, they came face to face with the critical difference between what is and what ought to be. It was a critical difference representing the divide between reality and fantasy, between what the former colonizers permitted heirs to do and what their people expected.

'We got caught up in the conflict of culture, of trying to graft the so-called sophistication of the European society to our African society,' Lieutenant-General Olusegun Obasanjo, former Nigerian head of state, suggested. 'The result so far has been an abysmal failure.'[2]

For the mass of Africans the euphoria generated by the *uhuru* celebrations of the early 1960s had long since vanished. In certain sectors there had been improvements: greater caring for the needs of children, the fight against hunger, resource development. But poverty, disease and sometimes early death still remained the general rule, even though black rather than white bureaucracies were now responsible for running the state.

By the 1980s the reality facing most Africans was that their reliance on outsiders had increased, not lessened. Food output per inhabitant was roughly 10 per cent lower than it had been a decade before. In contrast military expenditure by and for African states burgeoned. From 1950 to 1972 Africa as a whole had imported major weapons to the value of $1·2 thousand million annually. By 1979 continental tensions and rivalries had pushed annual weapon costs up to $15 thousand million. World military spending was running at about $410 thousand million yearly or nearly $1 million a minute – about 500 per cent more than the 1960–70 average.[3]

None of this was fortuitous. Even before Africa's rate of militarization began outstripping that of every other region outside the Middle East, the misjudgements of the western powers had created opportunities which the Russians gratefully seized. The fact that the Russians, with monotonous regularity, misused those opportunities or failed effectively to exploit them, was hardly attributable to western prescience. It was, rather, their sheer good luck which somehow they seemed unable to build upon.

The catalogue of western errors is a long one. France's efforts to subdue Algeria after years of anguished fighting finally collapsed and rocked the structure of the French state; the British–French invasion of Suez in 1956 temporarily split NATO, ensured a role for Moscow in a transformed African political situation and, in the view of some authorities, provided a cover for the Russian invasion of Hungary; the CIA-sponsored ousting of Ghanaian President Kwame Nkrumah set back the cause of pan-Africanism indefinitely without stabilizing either the country or its neighbours; British and Belgian manoeuvrings, in collusion with the white Rhodesian rulers of the defunct Central African Federation, to detach the wealthy province of Shaba (Katanga) from Zaire split not only the west but also the blacks of the region; the calculated tolerance displayed by successive British governments to the white minority who illegally seized power in Rhodesia in 1965 created conditions for a guerrilla war in which nearly 30,000 people were killed and 100,000 were maimed; Portugal's tortured attempt, with 200,000 men, to crush liberation movements in its African colonies, covertly supported by the allies until it too failed, made it easy for the Russians to champion the freedom fighters; American misconceptions in Angola and the Horn of Africa gave the Russians two prized footholds in the continent; and continuing western investment in and collaboration with South Africa identified the Americans and former colonial powers with the *apartheid* republic, whose discriminatory race policies remained a target of hatred among all Africa's black millions.

Inevitably, even moderate African leaders turned their gaze eastwards for the support that they felt they could not get in the west. A classic example was provided by Zambian President Kenneth Kaunda. In the 1970s, he risked his political life by entering a dialogue with South Africa's former Prime Minister B. J. Vorster, but by early 1980 had reached the limits of frustration. He concluded an arms-purchasing agreement with the Soviet Union. He was not the first to do so. He would not be the last.

And help they got. It was military help initially that hastened the transformation of Africa into a new area of conflict between the great powers. The effect was further to arrest the social and economic development which Africans needed above all else.

'The association of much of Africa, of Mediterranean countries such as Spain, Morocco and Tunisia, to say nothing of Israel, with Western Europe, was in the geopolitical interest of the west,' Henry Kissinger reflected in his memoirs in 1979. 'To thwart a relationship of these key countries with Europe would be the height of political folly.'[4]

For the American superpower and its friends that might have been true. For the Soviet superpower and its partners, because they took it to be true, it became a prime purpose to foil that 'geopolitical interest of the west'.

Aided by outsiders, abetted by some of their own rulers, playing host to scores of thousands of foreign troops from distant lands, shadowed by the threat of a South African nuclear strike capability, the people of Africa by 1980 had become involved in an all-out arms race without an end in sight.

The militarization of Africa by the end of the 1970s threatened crushing new burdens for its swiftly swelling population.

A simplified examination of the black man's social and economic burden shows why:

1. Annual spending on soldiers and their weaponry averaged about $34 per person or more than one-tenth of annual income.

2. Investment in teachers, schools and general education was using up an average $23 per person each year, at a time when know-how was Africa's prime need.

3. For every 100,000 African people there were 290 soldiers but only 46 doctors.

4. Public debts of the countries of sub-Sahara Africa alone, according to the World Bank, exceeded $17 thousand million in 1977. By 1979 military spending was running at an annual rate of $15 thousand million.

5. Since 1960 richer countries contributed each year an average of $5 per person to help poorer fellow inhabitants of the earth, compared with $95 per person spent on defence programmes.

6. The annual cost to the United Nations of international peace-keeping was about $135 million while member-states were spending in total 3,000 times as much on their own forces.

7. A woman in parts of rural Africa had to walk several hours a day to collect her family's safe water while one of the superpowers could deliver an intercontinental ballistic missile across the globe in a matter of minutes.

8. For the cost of a single one of those missiles fifty million hungry African children could be fed adequately and 340,000 primary schools could be built.[5]

There were few signs to suggest that the OAU had the authority either to settle dangerous disputes or to restrain the build-up of arsenals. There were even fewer indications of an east–west willingness to curtail direct or indirect intrusions.

If anything, the opposite was true.

The general military picture in sub-Saharan Africa in the early 1970s revealed that all the major outside powers had varying forms of collaborative agreements with key countries of the continent. In broad outline the east–west line-up showed that:

1. America had security assistance accords, including staging facilities, with Kenya, Zaire, Ghana, Liberia, Senegal and Somalia. Britain had training, overflying, supply and defence arrangements with Kenya and newly independent Zimbabwe, military missions in several West African countries, and training and supply agreements with most of its former colonies except Tanzania. France had defence and cooperation pacts with the Central African Republic, Gabon, Niger, Upper Volta, Ivory Coast, the Malagasy Republic, Senegal, Cameroon and Djibouti. Several lesser training and technical military cooperation arrangements, which fell short of full-scale agreements, were also operational.

2. The USSR had treaties of friendship, which included military aid, with Angola, Mozambique and Ethiopia. It also provided a range of assistance under specially negotiated deals to Guinea (Conakry), Guinea-Bissau, Mali, Nigeria and Uganda. Its treaty with Somalia had been repudiated at the time of the Ethiopian crisis and later the Americans took over. China had military aid agreements with Cameroon, Equatorial Guinea, Guinea (Conakry), Mali and Tanzania. Cuba had aid arrangements with the Congo (Brazzaville), Guinea (Conakry), Angola, Mozambique and Ethiopia.

3. Egypt, Morocco, Belgium, France and China have, at various times, sent arms or men into Zaire.

4. South Africa and Israel consistently declined to define their widely known military links. South Africa had rights to manufacture various types of missiles, armoured vehicles, and aircraft under French licence; she periodically received aircraft, radar, and electronic and other equipment from the Americans, British and West Germans, usually in clandestine fashion.

Since the Second World War, trading in armaments had become an instrument of big-power policy where valued investments or strategic interests were at stake. Global considerations transcended regional realities as in Zaire and Nigeria during the 1960s, or in Angola, the Horn, central and southern Africa in the 1970s.

With guns for sale and regimes to defend, the great powers were putting their prestige on the line by risking involvement in disputes which could lead to wider struggles. 'The former major colonial powers, the United Kingdom and France, the USA, the USSR and China are all, to a greater or lesser extent, striving to strengthen their influence in one part of the continent or another,' Frank Barnaby, director of the Stockholm International Peace Research Institute (SIPRI), wrote in mid-1969. 'To this end they do not hesitate to exploit African instabilities even by military means.'[6]

Zones of battle emerged in four of the continent's most explosive regions. These ranged from Morocco in the north-west to the Republic of South Africa in the subcontinental tip, and from the Horn in the north-east to central Africa to the west. Overall the lives of nearly 200 million people were affected. In each zone there was – and still remains – an east–west dimension, with the Russians or their friends on the one side and the Americans or their partners on the other, arming their respective protégés with major modern weaponry. Factors of strategy, of access to mineral resources, of contemporary and future alliances, were common denominators. So, too, was an ever-increasing Moslem involvement throughout, except perhaps, in the subcontinent.

A glance at the issues in the four troubled regions follows.

Western Sahara

Western Sahara, decolonized by Spain in 1975, became the object of bitter dispute among its three neighbours, Morocco, Algeria and Mauritania. King Hassan II and Mauritania each annexed parts of the territory in defiance of UN rulings and against Algerian protests.

Their coordinated invasion was resisted by Saharan nationalists who banded themselves into a hard-fighting guerrilla force, the Popular Front for the Liberation of Seguiet el Hamra and Rio de Oro (known by its Spanish initials as the Frente Polisario). Polisario guerrillas, radically oriented, were receiving Algerian weapons and money to support their demand for self-determination. Libya helped too. With few natural resources of its own, Mauritania hoped for whatever pickings were available if Western Sahara could be won, but in fact by 1979 conquest seemed impossible and Mauritania sued for peace. Mauritania at times was so hard-pressed by Polisario that French Jaguar fighter-bombers flew into action against the guerrilla columns advancing on the capital Nouakchott; and Morocco for a while sent 10,000 troops to defend the country. Later, Polisario guerrillas thrust into Morocco itself.

Nominally non-aligned but actually pro-western, Morocco felt compelling reasons for claiming Western Sahara just as it had once claimed all Mauritania. Spain's ex-colony possesses nearly two thousand million tons of proven, high-grade phosphate deposits. King Hassan knew that if any other country were to dominate Western Sahara then Morocco's hold over the world's phosphate market would be jeopardized. In the fashion set by the Arab oil producers, the King – between 1974 and 1975 – raised the price of phosphates on international markets from \$14 to \$68 per ton. Morocco and Algeria had already (in 1963) gone to war over a slice of disputed frontier territory rich in iron ore. The Moroccans lost. For their part Algeria, facing the Mediterranean, would stand to win access to the Atlantic if Western Sahara were to become independent.

International manoeuvrings on the issues involving nearly forty million people in the area were equally complex and hidden from public view. The Soviet Union had long been arming Algeria, a country with a socialist base, and the radical Libyans. But the Russians withheld open support for Polisario although they knew their military supplies to Algiers were filtering through to the guerrillas. Their formal neutrality in the dispute was the consequence of a wish to keep on good terms with Morocco. Moscow and Rabat, in March 1978, had signed a thirty-year agreement providing for credits worth $2 thousand million to develop the Meskala phosphate deposits in southern Morocco. The CIA reported: 'According to Morocco, combined trade and credit transactions under the agreement will total $10 thousand million by the end of the century, propelling Morocco into first place among Moscow's African trading partners.'[7]

Successive US administrations also fostered the Moroccans and Algerians alike, while trying to persuade Hassan to negotiate a settlement with Polisario. Rabat had first place in Washington's affections, among other reasons because of its support for the Egyptian–Israeli peace treaty and its continuing pro-western posture. But an interagency intelligence report, prepared for President Carter in late 1979, warned that Hassan, weakened by economic problems at home and engaged in 'an unwinnable Saharan war', was in danger of dethronement probably inside a year or so. Hassan's attempt to conquer Western Sahara was costing his exchequer up to $1·5 million a day. Disclosure of the intelligence appraisal swiftly followed a Carter decision to pump new weapons into Morocco, from reconnaissance aircraft to Cobra attack helicopters which Hassan doubtless needed for use against the Polisario guerrillas.

Despite the supply of those weapons, perhaps even because of Washington's refusal to recognize Hassan's claims to Western Sahara, the King's relations with the west showed signs of loosening in the years ahead.[8]

Central Africa

Central Africa, with fifty million people and fabled resources of rare-earth minerals, became a setting for east–west competition from the dawn of African independence. The triangular region from Chad at the apex, south-westwards to Angola and south-eastwards to Zambia, is the effective crossroads of the continent where northern and southern, eastern and western influences meet and where foreign interests clash. For a century, too, it was the scene for the interplay of French, Belgian, Portuguese and British rivalries. Independence brought the Russians and Americans along with their ideologies into the region; tempting some young states to choose sides in the hope of advancing their special interests.

Large-scale exploitation came only with the increasing demands of the great powers for strategic materials. The world energy crisis of 1973 gave the process of exploration and development a big impetus. Satellite reconnaissance by the United States disclosed in 1974, for instance, the likely existence of big deposits of rare minerals in a zone extending hundreds of miles between Zaire and the Central African Republic, themselves already endowed with uranium, diamonds, copper or phosphates. There were sizeable oil deposits in Congo (Brazzaville), Gabon, Cameroon, Chad and Angola; precious cobalt in Zaire and Zambia; uranium in Gabon and Chad and much else besides.

All this hastened superpower penetration either directly or through third and fourth parties. If the Cubans or East Germans could be termed the 'surrogates' of the Soviet Union, then the French in fairness could be seen as the standard-bearers of western interests, even though Paris invariably put its own needs first. If France felt free to intervene actively in Chad, Zaire and the Central African Empire (first for, later against, Bokassa), Cubans argued that there could be no valid reason for them to refuse the pleas of their Angolan and Ethiopian friends.

The new reality, specifically in Central Africa, was that the superpowers and their allies were engaged in attempts to cut each other out. The objectives of east and west alike, as Africans interpreted them, appeared to be essentially self-serving if not totally cynical, contributing little to the urgent need for the stability of a vulnerable region.

Two contrasting cases symbolize that cynical lack of care and understanding with which east and west approached the affairs of Africa. They also help to explain why political competition escalated inevitably into a full-scale arms race in a continent crying for socioeconomic, not military, development. Both situations also illuminate just why the Central African triangle has remained a zone of extreme tension, strife and intrigue.

The CIA, on the evidence of a US Senate Select Committee, set out to assassinate Patrice Lumumba who, in 1960, had emerged as the first prime minister of the newly independent Congolese state (Zaire). Lawrence Devlin, chief of station, cabled his headquarters in August: 'Whether or not Lumumba actually Commie or just playing Commie game to assist his solidifying power, antiwest forces rapidly increasing power Congo and there may be little time left in which to take the action to avoid another Cuba.' The National Security Council swiftly responded with a message authorizing Devlin to act as he thought best to secure the removal of Lumumba. President Eisenhower, on 18 August, allegedly approved an order 'for the assassination' of the African leader.[9] By mid-September Mobutu had seized power, Lumumba was in UN protective custody, and a CIA scientist had been sent with poisons intended to kill the ousted premier, who then briefly escaped. With CIA help, Mobutu's men rearrested him in November and had him moved to Katanga (Shaba province) where the CIA considered him still a menace to American policy, according to a dispatch to headquarters on 13 January 1961. On 17 January he was beaten up, then shot dead by Mobutu's men. The CIA, in testimony to Senate investigators, denied all complicity.[10]

In the case involving Soviet policy Moscow, by the early 1970s, knew in detail of the excesses being perpetrated by Macías and Amin, according to official British information. So, too, other communist governments were aware of the brutalities, murders and repression going on through the entire decade in Equatorial Guinea, Uganda and the Central African Empire. Yet against all principles of socialist ethics the Russians, by 1979, had sent in between fifty and 100 military advisers, trainers and weapons to build up the forces led by Macías and Amin. The East Europeans, mainly East Germans, also had gone into Uganda primarily to train and advise on general security and quasi-military matters, British authorities claimed. David D. Newsom, US under-secretary of state for political affairs, told the House Sub-committee on Africa on 18 October 1979: 'The indiscriminate supply of weapons and training by the communist nations to insecure and repressive regimes has sustained them and contributed to some of the most grisly crimes against human dignity ever perpetrated on the African or any continent.'

Castro's Cuba steered clear of Uganda and the Central African Empire but, according to the British, had sent up to 200 military advisers and trainers into Equatorial Guinea.[11] Cuban teachers and forestry experts, in fact, had joined a UN development programme in the country in 1973 but Havana announced the closure of its mission by March 1976.

Cynicism was by no means the monopoly of east and west. President Mu'ammad Gadafi of Libya, whose Islamic fervour was matched only by his avowed hostility to the western powers, communists and Israelis, was not above indulging in a form of imperial expansionism himself. He sent Libyan forces into the territory of Chad, his southern neighbour, and annexed 100,000 square miles of supposedly uranium-bearing desert along the frontier. He also armed and funded the forces of the left-leaning Chad National Liberation Front (FROLINAT) which won ultimate control of the country. The Libyans and Russians, swallowing their ideological hostilities, got together after Sadat's expulsion of the Russians in 1972. Drawn by dislike of the Egyptian leader, Moscow became Gadafi's main arms supplier – and sold him a complete nuclear-power complex, too. The man who hated Soviet communism permitted hundreds of Soviet military advisers and trainers and nuclear specialists into his country to train Libyan air, land and sea forces and to develop a nuclear-power industry.

Horn of Africa

The Horn of Africa, after the ravages of a revolution in the mid-1970s that saw Ethiopia and Somalia exchange their superpower sponsors, remained an arena for the practice of *realpolitik*. The military regime of Colonel Mengistu Haile Mariam pursued a programme of socialist land and economic reform with Soviet–Cuban–East German soldiers and specialists standing on guard and also providing massive aid. But Eritrean guerrillas in the north and Somalis of the Ogaden in the east, dreaming their separatist dreams, pinned down scores of thousands of Ethiopian troops committed to preserve the unity of their ancient state. Neither the Eritreans nor the Somalis lacked arms, funds or help. Material flowed in from their Moslem co-religionists in Saudi Arabia, the Gulf States and Egypt by way of the Sudan in the case of the Eritreans; and through Somali territory where President Siad Barre, pragmatically, had modified his constitutional obligations to unify the scattered elements of the Somali people within a Greater Somalian empire.[12]

In geopolitical scheming, time has limited relevance. What matters most is the fulfilment of objectives. By the end of the 1970s there was a clear-cut pattern to the objectives of the Americans (who were working in harness with the Saudi Arabians) – at least as perceived by the Ethiopians, the Russians and the Cubans.[13] In brief they suggested the American–Arabian counter-strategy had these aims:

1. To avoid overt involvement in the Eritrean and Ogadeni struggles to break loose from the Ethiopian grip, but without discouraging the secessionists from pursuing their goals.

2. To ensure that the Somali Republic did not provoke the Ethiopians, but instead focused on building up its own strength, helped by a US aid package that included $40 million in military supplies.

3. To extend the military capabilities of Ethiopia's two big neighbours, Kenya and Sudan, in a strategy of encirclement to contain radical Ethiopian–Soviet–Cuban influences within the confines of the Horn.

The new guard in Addis Ababa did not need to peer into a crystal ball to reach these conclusions when the book was there for them to read.

The Africa Sub-committee of the US House of Representatives, examining economic and military aid programmes for 1980–81, heard assistant secretary of state for African affairs, Richard Moose, testify on 28 February 1979 that nearby Arab states 'for years' had been funding and arming Eritrea's nationalists, with Washington indirectly backing their efforts. Sudan, for example, provided sanctuaries and training for hundreds of thousands of Eritrean refugees and guerrillas. Egypt sent supplies. Saudi Arabia financed Sudanese military needs with the Americans helping in arms and economic projects to the tune of $150 million over a five-year period. But by mid-1980 these complex arrangements seemed to be falling apart. Ethiopia's leader, Colonel Mengistu Haile Mariam, met President Jaafar Numeiry of the Sudan, in what seemed to be an attempt to reach a political reconciliation that would remove huge burdens from their respective economies; Mengistu by pledging limited autonomy for Eritreans he considered 'moderate' and Numeiry by freeing himself of the cost of sustaining the Eritrean sanctuaries.

In the Ogaden Somalia continued its support for the Ogaden insurgents but the Americans themselves would 'not provide arms in situations which fuel local conflicts'. Yet the Soviet invasion of Afghanistan late in 1979 and through 1980 brought an American reassessment and a search for base facilities in the Indian Ocean region and near the southern approaches to the Gulf. This yielded agreements with the Sultanate of Oman and the Republic of Kenya for access to their ports and airfields. Somalia's air and naval base at Berbera, abandoned by the Russians, sorely tempted Washington. Knowing this, President Siad Barre demanded $2 thousand million in long-term economic and military aid, plus political support for his Ogadeni claims, as his price for an agreement. It was too high and dangerous for Carter's men to contemplate. Yet Somalia, the world's fifth poorest land, had become the centre of mankind's biggest refugee problem with 1·3 million ethnic Somali nomads trekking eastwards from the Ogaden and other parts stricken for years by drought. Somehow they had to be fed, sheltered and helped to survive. Kenya was as anxious as Ethiopia over Siad's unrenounced expansionism. In December 1980, President Daniel Arap Moi and Mengistu, ideological rivals, signed an improbable pact pledging 'to coordinate activities in the struggle against Somalia'. So, when Reagan entered the White House, Siad was ready to settle for weapons worth $40 million predicated on a promise to pull all his troops out of the Ogaden.

Kenya in the meantime received help to establish 'a credible defensive military deterrent' through foreign military sales credits over three years totalling $44 million. New supplies covered the cost of missile-carrying anti-tank helicopters, a dozen 12F-5 airplanes and other equipment. Special economic aid in loans and grants would be worth $37 million.[14] In the aftermath of Afghanistan, however, the US aid programme was greatly expanded and, quite aside from rental and infrastructural costs, Washington planned to invest up to about $100 million in the modernization of Kenyan airfields and port facilities at Mombasa.[15]

Nor in the increasingly frenetic atmosphere that arose with the Iranian and Afghan crises did the Americans forget Ethiopia. To keep lines open to Addis Ababa, Washington arranged that small amounts of aid for agricultural development would continue to go to that country. Tough negotiations nevertheless lay ahead for the compensation of US firms nationalized by Mengistu's regime.

That, however, was like a man maintaining his insurance policy premiums to a company that had changed its directors and gone into a different business. More pragmatically, in case Gulf oilfields and Indian Ocean oil routes should be imperilled by the troubles in Iran and West Asia, the Americans blueprinted and began to implement far-reaching new geostrategic arrangements for the defence of their interests, from Australia to the African eastern seaboard and to the southern entrance to the Gulf of Aden. The Australians were sounded about prospects for a big new air and sea base near Perth on their west coast. Britain's tiny Indian Ocean island of Diego Garcia – jointly managed – became a scene of fevered activity with airfields, deep harbour, storages, workshop and other facilities, enlarged and fitted with the most sophisticated technological equipment from space-tracking stations to submarine-tracking gadgetry. The coral-island base appeared as a likely halfway house between Australia and Africa, with warplanes and warships beginning or interrupting their far-flung missions there and ending up in key African airfields and ports.

Controversy attended all these activities even before the Iranian revolution and the invasion of Afghanistan had peaked to provide a new and urgent rationale for all this movement, or impression of movement. Argument focused on the content of US policies in Africa, especially in relation to attempts to introduce to Africa a modern version of the great game played out by Imperial Russia and Great Britain in the nineteenth century over Afghanistan – the 'garden wall' of the Indian subcontinent.

Two American professors who testified before the sub-committee questioned the wisdom of the US counter-strategy in the Horn during the post-revolutionary period. John. W. Harbeson, professor of political science at the University of Wisconsin, warned that it could be 'dangerous for us to be increasing military aid to the Sudan and Kenya' rather than to increase economic aid to Ethiopia itself as a step towards reconciliation.

Tom J. Farer, professor of law at Rutgers School of Law, observed that the only way to a peaceful settlement he could conceive for the Horn and its sixty-seven million people would be to work for a loose political relationship between Eritreans, Somalis and Ethiopians. 'As far as one can tell this also is the solution preferred by the Cubans and Soviets,' he added. 'So one must ask the question: is it conceivable in any area of the world that a Soviet notion of a proper solution could coincide with our own or that our own interest and Soviet interests could coincide? It seems to me in this case that the answer is yes, although a case could be made that a peaceful settlement is more in our interest than in the Soviet interest.' [16]

Subcontinental Africa

Subcontinental Africa emerged as perhaps the world's most volatile zone of conflict after the Persian Gulf, not only because of the perils of east–west collision but also as the setting of a black–white struggle for power. [17] The issue of race, bound up with the geopolitical rivalries of the superpowers, had profound implications for multiracial societies everywhere.

Militarily South Africa was the dominant power on the continent, leading B. J. Vorster to boast on one occasion while he was prime minister that the country could 'smash its way to Cairo by breakfast'. After their experience in Angola at the receiving end of Cuban fire-power, South Africans might have been expected to be less arrogant. But contemporary appraisals nevertheless agree that the armed forces of the Republic dwarf those in the rest of sub-Saharan Africa.

The combined defence spending of the Angolans, Mozambicans, Zambians and Tanzanians in 1979–80 totalled around $600 million – or about 27 per cent of South Africa's defence budget. Those four African countries could mobilize about 130,000 servicemen, 595 mostly light tanks and armoured vehicles, about 120 combat aircraft and an assortment of naval craft that had seen better days.

In contrast, the South Africans maintained a standing force of more than 63,000 servicemen, most of them conscripts, out of a population of twenty-eight million (with blacks outnumbering whites four to one). But in an emergency nearly 500,000 could be mobilized. The South Africans possessed 250 ageing Centurion tanks made in Britain, 3,500 armoured cars and personnel carriers, a big array of artillery including howitzers that could fire nuclear-tipped shells, 416 combat airplanes, three submarines, a destroyer and three frigates. These statistics contained in *The Military Balance: 1979–1980* (published by the prestigious International Institute for Strategic Studies) did not necessarily tell the full story, according to recent projections by US academics. These last suggested that the Republic by 1980 had developed nuclear weapons capacity, with technological and material help coming, in various sectors, from individual western powers. Pretoria from time to time issued ambiguous statements on the subject but formally denied any intention of building nuclear bombs.

The collapse of Portugal's imperial rule had transformed the settled scene of white dominance. It gave coherence to the fight by Zimbabwean nationalists for black majority rule. On top of this came worldwide, as well as indigenous, pressures for an end to South Africa's management of Namibia. Historically, the struggles of the 1970s in Angola, Zimbabwe and Namibia would probably be seen as skirmishes preceding the day, or year, of reckoning for South Africa's white rulers.

There were few signs, meantime, that South Africa's military leaders meant passively to await that time of reckoning. They embarked, instead, on a carefully prepared campaign designed to destabilize, if not destroy, the governments installed in the northern territories despite the professed commitment of those black regimes to seek a form of coexistence with their powerful southern neighbour. Thus, in turn, Angola to the north-west, Zambia and Zimbabwe in the centre and Mozambique to the north-east, were assailed by land and air by the South Africans who, predictably, disavowed all responsibility.

Angola was a special case, sharing a border with the disputed territory of Namibia. Guerrillas of the South-West African People's Organization (SWAPO) for years had been operating from Angolan bases against a South African military force 20,000 to 30,000 strong. Claiming rights of 'hot pursuit', South Africa launched regular air and land raids against SWAPO bases and beyond, linking up periodically with UNITA (National Union for the Total Independence of Angola), the movement led by Jonas Savimbi, who had never stopped fighting the government in Luanda of the MPLA (Popular Movement for the Liberation of Angola). Angola's ambassador to the United Nations, Elisio de Figueiredo, for instance, charged in a letter to Secretary-General Kurt Waldheim on 29 May 1980 that the South Africans a few days earlier had bombed a southern Angolan town leaving 200 dead 'and countless injured with untold material damage and destruction'.

On the same day Prime Minister Robert Mugabe of Zimbabwe, in an interview with the BBC, asserted that South Africa was training three separate groups of insurgents for counter-revolutionary operations against Zambia, Zimbabwe and Mozambique. Each had a frontier with South Africa, Zambia via the Caprivi strip of Namibia. He identified the Zambian and Mozambican dissidents under training as the Machala Gang, after a former Zambian game warden hostile to Kaunda; and the Andrea Gang as part of what is known to be the Mozambique National Resistance Movement (MNR). Although Mugabe did not name the Zimbabwean dissidents it was at the time generally known that between 1,500 and 2,000 auxiliaries, loyal in Zimbabwe's pre-independence election period to Bishop Abel Muzorewa, crossed into the Republic for sanctuary, training and arms.

Earlier that month, on 23 May, Mugabe met President Samora Machel of Mozambique in Beira in order, among other things, to coordinate military action against the 4,500-strong MNR, which for months had been trying to disrupt communications between the two countries along their extensive, thinly guarded frontier. In the pre-independence period the white-managed government of Salisbury had been supporting, supplying and arming the MNR. Under the Mugabe–Machel agreement the two countries resolved to wipe out the dissidents, whose aim was to bring down the Machel regime. Mugabe, on 24 May, pledged publicly that Zimbabwe would clear these groups out of his territory and then it would be up to Mozambique to take care of them. 'Clearing them does not mean just whistling and then getting away,' he said. 'We can whistle in a much more thunderous and danger-ous way.'

Machel made a similar point on 30 May when his aides claimed that South Africa was training the rebels at a base south of the Beitbridge link with Zimbabwe in the northern Transvaal. The Mozambicans claimed to have detected South African military aircraft, carrying no markings, operating frequently over their territory, engaging in food and weapon drops, and periodically attacking vital installations from power plants on dam sites to road and rail links with Zimbabwe.

Involvement by the South Africans in pre-independent Zimbabwe, when Muzorewa was nominal head of government, was an open secret. Hundreds of South African regular soldiers and airmen, apart from mercenaries, had been integrated into the then Rhodesian armed forces up to the time that Mugabe was elected undisputed victor in the election.

Africa's race for arms, as an extension of east–west rivalries, brought new dangers of conflict in a continent where dozens of inherited fron-tiers were still in dispute.

The United States and Western Europe easily led the Soviet bloc in weapons delivered to Africa immediately before and after the years of independence. The Americans had much wartime material to give away and so, between 1946 and 1978, grant military aid exceeded foreign sales by $69 thousand million to $53 thousand million.[18] Then, as the imperial powers withdrew, they turned over to 'reliable' successors those installations and stocks that they could not easily take with them. Finally, the Europeans sought wherever possible to maintain the role of suppliers as a way of preserving their residual influence.

But when new power centres began transforming international relations the pattern of the arms trade changed too. Several young states of the Third World turned eastwards for their weaponry. They had picked up Moscow's signal of the mid-1950s, when the huge arms deal with Nasser's Egypt was negotiated, and the USSR began moving from a posture of continentalism to one of globalism.

Coincidentally, as the years of the Vietnam war rolled by, a syndrome of withdrawal from distant foreign entanglements became evident among Americans, evolving into something of a limited retreat from globalism. Consequently by the late 1970s, within a twenty-year time-span, the volume of Soviet bloc arms shipments to Africa at least began catching up with that of the west.

Broadly, factors of national security and international strategy inhibit supplier and recipient countries alike from disclosing the kind, scale and cost of weapons sold, supplied free, or otherwise transferred. Comparisons, moreover, are hazardous because of varying national statistical disciplines, fluctuating currencies and propagandist overtones. The random samplings that follow are presented, accordingly, for cautious consideration.

Between 1950 and 1972 the USSR shipped arms worth $180·3 million (31 per cent of the regional total) to North Africa, and $204 million (16·6 per cent of the regional total) to sub-Saharan Africa. Comparative American, British and French supplies over the same period were valued at $357·1 million (61·7 per cent) for North Africa, and $325 million (51·3 per cent) for sub-Saharan Africa.[19]

American authorities have claimed that between 1967 and 1978 the USSR delivered military goods worth $2·7 thousand million to sub-Saharan Africa, with Angola and Ethiopia receiving all but $400 million of the total. The Americans and other western nations over the same period sent in $1·66 thousand million, a figure which does not include US contributions for 1977 and 1978.[20]

Between 1976 and 1979, Algerian, Libyan and Moroccan spending on arms rocketed as turbulence intensified in the region. Along with Egypt, their arms bill totalled $4·4 thousand million in 1979 alone, with about 75 per cent of their weapons coming from the west. In 1979, too, South Africa, Nigeria and Ethiopia spent about as much, with the South Africans accounting for nearly half, Nigeria for $1·75 thousand million and Ethiopia for $550 million. The western powers were the main suppliers although South Africa makes many of its own weapons, usually under licence from western corporations.[21]

President Carter, in May 1977, announced a policy of restraint in arms transfer 'because of the threat to world peace . . . and the special responsibility we bear as the largest arms seller'. Initial claims later that total sales in 1978 had been cut by $700 million from the 1977 level to $8·6 thousand million were questioned within the administration itself on grounds of faulty calculation. The real reduction turned out to be just $66 million. Nevertheless sixty-seven countries had special weapons requests refused.

The USSR became the world's second largest weapons supplier after the Americans with sales of $5·4 thousand million, calculated to represent 27 per cent of the 1978 world total. Moscow puts out no statistics on the subject.

France supplanted Britain as the world's third largest arms exporter with a $2·2 thousand million, or 11 per cent, share of the market. The French transacted extensive business with South Africa, which produces armoured cars, Mirage F-1 fighters and surface-to-air missiles under French licence.

Britain in 1978 sent out a 15,000-ton Royal Naval vessel with a floating exhibition of British arms as a way of winning orders from Mediterranean, African and Latin American governments. Tanks, guided missiles and fast patrol boats were among the tempting items on display.[22]

In the shadowy world of international arms trafficking, the borders between politics and profiteering have become blurred. Most state authorities supervise the trade yet remain subject to the influence of armament makers who, in some countries, band themselves together into powerful lobbies. Their sales representatives at home and abroad may not necessarily resort to the techniques associated with the notorious 'merchants of death' in the pre-war years. But there is a long catalogue of cases indicating that prime ministers and princes, presidents and potentates have not been above accepting pay-offs and bribes to promote the interests of big corporations with aircraft, ships and major weapons to sell. The US Congress, after investigating precise instances, outlawed the practice. In Britain the Defence Ministry has its own sales division, with the resources of the arms industry always ready discreetly to help push British military exports in selected countries. France, West Germany and Italy have, from time to time, trespassed into what used to be Britain's imperial preserves.[23]

There was scope in the African context for quiet cheating by all governments seeking to sell arms and hungry for consumer markets and for new sources of raw materials. Zaire provided a classic case when the

British, Belgians and French worked with the black secessionists of Katanga, the white rulers of the Central African (Rhodesian) Federation and South Africa *against* United Nations resolutions designed to preserve the unity of the country. Nigeria's civil war in 1967 saw the British and Soviet Union arming the forces of the federal government, while President Charles de Gaulle's France was openly backing the rebels of Biafra.

In each situation the provision of European arms and the presence of European mercenaries amounted to a declaration of political support for the chosen side, with economic gain as the motive. Concerned Africans, for their part, saw the activities of the British, Belgians and French as neo-colonialism in the raw.[24]

The issue, above all others, uniting African countries since independence was the shared resolve to end white-minority rule in the subcontinent. The Russians, with everything to play for and nothing to lose, identified themselves totally with this aim and so, in African eyes, enhanced their credibility. The United States, with its own and allied European interests to protect, seemed slow to recognize the depth of African sensitivities on the subject. No amount of rhetoric could obliterate black suspicions that American associations with the former colonial powers implied an endorsement of 'white' attitudes towards Africa and that, in a struggle between black and white in Southern Africa, the Americans, at the end of the day, would resist revolutionary change if for no reason other than that the Russians would be supporting it.

The overall performance of the western powers, in contributing to South Africa's formidable build-up of military power, provides its own comment.

In August 1963 the UN Security Council called on all member-states to impose an embargo on the supply of arms to the South African Republic in protest against its discriminatory racial policies. This was a *voluntary*, as distinct from a *mandatory*, embargo. (A mandatory ban was ordered only in November 1977.) But voluntary or not, all the big powers, including the Americans, were honour-bound to observe it. They did not. Between 1967 and 1976 South Africa received armaments worth $500 million from the Americans, British, French, West Germans and Italians, among other westerners.[25]

The Americans and their European allies felt free to go on arming the South Africans with material defined as strategic equipment for defence against external threats, though there were few signs that South Africa was at the time menaced by any foreign power.

Aircraft, ships, tanks and electronic equipment, therefore, continued to reach South Africa from a variety of western manufacturers. In 1971 the newly formed government of Prime Minister Edward Heath re-asserted Britain's right to go on supplying South Africa with naval equipment. In the process, he precipitated a crisis within the Commonwealth. Even after the Security Council transformed the voluntary embargo into a mandatory ban, evasions continued. Italy, for instance, delivered an air defence system in 1979.

Not all the evaders were western nations. In late 1978 the government of Prime Minister Indira Gandhi, possibly through some administrative lapse, permitted at least one hundred old British-built Centurion medium tanks to reach South Africa. These tanks, surplus to Indian needs and bought in the early 1950s, were wanted by the South Africans for 'cannibalization' and for emplacement in concreted frontier posts.[26]

The collusion of western powers in transforming South Africa from a minor to a major military force served short-term purposes without resolving long-term problems. It averted the need for some governments to face agonizing options laden with emotional and commercial factors which could affect the political survival of leaders in office. It also, in theory, bought time for a process of diplomatic dialogue to be used in the search for a non-violent settlement of black–white relations.

Yet no one with an intimate, or even working, knowledge of the South African setting could see the white minority yielding its supremacy without a fight. Events such as the crushing of the Soweto uprising in 1976, the killing of Steve Biko in September 1977, and the consistent pattern of South African air and land attacks on Angola were taken by blacks as suggesting that their struggle would ultimately have to be a bloody and protracted one. Unbroken western associations with successive South African leaders were also interpreted by key black leaders as attempts to preserve overall western domination of the continent.

When high US envoys met with representatives of the former European colonizing powers in Washington, Paris and Brussels in mid-1978 to map new policies for Africa, Tanzanian President Julius Nyerere addressed a message to foreign governments. The message said those consultations would be concerned with two things:

'. . . with neo-colonialism in Africa for economic purposes, the real control of Africa and African states. That will be led by the French.

'. . . with the use of Africa in the east–west conflict. That will be led by the Americans.

'These two purposes will be coordinated so that they are mutually supportive and the apportionment of the expected benefits, and costs, will be worked out. It is at that point, the division of the spoils, that disputes are most likely to occur.'[27]

Part Two

The Communist Powers in Africa

4. The Soviet Union

Egyptian notables and foreign diplomats jostled in the Sudanese embassy, Cairo, for a word with the Sudanese Prime Minister Ismail al-Azhary on 18 May 1955.

But Gamal Abdel Nasser, then president of Egypt, had other matters on his mind. He sought out Soviet Ambassador Daniil Semyonovich Solod for a talk in an anteroom adjoining the reception salon.

'We want to have arms from you,' Nasser said to Solod in Arabic. 'What will be your answer?'

Solod replied that he would check back with Moscow. Three days later he called on Nasser and, during a two-hour meeting, reported that the Soviet government was ready to come to an agreement. 'It went on very simply,' the late Egyptian leader subsequently recalled in an interview with former *New York Times* correspondent Kennet Love.[1] He was surprised, nevertheless. Only a few months earlier the Kremlin had been denouncing his regime as fascist and calling on Egyptians to topple him. But, in the meantime, the Americans and British had sponsored the Baghdad Pact, an anti-communist alliance of mainly Moslem states along the northern tier of the Middle East. Cairo and Moscow bitterly opposed it.

Nasser said that, in the weeks following Solod's call, he had tried repeatedly to have his military needs fulfilled by the United States and Britain. The Americans, he claimed, kept stalling, as they had been doing for years. The British set unacceptable conditions. Both calculated that he was bluffing. He was not. On 9 June he warned President Eisenhower and Secretary of State John Foster Dulles – through US Ambassador Henry Byroade – that he was negotiating with the Russians but emphasized again that he would still prefer to deal with the west.

The warning went unheeded. It took his top military advisers two months to list the country's precise armament needs, arrange delivery dates, fix payments by way of cotton and rice supplies and then sign a complete agreement with Czechoslovakia, acting for the Russians. The deal was announced on 27 September.

Its effect was to tilt the west's centuries-old control of Middle Eastern affairs towards the east and create a new power balance in one of the world's strategically crucial regions.

In Washington that humid Thursday, 19 July 1956, there was no breath of wind.

Egypt's ambassador Ahmed Hussein was in Dulles's State Department office insisting yet again that Cairo wanted American, not Soviet, help to build the monumental Aswan High Dam. This was Nasser's dream project – his personal Pyramid – for bringing water, light and food to the parched and hungry millions in the Nile valley.

Hussein had been forewarned that Dulles would play Cairo's request as frigidly as he had played it long. The Americans, like the British, felt that they had been getting a rough ride from Nasser. Egypt's leader had opposed the Baghdad Pact. Then he had signed the arms deal with the communists. Sensing deadlock, Ambassador Hussein looked Dulles in the eyes, touched his pocket, and said: 'We've got the Soviet offers [to build the dam] right here.'

That gave the secretary of state his chance. He had Eisenhower's authority to direct anyone who said that sort of thing to go right back to the Russians.

'We've considered it all very seriously, knowing how important it is for Egypt, but I'm sorry,' Dulles told the envoy. 'Frankly the Egyptian economy seems to us overloaded and it doesn't make it feasible for the United States to participate. Therefore we are withdrawing our offer to help.'[2]

Nasser, angered but unsurprised by this second spurning, thundered at a rally near Cairo on 24 July: 'When Washington broadcasts the lie that Egypt's economy is unsound, I say to them "drop dead!"' Two days later Egypt nationalized the British–French Suez Canal Company and so aroused the implacable enmity of Britain and France.

Dulles set out to calm the anger of Anthony Eden (later Lord Avon) and Guy Mollet and to promote a reconciliation with Nasser. The British and French prime ministers were suspicious of the secretary of state's intentions. They were convinced that Dulles, in reality, was undercutting their interests and preparing to appease the Egyptians in order to avoid being tainted by association with European colonialism. In early October, then, British and French forces, colluding with Israel and defying the Americans, invaded Egypt.

The ten-day war that followed saw Eisenhower and Dulles shatter British–French assumptions that the Americans, or NATO, would somehow help preserve their world-wide imperial systems.

The Russians swiftly stepped in again. In 1955 they had been first in the field with an offer to build the Aswan High Dam. They renewed the suggestion. Nasser accepted. Aswan became the symbol of Muscovite willingness to help the needy nations of the Third World. Through the miscalculations of western leaders, the gateway to Africa had been opened. The Russians streamed through in the next few years to fan out to the eastern and western, northern and southern reaches of the continent.

Nasser died in September 1970, and Anwar Sadat took over. By this time the Soviet presence in Egypt was approaching 20,000 experts, advisers and instructors servicing Russian-built installations, supervising naval facilities, training Egyptian personnel in the use of sophisticated weapons and helping to defend strategic targets, like the Aswan High Dam, against the possibility of Israeli air and land attack. Arab–Israeli tensions were heightening.

Within a year Sadat and the Soviet leadership were quarrelling. Egypt's new leader wanted even more offensive weapons, with greater punch. Moscow countered by insisting that certain arms could be supplied only on condition that they would be used with Soviet consent. Then two things happened. In Cairo during May 1971, Sadat fired and later arrested several leading left-oriented Nasserites in top positions, suspecting a Moscow-sponsored plot to oust him. In Khartoum, Sudanese President Jaafar Numeiry, similarly, rounded up leading communists on charges that they, with Moscow's help, were conspiring to mount a *coup*. He had them executed.

The Russians, angrily anticipating a swing to the right in the Arab world, stalled on Sadat's arms deliveries. They declined also to ease the terms of his soaring debts. Like a manager dealing with a doubtful client, Moscow virtually foreclosed on Sadat's political and economic overdraft. Relations worsened as the months slipped by. Ultimately, on 18 July 1972, Sadat ordered all Soviet military and other personnel to leave the country. He took over all equipment and installations. Only a tenuous fifteen-year friendship treaty remained. Even that was abrogated by Cairo in 1976.

Sadat explained later: 'They [the Russians] attempted to exert pressure on me and bring me to my knees.'[3]

It was not the first or last time that Moscow discovered that countries in the shifting African setting were concerned less with the superpower contest and more with fulfilling their own aspirations.

The Soviet Union's 'discovery' of Africa after the Second World War came late, almost as if it were an accidental by-product of Moscow's primary interest in the Middle East. Soviet interest in the affairs of the

Middle East itself was initially something of a response to the steady US economic, political and strategic penetration of the region. Egypt proved to be the first target of opportunity when the Russians decided to challenge the domination of the western powers in spheres of influence they had long considered to be Europe's preserves. The Russians needed no lessons in recognizing new openings when they saw them. From the platform of Egypt it was not difficult to detect many such openings throughout the continent, especially because the Americans and Chinese, comparative latecomers too, had embarked upon their own voyages of political and strategic discovery from the mid-1950s onwards.

It became a central Soviet objective to match, if not to out-manoeuvre, Chinese and American activism in Africa and to develop a global reach. Thus the formula used by the USSR in leapfrogging into Egypt became the invariable pattern for penetrating other parts of Africa and the Third World. Alliances formed by the Russians did not always endure. But Moscow still could boast that it had helped build up its target states. When, on occasions, the Russians were invited to leave they did so, leaving behind visible structures which would testify to certain achievements and enhance the bargaining power of the countries concerned in future dealings with the west.

Africa had held a fascination for Russians long before the 1917 Revolution. Rivalry with imperial Britain moved Tsarist policy-makers of the nineteenth century to encourage an expansion of the Ethiopian empire, to seek territory in the Horn of Africa and to support the Afrikaners in their war with the British from 1899 to 1902. Ironically, Tsarist Russia, like the United States, had attended the Berlin Conference; and although both countries steered clear of the scramble for territory, they endorsed the final act which laid down the rules that were supposed to govern the continental carve-up.

Nevertheless, before and after the Revolution, it was Asia, with its huge populations edging on to the Moscow-ruled land mass, that attracted Russia's primary attention. The colonies in Africa were seen – correctly as it turned out – as fall-back bastions that would be developed by the Europeans only after the ultimate loss of their more lucrative Asian possessions. Lenin himself had set the ideological basis of Soviet policy towards Europe's global imperialist systems, observing, once, that 'the road to Paris goes through Calcutta and Peking'. Africa barely rated a mention.

In the last article he wrote before dying in 1924, Lenin noted: 'The outcome of the struggle [between communism and capitalism] will be determined by the fact that Russia, India, China and so forth, account for the overwhelming majority of the population of the globe. And this majority during the past few years has been drawn into the struggle for emancipation with extraordinary rapidity.' This led him to the conclusion that an alliance between the Soviet Union and the seething colonial masses would make 'the final victory of socialism' certain.[4]

From then on, the policy of the Soviet Union towards Africa in particular, and the Third World generally, fluctuated according to the personalities of the country's three outstanding leaders:

Joseph Stalin (1924–53)

Joseph Stalin had no time, no resources and no inclination to test Lenin's thesis that the colonies were indeed imperialism's 'weakest link'. He focused first on consolidating his regime and pursuing his policies. Then came his subjugation of the European communist movement, with his assault on social democracy as the enemy greater than fascism. Next he worked to repel and defeat the Hitlerian invaders. In his final phase he concentrated on reconstruction and building the industrial and military base for the post-war duel with the Americans. He shunted aside the revolutionary possibilities of rising nationalism in the shaky empires of Europe, never yielding on his own theory that colonial peoples had to rise and fight to win freedom for themselves. For him the Jawaharlal Nehrus, Kwame Nkrumahs, Sukarnos and Ben Bellas were servants of their indigenous upper classes and, by definition therefore, in league with their imperial masters. Somewhat like Dulles he seemed more comfortable dealing with the simplicities of a bipolar world in which the frontiers of the east–west cold war were neat, clear and uncluttered with the complexities of power balances – beginning, even then, to shift.

Nikita Khrushchev (1953–64)

Nikita Khrushchev was quick to recognize that nationalism was on the move in colonies around the world, including those in Africa. He rejected the isolationism of Stalin, set out to revive Lenin's concept of a communist alliance with the turbulent colonial societies, and announced at the twentieth congress of the CPSU in 1956: 'The new period in world history which Lenin predicted has arrived!'[5] Moving forward from Stalinism meant to Khrushchev reaching out into the world beyond the ring of encirclement with which the Americans had surrounded the Russians. Brash and ambitious, inventive and opportunistic, Khrushchev put forward the concept of 'peaceful coexistence' between the capitalist and communist worlds and evolved a programme designed to link the fortunes of the Russians with those of the Third World. Such an alliance, he argued, would tip the scales in the direction of socialism. It meant, of course, working with the very same nationalist leaders rejected by Stalin as the servants of colonialism.

Initially, at least, the nation-states emerging from the crumbling empires of Europe were ready to shelter under the umbrella of socialism if only to advertise their new-found independence of action. They had anti-colonialist tales to tell the Russians. For their part the Russians had anti-western confidences to relate.

The young developing countries needed aid on a vast scale to equip themselves for the rigours of competitive life in the twentieth century. Khrushchev seemed to have money to burn; lavishing economic help worth $5 thousand million in his decade of power. Thus began the Soviet thrust into lands spanning three continents, from Cuba to the South China Sea, with black Africa low on Moscow's list of priorities at the outset. But even Khrushchev, as extrovert as Stalin was dour, began to over-extend his country's resources at a time of austerity for Russians themselves and for their communist allies. Some of his spectacular boasts and extravagant initiatives aroused as much consternation among his own Politburo colleagues as they did abroad. 'Whether you like it or not, history is on our side,' he warned the Americans in 1956. 'We will bury you!' That did not exactly sound like a man professing a dedication to 'peaceful coexistence'. He was indicted by his own colleagues in late 1964, when he was removed from office because of misjudgements that included 'hare-brained schemes' for industrializing countries still semi-feudal. He continued to back governments which had outlawed communist parties. He had chosen as friends those who presided over precarious and unstable regimes.

Leonid Brezhnev (1964–   )

Leonid Brezhnev, Khrushchev's successor, set out from 1964 to modify the pattern of Soviet global activities. The magnitude and political power potential of the Third World were realities acknowledged by the Russians but the Brezhnev era brought cool, calm, cost-effective logic into dealings with this rising new force. There was a major, unexpected factor to project into the world-wide geopolitical equation and that was the role of China, now ideologically written off by the Russians as an ally. Key parts of Europe's old empires became settings for major wars, such as Indo-China, the Middle East and the Indian subcontinent. Meanwhile, Africa still remained low among the preoccupations of the superpowers. It was only when the Russians were expelled from Egypt in 1972 that Moscow began actively to search for alternative

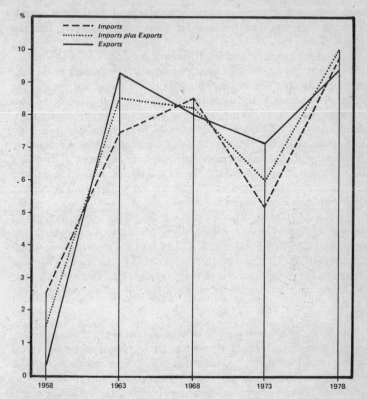

Fig. 8: Russian trade with Africa: percentage attributable to Africa, south of the Sahara, of the total trade between Russia and the developing countries
SOURCE: *Vnyeshnyaya Torgovlya SSSR v 1958, 1963, 1968, 1973, 1978 gg*, Moscow.

strategic, political and economic footholds. Realizing how easily Soviet clients in regional conflagrations could suck their superpower sponsors into full-scale confrontations (as over Cuba) Brezhnev constantly hammered the theme of east–west *détente*. In doing so he met with responses from the Americans, West Germans and others.

But the quest for *détente* did not mean that Brezhnev and his fellow-leaders for a moment lifted their gaze from the developing nations of Africa, Asia and Latin America. The Russians remained on the lookout for positions from which they could command vital sea-lanes and check or counter the spread of West European, American and Chinese influence. They insisted that *détente* should not and would not preclude them from supporting people and movements struggling for liberation or defending their territories against unprovoked 'imperialist' attack. That, at least, was their rationale for intervening in Angola, Ethiopia and Afghanistan.

Brezhnev himself offered the Kremlin's prescription for reconciling the concept of east–west accommodation with the pursuit of forward revolutionary policies in the Third World. '*Détente* does not in the slightest way abolish, and cannot abolish or change, the laws of the class struggle,' he told the twenty-fifth congress of the Soviet Union's communist party. To Kissinger and Brzezinski, to Ford and Carter, to West European and Chinese leaders, that was an unacceptable contradiction. As they saw it, *détente* was, or should have been, indivisible, involving the reduction of tension globally. There was little, though, that the west could do about it in the cases of Angola and Ethiopia, mainly because of their own mistaken policies in Africa.

It was a different story however, in late December 1979, when Soviet air and land forces invaded neighbouring Afghanistan and posed in the eyes of western and key Third World nations a direct threat to the oil resources of the Gulf and to the territory of Pakistan. Not all Russia's disavowals of these intentions allayed the fears of the Americans, Europeans and most Moslem states. Some African countries, too, joined the chorus of condemnation.

Alongside Brezhnev's interest in winning access to the raw materials of Africa and other Third World countries, there was the additional objective of building up Soviet trade. There were goods to be sold, especially capital equipment and armaments and, with both, the expertise of Soviet personnel. There were commodities and some scarce minerals to be bought, like bauxite, cobalt, cocoa, rubber and certain foods. Brezhnev consolidated the Soviet Union's shift from a continental to a global foreign policy, reinforced by a navy with a world-wide mission. He went ahead with the Khrushchevian programme of concentrating Soviet activity in what became known as the 'zone of national liberation'. It stretched from south-east Asia through India, Bangladesh, Afghanistan and Pakistan, along to the northern and southern tiers of the Middle East, and then across the Mediterranean to North Africa. The giant arc later was extended to resemble a horseshoe when much of black Africa was appended to the zone.

Brezhnev, like Khrushchev, occasionally stumbled. Several African leaders he chose to support were either toppled or broke with Moscow. Those overthrown included Ben Bella of Algeria, Nkrumah, and Keita of Mali in late 1968. Then Numeiry in 1971, Sadat, Siad Barre of Somalia and Macías of Equatorial Guinea expelled most, if not all, the Russians. President Ahmed Sékou Touré of Guinea restored relations with France, hoping to reduce his over-reliance on Moscow. The fall of Idi Amin of Uganda and Bokassa of the Central African Republic were further setbacks in 1979.

These reverses served to emphasize that the Russians, like the Americans, knew little of Africa and its people. The rigidities of their ideologies conflicted with their strategic aims in a variety of situations. Some Tanzanians related with high amusement the saga of a Soviet attempt to promote a tuna fish project in the clove-producing island of Zanzibar as a means of diversifying the economy of Africa's would-be 'Cuba' in the late 1960s. The Russians offered to set up a tuna processing plant after providing the ships that were to track and catch the fish. But, so the Tanzanian version went, the vessels could not keep up with the tuna fish and the only available replacements were being built in Japan. The scheme was abandoned.

Other Soviet miscalculations were on a scale matching those of the western powers. Moscow put its money, just as the British did, on Joshua Nkomo emerging as Zimbabwe's first internationally acceptable prime minister. Robert Mugabe, the clear-cut winner, had long been regarded as a bad risk because of his political identification with the Chinese. As things turned out, Mugabe emerged as his own man, a Zimbabwean first, a socialist second, and western powers were quicker to adjust to that reality than the Russians, even though they may have felt they could afford to wait and watch.

Over the years, though, it was true that the Soviet Union, through experience, built up a body of knowledge and a school of experts which helped its envoys to avoid some of the clumsy, often arrogant, diplomacy they had perpetrated in Africa in the past. Moscow came to learn the hard way that pure doctrine was no substitute, in the African context, for getting to know and trying to satisfy the yearnings of blacks for development and modernization.

The reality of their needs compelled most African states to accord greater priority to north–south economic issues than to east–west ideological ones.

As a new generation of leaders arose in Africa, there was a tendency among some to regard the USSR as a sophisticated, technologically developed industrialized state with interests and ambitions comparable to those of their own one-time European rulers and of the Americans. For the Russians to counter-argue, as they did, that the poverty of Africa was the heritage, and therefore the responsibility, of the former colonizers convinced few of the new leaders struggling for political and economic survival.

By the 1980s a new imperative presented itself to the Russians, if they wanted to achieve the destiny they and the socialist community professed to share with the Third World. The imperative was that Moscow would have to pay a price in development aid if that linkage was to be forged and to endure.

By 1980 there was a formidable Soviet presence in Africa, complete with air- and sea-lift capabilities. James Callaghan, when he was Britain's prime minister, said once, 'I'm sure they [the Russians] would like to establish a belt of friendly states across Africa from the Indian to the Atlantic Ocean.'

The idea of such a pro-Soviet belt across the continental waist has been 'an extension of their thinking and they're ready to take advantage of it', Callaghan added. Moscow already was strongly entrenched in Angola, on the Atlantic, in Mozambique on the Indian Ocean, and in Ethiopia edging on to the Red Sea. Between Angola and Mozambique lie Zambia, Zimbabwe and Malawi.[6]

The performance of Moscow and its communist partners worried the west and impressed some Africans. But few African leaders felt irrevocably committed to the Soviet system. Frantz Fanon, the Martinique-born psychiatrist turned writer who involved himself in Algeria's struggle for liberation, wrote in *El Moudjahid*, 5 January 1960, that Africans, being concerned only with anti-colonialism, remained neutral in the east–west power contest.

Our neutrality means that we do not have to take a position for or against NATO, for or against the Warsaw Pact. Within the framework of our anticolonialist combat, we take account only of the firmness of our commitment and the backing that this or that country gives us. And within this framework we can say that the peoples grouped under the label of Eastern countries are giving us very strong support and the so-called countries of the west are full of ambiguities.[7]

From the mid-1950s on, the Soviet drive into Africa was deep, selective and sustained. Moscow pursued four interlocking objectives – strategic, economic, ideological and political – with a zeal that often outstripped coherence, with a superpower's cynicism that often left the new breed of Africa's socialists and humanists confused and perplexed. The consequence was that the ebb and flow of Soviet influence in Africa came to depend more on the mistakes and misperceptions of the capitalist west than on the concepts of communism. Where the western powers blundered, the Russians moved in. When the Soviet Union failed its protégés, the Americans and Europeans came back. Invariably, ordinary Africans seemed doomed to play the role of eternal losers, servants to the follies of faraway foreigners.

The Soviet Union had four main goals in Africa, strategic, economic, ideological, and political.

The Strategic Goal

Strategically, the Soviet objective was to wrest from the west their old dominance of the world's key 'choke-points' controlling straits and waterways or located in anchorages along vital oceanic routes. Many Third World countries were, after all, colonized in the first place because of their strategic positions. Several in the early post-war years had provided the Americans with military bases and facilities. But as concepts of non-alignment hardened, especially during the Vietnam war period, and as intercontinental weaponry developed, quite a few of these bases became too costly politically to maintain and, in any case, obsolete. 'Choke-points' is a naval term describing strategic positions enabling the occupying power to prevent an adversary from entering or leaving a given sea or ocean area. The US maritime administration in June 1975 listed thirty-one sea-lanes essential for the free conduct of American foreign trade and twenty-three of them edge on to Third World territories. Equally the USSR's vital sea links through the Dardanelles, the Mediterranean and the Indian Ocean pass along North and East African, Middle Eastern and South Asian littorals controlled by Third World countries.

Some aspects of Moscow's penetration of Africa became understandable only when viewed against the background of the Soviet world experience. In the early 1960s, for instance, the Americans stopped what seemed then to be the Congo's (Zaire's) slide into a partnership with Moscow. They prevailed also in forcing the Russians to yield during the Cuban missile crisis. 'Never again!' Kremlin leaders vowed after their retreat.[8] And so they set about building up their power around a nuclear strike force and a blue-water navy, able to roam the seven seas and call in at all the continents. But they did this more or less on the cheap, without aircraft carriers, marine amphibious forces, tankers and transports. Their aim was to offset this deficiency by winning rights to use ports and airfields in distant lands. Africa, consequently, became a major area for Moscow to negotiate the use of anchorage, storage, refuelling and repair facilities, and air staging and overflight arrangements.

The Economic Goal

Economically, the Soviet objective was to aid and trade with responsive African countries, especially those strategically located. Moscow recognized that a top African priority was for coordinated programmes of development, for downstream industries needed either to process or manufacture indigenous primary products and for stable, inflation-proofed pricing for their commodities. Thus there was emphasis on long-term trading accords, coupled with technical help in the form of machines and equipment to advance the process of industrialization. Where possible the Russians funnelled their aid through the public sector of the receiving country, so consolidating the overall power base of the government concerned and establishing their own presence.[9] Arms sales were part of the two-way trade and from 1970 to 1980 made up about 50 per cent of total Soviet exports to Africa.

None the less, by comparison with total American–West European–Japanese business dealings, Soviet and East European trade with Africa was fractional. Through the 1970s Soviet–African dealings averaged 2 per cent of Moscow's total foreign trade.

Development loans usually were designed to finance African–Soviet trade on easy terms: a 2 per cent interest rate; a twelve-year redemption period beginning with the completion of a project or delivery of equipment; and repayment in local goods or raw materials, rather than in cash. Some countries, Egypt and Ghana included, rescheduled or defaulted on their repayments. Others had to keep borrowing more merely to service their debts. Generally Moscow resisted writing off or deferring money owing. This led to some embittered arguments, for instance with Guinea and Egypt. Other sources of friction developed because the Russians sometimes indulged in 'switch trading', or the re-export, at a profit, of goods supplied by debtors – a time-honoured capitalist practice.[10]

The Ideological Goal

Ideologically, the Soviet objective was to lure the fledgeling states and national liberation movements into alliance with Moscow and world communism against what were portrayed as the still-active forces of imperialism and neo-colonialism. This was a departure from the worldview of Stalin who, to the end, regarded the bourgeois leaders of the world's rising nationalist forces as tools of their foreign imperialist rulers. It was, instead, Leninism revived.

Ideology, then, became the handmaiden of power politics. The countries of Africa and the Third World, nominally neutral in the gladiatorial contest of the superpowers, had, as Lenin predicted, the resources and numbers to become a power centre in their own right. They possessed a bargaining potential in the strategic materials needed so desperately for the industries of the northern hemisphere. Arab oil producers in 1973 blazed the trail with their fivefold increase in oil prices, seizing at a stroke an annual $40 thousand million of the world's purchasing power. Moscow encouraged other primary producers to set up similar cartels for the commodities they had to offer. The Russians found some ready listeners, at least for a while, for their stirring anti-European and anti-American serenades. 'There were scores to be settled,' Daniel P. Moynihan observed in his study of the Third World's critical attitudes towards the west, 'internally and internationally.'[11] Moynihan, former U S ambassador to the United Nations and later a senator, suggested many of these Third World prejudices had their roots in 'British socialist opinion' as it developed from the nineteenth to the mid twentieth centuries.

The Political Goal

Politically, the objective was to extend Soviet influence by identifying with the needs and causes of the Third World. If any single factor helped to create a credible identity of interest between the Russians and the Africans, it was Moscow's total commitment actively to support the struggle to end white supremacy in the subcontinent. While the N A T O allies were building up the arsenals of the Portuguese before the 1974 upheaval, the Russians were arming and training the guerrillas of Mozambique, Angola and Guinea-Bissau. While British and American oil companies were evading sanctions imposed against the rebel Rhodesian government of Prime Minister Ian Smith, the Russians were funding and arming the Patriotic Front forces led by Joshua Nkomo and Robert Mugabe. While the western nations were safeguarding their big investment and trading stakes in South Africa and denouncing the system of *apartheid*, the Russians were keeping close contact with the country's resistance movements, especially the African National Congress, which had links with the outlawed South African Communist Party.

The Russians also made good political use of the anti-western radicalism inherent in those Africans whose only experience of subjugation was at the hands of Europe's colonizing powers. Whenever possible, it was a Kremlin aim to erode the influence of its European and American rivals, reasoning that any western loss would represent a Soviet gain. In its own fashion it resembled almost exactly the attitude of Washington's policy-makers towards Moscow's activism in Africa. A rationale for the Soviet approach to aiding and training people of Africa, Asia and Latin America was provided by Nikolai Sofinsky, deputy minister for higher and specialized secondary training, in an interview with a military journal in 1976:

Aid is granted according to the Leninist principles of proletarian internationalism . . . As you well remember, Lenin said that Soviet Russia must help the Mongols, Persians, Indians and Egyptians to go over to the use of machines, learn to ease their labour and switch over to democracy and socialism. Lenin said that more than fifty years ago. Since then, assisting the formerly oppressed and dependent peoples to overcome their backwardness in the spheres of economy and culture inherited from colonialism has been one of the main lines in the foreign policy pursued by the Soviet state.

In the twenty years to 1976 the number of foreign students trained in the Soviet Union has soared from 134 to more than 20,000, he said.

There was, of course, another consideration motivating Moscow's efforts in Africa and that was to counter the sallies of the Chinese into those regions of Soviet endeavour. The Chinese challenge began in the late 1950s with the Peking–Moscow ideological dispute, but then faded after the death of Mao Tse-tung in 1976. Peking's new rulers became more concerned with a programme to modernize their own industrial and social institutions, something Mao had neglected or failed to do in most sectors except in the development of a nuclear military capacity.

On the surface and measured against the scale of effort and invest-ment it seemed that, after a quarter-century, the Soviet Union had registered more losses than gains in Africa. Six alliances or special relationships – with Ghana and Mali in the 1960s, with Egypt, Sudan, Somalia and Guinea in the 1970s – had been either denounced or diluted. The Soviet bid for a foothold in the Congo (Zaire) in the early 1960s had been foiled by the Americans. Difficulties developed in dealings even with those regimes which professed a radical or Marxist–Leninist orientation, including Angola and Mozambique, Benin and Congo (Brazzaville). In the short-term as well as the long-term perspec-tive, the Russians, just like the westerners, did not always seem to appre-ciate African sensitivities over race and nationalism. Marxist–Leninist concepts found few takers among the peasantry and in the urban com-munities struggling to overcome the challenges of poverty, disease and the violence of great and sudden social change. The symbolism associ-ated with the 'ugly American' was occasionally transferred to Russians, whose aloofness in African settings concealed an impatience and lack of identification with the life-styles of the people they had set out to help.

The greatest loss to the Russians was, perhaps, in their credibility. This stemmed primarily from an indulgence in a widely visible political opportunism. Africans, through legend and sorrowful experience, tend to equate Europeanism with everything white, and whites with most things oppressive. Russians are no less white than Western Europeans. Broadcasts in a score of African tongues, taking up about thirty hours daily and beamed to different parts of the continent, may have suc-ceeded in convincing listeners that the politics of East European social-ists differs from the politics of the capitalist west. But what spoke even louder to millions of Africans was the military and political support

Moscow felt justified in extending to strong-arm regimes like that of former Ugandan President Idi Amin. During his eight-year term Amin stood accused by his own people of murdering thousands of his countrymen. 'In the developing countries as everywhere we are on the side of the forces of progress, democracy and national independence,' Leonid Brezhnev told the twenty-fifth congress of the CPSU on 24 February 1976. 'We treat them as our friends and comrades-in-arms.' Brezhnev would find it hard by any standards, though, to convince Africans that Amin represented progress and democracy.

There was, additionally for Africans, a detectable cynicism in the continued sale of Soviet arms to those African states like Guinea, Mali, Algeria, Ghana and Egypt, which for years had outlawed, gaoled, persecuted or even executed leaders of indigenous communist parties. The conclusion reached by those Africans dedicated to socialist concepts was that the Kremlin, in the interests of the state, would readily sacrifice its professed ideological precepts, despite the Leninist dictum that there was no substitute for a policy of principle.

Soviet policies in Africa, however, also yielded a series of gains which, if properly consolidated, could in time more than compensate for their setbacks. The extension of their political influence and physical presence from the Mediterranean littoral southwards to subcontinental Africa added an important new dimension to their posture as a global power. Their entrenchment in Angola gave them access to the South Atlantic on one side and to Zaire, Zambia and Namibia on the others. By establishing themselves in ancient Ethiopia, they won a platform from which they could address the Moslem north and the Bantu-speaking peoples of East and Central Africa. A twenty-year treaty alliance with Mozambique did more than oust a significant Chinese influence. It also carried with it facilities to use the country's modern ports and to develop new installations along a 1,500-mile Indian Ocean coastline. Mozambique's neighbours are not only Tanzania and Malawi but also Zimbabwe and the Republic of South Africa, heartland of white supremacy. Maputo and Pretoria, the Mozambican and South African capitals, are a mere 300 miles apart. Robert Mugabe's arm of the Patriotic Front guerrillas, while fighting to win power in Zimbabwe, had been based in Mozambique, a country with untapped deposits of iron and coal, gas and gold, bauxite, graphite and other resources.

If the Russians held their positions in Angola and Mozambique, they would be able crucially to affect the struggle for power building up throughout southern Africa. The region was more than the last redoubt of white supremacy. It was also the repository for money-spinning British, American and West European investments worth thousands of millions of dollars. Most important of all, it remained a treasure trove of scarce strategic minerals, from gold to uranium. It was here that the fears expressed by Callaghan, and subsequently echoed by Chinese authorities, took on a special significance. Consolidation of Mugabe's radically oriented regime in Zimbabwe in theory could provide the Russians with opportunities to influence a belt of friendly states from the Indian Ocean to the Atlantic, further isolating South Africa. They would also possess the potential either to cut the supply or to raise the cost of the minerals which were essential for the highly developed technological societies of the northern hemisphere.

Yet those were by no means all the benefits the Russians could claim to have achieved since the mid-1950s. In north-west Africa, on and below the bulge, they obtained naval and aerial staging facilities in the Republic of Guinea, Guinea-Bissau and Equatorial Guinea; on the offshore islands of São Tomé and Príncipe, and in Mauritania, they negotiated shipping and fishery accords; the governments of Benin and Congo (Brazzaville) profess a commitment to radicalism which has been sufficient to win them Moscow's military aid; and in Algeria, as a major supplier of arms, the Russians have preserved the degree of leverage necessary to permit them to head off the danger of a conflict with Morocco over the disputed future of the Western Sahara. Northwards along the Mediterranean rim of the continent, Libya, after Moscow's break with Cairo, became a client-state for Soviet arms. The Libyans, with petro-dollars to burn, over the years purchased more sophisticated weaponry than they could use for themselves, even allowing for their enmity with the Egyptians. They became, in effect, a provider of arms for Moslem fundamentalists and even non-Moslem radical movements, ranging from the Palestine Liberation Organization (PLO) to the Irish Republican Army (IRA). Nor did Gadafi confine himself to the role of arms dealer. When Idi Amin was struggling to save his presidency, Gadafi sent up to 2,000 militiamen by air to Uganda without telling his own general staff. The Libyan expeditionary force failed in its mission and, indeed, was soundly trounced.

Beyond Benghazi, Tobruk and Tripoli, concealed in the wadis and sand dunes of Cyrenaica, the Libyans built training camps and vast arsenals where militant Arabs and Africans were taught the arts of guerrilla warfare and where Soviet-supplied Kalashnikov rifles, RPG-7 rocket launchers, machine guns, land and sea mines were stored for judicious redistribution. Colonel Gadafi, Libya's head of government, for all his professed devotion to Islam and hatred of communism, was not above serving Soviet interests in the Arab and African worlds even though he might insist he took no orders from Moscow. The causes he supported and the operations he financed – anti-Egyptian, anti-Sudanese, pro-PLO, pro-IRA, even his own expansionist thrust into Chad – were those with which the Russians were identified. There were occasional inconsistencies which, somehow, Moscow found it possible to accept. Libya kept on arming the separatists of Eritrea and the champions of a Greater Somalia even after a regime with Marxist pretensions assumed power in Ethiopia. If these deviations annoyed leaders of the Kremlin they showed no signs of it in public, perhaps because Gadafi was too useful as a middleman.

When the Libyan leader, brimming with ambitions for his country, sought Soviet help to set up a complete nuclear-power generating complex, he was rewarded. In 1975 agreement was announced by the two countries for the purchase by Libya of an atomic reactor for civil power generation, with the Soviet Union supplying all the subsidiary installations and services including the training of technicians. The only condition set by Moscow was that Libya should accede to the non-proliferation treaty which provides for international inspection arrangements to guard against the production of nuclear weapons. Secrecy has surrounded the construction and subsequent activation of the plant but Libya's subsequent thrust into a region of Chad where substantial uranium deposits are suspected raised the eyebrows of scientists and experts in many capitals, including Moscow itself. The spectre of an unpredictable Gadafi brandishing a Libyan atomic bomb alarmed legislators in Washington, London and Paris, too, and it became a subject of secret discussion with the Russians in the London-based Nuclear Suppliers Club. This is a group of industrialized nations with an actual or potential nuclear-weapons capacity pledged to check the spread of nuclear weapons.

The Libyan episode served to underscore the fact that clients of the Soviet Union in Africa are not prepared automatically or permanently to subordinate themselves to the status of satellites. There had been evidence of this long before the Libyans and Russians were on speaking terms. President Sékou Touré of Guinea made his point when he barred Soviet aircraft from using Conakry's staging facilities during the Cuban missile crisis and the Ethiopian war with Somalia. Nigeria bought Soviet (and British) arms during the civil war of 1967–70 on purely commercial state-to-state terms without assuming any political commitments. The roof did not come crashing down when countries like Egypt, Somalia, Mali and Sudan exercised their right abruptly to terminate their close military and political relationships with the USSR. With good grace Soviet personnel quietly put away their tools and headed homewards.

There were, nevertheless, yet other gains, with a significance inversely proportionate to their lack of visibility. The Russians succeeded in developing interlocking networks of air and sea facilities criss-crossing the length and breadth of much of the continent and along its northern, western and eastern littorals. These systems deepened their penetration of Africa. They helped to build up invaluable infrastructures which, in times of emergency, could be transformed to state and military use.

Aeroflot, the national airline of the USSR, negotiated civil-aviation agreements with some twenty-nine of the fifty-two countries of Africa.[12] These accords were coupled with rights to overfly states between the Soviet Union and the African territories involved. The services were horizontal, vertical and diagonal; meaning that Soviet airplanes could fly in most directions and stage at authorized points. In some countries this included up to four or five different airfields. The arrangements, under economic-aid programmes, permitted more than the construction of modern airports modelled on Soviet standards. They also allowed for the development of electronic communications linking all Aeroflot points with Moscow, with each other, with fuel storage depots and maintenance and servicing centres and with installations accommodating technical personnel who included traffic controllers. During the Angolan civil war, for example, Aeroflot and Cuban transport planes staged, after their transatlantic flights from Havana, at Conakry in Guinea or in the Congo (Brazzaville) before completing their southward run to Luanda. During other crisis situations observed by American, British and French intelligence services, Soviet aircraft moved indigenous African units to flashpoint areas. At the time of the Ethiopian–Somali conflict, the facilities enabled Moscow to dispatch urgently needed arms and other military equipment from bases in the Soviet Union to the troubled areas.

Alongside the build-up of airfield and port installations, the Soviet Union constructed supporting road systems and supplied the transportation gear that went with them – trucks, buses and automobile fleets.

At relatively low cost, then, Moscow acquired an impressive air- and sea-lift capability and was able in Angola to keep the Luanda government, the Soviet and East-European contingents and the Cubans fully supplied. During the 1977–8 Ethiopian–Somali war, it was able at short notice to equip an entire division from southern Russia, and send 1,000 military and technical advisers, in addition to approximately 15,000 Cuban combat troops and a constant stream of supplies.

'It was a tremendous logistical performance,' a British official acknowledged. 'Not only did the Russians deliver the goods to the right places at the right times but they also organized the proper distribution to a variety of units, flowing in from different parts, each speaking their own language, all merging into a smoothly operating whole.'[13]

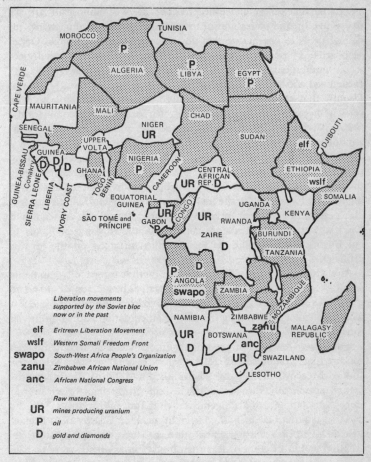

Fig. 9: Past and present recipients of Soviet military aid (shaded area)

That Ethiopian episode, and the Angolan affair preceding it, rated as case histories in their own right. They are dealt with in greater detail elsewhere in this book. Their importance lay in the fact that they dramatized what appeared to be the Soviet Union's activism when circumstances warranted it. It led some western authorities to view the developments as the start of a new imperialist, or counter-imperialist, phase in Soviet policy in Africa, with overtones of adventurism.

From the zero baseline which was its staging-point in the mid-1950s, the Soviet safari through Africa had come a long way by the 1980s.

The Russians were concerned to negotiate with almost all Africa's thirty-five littoral states and nearby islands precise arrangements for fishing fleets to operate up and down the Atlantic and Indian Ocean seaboards. These fleets, equipped with the most sophisticated electronic equipment, were able to work the waters within the widely recognized 200-mile economic zones, often within sight of the shores. Usually they were attended by modern support vessels able to keep track of western shipping movements, chart sea-bed formations for the Soviet Navy's own growing submarine force, and generally to serve as a mobile infrastructural component of the Russians' world-wide naval operations.[14] Possession of naval and mercantile anchorages along the East and West African coasts established a Soviet presence along the Indian and Atlantic Oceanic sea-lanes used by giant tankers carrying Middle Eastern oil to the fuel-hungry societies of Western Europe.

A persistent argument by the West Europeans, South Africans and Chinese was that this presence could allow the Russians suddenly to cut Europe's oil supplies. US authorities shrugged off the idea as artificial.

Any attempt to cut off or interfere with western oil shipments would be regarded as an act of piracy or war. 'The balloon would go up if that were to happen,' a senior State Department authority said. 'It would be like an attack on a friendly or allied nation and would invite total retaliation.'

There were few signs suggesting that the Soviet Union contemplated actions that would jeopardize the safety of vital western sea-lanes. Indeed Moscow, in exchanges with allied and Third World governments, specifically disavowed interest in disrupting American and European commercial arrangements with Arab oil producers. By the end of 1980 then, even among far-right members of President Ronald Reagan's entourage, it remained quite academic whether western retaliation would be total or less than total if interference were to take place. More relevant, though, was the fact that NATO military officers had prepared contingency plans for the defence of the South Atlantic sea-lanes in case of emergencies. Those routes are well beyond NATO's geographic limits which, in the south, stop at the Tropic of Cancer. 'We have our contingency plans for the defence of the South Atlantic sea routes,' Secretary-General Joseph Luns told a private meeting of the European–Atlantic group at the Palace of Westminster, London, on 29 October 1980. This implied, without proving, a degree of secret consultation with South Africa in contradiction of proclaimed NATO policy. Luns, more than once, had met privately with South Africa's Foreign Minister, Roelof 'Pik' Botha, and discussed a range of international political and strategic issues.

5. Cuba

For thousands of Cuban troops, teachers and doctors streaming into Angola during the 1975 civil war it was something like a homecoming.

'We are a Latin–African nation,' Fidel Castro told a rally of 1·2 million Cubans in Havana's Plaza de la Revolución around that time. 'African blood flows freely through our veins.'[1]

A certain romanticism marked Castro's reminder that race and culture were among the links uniting Cuba with Angola. Today's Cuba had to redeem the debt of blood and suffering owed to past generations of slaves torn from their African homelands over the centuries to toil in bondage through the Americas, Caribbean and West Indies. Nearly two-thirds of Cuba's ten million people are either Negroes or mulattos, the rest settled Spanish. Countless thousands of their ancestors, ironically, had been captured in Angola itself by the Portuguese for sale to the sugar-planters of Cuba.

It was full circle, then, when Castro's columns filed into battle against Angola's southern and northern invaders who had made common, if covert, cause with Agostinho Neto's internal foes.

The same emotive stress on slavery was evident nearly three years later during a Castro address to an Afro-Arab conference in Addis Ababa, at a time when Cuban forces were helping Ethiopia beat back invaders from Somalia. 'It must not be forgotten that there was slavery in Ethiopia until the [1974] Revolution,' he said. 'In the Addis Ababa exposition we have seen the iron and steel fetters used to chain tens of thousands of this country's citizens.'[2] A master politician was at work. He was reminding his listeners that his own people had shared their past.

Westerners could hardly object to Cuban efforts, between 1960 and 1975, to raise living standards in needy African and other countries. Those efforts indeed were praised in some West European, Asian and African capitals by officials who argued that in an ideal world east and west might well join together to tackle the herculean task of eliminating the misery, want and stagnation afflicting the lives of millions in the

Table 3: Western financial interests in fifteen key African countries (in million $)

Country	Date of Independence	Direct Investment United States[1]	Direct Investment United Kingdom[2]	Direct Investment Other W. Europe	Military Sales 1970–76 United States[3]	Military Sales 1970–76 France[4]	Foreign Aid United States[5]	Foreign Aid United Kingdom[6]	Foreign Aid France[6]	External Public Debt Outstanding 31.12.76[7]
Algeria	1962	—	—	s	—	22·1	—	-73·6	364·5	11,340·8
Chad	1960	—	—	s	—	s	6·0	0·1	22·0	250·0
Egypt	1936	s	s	s	17·1	148·2	1,275·0	49·0	72·1	7,866·2
Gabon	1960	—	—	s	0·2	—	10·9	-0·3	69·7	940·6
Ivory Coast	1960	—	—	s	—	—	123·1	0·3	73·5	2,220·8
Kenya	1963	s	207·0	—	—	—	167·9	-21·7	—	1,248·9
Liberia	1847	334·0	12·7	—	2·3	—	54·7	76·7	256·2	348·4
Mauritania	1960	—	—	—	—	s	30·0	0·8	6·8	619·1
Morocco	1956	s	—	s	443·7	154·0	373·5	20·7	173·1	3,152·5
Namibia	—	—	15·3	—	—	—	—	—	—	—
Nigeria	1960	535·0	467·0	—	12·1	—	56·0	190·1	14·4	1,420·4
Rhodesia	—	—	267·0	—	—	s	—	27·2	-0·6	—
South Africa	1910	1,670·0	2,343·4	846·0	349·0e	s	309·9	10·4	—	4,000·0e
Zaire	1960	200·0	12·0	1,000·0e	29·0	177·1	272·4	104·2	42·1	3,306·9
Zambia	1964	—	135·8	s	—	—	116·8	—	1·6	1,604·9
Totals for Africa		4,467·0	4,073·6	4,000·0e	904·1	750·0e	1,900·6	750·0e	1,250·0e	56,957·3

s = significant amount, but no data available   e = estimate.

Note: Figures are for 1974, 1975, 1976 or 1977. In many cases significant data may exist but are not publicly available, particularly with regard to direct investment and military sales. For instance, Business Week (6.11.78) reports that: 'The U.S. has a $6 billion book-value investment in South Africa and did $2 billion trade in 1977.' British companies have some $8 thousand million in fixed assets, according to the same source.

SOURCES: 1. US Department of Commerce, Survey of Current Business, August 1977; The New York Times, May–June 1978. 2. United Kingdom Board of Trade and Industry, Trade & Industry, 25 February 1977; Changing Patterns of International Investment in South Africa and the Disinvestment Campaign, Simon Clarke, London, September 1976. 3. US Department of Defense, Defense Security Assistance Agency, September 1976; Sean Gervasi, US Arms Transfers to South Africa, 30 May 1978. 4. Stockholm International Peace Research Institute, SIPRI Yearbook, 1977. 5. Center for International Policy, International Policy Report, Washington DC, January 1977. 6. OECD, Geographical Distribution of Financial Flows to Developing Countries 1969–75, 1976. 7. World Bank, Annual Report 1978, Washington DC.

backyards of the earth. But, soon enough, Cuban motives were questioned. The movements and activities of their civilian specialists and military advisers were tracked and in the eyes of the United States and other North Atlantic allied nations they became causes of concern, first in Angola, then in Ethiopia.

Cuban deployment of up to 50,000 combatants and civilians in the two countries – the communist world's biggest-ever overseas military venture – transformed the political map of Africa. The Cubans were denounced by Kissinger in 1975 as 'surrogates' of the Russians at a time when Americans themselves had become covertly involved through CIA cooperation with successive Zairean and South African invasion forces.

In time, a body of evidence built up suggesting that Kissinger's widely publicized accusation against the Cubans could have been based on a premature assumption. Castro's reliance upon, and coordination with, Moscow were never denied. But he disavowed having been asked or pressed by the USSR to move into either Angola or Ethiopia. For the first twenty years of his rule from 1959, Castro invariably projected a brand of Marxism suiting his own principles and his country's national and international interests. Neither Havana nor Moscow – and even Kissinger acknowledged this – *created* the Angolan civil war. Nor did they *incite* the Ethiopian revolution.

The most dramatic element in Cuban – and later Soviet – involvement in Africa during the 1970s lay in its scale, depth and essential success. There had been explicit forewarnings from Havana that Cuba regarded its commitment seriously.

Because US policy-makers like Kissinger and Brzezinski failed effectively to counter that commitment, they reacted with hostility and resentment. It was a reaction that appeared to be tinged with the frustration that flowed from the refusal of the Cuban David to yield to the American Goliath.

The failures of the Ford and Carter administrations boiled down to a central issue. Neither grasped the dynamic nature of national liberation movements, as in Angola, nor of national revolutionary movements, as in Ethiopia. Instead the Americans saw both as instruments of Cuban–Soviet expansionism. In Angola, the Cubans, long before the Portuguese collapse, had correctly perceived Neto's MPLA (Popular Movement for the Liberation of Angola) as the only liberation movement in the country with a national, as distinct from a merely regional, base.

In Ethiopia, the Cubans for two years had sought vainly to head off a collision with the Somalis and their serious military involvement began only after Siad Barre breached a solemn promise to Castro that he would not invade the Ogaden.

Cuba's centre-stage appearance in both countries came about first because of their internal conditions, which the western powers either failed to foresee or did nothing to prevent; secondly because the Cubans had invested years of hard, unsung, ground-level effort into understanding the problems of the developing nations from Latin America through the Caribbean, Middle East and Africa, then eastwards to Asia. It was an identification with a tri-continental spread and the results often showed up the Russians as much as the nations of the west.

While the Russians, for instance, were distributing armaments to handpicked customers, often at bargain-basement prices, the Cubans were telling Asians how to breed bulls. Long before fighting wars in black Africa, Castro was sending out builders' brigades to do the sort of work that the American Peace Corps had set out to perform. The spread of the socialist gospel was a top Havana priority, and functional field work accompanied the crusading. Cuban engineers helped needy clients in three continents to build roads and dams. Cuban teachers taught African children to read and write. With generations of experience to guide them, Cubans demonstrated sugar planting and refining techniques.

Fishermen shared their know-how with fellow Caribbean islanders. Basketball coaches and dance instructors followed scientists, miners, agriculturists and sports specialists to display the talents they had acquired in the years since Castro's revolutionaries emerged from the Sierra Maestra. Doctors and nurses ran hospitals penetrating stricken regions where disease was rampant.[3]

Impurities nevertheless soured the vintage of Cuban socialism. 'We are the standard-bearers of social progress and justice,' Castro told the Afro-Arab delegates at Addis Ababa in September 1978. At that time Cuban military instructors were helping train the forces of Uganda's President Idi Amin, branded by his own people as a genocidal murderer. It was also when about 200 Cuban military and technical men were aiding the regime of President Francisco Macías Nguema, whose reign of terror in the former Spanish colony of Equatorial Guinea forced one-fourth of his 340,000 people into exile. It was hard to discover which specific principles of 'social progress and justice' motivated Castro to lend a helping hand to rulers as dubious as these.

Angola and its aftermath generated American hostility towards Cuba for its role in Africa in two distinct phases:

1. Kissinger, humbled by congressional rejection of his plans for the civil war in Angola to continue, ended his term by making total Cuban military withdrawal the precondition for normalizing Washington's

relations with Havana. The new Carter administration, in conciliatory mood and anxious anyway to dissociate itself from Kissinger's failed policy, cancelled that precondition early in 1977.

2. Carter began his term by sending a message to Castro which said in effect that the past was the past and that Angola need not stand in the way of normalization. But his offer of a measured approach towards friendship embodied what he believed to be an informal understanding that Castro would cut back the Cuban expeditionary force (which Kissinger and the CIA had suggested was about 15,000 strong). Yet within months the process of conciliation had gone awry and, by November, the president was describing the reinforcement of Cuban troops as 'a threat to permanent peace . . .'.

The Castro brothers, Fidel and Raúl, in turn proclaimed defiantly that Cuba would not withdraw from Africa as the price of a deal with America. In Havana, Fidel told two US congressmen in early December 1977: 'If the issue of Cuban–American relations is placed in the context of Africa, the restoration of relations will not advance.' Raúl, speaking in Luanda on 5 December, observed: 'American governing circles which try to make the withdrawal of Cuban internationalist troops from Angola a precondition for the future improvement of relations with our country are wasting their time.' What, then, went wrong?

Undoubtedly the absence of direct man-to-man communication between the two presidents was a handicap; it compelled each to address the other through third parties, often with axes of their own to grind, or publicly through the media. There were, additionally, internal political and external diplomatic pressures on both leaders limiting their freedom of movement. Finally there was the ever-present danger of clandestine provocations calculated, in an atmosphere of mutual suspicion and a clash of interests in Africa, to bring about defensive yet damaging acts of retaliation. Some senior Havana authorities, hardened by the lessons of years of anti-Cuban conspiracy, were convinced that their withdrawal programme, and with it the normalization process, were deliberately and cleverly sabotaged.

Carter's initial policy of conciliation had brought an easing of US restrictions on travel to Cuba, establishment of low-level diplomatic missions in the two capitals and a resumption of informal dialogue. Scores of American congressmen, entrepreneurs and public figures paraded through Havana, many to meet, speak and be photographed with the bearded apostle of anti-capitalism, still an imposing figure in his guerrilla battledress. Vice-President Carlos Rafael Rodríguez, a colourful personality in his own right with a long record of communist-party activism and a theoretician's reputation, sometimes deputized for him.

The generalized account that follows, giving the version of 'insiders' about informal American–Cuban exchanges on Africa, was pieced together by the author from information gathered in talks with Americans and Cubans alike who participated. All insisted on anonymity.

The Carter Signals to Castro

The president entered the White House ready to distance himself from the Cuban policies of five predecessors. The road to reconciliation, after twenty years of sterile rhetoric and acts of subversion, seemed open if there could be reciprocity in settling outstanding issues. It must have been plain to Castro that Africa was a major preoccupation of the new president. Carter, again, hoped to abandon the confrontational attitudes of the past and instead to seek to reduce superpower competition in a continent which needed, above all, peace and stability to meet the rigours of late-twentieth-century life. Moderation from east and west alike was required, therefore, if this were to become a shared aim. Had not Carter already accepted the concept of black majority rule in the white bastions of the subcontinent; repeatedly stressed the need to respect human rights; and sought an east–west limitation of arms sales to Africa and of naval demonstrations in the Indian Ocean?

Yet observers in the White House were soon dismayed that their gestures were yielding few comparable responses from either Havana or Moscow. The first invasion of Shaba in Zaire by Angola-based Katangans took place as Cuba was reinforcing its Angola garrison. Next came Cuba's involvement in Ethiopia, small to begin with but swiftly escalating, with Soviet help, to vast proportions. The strategic balance in the Horn had been transformed. All this posed questions about the true nature of Cuban objectives in combat zones thousands of miles from home. Committed as he was nationally and internationally to removing cold-war rivalries from the African setting, Carter was gravely embarrassed by these developments. He faced a rising clamour for effective counter-action.

The president had been jolted, in particular, by CIA estimates in November which indicated that Cuba had sent an extra 4,000 combatants into Angola, bringing the strength of the garrison up to some 19,000, in addition to nearly 5,000 civilian technicians. Washington related this to a possible Cuban involvement in other southern African countries, notably Zimbabwe, then a region of tremendous volatility with explosive racial complexities.

A situation was seen to be shaping with implications threatening race relations on a global scale. East–west *détente* was at risk. Equally disappointing to Washington was the catalogue of misleading, unreliable statements of Cuban–Soviet–Ethiopian intent, politically as well as militarily.

For Carter, prepared as he was to take the political risk of restoring relations with Cuba, Havana's credibility had begun to assume a threadbare look. White House planners were asking if the establishment of normal relations with the United States was an objective Castro shared. By the spring of 1978 the drift among some of the president's top men was towards the conclusion that normalization did not matter especially to the Cuban leader and Carter was so advised.

The Castro Response to Carter

Cuban leaders reacted seriously to Washington's complaints. They attributed some to honest misunderstandings, others to circumstances beyond their control, several to differences in principle and outlook unlikely to be reconciled. On certain issues expressions of concern were coupled with indignant protests against what they saw as deliberate American misrepresentations of their activities in Africa.

Angola

The Cubans recalled that when Kissinger demanded total withdrawal from Angola they had advised Washington through Canadian, British, French and Swedish envoys that Cuba had a precise accord with Neto to defend Angolan frontiers until Angolans were strong enough to do the job themselves. It was Havana's duty to respect that promise. Meanwhile withdrawals had begun and, by April 1977, about half the expeditionary force had gone. The size of that force was ultimately disclosed by Castro himself to have been 36,000 at its peak.[4]

In March 1977 Castro was in Africa when something occurred that he claimed had been totally unexpected. The first Katangan thrust into Shaba was launched, bringing into Zaire French and Moroccan troops who, after pushing out the Katangans, stayed on for months. Spurred by the French, Mobutu spoke explicitly of crossing into Angola again. For Neto, this revived dangers of a new Zairean invasion.

For Castro it meant that withdrawals had to be stopped and reinforcements brought in because Cuba was resolved to honour its pledge. France, Britain and Belgium were warned at once that any Zairean attack on Angola would meet with Cuban resistance.

On his return to Havana, Castro sent word again to Washington – via the French – that Cuba had had absolutely nothing to do with the Katangan attack and would not want it to disrupt the normalization process, but that Mobutu's threats had to be taken seriously and this was why the withdrawal programme had to be reversed. Washington, however, assailed Cuba for failing to fulfil its informal commitment to withdraw. Castro resented this as a misrepresentation. He remarked sourly to more than one visiting American that a 'Kissingerian flavour' seemed to have crept into some of Carter's misstatements: 'How could he find it possible to praise France and Morocco for sending troops to defend Zairean territory and yet, at the same time, attack us for doing exactly the same thing in Angola and Ethiopia? He knows we support the territorial integrity of states.'

In talk after talk with U S visitors Castro and Rodríguez stressed that:

1. Without Cuban troops Angola would soon become a victim of outside aggression.

2. Since 1975 Cuba had been protecting the Cabinda enclave, worked by Gulf Oil, and indeed in 1975 had beaten back Zairean–French attempts to seize it.

3. Cuba's sole mission in Angola was to safeguard its frontiers but not to tangle in its internal conflicts; if Nino Alves and José van Dunem had succeeded in their counter-revolutionary attempt of May 1977 to topple Neto, Cuba would have pulled out completely.

4. Havana had made considerable economic sacrifices to help the Angolans and in 1977 all aid was free; but the Angolans paid for some assistance in 1978 because Cuban resources were not unlimited.

Ultimately, though, neither Angola nor Ethiopia would need Cuban help and then would be the time for Cuba to go.[5]

Ethiopia

Castro and Rodríguez, in most discussions on the subject, maintained that the Carter administration failed to realize how long and hard Cuba had resisted repeated pleas from Mengistu to provide military help. Nor did Washington register, as they saw it, the intensity of Cuban efforts to reconcile Mengistu and Siad Barre, both professing socialist affiliations. During his 1977 journey to Africa, Castro met Ethiopian, Somali and South Yemeni leaders in Aden, hoping to help them dilute or drown their differences within a southern Red Sea confederation. In that way, Castro reasoned, Siad's ambitions to annex the Ogaden might have been contained. (Plainly disenchanted with Siad, Castro in 1978 was telling visitors: 'The Mexicans have more right to Arizona than Somalia has to the Ogaden.') In Aden Castro proposed the formation of an Ethiopian–Somali–South Yemeni commission to take the confederation project further. The South Yemenis countered with the suggestion that Cuba, too, should join the group as its fourth member. Siad refused both propositions and the talks broke down. But the Somali leader pledged solemnly that he would not pursue with force his claims on Ethiopian territory. By early July, Somali irredentists in the Ogaden were intensifying their campaign to unite with Somalia. By the end of the month Siad's forces had invaded. He had become, in Castro's words, 'the great deceiver no one [not even Americans] should trust'.

Before July a small group of Cuban advisers was helping Mengistu plan the remodelling of Ethiopian armed forces. But when irredentist activity increased Mengistu appealed again, more urgently, for at least 300 Cuban specialists – specifically tankmen – to hurry to the zone and to help direct defensive operations, without involving themselves in battle. His request was met. Then, when Siad invaded, Mengistu's S O S for aid confronted Cuba, as Castro put it, with a tremendously 'difficult moral problem'. It was whether to stand idly by and watch Ethiopia disintegrate or whether to help defend its frontiers which, in O A U terms, were supposed to be sacrosanct.

To some extent the situation on the ground provided its own answer. The Cuban specialists were in the fighting zone. They were authorized to become operational. Washington was immediately advised. Siad broadcast the claim that 20,000 Cubans were in the field. The Cubans insisted that only their 300 specialists were engaged. In a later battle for the key town of Harar, Siad blamed the Cubans for the loss of 4,000 of his fighters. Havana told Washington that no Cubans were present.

Cuban leaders insisted that Washington was advised as Cuban involvement increased. Nevertheless the Cubans acknowledged that, against their wishes, a good deal of public dissembling did take place. Castro wanted to disclose the Cuban role in detail at all stages but Mengistu would not have it. Thus misleading accounts appeared. Mengistu, in Havana's version, felt a need to maximize the Ethiopian role and to minimize the Cuban one, and there was little Cuba could do about it except to keep Washington as fully informed as security factors allowed. Castro and Rodríguez neither expected nor got Washington's approval. Both sides knew that their differences on principle were almost impossible to reconcile. Still, Cuban leaders hoped that Carter would try to understand how unwillingly the Ethiopian commitment had been assumed; at the expense, indeed, of other important political objectives. They had worked for a Mengistu–Siad reconciliation and faced with Siad's intransigence were still working for an Eritrean solution within the confines of Ethiopian unity.

Despite what Castro called 'lying American claims' that Cuban units were fighting their former Eritrean friends, Cuba had not and would not take part in Mengistu's attempts to crush Eritrean separatism. In principle, to be sure, Cuba opposed such separatism in a land with

eighty or more distinct ethnic groups. It favoured an Ethiopian confederation in which autonomous regions could coexist. Without that
unity and a Red Sea outlet, Ethiopia could hardly survive.

Cuba and Southern Africa

Castro and Rodríguez at different times, with different visitors, were
emphatic that they had refused many requests for combat aid from
heads of African governments involved in the Zimbabwe–Rhodesia
struggle and other southern African problems. Their only commitment
was to help train Patriotic Front and SWAPO guerrillas struggling
for Namibian statehood. But Cuba's options remained open. Cuba
favoured, first, a negotiated peace settlement that would ensure black
majority rule and, secondly, self-liberation by the Zimbabweans, if a
political solution either proved impossible or were to break down.

If, however, Zambia and Mozambique were to be attacked by a
Zimbabwe under effective white-minority control, a situation would
doubtless arise in which Cuba would be pressed for help not only by the
victims but also by concerned neighbour states.

Cubans argued that their presence in Angola, ironically, had yielded
a positive spin-off exploited by the Americans and British in dealings
with white Rhodesians and South Africans. The fact of that presence
was a useful, restraining influence. It also stimulated American–British
thinking and action. The South African and Rhodesian whites had been
impressed by the Anglo-American argument that if they went too far,
declined all compromise, they might find themselves in confrontation
with the Cubans. In that sense there was a confluence of Cuban,
American and British interests, for all wanted, or said they wanted, an
end to white domination.

In Zimbabwe, whether before or after a political settlement, Cuban
actions would be conditioned by respect for the attitude of the Patriotic
Front and the five front-line states (Zambia, Tanzania, Botswana,
Angola and Mozambique). There had to be limits to the degree of
Cuban involvement in Africa. There was no wish in Havana to preside
over a transfer of Cuba's population to Africa. Carter ought to under-
stand that Cuba's preference at all times was for negotiated solutions in
Africa's trouble-spots.

Against what was taken to be an American failure to understand
Cuban motives and difficulties, Castro and his colleagues, by the end of
1977, concluded that Carter had authorized a deliberate campaign
against Cuba's policies in Africa. With dismay, surprise and anger they
spoke of a map that Brzezinski and Hamilton Jordan, Carter's chief of
staff at the White House, had 'planted' in the media purporting to

portray just how extensive Cuban activities in Africa had become. In a dozen coastal states – not counting Ethiopia, where a big build-up was under way – the map showed more than 26,000 Cuban military and civilian personnel to be in place. As Havana's leaders described it, phantom Cuban contingents were shown in countries where their people had never set foot. This, as they saw it, was reprehensible behaviour by Carter, someone from whom they had expected greater balance and less bias than his predecessors had displayed.

Rodríguez summoned Lyle Lane, head of the US mission, and demanded that he ask Washington what lay behind the issue of information so false. He posed three questions:

1. Did President Carter feel that he had to act tough towards Cuba as a way of winning congressional ratification (then pending) for the new Panama Canal Treaty? If so, he ought to know that Cuba did not think much of being used.

2. Had President Carter abandoned his policy of normalizing relations with Cuba? He had that right but Cuba ought to be told because it, too, could revise its own attitude.

3. Could there have been some misunderstanding in Washington about Cuban aims and actions in Africa? Havana would be glad to remove any misapprehensions.

Lane and others were shown in detail where the US Defense Department map was false. The envoy said that the material was based on CIA reports. It left the Cubans with no other conclusion but that American intelligence-gathering in Africa was wildly wrong. That, they said, was Carter's problem and not theirs.

The explanation for Cuban activism in Africa after Angola may have impressed some elements in the Carter administration but it left the president unyielding. At mid-term in his presidency, Carter had wider considerations to ponder. His popular rating had sagged. The recalcitrance of Congress worried him. The Ethiopian episode found the Americans, yet again, on the losing side.

Haunted by the hairline passage of the Panama Canal Treaty, which underlined the gathering strength of the conservatives in Congress, Carter wanted also to chart a strategy for achieving the central objective of his international policy. This was to secure ratification of the second-phase Strategic Arms Limitation Treaty (SALT 2), which was then approaching signature. It seemed to him and his advisers essential, therefore, to divest himself of any left-leaning image. The Cuba factor was a ready instrument.

'They [the Russians and the Cubans] take advantage of local disturbances,' he told a Washington news conference. '[They] move in with massive intrusion, both of military weapons which contribute to further bloodshed among the Africans themselves, and when they are permitted by the local governments, they send in large quantities of troops.'[6]

The administration thereupon sought to back up its verbal denunciations of Cuba with deeds. Arguing that Cuban military collaboration with the Soviet Union had compromised its non-aligned status, the Americans called on member-nations of the non-aligned movement to dismiss the Castro regime from their ranks. The attempt failed. Cuba played host to the ninety-five member-nations and member-groups of the movement in Havana during September 1979, with Castro presiding. Most African, Asian and other non-aligned countries endorsed not only the Cuban presence in Angola and Ethiopia but also Cuba's overall programme of aiding and training developing countries and liberation movements. 'On an almost daily basis Carter has been expressing concern over Cuba's role in Africa,' Leslie Harriman, Nigerian ambassador to the United Nations, told a correspondent. 'Cubans have never attacked any sovereign state or crossed an internationally recognized boundary. What they have done is to assist oppressed people gain their self-determination from colonial masters.'[7]

Castro had a ready answer to Carter's charge that 'Cuba is used by the Soviet Union as surrogates in several places in Africa'.[8] He told an American television audience: 'Do you want to know if the Soviets asked us to go there [into Angola]? The Soviets absolutely did not ask us. They never said a single word in that sense. It was exclusively a Cuban decision.'[9]

Explaining their military involvements in Africa, Cuban leaders stressed repeatedly that they had conformed fully with principles laid down not only by the non-aligned movement but also by the OAU. Cuba and Yugoslavia were the only two communist states which had been charter members of the non-aligned movement when it was founded in 1961. Three of its principles were:

1. To seek actively to end what was called 'imperialism', 'colonialism', 'neo-colonialism' and 'racism'.

2. To provide support for any member-government or group which appealed for help to preserve its independence or to achieve liberation.

3. To respond to requests for defence aid by any member-state whose territory was threatened or violated by an aggressor.

The Cubans insisted that in Angola they had responded to a plea for combat help *after* the intervention of Zaire, South Africa, European mercenaries and the CIA. Their entry into the Ethiopian conflict had answered a plea for support from the Dergue *after* Somalia invaded the Ogaden. They argued further that they had followed a precedent established by the United States itself two centuries earlier.

'The right of recourse to violence to achieve or defend independence, in fact, has been historically sanctioned as far back as the US Revolution of 1776,' Dr Gordon Adams wrote in 1978. 'Moreover it is clear that nations involved in such struggles have historically had the right to appeal for foreign support. The United States, itself, did so in the eighteenth century.' [10]

Senior US authorities in Washington, London, Brussels and other capitals acknowledged frankly to the author at the time that it was difficult, given the circumstances, to challenge the right of the Cubans to intervene as they were doing in Angola and Ethiopia. In office presidents Gerald R. Ford and Jimmy Carter consequently did what they thought was the next best thing. They attempted to rally world opinion against the communist states for intruding in the affairs of a distant continent where, supposedly, they had no historic interest or contemporary business.

Thus, former President Ford:

Africa will loom ever larger in our lives for the rest of this century. The Soviet Union is waging an undeclared war, the resources war. Africa is the battleground because from it come many of the resources and raw materials essential to western society and especially to the United States . . . [11]

And Carter:

There is no other country that acts in harmony with, or under the domination of, the Soviets any more than the Cubans do. [12]

This was a far cry from Carter the presidential candidate arguing in 1976 against Kissinger's global approach to Angola:

I think that the United States' position in Angola should be one which admits that we missed the opportunity to be a positive and creative force for good in Angola during the years we supported Portuguese colonization. We should also realize that the Russian and Cuban presence in Angola, while regrettable and counter-productive of peace, need not constitute a threat to US interests, nor does that presence mean the existence of a communist satellite on the continent.

The president's transformation left two crucial issues unanswered.

One was whether Castro took his orders from Brezhnev or whether Brezhnev took his cue from Castro. There was a formidable body of evidence to suggest that Castro, in Ethiopia as well as in Angola, acted according to his own lights and swung his sponsor along with him.

The other issue was posed by Paulo Jorge, foreign minister of Angola in 1978 and quoted by Gerald J. Bender, assistant professor of political science at the University of California:

How does the United States distinguish between the type of foreign aid Cuba is providing Angola and that provided by the United States to other Third World countries? You have more military instructors in Saudi Arabia and Iran than we have Cubans and Soviets combined. We don't criticize Iran's or Saudi Arabia's right to choose their helpers, nor do we criticize your country's right to provide that assistance. We frankly have a hard time understanding the standards of international diplomacy the United States applies to judge us. Perhaps this is because as a young nation we are inexperienced. But it appears to us that your country is being extremely hypocritical, if not punitive, in its attitude towards us.

Andrew Young could not have known it at the time but he had begun running counter to Brzezinski's views when he said on television in January 1977: 'There is a sense in which the Cubans bring a certain stability and order to Angola.' The statement brought down the wrath of critics, from congressmen in Washington to politicians in Pretoria, on his head.[13]

In a talk with the author exactly two years later the former ambassador elaborated his view. The Portuguese in pre-independent Angola filled most of the key posts in the colony. They had done little to prepare Angolans for a transfer of power; it was as if, unconsciously, they were creating the conditions that would satisfy what most whites in subcontinental Africa believed – that blacks were incapable of running a sophisticated modern society. US authorities, according to Young, were well aware that when civil war erupted most of the 500,000 settled Portuguese simply cut and ran from Angola, taking just about everything movable – more than 20,000 trucks used for internal food distribution, consumer goods from stores, medicines, drugs, office equipment; all were shipped back to metropolitan Portugal at state expense. The departing settlers also burned most government records, ripped out telephone wires in key public offices and generally pillaged the land.

From late 1975 the Cubans moved in with technicians of all kinds in an endeavour to restore order out of the mess that the Portuguese had left. Thousands among their expeditionary force were medical personnel, construction workers, engineers and agriculturists, housing specialists, road-builders and teachers. Their purpose was to help the Angolans take over the skilled jobs suddenly abandoned and, Young reported, by 1979 this was proceeding apace. Those elements of the combatant units not engaged in southern and northern frontier defence operations against the South African and Zairean infiltrators were helping, too, on the farms, in the towns, along the coast. Years of hard reconstruction nevertheless remained, alongside the need for constant vigilance, and action, as South Africa continued to raid and bomb as well as to arm internal enemies of the Luanda government.[14]

In contrast with functional aid provided in other African lands by the USSR, the American Peace Corps, and the countries of East and West Europe, Cuba's commitment in Angola and elsewhere had, immediately, more meaning to Africans in hovels and high places alike. Stressing their own African heritage Cuban field-workers lived with and like the Africans they trained, without demanding the best local accommodation available. Just as the Chinese did, they openly acknowledged that they, like the Africans, were an underdeveloped people.

The support and specialist services they provided precisely identified them with the workaday problems of the seventeen or so African countries that they had been helping since the early 1960s. Their experience enabled them to form political as well as social judgements, and to chart programmes, well in advance of their Russian friends or western antagonists.

The Russians derived much of their information either from books or from briefs written for them by specialists as removed from the realities as were the polished diplomats of the west. African friends would tell Moscow what they thought Moscow would like to hear. On such fragile foundations Kremlin policies were evolved – only to be reassessed in the light of insistent Cuban advice.

Because their own diplomats and intelligence operatives were totally detached from direct contact with men and women on the dirt roads of Africa and in mud-hut villages, the judgements of American, British, French and other western authorities were little better than those of the Russians. The intelligence operatives, like the CIA and KGB, worked closely with those local security agencies ready to cooperate, and invariably fed into their foreign counterparts 'party-line' material. Links between the CIA station in Pretoria and South Africa's former Bureau of State Security (BOSS) were close through the 1960s and early 1970s and should have provided a demonstration of how Washington came to be sadly misinformed about the true state of affairs in Angola before and after independence. It was only after the event, for instance, that Washington learned that Cuba would have gone into Angola's struggle alone, even if Moscow had declined to support that venture, according to US *and* Cuban authorities.

In the Horn of Africa it was Cuba, not the USSR, which set the pace in pressing for a political settlement between the Ethiopians and Eritreans and which proposed an Ethiopian–Somali–South Yemeni confederation of socialist states. Both initiatives almost certainly had the blessing of the Kremlin but the fact that Castro took the lead told its own story. In the same way Castro, not Brezhnev, called attention to the condition of the Ethiopian people after the disappearance of Emperor Haile Selassie:

> What did imperialism and its ally, the feudal regime, leave behind in Ethiopia? A total of 150,000 lepers, 400,000 victims of tuberculosis, 6,000,000 malaria victims, 14,000,000 people with various types of eye infections, hundreds of thousands of people who starved to death during the droughts, a 95 per cent illiteracy rate and 125 doctors [for 30,000,000 people].[15]

As Cuba helped its Angolan and Ethiopian protagonists overcome their challengers, the CIA estimates suggested that the two campaigns from 1975 to 1978 cost at least 1,500 Cuban lives. Resistance by Jonas Savimbi's UNITA, financed by the South Africans and, according to his own claim, by the Chinese too, ground on. Egypt, Saudi Arabia and other Islamic states kept the flames of Eritrean separatism alive in the 1980s.

Then came the second Shaba affair.

The first Shaba episode, in March 1977, was no unlucky incident that simply happened to disrupt Cuban withdrawals from Angola and so derail the train of Cuban–American normalization. Cuban authorities privately expressed their conviction that the Katangan invasion was too well timed yet too loosely organized not to provoke questions. In the highly conspiratorial setting of the Zairean–Angolan–South African–Rhodesian quadrant the stakes were high and there were agents in abundance to make mischief. But Havana's own theory was that there had been an intercontinental dimension involving anti-Castro exiles in Florida who had a vested interest in wrecking Carter's initial hopes of restoring relations with Cuba. If Castro himself or Rodríguez possessed firm evidence of a plot they did not produce it. But aides spoke openly of it to the author, long after the event, with no apparent political yield in prospect.

Certainly the region was rife with suspicion of international plotting. In February 1977, weeks after Carter's inauguration, 'Cobra 77' was disclosed: the code-name for an invasion of Angola, allegedly being planned for late 1977 by South Africa, Zaire, France and a mercenary band. No such invasion took place, perhaps because there was no plot, perhaps because it was prematurely revealed. What did take place, though, was a series of cross-border attacks on Angola by the South Africans and the Zaireans, partly in support of Savimbi's continuing resistance, partly to destabilize the Neto regime. Then, again, international publicity attended the operation of a West German company called Orbital Launch and Rocket Corporation which, with CIA help, rented 100,000 square miles of Shaba territory for missile-firing tests, missiles which could be targeted on Angolan strong points. The puzzle about the Shaba affair was that it was organized so badly. It could never have succeeded (and therefore should never have been undertaken) unless there had been some other objective in mind. If that other objective was to disrupt the Cuban withdrawal then it succeeded.

Shaba, a province of Zaire, used to be called Katanga. Its Lunda tribespeople dominate the south-eastern reaches of the country, spill over into Zambia and, nowadays, into Angola too. A history of shifting allegiances since the sixteenth century qualified the Lunda for the role they played in the post-colonial era as black Africa's true surrogates who, since 1960, served seven different sponsors, usually white. Their causes may have changed but their mission remained constant. It was – and is – to win ultimate control over the enormously rich mineral resources in the land of their fathers. About one-third of Africa's copper is mined in Shaba. The territory produces three-quarters of the world's cobalt. It has zinc, cadmium, tin and, for good measure, the uranium of Shinkolobwe.

Up to 400,000 in number, the Katangans in north-eastern Angola, banished from their homeland in the early 1960s, were the creatures of Belgian colonialism. Initially they were trained to serve as the gendarmerie of the key Congolese (Zairean) province that earns half the country's foreign revenue. With independence in 1960, they became the military arm of Moïse Tshombe's failed attempt to establish Katanga as an independent state – an attempt backed at the time by Belgium, Britain and the abortive Central African Federation, run by white Rhodesians. The United States, eager for a share in the territory's resources, opposed separatism and ultimately won a share of its mineral wealth by backing Mobutu. Intrigue and counter-intrigue surrounded the Katangans through the years. The downfall of Tshombe saw them seek sanctuary in Portuguese-ruled Angola, where they came to be used against the liberation movements. But Mobutu remained their arch-enemy. After Angolan independence, with Zairean troops attacking Neto's forces, Neto set them free to counter-attack the Zairean invaders. Sometimes they operated on their own. At other times they were led by mercenaries – French, Belgian, it did not matter who.

Shaba One, with Castro in Africa, caught the Cubans offguard.

Fourteen months later, in May 1978, Havana was better informed. One week before the second Shaba invasion by the well-trained Katangans, Castro personally called in Lyle Lane and warned him that something was afoot. The Cuban leader, according to R. Roa-Kouri who was Havana's ambassador to the United Nations, told Lane he was trying through the Angolans to head off another imminent Shaba venture. The Cubans, however, could not themselves intervene in Angola's internal affairs. It so happened that Neto, already stricken with cancer, was in Moscow for medical treatment. 'This probably was a determining factor in our not preventing the second invasion,' Roa-Kouri told the author.[16]

The attack took place. Immediately Mobutu charged that the Cubans had not only arranged it but also taken part in it. Carter repeated the accusation but said nothing about the forewarning sent to Washington by Castro. Again and again the president blamed the Cubans for an affair which degenerated into a Katangan rampage of killing of blacks and whites indiscriminately. French, Belgian and Moroccan paratroopers hurried to the scene and beat back the attackers. The rescue force then stayed for about a year to ensure the continued stability of the province and its continued mineral output. Under congressional pressure Carter found it hard to support the intelligence data he claimed to possess, establishing that Cuba actually had promoted the invasion. Gradually he backed away from his charges.

The tale of the Katangan soldiery was a sorry one. The United States was not guiltless of seeking to exploit their fighting skills. There was the long-concealed episode of 1964, when anti-Castro Cubans were hired for a special role in Zaire. At that time former Secretary of State Dean Rusk had demanded to know why 'the movement of Katangan gendarmes from Angola' could not be used to help crush a threatened communist takeover in a land riven by rebellion. Details emerged in a series of hitherto secret papers declassified in mid-1978 at the library of the late President Lyndon B. Johnson in Austin, Texas.[17]

Castro embodied the survival instinct of his people, who had lived through more than slavery. They had endured prolonged nineteenth-century liberation struggles against Spanish masters; a twentieth-century guerrilla war; and subsequent big-power attempts to tame a revolution that had begun going its own way.

From the outset Havana's far-out radicalism aroused the hostility of the nearby American giant and the doubts of the distant Soviet patron. Yet both the hostility and the doubts produced results opposite to those intended. In turn, the Bay of Pigs invasion, the Cuban missile crisis, acknowledged CIA conspiracies to assassinate Castro, an effort by Moscow to oust Castro, and trade restrictions by both superpowers had the effect of stabilizing the regime, of extending its influence abroad, and of rallying Third World sympathy. Ultimately, though, the most serious outcome was that Washington's lack of flexibility drove Havana to shelter beneath Moscow's protective umbrella.

Through most of the 1960s, as Havana-born Professor Jorge I. Dominguez of Harvard University noted in 1978, Cuba had been going its own way. Fundamental differences with Moscow had surfaced over

Castro's initial neutrality in the Sino-Soviet ideological conflict. Havana also assailed Moscow for yielding to US demands for the removal of its missiles from the island in 1962. And the Russians, recognizing then that Castro was no Muscovite lackey, had promoted their own 'micro-faction' inside the Cuban communist party, for the purpose of eliminating Castro and his entourage.[18]

By 1968 Castro had lost more than his friend and sometime revolutionary conscience, Ernesto Ché Guevara, killed in the bushlands of Bolivia. He had also lost the illusion that Latin America was ripe for Cuban-type socialism. More serious was Soviet curtailment of oil deliveries to Cuba. China had already cut back sugar purchases and rice exports. US trade sanctions were hurting. In Prague, the liberal spring was blooming but was to wither when the tanks of August began rolling through the land. Castro and his fellow-leaders knew they could no longer procrastinate. To them this was a Playa Girón (Bay of Pigs) that worked – and so had to be seen as a watershed in inter-socialist relations. Accordingly Castro's party endorsed the Warsaw Pact invasion. The survival of Cuba's own revolution was guaranteed.

By singing Soviet tunes Castro alleviated Cuba's more urgent troubles. He became more pragmatic in state relations with Latin American and Caribbean neighbours and, by the end of the 1970s, he had rallied eight regional fellow-members or observer-governments to the talks of the non-aligned in Havana. He was in 1979 elected leader of that movement for a three-year term, with a personal prestige that was extraordinary for the leader of ten million people. He was able to evolve a foreign policy nationally based, yet globally oriented, distinctive from that of Moscow, yet dovetailed with the objectives of the Soviet Union, at least in geopolitical terms. More specifically, Castro turned from Latin America towards Africa for a freer, fuller expression of Cuban achievements and abilities in a setting more appreciative of help and, in time, more promising of reward.

In choosing Africa early, Cuba's leaders demonstrated greater prescience than either superpower. Their choice was made in the early 1960s. They identified with the sensitivities not only of the Africans themselves but also of their own domestic constituency of blacks and black-Spanish descendants. The backing of that constituency, especially in Oriente province, had been crucial to Castro's long march through the Sierra Maestra to power.

Cuba had little to risk in exporting know-how and personnel, and everything to gain, particularly because their overseas involvements instilled a sense of mission into the rising generation which had missed the revolution at home. Moreover, Washington's growing interest in a promising continent needed to be challenged.

Cuba and the Soviet Union together developed an infrastructure of air, land and sea communications, reinforced by East European contingents, giving socialist nations and Cuban forces a mobility and influence throughout the continent that could not easily be nullified. The socialist states insisted that they sought no investment stake and no privileges for the multinationals they did not possess. They wanted – and seized – the chance to spread their ideological precepts. In using that opportunity they were able to make life harder for those they branded as 'imperialists' and 'neo-colonialists' – the nations of the west.

When Castro presided over the Havana summit of the non-aligned movement in September 1979, a central issue dominated the proceedings. It was whether the socialist bloc under Moscow's leadership could be regarded as the 'natural allies' of the group or whether any attachment to a power bloc would be alien to the spirit of the movement. Castro maintained that such a linkage was not only logical but inevitable. And he used his chairmanship to tilt policy accordingly. The late President Josip Broz Tito of Yugoslavia, his veteran predecessor as leader of the movement, stubbornly battled for a confirmation of the original articles of faith which had inspired the founding fathers of non-alignment. The struggle for the soul of the movement assumed the aspects of a duel between a partisan of the past and one of the present, each with storied achievements to strengthen his case, both resolved not to push the issue to the point of splitting the movement. It turned out to be Tito's last duel, one he did not win. In the spring of 1980 Europe's only surviving Second World War leader, still heading a state, died.

Castro's thesis that the movement must become the political instrument of developing countries in their struggle for a new international economic order commanded greater acceptance than Tito's case for a clinical neutrality between east and west.

For Africans, in particular, Castro's message seemed more sensitive to the needs of the times. The escalating east–west scramble for Third World energy resources and raw materials could be a process that would enhance the negotiating power of the developing countries, a power which member-countries ought to use.

Beset by their own problems, seeking to bridge the ever-widening technological gap, coping with their population and food problems, Africans had no cause to become involved in the intricacies of the great east–west divide.

Global solutions involving a fairer distribution of the earth's resources were essential, Castro argued. His emphasis was neither on Soviet tanks nor on US marines but on what he portrayed as the more insidious pressures of the multinational conglomerates, the established and powerful financial institutions of the west, racism, neo-colonialism and the need for the Arab oil producers to lower their prices for fellow-members.

All in all, the outcome suggested that the movement had advanced towards the concerns of north and south, in economic terms, and away from the political issues of east–west rivalries. By clever stage-management and far-sighted focusing on worrying issues – with suggestions that the most acute of those worries were western in origin – Castro encouraged the non-aligned states to adopt the concept expressed by a Jamaican diplomat in 1976: 'Socialist countries are the traditional and natural allies of the developing countries.'[19]

Castro made no secret of his belief that a new correlation of forces would emerge if there were to be a union between the world socialist community and the people of the collapsed or collapsing empires of Europe.

Victories in Angola and Ethiopia, plus unremitting aid in parts of Africa, Asia and Latin America, had thrust Fidel Castro into temporary leadership of the Third World against US wishes. But in southern Africa his Angolan friends were still under attack. In the Horn of Africa, Eritreans and Somalis were finding new friends.

Most important of all, though, was the fact that a crisis even then was building up in south-west Asia. It reached a peak on Christmas Eve 1979, when Soviet ground and air forces moved into Afghanistan, the buffer state separating the USSR from Pakistan.

That development transformed the world scene almost overnight. East–west relations deteriorated. The non-aligned movement split, with even Moscow-oriented states like India assailing the intervention as inadmissible. Castro and his colleagues were shaken. At first they remained silent and then grudgingly endorsed the Soviet action. Plainly it was an endorsement that stemmed more from socialist solidarity than from socialist convictions.

6. China

Old China's links with Africa pre-dated those of Europe. They reach back into the fourteenth century when Cheng Ho, a noted explorer, told of his travels along the east coast. The gap that followed fifteenth-century exchanges with Egypt coincided with the period of European expansionism through Asia, around the rim of Africa and deep into the western hemisphere. The slave trade that scarred Africa did not leave the Chinese unmarked. Imperial Europe's dominance saw Chinese workers indentured for service in various labour-hungry territories wherever the work was hard and dangerous. If, by the late nineteenth century, slavery had been formally abolished, the use of ill-paid Chinese – and Indian – labourers was an easy substitute. Six thousand Chinese worked on railroad construction in Canada. Up to 100,000 Chinese were shipped to South Africa, after the discovery of the Wit-watersrand gold reefs, to work in the mines. Today their descendants run some of Johannesburg's best Chinese restaurants and backstreet grocers. Under South Africa's unique race laws Chinese, unlike Japanese, do not rate as honorary whites – trade with Japan is bigger business than non-trade with China.

Chou En-lai in 1964 crisply summed up his impressions after a journey through ten friendly African states. 'Revolutionary prospects are excellent throughout the African continent,' the prime minister of China told journalists in Somalia before flying home.[1]

He could not know then that ten years later his country would be airlifting hundreds of tons of arms and scores of military instructors into Zaire for what the world took to be a counter-revolutionary cause.

Zaire's President Mobutu in the early 1960s had been denounced by the official New China News Agency as a 'neo-colonialist swindler and puppet' of the Americans who 'connived at the murder' of the country's first prime minister, Patrice Lumumba. But in 1974 Mobutu was providing soldiers, bases and sanctuary for Holden Roberto's movement in its contest for power in Angola against the radical forces of Agostinho

Neto. Peking and Washington were supporting Roberto, not least to thwart Neto's Soviet and Cuban patrons.

Chinese authorities offered an epigrammatic rationalization to explain their transformed role. 'The enemy of my enemy is my friend,' officials would recite. China, indeed, had become the enemy of the USSR. Quarrels first over ideology, then over state interests, escalated from rhetoric to military reality. There were troop concentrations along much of their disputed 4,000-mile frontier. Fighting flared in March 1969 over rights to islands in the Ussuri river. Fears of a Soviet pre-emptive nuclear strike led the Chinese to construct huge nuclear-proof shelter systems beneath most of their major cities. Richard Nixon and Henry Kissinger took the dangers of a Sino-Soviet war seriously enough to commission a National Security Council study in 1969 of the options open to the United States if such a contingency should arise.

The breach between the erstwhile communist allies was the most important political development since the People's Republic proclaimed itself the lawful government of China in 1949.

The event altered the correlation of world forces. The Chinese emerged from a brooding isolation first imposed by the Americans, only to face Soviet attempts to re-encircle them through an Asian security system of military and other alliances. Under Nixon the United States began to recast its world policies in a way which would ultimately permit Washington to play its newly acquired 'China card' against the Soviet Union.

Before Nixon's historic presidential visit to Peking, Chou, in one of the most significant turnabouts of the times, disclosed the depth and evident seriousness of the Chinese political transformation, during a conversation with General Alexander Haig in January 1972. Haig then was Kissinger's deputy and later would become Nixon's chief of staff at the White House. During the last stages of the Watergate affair, he was entrusted with the task of preparing all the complex logistics for the flamboyant Nixon trip the next month. He had two long discussions with Chou – on the India–Pakistan fighting and on the Vietnam war.

'In the Great Hall of the People I recall vividly Prime Minister Chou's words,' Haig said in an interview with the author in May 1979, when he was nearing the end of his term as supreme commander, allied forces, Europe (SACEUR). 'He urged: "Do not leave Vietnam . . . and do not withdraw from Southeast Asia."' But, Haig made clear, Chou underlined China's moral backing for the North Vietnamese, arguing that a rapid end to the fighting was essential if Soviet influence in Indo-China was to be checked. On the India–Pakistan crisis Chou said that he supported US policy because of its evident pro-Pakistan overtones.[2]

The complex Sino–Soviet ideological and inter-state quarrelling would tear the global communist movement apart, split national parties and torment individual adherents who found themselves forced to choose between Moscow and Peking.

United, the USSR and the People's Republic of China would have been able to concert policies and actions against the American-led west and to line up a majority of Third World countries in opposition to what both portrayed as 'imperialism and neo-colonialism'. Divided, they dissipated their energies by undercutting each other.

Western powers were beneficiaries because the disarray of their challengers transcended their own contradictions and disunities. There were some African countries, too, which derived secondary gains by becoming targets for the competing attention of the Chinese as well as of the Russians and Americans.

China followed the Russians into Africa in 1956. By definition, countries of the Third World which either had received or were nearing independence seemed to offer the best hope for fulfilling Lenin's prophecy of the 'final victory of socialism'. The perception may have been accurate. But the irony was that the process of translating perception into practice generated one of the major quarrels which split Moscow from Peking.

Peking's obsessive concern with a need to blunt Moscow's thrust towards globalism was rooted in the bitter disenchantment of the 1950s. Mao and Chou then witnessed the rash, brash, opportunist, and extravagant aid lavished by Khrushchev on Third World countries like Egypt. They considered it a betrayal of revolutionary principles. Loyal to their interpretation of Marxism and Leninism, they reckoned the needs of their own land had been subordinated to the developing global designs of the Soviet state.

They had fought a rough and tough civil war at immeasurable sacrifice in the socialist cause, and without much help from Stalin's Russia especially during the years of world conflict. They believed China then had absorbed much of the striking power of the Japanese which otherwise might have been aimed at the Russians. Now they were watching Khrushchev's Russia funding grandiose projects for regimes, like Nasser's, which fundamentally were more nationalist than socialist. Revolutionary China's needs for development meanwhile were being downgraded.

They were suspicious that the Russians might deliberately have been slowing the pace of Chinese development for state interests. Aid received from Moscow was, in Peking's view, circumscribed, selective and insufficient in the light of the burden China had borne in Korea and was ready to bear elsewhere if needed. A test-case arose in the context of China's wish to start a nuclear-weapons programme at a time when its leaders felt they were being encircled by American power. Moscow's blunt refusal to share nuclear-weapons secrets was taken to signify distrust. It became known in Peking that Soviet leaders were asking their western counterparts through diplomatic channels: 'How would you like it if you were to wake up one morning to find your neighbour possessing nuclear weapons pointing at you?'

It was in the mid-1950s, therefore, that the feud began secretly to fester. Events proved that not all the attempts by the Russians at reassurance could cool the fever. By 1963 the storm had burst and from then it was all-out hostility bred of suspicion, rumour and fear. Fear turned into rivalry. And rivalries were transplanted into the Third World, splitting the theory and practice of socialism everywhere.[3]

China approached Africa with economic aid and political and strategic policies shaped by her own revolutionary and post-revolutionary experiences. By 1956, when the first Chinese mission was established in Cairo, differences with the Russians had begun to develop behind a façade of unity.

In aid, policy rested on eight principles publicly defined by Chou in 1964. These emphasized the need for self-reliance, functionalism, training, reciprocity, fairness and the absence of conditions. The focus, in the first quarter-century of Chinese involvement, was on helping mainly the poorer states of black Africa. Initially military assistance, including training and weaponry, was provided to insurgents, dissidents and liberation causes approved and often driven on by Peking.

The involvement of the Chinese in Africa from 1956 to the start of the 1980s fell into three distinct phases: at the outset revolutionary; then competitive in an anti-Soviet sense; finally evolutionary after Mao's death when problems of domestic modernization and leadership assumed precedence.

The pursuit of Chinese vital interests abroad was conditioned by external pressures. It would be for history to judge whether Chinese attitudes produced those external pressures or whether external pressures shaped Chinese responses. On one thing there could be little doubt: Chairman Mao and Chou brought a new awareness of Third World importance into Chinese foreign policy-making five or six years after establishing communist supremacy on the Chinese mainland.

The Phase of Revolution (1956–64)

The first, revolutionary, phase lasted from 1956 until about 1964. Shunned by the Americans, excluded from the United Nations, the

Chinese set out to break loose from their isolation around the mid-1950s and thus to lessen their reliance on the Russians. The first Afro-Asian conference in Bandung, 1955, was a turning-point. Chou's elegant diplomacy impressed leaders like Nasser and observers representing some of Africa's key liberation movements. Within thirteen months, Egyptian–Chinese diplomatic relations were established, to the further anger of President Eisenhower and Dulles who already had been dismayed by Cairo's arms deal with the Soviet Union.

But the early years of their presence in Africa showed the Chinese to be still flushed with the success of their Long March to power. Mao and Chou preached greater radicalism in those African countries where the Russians seemed ascendant, and practised scarcely concealed subversion where the western powers were dominant. They tended, long before the cracks in the façade of Sino–Soviet unity became visible, to assail Moscow's concessions to concepts of coexistence, and openly criticized Nasser when he outlawed and gaoled Egypt's communists, a development that left Kremlin leaders swallowing hard but staying silent.

North Africa, a zone of magnetic attraction for Peking because of Algeria's liberation struggle, in the late 1950s was another setting for Soviet heresies, as the Chinese saw them. Needing friendly relations with France and concerned to avoid embarrassing the French communists, Moscow encouraged a negotiated settlement in Algeria. Peking, in contrast, urged the Algerians to fight on to the end and provided money and arms for their cause. In sub-Saharan Africa, China encouraged dissidents and insurgents in independent states under western influence, as in the Cameroon and Congo (Zaire) in the early 1960s, when the Russians were displaying greater pragmatism.

The Phase of Competition (1964–76)

The second, competitive anti-Soviet phase lasted from about 1964 until about 1976. Public disclosure of Sino–Soviet differences preceded Chou's 1963–4 voyage of discovery. The Chinese leader made it plain that Africa would become a region of competition not only against the west but also against what Peking took to be the sacrifice of revolutionary principles by the Soviet Union for the sake of advancing its state interests. The Chinese spared little in a campaign to undermine the influence of the Russians wherever and whenever possible. Something of a pause developed with the outbreak of the Cultural Revolution in 1967, because the Chinese withdrew all their missions from Africa, except in Cairo, then the seat of the Afro–Asian movement.

From the start of Nixon's presidency in 1969, the Americans and

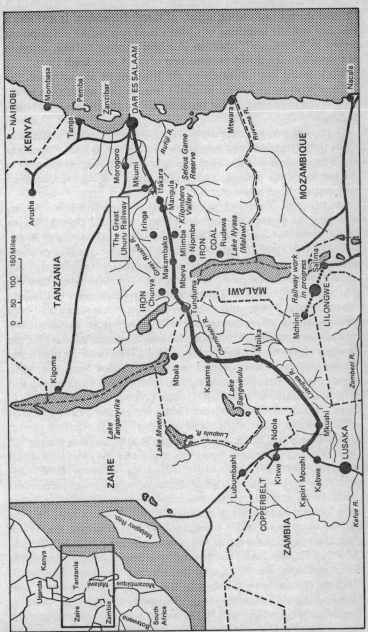

Fig. 10: The Tanzanian–Zambian Great Uhuru (freedom) Railway
SOURCE: R. Hall and H. Peyman, *The Great Uhuru Railway*, Victor Gollancz, 1976.

Chinese started exchanging signals of future friendship. It was also a year that saw the launching of China's most spectacular development project in Africa, the Tanzanian–Zambian freedom railway, designed as a riposte to the Soviet construction of the Aswan High Dam.

While losing out ultimately to the Russians in Mozambique, the Chinese were invited in by Machel's two neediest neighbours to aid them in the costliest and most venturesome enterprise ever undertaken in Africa.

The newly independent people of Zambia and Tanzania in the early 1960s were trying hard to interest the Americans, British, Canadians and others in financing a rail link giving landlocked Zambia an outlet to the Indian Ocean through Tanzania's port of Dar es Salaam. They were turned down repeatedly.

'British corporations, white settlers and civil servants joined in discouraging the project,' George Ivan Smith, a special United Nations envoy on the spot, recalled. 'Their views influenced successive World Bank and UN specialist teams in reaching negative conclusions about the feasibility of the scheme which possessed the most profound political implications for the countries concerned.' Ivan Smith, who then was UN Secretary-General U Thant's personal representative in East and Central Africa, forecast at the time that a western rejection would have consequences similar to those which followed American–British miscalculations over Aswan. These miscalculations had made it easy for the Russians to move into Africa in strength. 'By June 1964, my hunch was coming true because I received several indications from Tanzanian friends that the Chinese would step in if the western governments and institutions declined,' he said. 'Of course I reported all this at once to U Thant. Around that time, too, I ran into a fairly senior British diplomat and suggested to him that he ought perhaps to take the railroad project more seriously but he dismissed it abruptly as a "political fantasy".' [4]

Chou's journey through Africa was historic for the proof it provided of China's political interest in the awakening continent. It led ultimately, too, to the construction of the freedom railway, a monumental showpiece in international aid which has yet to be surpassed by other major outside powers. When he was in Egypt, Nasser's men, perhaps mischievously to check his reactions, took him to inspect the Aswan High Dam project nearing its formal opening ceremonies by Khrushchev. The Chinese leader displayed close interest, putting questions to Soviet technicians on the construction site, and was clearly impressed.

Peking did not have to wait long for the opportunity to show that China could build something bigger and better in Africa for Africa. A Tanzanian mission, led by Vice-President Rashidi Kawawa, and including Foreign Minister Abdul Rahman Mohammed Babu, who had old links with the Chinese, visited Peking in June and the Tanzam railroad project was discussed in broad outline. By the time President Julius Nyerere flew to China on a state visit in February 1965, the Chinese leadership were ready with an offer to undertake an independent survey of the best route and with assurances that they would be willing to help if appropriate agreements were reached with Zambia as well as with Tanzania.

Ivan Smith remembered being told by a senior member of Nyerere's entourage that Chou seemed to anticipate the concerns of some of the Africans. 'He escorted Julius one day to the rooftop of a building in Shanghai and called his attention to a large zone of slum-dwellings. Then the prime minister turned to the president and remarked simply, "You can see how most of our people live – we have no wish to take over any more slums in Africa."' Chou was making the point that the Chinese would pack their bags and go home after the job was done and not seek to take over and communize them as western governments, white settlers and elitist Africans suspected.[4]

In the months that followed President Kenneth Kaunda, more than Nyerere, tried anxiously again and again to interest western governments, and even Japan, in backing the scheme as an alternative to taking up Peking's offer. But Washington, London, Bonn and Tokyo were not to be moved. Perhaps they hoped that the Chinese would bog themselves down in a doubtful and costly venture.

By 1969 one of the world's most spectacular construction projects had been launched. China poured up to 350,000 tons of cement, 325,000 tons of steel rails, untold numbers of locomotives, trucks and other rolling stock into clearing the route, tunnelling through mountains, building bridges, hacking through woodlands, draining swamps and bulldozing huge mounds of earth. Scores of Chinese died in the alien territory from disease, snakebites and accidents.[5] A thirty-year interest-free loan financed the project.

There were sharp contrasts as well as striking similarities of aim and purpose in the Soviet and Chinese construction of their showpieces in Africa.

In Egypt, Soviet personnel, like their western counterparts, could count on more advanced technology and therefore had no need for a mass labour force that would be difficult to organize and discipline. The skills of Soviet technicians also implied high standards of specialist training and richer life-styles than those attained by most of their local collaborators. They required and received better accommodation, food, transportation and other privileges than those with whom they worked. Barriers soon arose and caused some hostility. The High Dam itself was an essay in modernization, highly visible, a sophisticated dramatization of the Soviet Union's own progress from poor beginnings.

In Tanzania and Zambia, on the other hand, the Chinese and Africans relied more on manpower than on the use of machines and equipment. Life in the bush entailed hardship and tremendous stamina. The Chinese lived at levels no higher than those of the Africans, in tents or huts or in the open, preparing their own meals, cultivating vegetables when they were static, requiring their co-workers to do nothing they themselves would shirk. They transmitted their know-how and experience freely, without arrogance, training loco-drivers, welders and surveyors as they went along. Their methods were functional, their behaviour controlled, even austere, to a point that led Kaunda to reflect in public, with controlled surprise, that 'We have yet to see a Chinese-coloured baby.'

Then there were the similarities. Aswan, like the railroad, was after all a showpiece. Both were undertaken because the western powers had rejected the commitment. Each was fashioned to suit the needs of the recipient. Moscow and Peking, alike, went into their respective ventures for reasons of prestige, to outflank their rivals and to advance their own national interests.

In building the Aswan Dam the Russians were doing more than consolidate the arms agreement they had reached with Nasser. They were also moving into a traditional, yet discontented, sphere of western influence. The enterprise enabled them to establish a platform from which they could demonstrate some of the talents they were prepared to put at the disposal of all Africa and thus to stake claims to the resources and friendship of African nations.

Chinese motives in building the freedom railroad were in part to outshine the Russians by displaying their own developmental capabilities. They were concerned also to have a countervailing presence along the African littoral of the Indian Ocean which, more and more, had been attracting the active attention of Soviet and American oceanic strategists. They had, finally, a growing interest in access to some of the continent's scarce strategic commodities, particularly copper. China is considered by western authorities to be a veritable El Dorado of untapped minerals but it is, and has been for years, short of copper. It produces less than half its annual need of about 325,000 tons. Zambia and Zaire, straddling Africa's copperbelt, by no means fortuitously became Peking's new friends in the early 1970s and copper sales featured in the various trading and offsetting economic accords which bound them.

China's activities in Africa quickened from 1969 not only because of the Nixon–Kissinger interest in normalizing relations but also because the momentum of the Soviet drive towards globalism was gathering pace.

Thus the polemics of the Sino–Soviet contest reached new degrees of intensity, and from polemics to political action was an easy step. Brezhnev in mid-1969 floated his plan to form a security system in Asia based on a series of interlocking bilateral or multilateral alliances. Inevitably, Mao and Chou interpreted the move as an attempt again to isolate China, a purpose the Russians disavowed. The scheme was greeted with a thundering lack of enthusiasm but for years remained on the international agenda. Chinese hostility consequently grew and led to the expansion in Third World testing-grounds of aid programmes, military as well as economic. This led the Russians, in turn, to increase their own commitments. So rivalries escalated.

By 1976–7 African demands, especially in the sub-Saharan countries, for China's low-cost services were at a peak. An estimated 21,000 Chinese engineers, builders, transportation specialists, doctors and project technicians were working in various parts of the continent. Some were provided free, most at a subsistence rate valued at about $100 monthly paid by the recipient country. In contrast, a CIA study claimed Soviet technicians were being employed at salaries valued up to some $1,650 monthly, in less-needy countries. Peking's cumulative total of economic aid in the sub-Saharan region, worth about $2 thousand million, was, however, beginning to taper off because of constraints at home. It was more than double the Soviet contribution, CIA figures suggested.[6]

Politically, the Chinese aim was to foil what was portrayed as the Soviet Union's pursuit of world hegemony. For some time the United States, as the only other superpower, was also accused of seeking the same objective. But as the struggle evolved Peking, in special situations, lined up with the Americans or their friends in opposition to the Russians. China's leaders themselves disavowed any hegemonistic pretensions but did not conceal an ambition to lead the Third World. Strategically, the Chinese strove to circumscribe superpower aspirations by mobilizing the Third World to play a balancing, almost a controlling, role. Drawing from the experience of the Chinese communist advance to supremacy at home, Marshal Lin Piao, minister of defence, who died in an air crash after a failed conspiracy to oust Mao, offered a definition in 1965:

Taking the entire globe, if North America and Western Europe can be called the 'cities of the world' then Asia, Africa and Latin America constitute the rural areas of the world. Since World War II, the proletarian revolution movement has for various reasons been temporarily held back in the North and West European capitalist countries while the People's Revolutionary Movement in Asia, Africa and Latin America has been growing vigorously . . . Comrade Mao⁻

Tse-tung's theory of the establishment of rural revolutionary base areas and the encirclement of the cities from the countryside is of outstanding and universal practical importance for the present revolutionary struggles of the oppressed nations . . .[7]

Lin died in disgrace. His global strategic theory remained to be repudiated. However the process of 'the encirclement of the cities from the countryside' was halted and the Chinese, instead, set out to collaborate with 'the cities of the world'.

The Phase of Modernization (1976–)

The third, evolutionary, phase of Chinese policy took shape after Mao's death in September 1976. New leaders intensified their efforts to limit Soviet influence around the world, dashing any hopes Moscow may have entertained for some *rapprochement* after the disappearance of Mao. Chairman Hua Kuo-feng reaffirmed his old leader's 'Three Worlds' concept: the formation of an 'anti-hegemonist' front of all 'Second [industrialized] World' and 'Third [developing] World' countries against the 'First World' superpowers (meaning the Soviet Union and United States).

A prolonged reappraisal of home and foreign policies led Peking to recognize the need to improve economic and political relations with Washington as a means of speeding a sustained programme of modernization reaching into the twenty-first century. Every sector of the nation's endeavours was scrutinized for its technological, social, political and economic content – and most were found wanting, particularly in the armed forces. A major conclusion reached was that resources had to be readjusted or diverted to meet the new priorities. Gradually it became clear that in given situations China shared an interest with the Americans to check the spread of Soviet influence. A wider range of options thus became embodied in China's world role, distinguishing it from the radicalism and isolationism of the 1960s.

The practical effects of this transformation were far-reaching. On the one hand, Peking's foreign policy became more outgoing, with Hua and his lieutenants searching for new friends among old foes, visiting once-hostile capitals, even burying the hatchet with the Emperor of Japan, long branded as a war criminal by Peking. Vice-Premier Teng Hsiao-ping called on the monarch during an October 1978 mission to Tokyo to ratify a treaty of peace and friendship. On the other hand, China curtailed its overseas aid programme and by the end of the decade had become virtually a spectator in sub-Saharan Africa with areas of conflict turned into zones of retrenchment. Statistics issued in two dozen black African states showed that through the first half of the 1970s they had Chinese aid commitments exceeding $1 thousand million; by 1980 total assistance had been cut back to a quarter of that amount and aid and advisory personnel nearly halved to about 11,000.

China's retreat from activism in Africa, however temporary, was not altogether attributable to the demands of the new Long March towards a modernized, socialist-based society. A series of resounding political errors played their part too. They were rooted, in the main, in the worsening Sino–Soviet relationship immediately before and after Mao died. Several sorely pressed African leaders began to question whether Peking was truly concerned with helping them or whether the real purpose was to hit and hurt the Soviet Union. There was no mistaking their conclusion, at least so far as Angola, Mozambique and Ethiopia were concerned. In turn each of those countries enshrined that conclusion in full-scale treaties of alliance with Moscow. Peking, like Washington, was left outside looking in, at least for a while until the capacity of the Russians to fulfil black Africa's needs could be measured and found wanting.

China's setbacks in Africa flowed from faulty perceptions of the implications that would follow the disintegration of Portugal's empire. Angola turned out to be the watershed. Cuban–Soviet involvement dramatized the depth of their readiness to intervene in the continent on the side of allies facing emergencies. Because the Havana–Moscow involvement succeeded, at least in the sense that it won the endorsement of the OAU, the Cubans and Russians later were encouraged to calculate that they would be able to repeat the performance in the Horn of Africa where the shaky Ethiopian state was under attack. They reckoned it would be safe to assume a commitment to stand by Mozambique, too, in the aftermath of independence. Transformation of Angola and Mozambique from colonial into radically oriented socialist states, with Zimbabweans in between in the grip of insurrection, heralded a dangerous new phase of struggle against Africa's last bastion of white supremacy in the south. To the Republic of South Africa's black neighbours, then, the sponsorship of a great power, even better a superpower with air, land and sea offensive and defensive capabilities, was essential. In military terms it had become clear that the Soviet Union, possessing a far more sophisticated arsenal, could outperform China. All this, however forbidding a prospect, was recognized by the Africans and not all the anti-Soviet rhetoric of the Chinese could counteract that appreciation.

From the mid-1970s on, the idea of attacks on Angolans and Mozambicans by their white-ruled South African and Rhodesian neighbours ceased to be a worst-case scenario. The attacks had, indeed, begun. A South African invading force had lunged to the very outskirts of Luanda, the capital, during the Angolan civil war. Former Rhodesian Prime Minister Ian Smith's security forces had unleashed the first of more than 350 land and air assaults deep into Mozambique. The promised protection of a Soviet-supported military umbrella therefore was a source of comfort to the Angolans and Mozambicans struggling, as they were, to consolidate their hard-won independence. General Haig, in talking with the author, reported that NATO had evidence indicating that a Soviet-armed and Cuban-trained Ethiopian force of brigade strength was being made ready in 1979 to move into Mozambique if needed to repel any invaders. Other US diplomats disclosed that Ethiopian air force squadrons, equipped in turn by the Americans and Russians with jet fighters, were available to provide air cover for Mozambique, if invited. Against this background Chinese offers to go on supplying the Mozambicans with ageing small arms and field weapons were hardly alluring.

Militarily, then, the Chinese were in no position to compete with their Soviet antagonists in the situation as it was. But they compounded their difficulties by aligning themselves during the Angolan crisis with Mobutú's Zaire, with Kissinger's protégés Roberto and Savimbi, and so, by proxy, with the white mercenaries fighting Neto and, most damagingly, the South Africans. Politically, for a country professing to be the true defender of the socialist faith it was an inexplicable decision – except in the context of Peking's feud with Moscow, a feud that had little relevance to African leaders at bay.

André Malraux, the French writer and former cabinet minister, has related how Mao told him somewhat contemptuously that Alexei Kosygin, the Soviet prime minister, had once observed that communism was a way to improve people's living standards. Then the venerable helmsman sarcastically added, the remark was like saying: swimming was a means of putting on a pair of trunks. As things turned out he might have added: 'Africa is a continent for outside powers to kick each other in the teeth.' Until the mid-1970s Chinese leaders, familiar with the fields and rivers and mountains of their own land, had displayed what seemed to be a genuine identification with Africans and their problems. China's standing in lands like Zambia, Tanzania, Mozambique and elsewhere was high if not pre-eminent. The government of President Samora Machel in Mozambique was distinctly Maoist in orientation. Chinese development techniques, from rural to urban construction, had become a widely accepted model. Soviet methods and attitudes, by contrast, had aroused resentments. In November 1975 Foreign Minister Joaquim Chissano of Mozambique had publicly rebuked Moscow saying that the provision of aid did not give the Soviet Union the right to dictate the policies of his country.

But by then the Angolan civil war had flared. Africans witnessed a strange alliance of Zaireans, Americans, South Africans and white mercenaries – with Peking's support – closing in on Neto. Only the Cuban–Soviet intervention saved Neto from defeat and, because of the South African connection, the OAU vindicated Neto's survival no matter who had helped him. Chinese support for Holden Roberto, through Mobutu's Zaire, was remembered but not forgiven.

There was a gulf between the public and private positions taken by the Chinese over their blunderings in Angola, Mozambique, Ethiopia and sub-Saharan Africa generally. In public Peking continued its insistent accusations against what it portrayed as the sinister designs of the Soviet Union to achieve global hegemony. The authoritative *Peking Review* in early 1978 asserted that the Russians were playing their usual trick of division and disintegration throughout southern Africa just as they had done in Angola:

[The Soviet Union] is sowing dissension among the Frontline countries, infiltrating into the liberation movement to split it by supporting one faction and attacking another and waiting for an opportunity to stir up another fratricidal war among the Africans. Thanks to Angola, the people of Southern Africa are fully aware of the consequences of Soviet interference in the liberation struggle . . .[8]

Privately, Peking took another tack. In late 1978 a top member of the Peking hierarchy was journeying through the states of southern Africa, quietly taking soundings in an attempt to mend political fences. But the outbreak of China's war with Vietnam blunted his efforts as several African leaders openly sided with Hanoi, portrayed periodically as the innocent victim of unprovoked aggression.

From Peking came informal word through responsible officials in late 1979, acknowledging, as one said: 'We made mistakes in Angola, perhaps because we simplified the issue, reacted blindly, without proper analysis, to the position taken by the Russians. As the Angolan civil war went on, the affair became for us more and more of a fiasco. When we recognized this we tried more than once to normalize relations with the Luanda government but our approaches were premature.'[9]

It was not surprising that Peking's approaches were considered premature by Luanda. The Chinese tradition in today's world is to abide by old friendships whenever possible. Thus because Mobutu in Zaire was seen to be in dire economic straits, as well as heightening political difficulties, a delegation from Peking visited Kinshasa to preserve and indeed advance relations with one of Africa's most strategically placed states. So, too, with Somalia after President Siad Barre's failed attempt to annex the disputed province of the Ogaden. After the Soviet Union abandoned its position in Somalia for the bigger prize of friendship with Ethiopia, the Chinese moved in to demonstrate there would always be a socialist alternative to the Russians. By the start of the 1980s disenchantment in Mozambique, over the scale and kind of Soviet development aid, had deepened and western help was solicited. New openings for China appeared.

It all went to show that in world affairs neither friendships nor enmities are permanent – but only the vital interests of nations.

Today there are few places where a nation's interests are more vital than in trade. Its practitioners rarely recognize ideological or other frontiers. That is why China and South Africa set about developing a commercial relationship through the entrepreneurial laundry of Hong Kong. The British colony – the bazaar of Asia – by 1980 had emerged as a booming market-place for the merchandise of two of the international community's least likely business partners. South Africa had maize, as well as chrome and other scarce minerals to sell. The Chinese had low-priced finished goods and textiles to export. Statistics provided by the International Monetary Fund showed that from 1973 to 1980 the value of South African–Hong Kong trade had soared from $108 to about $340 million (gold and diamond sales excluded). By the accounts of middlemen, representing both sides, a big although unquantified proportion of this trade involved the Chinese buying from and selling to the South Africans. Officially neither Peking nor Pretoria acknowledged this trade. Commodities were shipped through Hong Kong in ways that avoided identification of their origins. Peking was sensitive to the fact that dealing with race-conscious South Africa would win few friends in Africa or Asia. Pretoria was aware that Taiwan, a military as well as an economic ally, would not appreciate commerce with its mainland Chinese rivals.

Part Three

The Western Powers in Africa

7. The United States

In late 1976 Henry Kissinger was shuttling back and forth through Africa, in search of peace in his time for Zimbabwe, Namibia and maybe even in the turbulent Republic of South Africa. For six months he had been immersed in the issues.

Between Lusaka, in Zambia, and Pretoria, on 17 September, a 'senior US official' was telling the attendant corps of Washington diplomatic writers aboard the plane that the secretary of state intended meeting representative black leaders in the US embassy during his brief stay in South Africa. Because the US embassy is American territory, the South African colour bar, or any ban on free speech, could not be invoked. There could, therefore, be a totally frank exchange with Kissinger on the unfolding pattern of events in the *apartheid* state.

The 'senior US official' was reminded by a correspondent that there were precedents for visiting statesmen to ask for and receive facilities to confer with prominent nationalists, in whatever country, gaoled for their political beliefs. Had Kissinger requested South African permission to meet with Nelson Mandela, Walter Sisulu and Govan Mbeki, among the group of black resistance leaders languishing for life on Robben Island, South Africa's Alcatraz?

'Good God, no!' the senior US. official exclaimed. 'They're just a bunch of goddarned radicals!'[1]

Months after his presidential inauguration, Richard Nixon presided over a National Security Council discussion of future US policies in southern Africa. The major options that 17 December 1969 were embodied in the fat and famous document known as NSSM 39 (National Security Study Memorandum 39). Its central assumption, on which Washington would predicate future actions, was that 'white rule is here [in Southern Africa] to stay'.

At one point in the proceedings William P. Rogers, who preceded Kissinger as secretary of state, urged closure of the US consulate in Salisbury, Zimbabwe. Then Rhodesia, the British colony was in a state of rebellion; and the United Nations had imposed economic and political sanctions, which were supposed to be all-embracing.

Roger Morris, a Kissinger aide who had initiated N S S M 39 but who later resigned in disenchantment, has recounted what then followed at the N S C meeting.

'Having otherwise been a quiet listener to all this, Vice-President [Spiro T.] Agnew read from prepared notes a fervent statement pointing out that "South African independence" in 1965 [*sic*] was similar to the United States in 1776, when black inhabitants did not have the vote. He expanded on the original provisions of the U S constitution, counting only a fraction of slaves for purposes of apportionment.

'After Agnew ended, there was an embarrassed silence, and Nixon leaned forward to admonish: "You mean Rhodesia, don't you, Ted?" '[2]

Four years before, to the day, Harold Wilson as prime minister and Lyndon B. Johnson were comparing their international problems in the intimacy of the Oval Office of the White House. Wilson was wringing his hands over the crisis Rhodesia's Ian Smith had precipitated the month before (11 November 1965) by leading his 250,000 white followers into rebellion, hoping thus to preserve white supremacy. Johnson's concern was with Vietnam, relating in particular to his need to rally international backing for America's position of total commitment against the northern communists.

Each situation would yet take an immeasurable political toll and haunt not only the two leaders but also their successors. Wilson and Johnson needed each other, yet not to the extent of complete political surrender. The British intended banning oil supplies to Rhodesia, for which U S compliance was essential. Even before their meeting Johnson, forewarned that the British request would be posed formally, countered with his own question: 'When is the first battalion of British troops going to reach Vietnam?' But on hearing Wilson's personal pleading he displayed greater understanding.

The Labour government was hanging on to power by its fingernails with a House of Commons majority of three. Left-wingers would rather see their government fall than back a British combatant role in Vietnam. In the end a deal was struck. Wilson promised rhetorical support of the U S position in Vietnam. Johnson promised U S oil firms would join the embargo.[3]

As things turned out oil companies of both Britain and the United States cheated. A British state investigator showed that through a complex inter-company swap system oil, through the years, still reached

Smith, with the connivance of British, American, and French oil executives and government officials.

Andrew Young, while still ambassador to the United Nations, told the author in January 1979 that the US government 'knows the American companies are guilty but we're too scared to do anything about it'.

November 1956 was a month to remember. It saw the culmination of two interacting crises, both with world-wide implications. British and French forces, colluding with Israel, occupied the Suez zone of Egypt, hoping to regain control of the Canal and to topple Nasser. Under cover of the consequent international commotion, Soviet tanks rumbled into Budapest and crushed a regime that was displaying deepening tendencies to assert Hungary's suppressed nationalism.

The secretly planned British–French Suez attack rocked and nearly wrecked the trans-atlantic alliance. President Dwight D. Eisenhower, on the point of re-election for a second White House term, felt deceived by his allies; although British and French leaders at the time insisted the Americans knew all along that the ultimate use of force had never been excluded. Eisenhower and John Foster Dulles led UN efforts for peace and the withdrawal of the invaders. Selwyn Lloyd, then foreign secretary, related that 'the almost ferocious way' in which Eisenhower and Dulles mobilized the opposition deeply worried the British government.[4]

Largely through the Eisenhower–Dulles initiatives, the British and French ordered a ceasefire on 6 November *before* they had won complete control of the Canal. They continued, however, to resist withdrawal. The day before the ceasefire Marshal Nikolai A. Bulganin, Soviet prime minister, warned Britain, France and Israel that they, like Egypt, could be attacked – but from afar, with missiles. He invited Eisenhower to join in sending a combined Soviet–American peace force to Egypt for the purpose of heading off the danger of the Third World War. Eisenhower showed no interest in what seemed in Washington to have been a public relations exercise.

While all this was going on another, more personal, drama occurred. Dulles in the small hours of 3 November was stricken with abdominal pain, rushed to the Walter Reed Hospital in Washington, and underwent surgery for an intestinal cancer condition which eventually, three years later, claimed his life.

On the morning of Saturday, 17 November, he was up and about early in his hospital suite. Herbert Hoover, Jr, acting secretary of state, and a hospital nurse were with him. He was expecting visitors.

Selwyn Lloyd arrived, accompanied by Britain's newly-appointed ambassador to Washington, Sir Harold Caccia. Lloyd's version of what then occurred has an apocryphal ring but Caccia has confirmed its details. And the sense of it, on the evidence of the French foreign minister of the day, Christian Pineau, was conveyed by Dulles to Pineau personally in wholly different circumstances.[5]

Lloyd, who later became Baron Selwyn Lloyd, reported: 'Dulles said at once with a kind of twinkle in his eye, "Selwyn, why did you stop? Why didn't you go through with it and get Nasser down?"'

'If ever there was an occasion when one could have been knocked down by the proverbial feather, this was it. Dulles was the man who had led the pack against us, supported the transfer of the matter from the Security Council to the General Assembly, and pulled out every stop to defeat us. And here he was asking why we had stopped. I replied, and Caccia bears this out, "Well, Foster, if you had so much as winked at us, we might have gone on." Dulles replied that he could not have done that.'[6]

Dulles, in friendly mood, recapitulated what had occurred throughout the Suez crisis. Purportedly he said that the only difference between the Americans and the British and the French 'had been over method'.

These vignettes reveal more than the attitudes of hierarchical ignorance towards Africa. They also distil the ambiguities and cynicism of some powerful Americans towards the continent since Franklin D. Roosevelt. From Roosevelt to Ronald Reagan, a period spanning eight presidencies, American–African relations have drifted from prolonged demonstrations of monumental unconcern to brief, romantic encounters.

The US approach to Africa fits into two distinct phases: the pre-colonial period, beginning with Roosevelt in the Second World War and ending with the 'Year of Africa' in 1960; and the post-colonial phase from 1960 onwards. The one constant thread running through the pattern of the two periods was Washington's deference to the primacy of West European interests in its imperial and post-imperial playgrounds.

The Pre-colonial Period (1941–60)

From the time that Americans entered the war, Roosevelt urged his European allies to recognize that the days of their empires were numbered. He spoke for the liberation of India, and other Asian and African colonies, whose peoples, he argued, were entitled under point three of the Atlantic Charter to run their own affairs, achieve higher living standards and salute their own chosen rulers. It was the music of the brave new world for which the allies claimed to be fighting. Yet it was not all the impulse of idealism. Inevitably, American national self-interest excited a wish to share in the long-closed monopoly markets controlled by the metropolitan powers. The British system, for instance, embodied a formally structured imperial preference system that gave British exporters privileged treatment and British importers special access to raw materials. Roosevelt's insistence on achieving the dismantlement of these arrangements so irked the late Sir Winston Churchill that he was moved to growl in 1942: 'I have not become the King's [George VI's] First Minister in order to preside over the liquidation of the British Empire.'[7] However, Churchill was witness to the process of liquidation, as leader of His Majesty's Opposition, when in 1947–8 transfers of power began in subcontinental India, in Burma and in Sri Lanka (then Ceylon).

The anti-imperialist words of Roosevelt and his secretary of state, Cordell Hull, were hardly matched by the deeds of their administration. In 1942 for instance, the president and Hull were ringing the bells of liberty for 'all peoples, without distinction of race, colour or religion'.[8] But, at about the same time, American military men, with General Dwight D. Eisenhower as allied commander in North Africa, were under orders to avoid offending the Free French, who claimed sovereignty over the Moroccan and Algerian colonies. Somehow Washington had to balance professions of friendship for the colonial powers with proclamations of support for the aspirations of the colonial people. As policies unfolded over the years, successive administrations simply accorded precedence to America's allies in Europe over Washington's paper promises to the subject colonies.[9]

President Harry S. Truman claimed to share Roosevelt's anti-colonialism. But events spared him the pain of translating principle into practice. A sequence of seemingly unrelated developments, thrust into the equation of the times, contributed to a world-wide climate of distrust, insecurity and fear. Soviet armies dug themselves into strategic bits of Europe, far west of their frontiers, where they would stay for decades. The Middle East was aflame and turmoil crept along the North African littoral. By 1949 the Russians had test-fired their own hydrogen bomb, ending America's atomic power monopoly. War flared in Korea. For a while disaster loomed over the Indian subcontinent as Britain split its 'jewel of Empire' between feuding Moslems and Hindus. Mao Tse-tung's armies were moving across mainland China. Soviet communism, indeed world communism as Truman perceived it, was on the march and had to be contained. The wind-up of empires could wait, he reasoned, because there were more pressing priorities.

Truman's mission against that background was to rebuild the economic strength and defences of the western powers against the challenge from the east.

First he launched the $17 thousand million European Recovery Programme – usually called the Marshall Plan – to help the war-bruised lands of the Old World back on to their feet. The formation of the North Atlantic Treaty Organization (NATO) followed in 1949. The flow of reconstruction funds and military aid into Europe enabled the colonizing powers to tighten their grip, at least temporarily, on their colonies, particularly in Africa. France provided the most dramatic illustration of the process. Roughly 40 per cent of US military help allocated to NATO went to the French who, in turn, diverted most of it to the costs of attempting to maintain their empire. After their defeat at Dien Bien Phu in 1954, they turned from Indochina to devote all their energies to winning the battle for North Africa. Because NATO's zone of responsibility embraced Algeria – as part of metropolitan France – Washington said little or nothing when the French committed an initial 80,000 soldiers, sailors and airmen, using US material, into the fight to preserve France's most prized imperial possession. The Truman administration and its successors might have kept silent about the depth of indirect US involvement in the French–Algerian war, but the Algerians knew and they remembered for decades afterwards.

The French were by no means alone in diverting resources made available by the Americans for purposes of 'containing' Soviet communism. American weapons in the 1950s found their way, for instance, to Belgian military bases in the Congo. Portugal ultimately would use American weaponry – including napalm and chemical warfare instruments – in Angola, Mozambique and Guinea–Bissau. The Americans tried hard, but vainly, to check whether any of their equipment had been used by the British and French in their joint invasion of Suez in 1956.

Eisenhower moved into the White House a month before Stalin died in March 1953. Profound changes in the balance of world power followed, as the decline of Europe's colonial empires gathered pace, especially in Africa. Younger, more dynamic Soviet leaders posed new challenges to the west that were both serious and subtle as they strove to surmount the walls of 'containment'. At home, Eisenhower's difficulties were deepened by division and distrust generated by the dramatic assaults of Senator Joseph McCarthy against American diplomatic and political establishments.

Americans felt haunted by the spectre of communist expansionism.

Dulles fed their fears with his talk about liberating East Europe from Soviet domination; his readiness to indulge in dangerous confrontation with Soviet and Chinese adversaries; his emphasis on America's nuclear supremacy; even his pressure on allied nations to sacrifice more for the shared security needs of the west, on pain of an 'agonizing reappraisal' of transatlantic links. American officials seemed preoccupied with how they could weaken their adversaries in the east–west struggle. Distorted perceptions were passed on to Third World countries whose own leaders were seeking ways of disengaging from cold-war involvements. Dulles' proclaimed disdain for non-alignment helped Khrushchev in his search for friendship with the infant states of the Third World.

Conceptually, Stalin's innovative successors seemed quicker than their western counterparts to recognize the openings for friendships presented during the 1950s. US leaders, having organized the North Atlantic, Central, South-East Asian and Australian–New Zealand–American Treaty Organizations (NATO, CENTO, SEATO and ANZUS) seemed concerned primarily with holding those lines.

Africans, during those years, were warned to beware of would-be communist seducers. In scholarly style, Assistant Secretary of State Henry A. Byroade spoke in 1953 of what he said would be 'one of the great tragedies of our time', if Asians and Africans, approaching independence, should be lured fatally by the new Soviet imperialism, and thus return to an 'age of slavery infinitely more miserable than they have ever known before'.[10] George V. Allen, who succeeded Byroade, attempted in 1956 to do the splits between pro- and anti-colonialism. 'All of the so-called colonial powers represented on the continent of Africa are our friends and allies in the worldwide contest between the Free and Communist worlds,' he said. 'A strong, free and friendly Africa is extremely important to US security.'[11]

Both officials demonstrated that the US interest in Africa was primarily geopolitical in content, without evident concern for African needs; and that US awareness of the African experience lacked sensitive understanding. The blacks knew more about racism than about communism. Therefore talk of the red peril was almost certainly academic for those Africans whose only contacts had been with oppressive whites.

Britain and France, in attacking Egypt, achieved none of their national objectives but they presented the American and Soviet superpowers with opportunities which each seized with varying degrees of gratitude. That event, viewed historically, almost certainly represented the starting-point of the superpower contest for Africa.

Suez enabled the Americans to renew, at least temporarily, their anti-colonialist credentials, because they denounced the undertaking so vehemently and worked so vigorously to thwart its fulfilment. It opened the way, furthermore, for Eisenhower to launch his Middle East doctrine – a doctrine approved by Congress, which empowered the president to intervene militarily and economically in certain circumstances. In effect the United States inherited the roles that Britain and France had played in the past. In time, this turned out to be a mixed blessing; for inheriting political influence was one thing, but paying to preserve it was somewhat more costly. A third by-product, at least in Britain's case, was to shatter any residual imperial illusion of independent British action. The administration's rationale was verbalized by Vice-President (as he then was) Richard Nixon in a campaign speech:

In the past the nations of Asia and Africa have always felt we would, when the pressure was on, side with the policies of the British and French Governments in relation to the once colonial areas. For the first time in history we have shown independence of Anglo–French policies towards Asia and Africa which seemed to us to reflect the colonial tradition. That declaration of independence has had an electrifying effect throughout the world.[12]

The Suez affair transformed British–French decolonization in Africa from an orderly process into a headlong rush. It gave African affairs greater importance in the United States. But Eisenhower and Dulles were too involved in the global contest with Russia and China to care much about regional problems, unless they possessed a precise strategic content. Also the US administration wished to steer clear of issues which might imply a shared American–Soviet outlook. In early 1957, for instance, Nixon made an eight-nation journey through Africa and performed the remarkable feat in his report of not once referring to the two major issues which for years had been preoccupying the continent. One was the French–Algerian war now moving towards its climax; and the other was universal hostility towards the strict racism embedded in South Africa's policy of *apartheid*. In each case, Moscow was proclaiming its support for the Algerians and the blacks of South Africa.

If, however, American leaders were prepared to look *past* Africa's most painful problems, there were some of their politicians who were not. In mid-1957, a handsome young Bostonian Democratic senator named John F. Kennedy focused national attention on the failure of the president and his men to evolve a consistent, recognizable policy towards the grinding, blood-soaked Algerian war. Kennedy questioned the credibility of an administration which had long claimed to identify itself with the Algerian independence movement while still arming the French enemies of liberation. The United States, he argued, was deceiving only itself if it thought that double-dealing with both sides would satisfy either. In reality, he maintained, basic US policy favoured the French colonialists.

The Kennedy intervention was a *tour de force*, but it changed little, until 1960, the 'Year of Africa', split the contemporary story of the continent in two.

The Post-colonial Period (1960–   )

The impact of independence upon Africa in 1960 was like that of a tropical storm; some of the seventeen newborn states were swept by euphoria, others were engulfed in conflict. The world's big nations, watching expectantly, prepared themselves for a new scramble if a power vacuum should form in one of the continent's strategic settings. They did not have long to wait. Strife, mutiny, separatism and general political mayhem gripped the Congo, that chunk of real estate in the heartland of Africa, a storehouse of strategic minerals, which King Leopold II of the Belgians had seized in the nineteenth century.

The material and strategic resources of the Congo (now Zaire) had long been coveted by outsiders. When law and order collapsed within a week after Independence Day (30 June 1960) and Moïse Tshombe proclaimed the secession of Katanga, rich with uranium and copper, an almost unprecedented display of international power politics followed. The duly-elected prime minister, Patrice Lumumba, appealed first to Eisenhower for help to defeat Tshombe's separatism; then to the United Nations; next to the Afro-Asian group; fourthly to fellow-Africans; and finally, in desperation, to the Russians.

Moscow provided sixteen transport planes, some land vehicles but no troops. Meantime the Belgians, British and French were giving under-cover backing to Tshombe's breakaway venture, primarily because they owned the biggest stake in Katangan resources, which at the time were contributing up to 60 per cent of the country's revenue. The Americans, themselves eager to share in the country's raw wealth, supported Congolese unity and identified themselves with UN intervention, which was seen in Washington to be the best way of keeping the Russians out. The first head-on collision between east and west interests in Africa had begun and it took up to five years before the country was stabilized. It has sunk progressively into deeper debt ever since, with US and western governments and institutions owed thousands of millions of dollars.[13]

The Congo affair, dramatizing the sort of geopolitical competition that independent Africa might expect, stirred Eisenhower in his final days to initiate a more activist policy, identifying the Americans with the United Nations in the approach to Africa. He offered American participation in an international programme to help promote the economic and military security of the awakened continent.

Eisenhower's policy on Africa, coming at the end of his second term, was too late to be effective. Kennedy's personal concern, laced as it was with a strong dash of idealism, was too briefly expressed in his tragically foreshortened presidency. From an African standpoint, his performance never fulfilled its promise.

The 1960s were years of tears and transition both within and between nations and, initially, Kennedy was at the centre of the scene. The tidy frontiers of the east–west conflict had begun to blur. Areas of instability widened.

In Europe the foundations of the French Republic shook as de Gaulle, defying the die-hards of empire, negotiated peace and the transfer of power with the Algerians. Brezhnev took over from a discredited Khrushchev in the Kremlin and by 1968 sent Warsaw Pact invading forces to subdue a rebellious Czechoslovakia. The Middle East endured a new Arab–Israeli war. Americans suffered the assassinations of their president, Martin Luther King and later Bobby Kennedy, and the civil-rights movement erupted into race riots almost beyond the control of Lyndon B. Johnson.

In the Far East, China finally parted political company with the Russians to transform the world power balance. The limited American intervention in Vietnam, authorized by Kennedy, escalated into a war that would not end until 1974.

In Africa a trail of turbulence zigzagged up and across the continent with the Sharpeville massacre in South Africa, liberation movements in the Portuguese colonies, white rebellion in Rhodesia (Zimbabwe), *coups*, counter-*coups* and mass killings by vengeful or tyrannical dictators.

Yet more and more emergent nation-states of Africa, the Middle East and Asia were disengaging from the east–west conflict, determined in their own interests to deal separately with either power or with both. Advances in military technology, from sputniks to intercontinental nuclear rocketry, rendered obsolete the strategic value of establishing, or even maintaining, sophisticated forward bases in foreign lands far from home.

The Americans withdrew from Morocco, Tunisia, Algeria and Libya and set out instead to evolve more balanced relationships with countries of the New Africa.

At his 1961 inauguration Kennedy offered the promise Africans had waited years to hear: 'To break the bonds of mass misery we pledge our best efforts to help them help themselves . . . not because we seek their vote, but because it is right.'

Like Roosevelt before him and Carter later, John F. Kennedy discovered soon enough that moral intentions and political realities rarely mixed in the affairs of states. First came the failed American attempt to invade Cuba at the Bay of Pigs in April 1961; then the near-apocalyptic Cuban missile crisis of 1962; next the build-up of the Vietnam tragedy. The young president, who had become the symbol of hope for many, began his term by lining up periodically with African and other Third World countries in key UN votes. But even this was halted when, of all ironies, it came to Algeria, whose cause he had himself spotlighted in 1957. Kennedy knew that de Gaulle was moving towards a settlement which could be jeopardized by adverse UN votes. So began a series of erratic postures affecting Africa. Outsiders, expecting better from the president, found US policies hard to understand.

On the evidence of foreign envoys who discussed the issues with him, Kennedy was resolved to crush Katangan separatism even if American forces had to be used. But the suspicion persisted that he was moved more by a determination to pre-empt the efforts of Belgians, British and French to detach and to monopolize Katangan resources than by any commitment to the Congolese themselves.

At another point, a US vote was recorded against a Security Council resolution demanding a stop to the supply of weapons which Portugal could use in its African colonies. An American statement explained that Washington had already ordered such a ban. It therefore seemed pointless for the Americans to vote against the resolution – except for the fact that they were seeking to renew their lease on the Azores Island bases. Portugal at the time needed friends. There was no evidence to suggest the Azores bases would have been denied to Washington in retaliation for a vote on principle in the Security Council. Yet Kennedy knew well that US arms *were* being used in the Portuguese colonies. Would a more robust, less expedient, stand by Kennedy then have helped to shorten the prolonged agonies of war in the Portuguese colonies if Lisbon's access to arms had been curtailed?

South Africa and Rhodesia offered further examples of Kennedy's ambivalence. A 1963 Security Council resolution imposing a voluntary arms embargo on South Africa, whose white rulers were intensifying their racist policies, was supported by Ambassador Adlai Stevenson: yet certain big arms contracts had recently been concluded with Pretoria and were being fulfilled.

The Americans similarly insisted on supporting Britain in rejecting

African protests against transferring all air and land weapons to white-ruled Rhodesia, when the Central African Federation, of Northern Rhodesia (now Zambia), Southern Rhodesia (now Zimbabwe) and Nyasaland (now Malawi), was dissolved in 1963. If those air force planes and army weapons had been shared equally among all three partners, the white Rhodesians, who soon rebelled against British rule, would not have been able to sustain themselves militarily as they did for fourteen years from 1965.

Kennedy in 1961 had bravely promised 'those people in the huts and villages of half the globe struggling to break the bonds of mass misery' that they could count on American help. It was rough enough for him – and them – to go back on that promise, in response to the intervention of bigger world issues. It was even rougher that the president felt compelled to retreat from other political commitments and attitudes which he had seemed to share with Africans, Asians and the world's less-privileged. A certain respect for Kennedy persisted nevertheless. It lingered on long after Dallas, Texas.

Assassination took Lyndon Johnson into the White House. War in Vietnam drove him out, five tumultuous years later.

In between, even the Great Society he contemplated, and less grand institutions, shuddered under the strain of violence in the cities, rising racial tensions, campus dissent, anti-war protests, and a tumbling currency. Europe, the Middle East and Asia had their share of troubles. So, too, did Africa. Each crisis, in its way, crossed Johnson's Oval Office desk. Reared in the relatively liberal Democratic tradition, he was sufficiently attuned to the needs of the times to identify his administration at least in principle with the proclaimed universal war on want, the true independence of African states, the resistance to white minority rule. Yet with the war in Vietnam cruelly totting up its daily body-counts, he carefully avoided assuming any major African commitment in cash or in kind that would imperil a presidency becoming increasingly confused.

The Johnson strategy towards Africa was to conduct a holding operation until time and circumstances would allow Washington to become more active. Thus support for British passivity in the Rhodesian crisis continued. American arms went on flowing into Portugal, with the CIA and others fully aware that US weaponry was in use against the African independence movements. The voluntary UN embargo on military sales to South Africa in 1963 did not stop regular leakages and high-level cooperation in nuclear technology. Investments by US banks and multinationals in strategic and profitable South African enterprises increased. Crumbs of comfort were occasionally thrown at American and other critics of these policies, when the administration supported UN resolutions denouncing *apartheid*.

But Johnson's holding operation for Africa could succeed only for as long as an obliging continent, and world community, stood still. Neither Africa nor the world would oblige.

First, in 1964, the Americans joined the Belgians in a controversial airborne rescue of white hostages held by Congolese rebels, supported by white mercenaries, in the northern city of Stanleyville. Next, the Vietnamese conflict began to escalate with U S air, land and sea forces becoming increasingly involved. Finally, in early 1965, American troops flew into the Dominican Republic to cut short an attempt to reinstall the deposed President Bosch. Even friendly African governments began to reassess American words and deeds, recalling old Soviet charges of neo-colonialism.

When the Nigerian civil war flared in 1967 it was an open secret that clandestine shipments of U S arms had reached the separatist Biafrans months before they launched their dash for an independent status. There was a smell of oil in the air which French, as well as American, companies had sniffed – oil in the region that would have been Biafra if the breakaway movement had been successful. At the time British interests possessed, or hoped to acquire, the major exploration and development rights. Despatch of American arms to the Biafrans suggested some U S oil interests were hoping to supplant the British as the major concessionaires. De Gaulle at the time staked France's claim for a share in what later turned out to be Nigeria's bonanza by associating himself publicly with the Biafran secessionists.

The British protested to both their allies. Official Washington, unwilling to offend their friends in London, subsequently declined to supply military goods either to the Lagos central government or to its challengers, adopting a stance of formal neutrality. France, working through South Africa and nearby francophone states, continued its arms flow. The British and the Russians sided unequivocally with the Lagos government, providing all the weapons needed, arguing they were doing so for the cause of the unity of the Nigerian state.

About the only positive outcome of the Kennedy–Johnson decade relating to Africa had more to do with people than with governments. A relationship developed between those in both continents leading the cause of black advancement and black consciousness: the intellectuals and activists of the American civil rights and African liberation movements. There was a cross-fertilization of ideas and experience among the disparate elements in the many movements involved. But there were perils implied by external pressures to isolate the protagonists and so to impose upon them the taint of racism.

A clash of two racisms – black and white – unfolded on the television screens across continents, involving civilians as well as soldiers and identifiable kith and kin. How would scenes like these affect faraway onlookers, whether whites with centuries of supremacist attitudes to suppress, or blacks with countless scores to settle and scars of humiliation to heal?

Richard Nixon, with Kissinger at his side, began the 1970s showing no signs that he foresaw challenges of this dimension. Both were men predisposed to accept the central thesis of NSSM 39: 'The whites are here to stay.'

The Kissinger Years

Kissinger did not really 'discover' Africa until Angola came along. The secretary of state, his gaze lifted beyond the bounds of continentalism, needed the world as his stage. He saw the countries and regions of the Third World, Africa included, only against the background of the transcendant problem of maintaining an American–Soviet power balance. Because of the constraints imposed by the certainty of mutual destruction in a nuclear shooting-match, Kissinger concluded that superpower rivalries henceforth would be played out in key regions of the world. That explained his continuing emphasis – *after* Angola mainly – upon the need to create and preserve regional power balances as a means of reinforcing the global balance. 'If strategic forces are today less important, regional balances gain more significance,' he said in 1975. 'In these circumstances our task is to find ways to restrain Soviet power over an historical period . . . by balancing off Soviet power around the world through a combination of political, military and economic means.'[14]

From 1969 to 1974 frustrated Africans remained, for broad US policy, in a condition of benign neglect. Kissinger, working on behalf of Nixon and later Ford, was almost wholly concerned with Indo-China, the SALT 2 negotiations, the breakthrough to China, and the Middle East where, by 1972, he had pushed Sadat into breaking with the Russians. Equally he was burdened by the Indo-Pakistani war, while the Watergate scandal, with all its implications, constantly haunted him. One of the great attributes of political leadership and statesmanship is an ability to delegate, but this Kissinger found hard to do, especially when a personally-sponsored policy was involved. Kissinger often argued that the United States had few, if any, vital national interests to defend in black Africa and this was yet another factor contributing to his apparent lack of concern.

The truth seemed to be that Africa, as a platform, had little appeal to a man who enjoyed strutting from one great world crisis to another. Africa, indeed, was not yet ready for a latter-day Metternich, even though shades of Bismarck hung memorably over the continent. Besides, he knew little of African history or the contemporary conditions of the continent, beyond the fact that they were sad and inequitable. Andy Young put it into words: 'Kissinger, just like John Foster Dulles, didn't know much about Africa.'[15] And on a later occasion, Young added: 'The Senate doesn't give a damn about Africa and it doesn't know a damn about Africa.'

In itself Angola, as Kissinger told congressmen, was not important to US interests. What was important – although he did not concede this – was that the event drove a coach and horses through the Africa policy he had adopted in 1969.

Kissinger had ignored the advice of Africanists in the State Department – men like Ambassador Nathaniel Davis – to view Angola and its implications in *African*, rather than in *global*, terms. He argued that Angola was irrelevant in itself. It had become the chosen setting of Cuban–Soviet involvement. The setting might have been Andorra. What, he argued, was important was that the venture had been undertaken in an area beyond the normal and acceptable area of influence either of the Cubans or the Russians. To congressmen, that seemed an *ex post facto* rationale because it had been established to their satisfaction that Kissinger himself had presided over the prior intervention of CIA men, helped by Zairean and South African troops, to back the side he hoped would win. If Angola rated so little importance, they wanted to know, why all that covert action and outside interference? And further, if Kissinger had not authorized or organized prior intervention, was it at all sure that the Russians and Cubans would have gone in? And finally, were not Americans, like the communists, involved thousands of miles from home, too?

Angola was judged to be a disaster of Kissinger policy by most US pundits, by the Congress of the day and by the Carter administration not only because the policy failed but also because the civil war and secret US intervention were held to have been encouraged by the secretary of state. That judgement had yet to be answered (at the start of the 1980s) but doubtless will be, somehow, in a second volume of Kissinger's memoirs. His arguments will need to be convincing, if Angolans and other Africans are to shed their conviction that the blood of civil war dead and wounded has stained his reputation.

Ever resilient, the great improviser, Kissinger after Angola exercised what Engels once described as the highest form of freedom – recognition of necessity. For him the necessity was to revise his tactics in Africa without altering his overall objectives in the east–west contest.

In the aftermath of his Angolan débâcle Kissinger, in Lusaka, Zambia, on 27 April 1976 offered a ten-point programme as a starting-point for a new, coherent, more progressive African policy. It centred on the future of Zimbabwe, because Americans and British alike feared that neighbouring Angola would become a platform for Cuban intervention and a sanctuary for Soviet-armed Zimbabwe guerrillas. In September 1976 he shuttled through southern Africa in an effort to produce a settlement. With the help of then Prime Minister Vorster, in Pretoria, he talked Ian Smith into accepting the inevitability of black majority rule by the end of 1978. But this blueprint for a transitional administration left control of the police, with law and order generally, in white hands. Nothing could have been more unrealistic if he had been sensitive to the hostility felt by the Zimbabwe Patriotic Front and most blacks towards their white rulers. What was worse, homeward-bound, he stopped over at Dar es Salaam and sent a signal suggesting, misleadingly, that the five front-line presidents would accept the blueprint. Smith was taken in by the carefully-contrived bit of ambiguity. African leaders were never able to swallow such a proposal. Subsequent negotiations in Geneva fell apart. The two sides were more distant than before. The war intensified. Kissinger with classic deviousness had chalked up another failure.[16]

It was plain that Kissinger, under President Gerald R. Ford's instructions, hoped to recoup the fortunes of the administration in an election year during which opposition Democrats were making hay of Washington's problems in Africa. His declaration in Lusaka, his safari to Pretoria, his support for black majority rule, set a few tom-toms beating. It was heavy, orthodox, middle-of-the-road stuff which even right-wing British Conservatives had for years accepted.

Some double-talk became evident. Kissinger called for 'a peaceful end to institutionalized inequality in South Africa'. US policy, he stressed in Lusaka, was 'based upon the premise that within a reasonable time we shall see a clear evolution towards equality of opportunity and basic human rights for all South Africans'. At the same time American multinationals and banks were investing heavily in South Africa's money-spinning mines, industries and other enterprises – reinforcing the barricades of *apartheid*.

In a year that saw black–white tensions reach flashpoint in Soweto, Langa and Alexandria, it was hard to believe Kissinger seriously imagined South Africa's white rulers could be 'encouraged or persuaded' peacefully to eliminate racial inequality or to introduce 'equality of opportunity' and 'basic human rights' – and 'within a reasonable time', too.

'Equality of opportunity' implied the chance for blacks to be elected to parliament and for all discrimination enshrined in the statute books to be removed. 'A reasonable time' implied, say, five or ten years. No South African inside or outside the government considered that there was the remotest chance of this happening peacefully in the foreseeable future. It was impossible to escape the conclusion that Kissinger was indulging in electoral rhetoric if indeed he was not demonstrating his absolute ignorance of the subject.

President Carter's Retreat

President Carter and his key men entered the White House seemingly determined to remove the ambiguities that marked American policies toward Africa; specifically to approach issues as they arose in a mood of enthusiasm and idealism rather than for their impact on American–Soviet relations. Initially they made some headway, not least because Carter's imaginative choice of Andy Young as his linkman with the Africans and other Third World peoples had a double effect. It dramatized his attempt to distance his policies and priorities from those of Kissinger and it established a significant, if emotional, relationship between the civil-rights movement in America and the cause of black consciousness and progress in Africa.

But the pressures of home and foreign politics made the president's aims in Africa hard to achieve and it was not long before these were shelved in mutual disappointment. By 1979 the US Senate was pressing Carter to lift sanctions against Rhodesia in advance of a political settlement, mainly because of Soviet–Cuban advances in other parts of the continent. Around the same time, Carter found himself retreating on the issue of human rights as they related to America's more stalwart friends in Africa like Zaire, which had a key role to play in the rivalries of the superpowers.

The cynical mutterings of senior French authorities that 'Andy Young is not a policy' were not quite true, as Young had come to be regarded in the Third World at least as a symbol of American good faith. Nevertheless those mutterings reached the White House soon enough and were exploited by opponents, such as Brzezinski, who never quite reconciled themselves to the freewheeling style and un-orthodox diplomacy practised by Young. The southern Baptist president, convinced when he took office that north–south relations were more important than the west's 'inordinate fear of communism', had given a doctor's mandate to his black friend.

The envoy set about prescribing remedies based on the idea that 'African solutions for African problems' were best. As he planned it, the

Carter administration, unlike its predecessor, would not approach black Africa in fear of, or rivalry with, the Soviet Union, but only in order to help or work with individual countries or groups of countries. Americans, with their multiracial experience, had a contribution to make in certain African situations, he considered, and one formula he constantly favoured was to cool heated passions by listening and talking for hours on end, whether the setting was in the plush surroundings of UN headquarters or in the bar of some mediocre hotel in a remote capital, where he could meet official or unofficial Africans in private. The author was able to observe Young's style of conference operations more than once, especially at gatherings relating to African problems. The Malta talks on Zimbabwe in 1978, when the Americans and British were attempting to 'sell' their failed settlement plan to leaders of the Patriotic Front, provided a memorable occasion. Former British foreign secretary David Owen, was staying in the detached elegance of the British high commissioner's residence, away from the frenetic conference atmosphere in the island's scattered hotels where the delegates were accommodated.

Young chose the hotel where Patriotic Front leaders were living. He arrived near midnight on the eve of the conference, dropped his bags and all protocol in his hotel room, descended to the bar, introduced himself to some of the black guerrilla leaders, ordered rounds of beer and immediately got down to listening, talking, arguing, agreeing, into the small hours. The Zimbabwean guerrilla commanders and political leaders got to like him.

If Jimmy Carter's disparate critics agreed on any one thing, it was on the aura of innocence he projected about the nature of the big bad world and, in particular, the designs of America's principal adversaries – the Russians. But there was nothing naïve about the way the president set up the quartet of foreign-policy and security advisers whose job it was to keep him advised and informed, in as balanced a way as possible, of what American policy should be in dangerous times. Carter had chosen Young, knowing that somehow somebody had to repair America's damaged relations with Third World nations after the disasters of the Kissinger period. And later, in mid-1979, the president acknowledged that Young had done so with fifty Third World countries.

But Carter also wanted Young to be balanced by a cautious, middle-of-the-road, yet resolute secretary of state with experience in government and a mature and mellow background, and so appointed Cyrus R. Vance to the job, only to see him resign in April 1980, because of differences over Iranian policy. Harold Brown as defence secretary shared the president's views about the need to check the spread of nuclear weapons. He also professed a commitment to limit the strategic arms race and to reduce force levels in Europe. Like Young, both Vance and Brown were card-carrying liberal Democrats dedicated to the concept of *détente,* although not at any price.

To coordinate, sift, and assess the recommendations of Young, Vance and Brown, Carter brought in Brzezinski, the academic from Columbia, as his adviser on national security affairs. From the moment he took office, Brzezinski, just like Kissinger, was directed by the belief that US policy towards Africa had to be related to general policy towards Moscow – not, as Young and his fellow-Africanists in the State Department would have wished, seen rather in a regional and African focus. When Young talked publicly of the Cubans exercising 'a stabilizing influence' in Angola, he was really addressing Brzezinski and Carter as much as he was the world at large. When he suggested that the British 'had practically invented racism' he was really protesting against Brzezinski's bid to win Carter's support for London's tendency to appease the rebel rulers of Salisbury.

The tussle between Young and Brzezinski began almost as soon as the Carter team took office. And, as Young freely acknowledged after resigning, the issue centred on the Cuban role in Africa. 'I think he [Brzezinski] believes whether it be in Angola, or the Vietnamese in Cambodia, we should try to make them pay a price for their intervention,' Young reflected. 'I think when we make them pay a price, we also pay a price. We pay a price in disturbed and disrupted relations.'[17]

The contest between the two men was played out on two levels. Few outsiders could be sure of precisely what was happening behind the scenes. But on the basis of information from one of the two men, it was a sustained, often one-sidedly bitter, devious and unending feud. Young in cabinet or in White House sessions invariably spoke his mind just as he did in public. Brzezinski in such encounters stayed silent, using silence almost as a weapon. But he, and those around him, knew that he had one big advantage.

Most mornings, around 8.15, he had a twenty-to-thirty minute private briefing session with the president, at which he pressed his own views and those of his colleagues. Young believed that, in those morning sessions, his own ideas were hacked about a great deal. In contrast Brzezinski, according to White House insiders, made a point of conveying to Carter how hard he and Vance were trying to work together. The fact that they had to try so hard to harmonize told its own story.

It was soon clear that Young was losing ground to the subtler Brzezinski in the battle for the presidential ear. Almost daily, Washington was denouncing the scale and kind of Soviet–Cuban activity in Angola and elsewhere in Africa, just as if the Kissinger era had not ended. And when Soviet–Cuban intervention began in the Horn of Africa, the onslaughts intensified. Whenever possible, Young sought to cool the temperature. Brzezinski, for his part, did the opposite. An angered Castro, for instance, was convinced that it was Brzezinski, with Hamilton Jordan's help, who during November 1977 had planted a map in the media misrepresenting the extent and nature of the Cuban presence in Africa.[18]

Young considered that this totally undercut his attempts to convince African countries that Washington had abandoned its anti-Moscow line and that instead it was looking at problems pragmatically outside the context of superpower considerations. Young repeatedly argued, in-house and publicly, that the force of African nationalism would never permit Moscow to maintain anything like a permanent position in most African countries. He cited all the cases where the Russians had been invited to go. He cited, equally, all the cases where, as a consequence of colonial and western misconceptions, the Russians and others had been invited to come. Andy Young's contention was that the Cubans and Russians were strengthened in Africa when Brzezinski's leaks and briefings provided a cover for renewed South African air and land raids on Angola, as if Pretoria knew that it could count on 'friends' in the White House. It was not by accident that Carter initiated a correspondence with Vorster first, then with Prime Minister Pieter Botha.

The fine hopes of the early Carter years had by the start of the new decade been badly battered. Angola remained unrecognized and both Angola and Mozambique felt an increasing need for Cuban–Soviet protection following attacks on them by South Africa that were unchallenged by the west. Frustrations over the fall of the Shah of Iran and the emergence of irrational rule in Iran spilled over into other areas of US politics. The Soviet Union's thrust into Afghanistan was the signal for a full-scale revival of the kind of hostilities, without open warfare, that marked the dark days of the cold war. There were divisions among the allies. Carter was approaching humiliating defeat by Reagan in an election he yearned to win.

Carter's defeat concerned African leaders less than the election of Reagan, who had pledged to arm the foes of Angola's socialist government. The shifting policies of the defeated president had merely confirmed the tradition of an ambivalent, indeed erratic, American approach to the problems of the continent. Reagan's advertised attitude, in contrast, signalled greater consistency in resisting latter-day African radicalism that could be seen to serve Moscow's aims. If there was a common denominator between the two U S leaders it lay in their shared perception that Africa had become just another setting where the influence of the communist powers had not only to be thwarted but also removed.

This shared perception rested on a reading of American vital interests in Africa. In pursuit of those interests Carter, conforming with the inherent liberalism of the Democrats, started with a commitment actively to collaborate with Africans in their cause to cleanse the continent of minority white rule. Reagan began imbued with a conservative Republican's sense of mission that it was essential to check the Russians in their real or imagined drive for strategic bases and control of strategic resources.

What, in fact, were America's vital interests in and around Africa?

The Strategic Dimension

The central aim in the words of former Defence Secretary Donald H. Rumsfeld was 'to maintain an international order' assuring the preservation of U S physical and economic security and of its political system. Conversely, the proclaimed goal of the Russians was to replace the old international order with something deemed to be better, more just and no longer dominated by the west.[19]

Strategically it was essential for the U S navy to retain access to those straits and choke-points linking major oceanic routes. In the age of space exploration, it was crucial for a global power to develop a world-wide infrastructure, with facilities for anything from guided-missile systems to meteorology.

In the context of superpower confrontation, Africa commanded special U S interest because of the extensive facilities that the Soviet Union had won in that great landmass for overflying rights, use of airfields, and ports of call, and even naval repair, victualling and docking arrangements. Because of the need to preserve regional balances, and the rash of little local wars in which east and west became involved by proxy, facilities of this sort assumed a special significance, not only in Africa but also in nearby regions such as the Gulf and the Arabian Peninsula. During the Iranian and Afghan crises of 1980, Washington negotiated air and naval facilities in Kenya, Somalia and Egypt.

The Economic Dimension

Until the wind-up of the imperial systems in 1960 the metropolitan powers of Europe had effectively excluded the United States from their closely guarded markets and resources in Africa. But the post-colonial period brought a steady flow of American investment, trade and aid to all the continent. It was a flow that became a torrent after the energy crisis of the early 1970s created a seemingly insatiable demand for Nigerian, Algerian, and Libyan oil and gas and a stake in new fields opening up from the eastern to the western seaboards. In parallel the requirements of the new technology in the lands of the industrialized north generated intense interest, and competition, for Africa's minerals and other scarce commodities. A mix of political and humanitarian motives also spurred successive US administrations progressively to increase economic, development and food aid to favoured and occasionally stricken countries.

The following random figures tell their own story:

In the eighteen years up to 1978 private US investment in Africa (excluding the Republic of South Africa) had soared more than five times, to $3·4 thousand million;[20] by 1980 the level had reached roughly $6·5 thousand million.

Comparative figures for South Africa showed a jump in direct US investment from $286 million in 1969 to about $2·5 thousand million in 1980.

The annual US trade deficit with Africa as a whole at the start of the new decade was in the vicinity of $40 thousand million.

In this light, Ambassador Young, reflecting the attitudes of the American-African constituency he represented, suggested that the expansion of business with Africa had become a vital national interest challenging investors and policy-makers alike. As he saw things new oil and resource discoveries, coupled with exploration facilities financed by the World Bank, offered fine opportunities for the investment of thousands of millions of dollars of available private capital. South Africa, initially the main source of US investment and trading income, had easily been outpaced by the rest of the continent. Young foresaw possibilities for ever-increasing American investment in black-ruled states. 'The United States is starting late but we have none of the colonial baggage to carry,' he wrote in *Foreign Affairs*, early in 1981. Quite apart from existing foundations supplying food and other aid, 'we have', he observed, 'a population of twenty-five million Americans of African descent'.

If President Reagan picked up the burden of that message he displayed at least initially few signs of it. At the start of his term of office he served notice of his expectation that private business should and would lead Americans to economic recovery. Authoritative suggestions from administration leaders that the country was entering a phase of free-for-all business activity were taken by US multinationals to mean that they could take full advantage of the opportunity to participate in the expanding economies of key African countries. But the administration stressed a central qualification. It was that all trading and aid policies had to be related to the nation's overall national and international strategic interests. At a time when adversary politics on a global scale was supplanting the phantom objectives of east–west *détente,* Africa's real interests looked certain to suffer. Suffer they did as Reagan increased U S military spending by $30 thousand million; cut back President Carter's budgetary allocation of a big increase in internation development aid; and focused most attention on those African countries that supported the broad thrust of Reagan policy, which was to roll the Russians out of Africa and, it was hoped, the Indian Ocean, Middle East and south-west Asia.

The Reagan formula left the U S about fifteenth in the league of seventeen western countries contributing a percentage of their gross national product to development aid. It assumed an even more unfortunate appearance in the context of *Global 2000*, a report prepared for the president by the Department of State and the Council on Environmental Quality as a signpost to the last two decades of this century. The researchers who produced the report maintained that by AD 2000 the world's population would have increased to about 6·35 thousand million, a 50 per cent rise. Nine-tenths of this increase, the report forecast, was likely to take place in the poorest countries of the world. Food, water and fuel shortages could be expected. Around 40 per cent of forest cover in poor countries would probably vanish because of the needs of people for heat, light and homes.

The Political Dimension

South Africa sought long and hard to persuade Washington, London, Paris and other key allied capitals to defend the sea-lanes around the Cape of Good Hope. These are routes used by giant tankers carrying Middle Eastern oil to the refineries of Europe and America. Pretoria pushed the argument – and unsuspecting politicians in the Congress, Britain's parliament and the French National Assembly picked it up – that Soviet warships in the Indian Ocean could easily disrupt western oil supplies unless some shared defence system was set up. But perceptive State Department diplomats immediately labelled that rationale as specious. For a Soviet naval vessel to stop, attack or otherwise interfere with western-bound shipping on the high seas would be tantamount to aggression and inevitably invite retaliation. If, so the counter-argument ran, Moscow meant to precipitate a war it would go all out and nuclear conflict would soon rage over more strategic centres.

Nor, in the view of State Department authorities, was it conceivable that the Russians would set out deliberately to force or in other ways induce African countries to withhold raw materials, including essential minerals, from the west.

African countries must sell their minerals as they cannot eat them. Plainly the Russians would try to raise the cost of access to those minerals. But that was something that had to be expected in the process of competitive coexistence.

General Alexander M. Haig took command of US foreign policy as Reagan's secretary of state. Earlier he had, briefly, contemplated contending for the Republican presidential nomination, abandoning the attempt when it became evident Reagan could not lose. But in settling for the first position in the cabinet, then asserting his managerial authority in some aspects of defence and economic policies, as well as in foreign affairs, he left few in doubt that his gaze was fixed on the 1984 presidential contest. Haig gave up his key post as supreme commander, allied forces, Europe (NATO's SACEUR), because he felt he was being denied direct access to Jimmy Carter, although the president's men ascribed his resignation to political ambitions.

Before resigning Haig, in a long talk with the author on the affairs of Africa (11 May 1979), spoke frankly about the geopolitical importance of the continent in the east–west context; about his concern over the advance of Soviet influence; about 'the constant dynamic turmoil' he foresaw as a consequence of the 'unnatural Europeanization' of Africa; and about his feeling that although *apartheid* was 'not good' it nevertheless was pointless to ask South Africa 'to commit suicide'.

During the interview Haig was in philosophic mood, expressing himself calmly, coherently. His replies revealed some factors likely to shape the new administration's approach to Africa in the years ahead (granted that promises of politicians do not always relate to an ability to fulfil them).

Excerpts from the interview follow in question-and-answer form:

Q: As an American general and as SACEUR how do you perceive the economic, strategic and political importance of Africa in today's world?
A: In a geopolitical sense Africa has become increasingly important as definitive limitations on raw materials are beginning to have such profound influence on the industrial and economic well-being of the industrialized states. These raw materials [always] have formed the growth of western industrialized societies. Beyond that, roughly 70 per cent of raw materials providing for our sustenance circumvent the continent. With the world in a state of flux and nonaligned states unfortunately becoming targets of east–west competition, Africa now is a vitally important area.
Q: If Africa's resources have become increasingly important to the west, are they not just as important to the Soviets?

A: Unquestionably. If you add to the minerals the agricultural failings of the Soviets, the potential grain contributions from a rich, vast and as yet largely untapped area, Africa becomes a prize of inestimable value to the east as well as to the west.

Q: Hasn't the ultimate answer got to be a process of east–west sharing in the development as well as in the use of Africa's resources, without each side trying to deny to the other access to those resources?

A: Our experiences to date make that a naïve objective. Broadly the west would welcome constructive eastern participation in development of the Third World. But, in the current environment, political objectives would dominate. Thus far, the almost exclusive Soviet contribution has been in the form of vast amounts of armament, military advice, directly or through proxies and, more recently, through direct military activities. The objective is indeed desirable but there have to be fundamental understandings and agreed guidelines if the needs are to be met.

Q: The big-power contest right now looks very much like the old scramble for Africa, when Africans really need to overcome their poverty and achieve true independence . . .

A: I wouldn't assess it as a struggle in the classical nineteenth-century sense. The west has been largely traumatized as a consequence of the colonial past and its disastrous outcome.

Q: Traumatized? Even by the pre-colonial period, the period of slavery?

A: That's right. My concerns today would be focused more sharply on the vacuums created, offering openings to inorganic Soviet imperialism. By 'inorganic' I mean an imperialism without an imperialist base, built exclusively on armaments, subversion and force. The Soviets have never accepted colonial models but have insisted on total client-state relationships (as in Ethiopia, Yemen, Afghanistan). African [and radical Arab] states are not comfortable with this. We've seen them rise up.

Q: Linking events in Africa today with the past, isn't much of the trouble attributable to the heritage of the Berlin Conference, when artificial frontiers were drawn to split whole nations and create chances for outsiders nowadays to exploit crises?

A: You're absolutely right. That's why there's going to be constant dynamic turmoil because nothing was ever natural about the Europeanization of Africa.

Q: Do you agree the focus of danger in Africa has moved south?

A: Yes. The novelty lies in the Soviet ability [to intervene]. They've been largely unchallenged and that generated a momentum of its own. When Angola first occurred, America was rather sluggish in challenging a situation that was murky. It's when a situation is ambiguous that it lends itself to low-risk amelioration – Kissinger made the point. The dangers of attending the problem grow tremendously and sometimes we recoil.

Q: Didn't the US cook its own goose by seeming to be associated with South Africa's intervention and in Africa the South Africans are –

A: Anathema.

Q: Right. And, of course, Pretoria claimed they'd got the nod and wink from

Kissinger, making it easy for the Cubans, in some African eyes, to pose as saviours?

A: There are two realms when you analyse these situations. One is rather brutal, geopolitical or a purely power realm. The other . . . you have to be very, very careful about. I don't want to be a proponent for amoral outlooks but there is need to ask yourself about what is moral. It's become almost faddish not to be a proponent of national interests today. If we have faith and confidence in our perceptions of social justice, the role of the individual in the state, it seems we must be less self-conscious about applying policies designed to further our national interests.

Q: Ends justifying the means?

A: That's it.

Q: What's to be done about South Africa?

A: South Africa's a more complex problem. It's a victim as well as perpetrator of its own problems. They've become a victim of our compulsive preoccupation with a search for social justice. No nation is going to influence another to commit suicide. *Apartheid* is not good. I'm against the suppression of these things in any environment but you've got to know where it's going to lead you and we've now created a situation in which our South African friends whatever shortcomings they have, are so profoundly alienated that they're going to do the worst for themselves. . . .

8. France

There was nothing delphic in the message Réne Journiac* brought the emperor in Bangui from Valery Giscard d'Estaing on Wednesday, 1 August 1979.

Jean Bédel Bokassa's involvement in the April massacre of the innocents – when more than 100 schoolchildren died – had been proven and would be announced in sixteen days by the investigating panel of African and French magistrates. The Elysée Palace had been advised in advance of the findings. It would no longer be possible for Paris to support him and abdication was the only way out. He could retire to France in comfort. Perhaps a pension might be arranged.

Emperor Bokassa listened in silence to the presidential envoy until he could bear it no longer. He lashed out angrily with his imperial cane at Journiac. Giscard's adviser on Africa recoiled, his arms upraised to ward off the blows. Bernard Bongo, president of Gabon, whose attendance had been pre-arranged by the French, held Bokassa back.

Journiac hurried to the French embassy and telephoned Giscard. In turn, the French leader rang the man he used to address as 'my dear relative'. Bokassa slammed the phone down on his only sponsor.

The first and last emperor of the Central African Empire, in striking Journiac, had assaulted the dignity of France.

Fifty days later, while Bokassa was visiting Libya, 1,000 French troops flew in to Bangui and restored David Dacko to the presidency that he had been forced in 1967 to yield to Bokassa. For the tyrant with an uncontrollable temper it was the end. But for the French and their connections in Africa troubles were just beginning.[1]

The *coup* had been planned as a quiet affair. It was carried out with all the aplomb that the French had displayed in the dozens of recorded and unrecorded interventions they had staged since the colonies of

* In February 1980, Journiac died in an airplane crash in mysterious circumstances during a mission to Africa.

francophone Africa were granted nominal statehood in 1960. Initially, too, 'Operation Barracuda' seemed to have been a singular success. Those African leaders who for years had looked upon Bokassa's despotism with disgust, acclaimed it, in private at least. Publicly most were discreetly silent.

Almost immediately Dacko made life difficult for the Elysée Palace with a series of utterances that contradicted the portrayal of events presented by Paris. First, he disclosed that he had flown into Bangui with the French takeover contingent. 'Some countries call upon the Cubans,' he told journalists next. 'Why shouldn't we call upon French troops, since they are our friends?' Later, he said, 'if the life of the country requires it they [the French force] will remain for more than ten years.' These were matters of policy that French ministers had been trying to obscure in formal explanations to the National Assembly and to the public. In yet another display of political innocence, Dacko announced his intention to establish diplomatic relations with South Africa in return for economic aid. It was an announcement certain to anger most of the states of black Africa committed, as they were, to support the struggle to end white-minority rule. The following day Dacko, under French pressure, withdrew the statement saying that it had been intended as a joke. The people of his country, he explained to disbelieving journalists, were in need of levity and relaxation and that was why he had made his joke. Pressed to repeat his explanation Dacko insisted: 'I am serious. It was a joke.' For quite a while after that there were no more news conferences.[2]

For Giscard the damage had been done. After denying that France, for months, had plotted the downfall of a regime it had been financing for thirteen years, the president and his spokesmen sought to brazen it out. They acknowledged helping to remove the emperor. Then they contested a documented report that Giscard, while finance minister in 1973, had accepted as a gift from Bokassa a package of thirty carat diamonds worth (at the time) more than $250,000. On 27 November 1979, the president acknowledged on French television receiving some diamonds but 'categorically and contemptuously' denied that they had been worth as much as the weekly *Le Canard Enchaîné* had suggested. In effect he was saying the diamonds he had accepted from the emperor were only small ones. It was as if he had borrowed from the logic of St Augustine's aphorism: 'Give me chastity and continency, but not yet.'

Finally the overworked presidential entourage at the Elysée claimed credit for organizing a little *coup* in which not 'a drop of blood had been shed'. François Mitterand, then opposition socialist leader, retorted scornfully: 'What do they mean, no bloodshed? Blood was flowing for years and it was known in Paris!'[3]

Beyond the confines of French political jousting the affair assumed more serious implications. France's role in the African francophone states and, later, in Zaire, attracted closer scrutiny and generated heated disputes. The role of Paris, with its economic, strategic and political connotations, was seen to be complex and subtle. The structure of French relationships enabled the president's men to influence events and policies in the former colonies with a simple admonition, a temporary cutback in aid, perhaps a well-timed military feint.

To some it may have seemed as if Giscard was simply following a long French tradition in going it alone in Africa when he and his Elysée Palace entourage calculated French, or European, interests were being threatened. '*Vive la France!*' a US State Department official exclaimed when asked to comment on the *coup* that ousted Bokassa. But among more thoughtful African authorities, especially those in the francophone countries, the affair served only to highlight the cynicism characterizing France's overall approach to the troubled continent, whether it took the form of selling nuclear technology to South Africa or peddling arms to some of Africa's most reactionary and oppressive regimes.

Giscard became president a year after the 1973 oil crisis, an event that led him to support the cause of Islam (and, predictably, access to Islamic energy sources) within his global design. Borrowing from Metternich, as the distinguished French socialist Claude Bourdet has noted, he fashioned his own version of a Holy Alliance: one that would unite the technology of Community Europe with the oil of Araby and the minerals of Africa. He considered, as the Chinese did, that such a combination would be able effectively to challenge what he saw as the hegemony of the superpowers.[4]

The French pursued their goals alternately with panache and arrogance, sometimes offending the susceptibilities of the Russians, Americans and their own European partners like Britain and Belgium. They earned for themselves a reputation for behaving as if they were the *gendarmes d'Afrique*, resurrecting their self-assumed nineteenth-century '*mission civilisatrice*'. Like policemen or missionaries everywhere they had successes and resounding failures. Giscard offered a rationale to a summit conference of leaders of French-speaking African states in Paris on 22 and 23 May 1978: 'In the field of politics Africa must be for the Africans,' he said. 'In economics Africans would impoverish themselves if they limited their interest to their continent alone.' Even then, and in retrospect, too, the president's words had a hollow ring against a background of sustained, carefully organized French political, economic and military interventionism and he may well have realized it when he sought to justify French actions: 'It also means that you protect Africa from the non-Africans who want to sow disruption or, sadly, violence. The objective of French policy is that the Africans can themselves control the problems of Africa.' France, he emphasized, would not permit the superpowers to carve up the continent between them and so lay waste to it. Initiatives were the right of Africans.

Nevertheless the record showed the extent of French involvement.

All but three states of francophone Africa signed accords providing for French military advice, training and arms. Five among them, Ivory Coast, Gabon, Senegal, Togo and the Central African Republic, gave the French base rights, with Djibouti joining in later. Bases also were acquired in five offshore island-territories.

Most states adhered to the franc zone (Communauté des Francs Africains), a currency system managed by the Bank of France and vesting effective control of francophone monetary policies in Parisian hands. On occasions, as when France entered the European monetary system, Paris failed to consult zone members although their interests were crucially involved. The system permitted the free flow of French capital into French Africa and repatriation of profits from investments, yet without allowing African governments to ensure those investments met their national needs. Overall the aim was to preserve old arrangements under which Africa's primary products and raw materials could be extracted for profitable downstream development in metropolitan France while French manufactured goods could in turn be marketed in Africa. French protestations that African industrialization was being promoted hardly squared with the figures. In 1979, for instance, France exported goods worth about $4·6 thousand million to francophone countries and imported roughly $3·1 thousand million from them.

Some African leaders denounced the system as colonialism with a false beard. President Shehu Shagari of Nigeria told an OAU summit meeting in Lagos on 28 April 1980: 'We are the victims of mass exploitation . . . it is unrealistic for the developed world to sustain their standard of living by buying our raw materials cheaply and selling us their manufactured goods at high prices determined unilaterally by them.'

In the first three years of independence beginning in 1960 France was 'invited' to protect incumbent governments threatened by internal challengers, according to Alain Peyrefitte, French information minister. The countries needing French help, he said, included Chad, Cameroon, Congo-Brazzaville, Mauritania, Niger and Gabon, some of them more than once.[5]

In February 1964, French troops again flew into Gabon to restore its toppled and imprisoned President Leon M'Ba twenty-four hours *before* help was formally requested. Gabon produces uranium, oil and manganese, mostly for France. The United States denied French charges that it had instigated the plot against M'Ba.

In the 1967–70 Nigerian civil war France sent arms to the Biafran separatists through neighbouring francophone countries and President de Gaulle proclaimed political and moral support for the Biafran cause. The British government, which knew extensive oil resources were located in the region called Biafra, was angered. Former Prime Minister Harold Wilson and his cabinet had no doubt that the French leader had been motivated by something more than his familiar allergy to the 'Anglo-Saxons'. They were convinced de Gaulle had scented oil and was hoping for the lush concessions which a victorious and grateful Colonel Odumegwe Ojukwu might have been expected to grant so important a backer. British-based firms possessed options on those concessions.

In 1967 a 2,500-strong French expeditionary force moved into the landlocked desert state of Chad where, three years before, Christian–Moslem civil war had flared. Thirteen years, several *coups* and counter-*coups* and thousands of lives later, the French pulled out with their mission still unaccomplished and with a Libyan invasion force helping to underpin the claimed authority of President Goukouni Oueddi's regime. Giscard conceded defeat on the advice of Martin Kirsch, successor to Réne Journiac. Chad, Africa's fifth largest territory and yet one of the poorest, is said to be endowed with enough oil resources to sustain itself plus considerable uranium deposits in its northern frontier region marching with southern Libya. Both factors were among the reasons for French and Libyan intervention. Yet, while the two countries were supporting opposite sides in the civil war, France was supplying Libya with some of the arms, including Mirage fighters, operating against the friends of the French. Old religious and ethnic feuds, fanned by outsiders, divided the people. Until early 1980 the government in N'Djamena, the capital, was dominated by the two million Christian and animist black southerners who are mainly farming folk. But the northern Moslems, with Libyan support, gradually gained ground and after a series of brief alliances, failed peace talks, massacres and counter-massacres, they won control of the capital. Behind the duel lay big stakes, quite apart from Chad's real or imagined resources. Libya's Colonel Gadafi saw the country as a vital link in a chain of Saharan states extending from the Atlantic to the Red Sea. For Gadafi, Chad was also a bridgehead into black Africa where he aimed to spread his revolutionary Islam-based ideology. Uranium in the Aohzou strip in the north, under Libyan occupation, would help Gadafi's dreams of nuclear development, long reliant upon Soviet and French help. Oil in the south would contribute to the modernization of the black farming communities where memories and legend live on about centuries of Arab slave raids. It was only in 1926 that French colonial rulers finally ended the slave trade.

From 1975 onwards France sent forces into action against Polisario guerrillas seeking self-determination and statehood for the Western Sahara. The former Spanish colony had been 'annexed' by neighbouring Morocco and Mauritania but the Polisario movement, with Algerian backing, thrust deeply into both countries compelling Mauritania to sue for peace. The French, in defending the Mauritanians, remained tied down, with their Jaguars bombing Polisario bases and columns.

There were many other freely-assumed obligations for the French to fulfil besides. Giscard lifted his gaze southwards, beyond francophone Africa and West Africa, towards Zaire, Zimbabwe and the Republic of South Africa. Even that was not enough. A twenty-seven-unit French fleet including a nuclear-powered submarine with nuclear-tipped missiles aboard patrolled the Indian Ocean and the waters below the Arabian peninsula.

French paratroops intervened in Shaba (Katanga) in 1977 and 1978 with the support of contingents from francophone states. Ostensibly their purpose was to rescue whites threatened, or attacked, by Katangan exiles who had returned to their homeland from north-eastern Angolan bases. France's actual mission, however, was to prop up the shaky regime of President Mobutu and so advance French ambitions for a greater stake in Katanga's fabled resources of copper, cobalt, uranium and other minerals.

Beyond Zaire, the French had been consolidating their relations for years with South Africa, by selling sophisticated air, land and sea equipment and arms worth millions of dollars to the white supremacist government.

Additionally the French negotiated a $1 thousand million contract for the supply and construction of a nuclear power complex to the South Africans. France's controversial deal was about the biggest concluded with the South Africans. It aroused immediate criticism from several African governments coinciding, as it did, with persistent reports that the government of Prime Minister P. W. Botha had all but completed a nuclear-weapons programme. Officials in Paris expected to ride the storm. South Africa was not party to the world treaty to stop the spread of nuclear weapons and some of its major research establishments were therefore closed to international inspection and safeguards. Informally, the Americans tried in vain to dissuade the French from going through with the contract until and unless South Africa did sign that treaty and so subject itself to checks against cheating.

In defiance of UN resolutions banning arms sales to the South Africans, the French made blueprints and licences available to the Pretoria government for the production of Mirage fighters, Panhard light tanks and guided missiles.

Even after announcing in 1978 (for the third time over the years) a formal cut-off of weapons supplies by the French, these arrangements remained operative. The French company, Total, was among the first (alongside British and American firms) to break the international oil embargo months after it was imposed in late 1965 on the breakaway government of Rhodesia's Ian Smith.

By the start of the 1980s French military domination of most of francophone Africa was complete. A network of interlocking agreements placed garrisons or 'training missions' of varying sizes in twenty-two countries (including Zaire); authorized France to intervene in certain cases against external aggression or internal disorder; provided for base facilities in eleven territories, two of them not yet independent.[6]

Overall, France's military presence in and around Africa – exceeding 15,000 soldiers, sailors and airmen – appeared modest compared with Cuba's 35,000-strong force. But surface comparisons were misleading. Ever since 1964 a highly-trained, specialist *force d'intervention* had been available in southern France to serve at short notice as a mobile reserve. Its specific mission was to deal with any emergency that might arise in Africa. The Eleventh Airborne Division, complete with paratroop, marine and infantry and artillery brigades, had seaborne, amphibious and armed elements, plus about 220 aircraft at its disposal. It also maintained a forward element on permanent alert in Senegal.

Existence of this out-of-sight force was no secret to francophone and other African governments. Its importance lay in the deterrent effect it was to exercise on would-be trouble-makers, for France's capacity to deal swiftly with sudden crises in Africa was plainly enhanced by these crack units.

Against that background France's failure to prevent Libya's conquest of Chad was seen to be a deliberate act of policy and so aroused dark suspicion. It was labelled as the most serious setback for French prestige and policy in Africa since the Algerian war; and it also spread alarm among Chad's, and Libya's, neighbours who for years had been witnessing Gadafi build up with Soviet as well as French weaponry an unrivalled record of interference in the affairs of target states near and far. Official French condemnations of the prospective Libyan–Chad 'merger' left most OAU governments unimpressed. From Nigeria to Sudan, from Tunisia to Egypt, persistent speculation ranged from theories that Gadafi had 'bought' Giscard's acquiescence with a few barrels of oil, to suggestions that

Chad might yet be divided into Libyan and French spheres of influence.

The contemporary French thrust through Africa – a century after the Conference of Berlin – was three-dimensional. Its economic, strategic and political elements were inseparable. Giscard had a traditional view of French interests, reared, as he was, by a banker-father Edmond and related through his wife to the Schneider family of steel barons.

The Economic Goal

In economic terms, France's approach remained as acquisitive as it was in the nineteenth and early twentieth centuries yet, because of its sophistication, considerably more efficient. Where the entrepreneurs of the past set out to amass great fortunes in the name of civilizing Africa's 'savages and heathens', the huge trading companies of today say they are doing so in the name of African 'development'. The Compagnie Française de l'Afrique Occidentale, for instance, is in the business of buying and selling anything from coffee to Caravelle airliners. A questioner asked Giscard over German television in early October 1979 whether France sought to derive economic advantage from its military presence in Africa. The president was irked, describing the question as 'insulting and stupid'. French intervention, he explained, had taken place in countries 'among the twenty-four poorest in the world. They have no natural resources, no mineral resources and live on French aid.'

Giscard's reply may have silenced his questioner but it was not quite accurate. In Gabon, Niger, Chad, Zaire and the Central African Republic, to name just five, oil, diamonds, manganese, cobalt and copper were among resources either being developed or coveted by the French. Nearly 100 per cent of the uranium used in French nuclear power and military-weapon plants came from African territories, among them Niger, which is one of the world's major producers.

The Strategic Goal

Strategically, successive French presidents in the post-war period tended to view Africa as an extension of Europe with its untapped reservoirs of raw materials vital to the economies and the strength of the Old World. It was the obverse of the Leninist dictum French officials were frequently heard recalling: 'The nation that holds Africa, holds Europe.' In an age of energy shortage, of nuclear development whether for civil or military use, of technological advance, Africa's oil, uranium, cobalt, phosphates and other scarce minerals possessed an immeasurable importance.

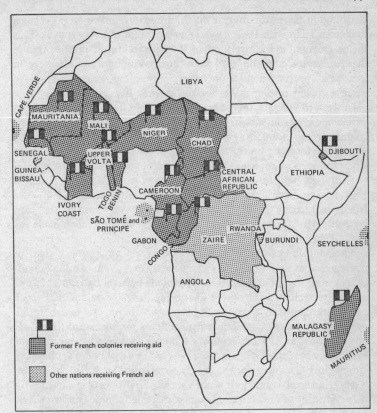

Fig. 11: French influence in black Africa
SOURCE: *US News & World Report*, 31 March 1980.

Without access to Africa's uranium there would have been no credible *force de frappe*. There were other factors which the French considered validated their perception of Africa's strategic value. The Central African land mass, a triangle from Zaire in the south to Djibouti in the north-east, then westwards through Chad and Niger and back to Zaire, formed a buffer zone against Soviet–Cuban penetration. To the north along the Mediterranean littoral and to the south in Angola and Mozambique, on the Atlantic and Indian Oceans, there were by the 1980s centres of socialist, although not necessarily totally committed Muscovite, influence. The francophone system, French authorities argued, blocked a link-up of direct lines of communication between those bases.

Against that background, and for all their other differences, Paris and

Washington shared an interest which turned out, fortuitously perhaps, to be consistent with Henry Kissinger's concept of 'relay states'. This theory emerged in the aftermath of Vietnam and rested on the premise that Americans could be freed from the need militarily to intervene in east–west confrontations if only there were other countries ready to assume greater responsibility for anti-communist resistance.

In western capitals, including Washington, Giscard and his envoys gave allied governments an impression of being willing partners in the common cause of holding back the advance of Soviet–Cuban influence, even while insisting on the right to act in their own national interests when the need might arise. The Americans, with little experience and virtually no political tradition of working with Africans, accepted French assurances and tended on the whole (after memories of Suez faded) to identify French national interests with those of the west generally. In African capitals, on the other hand, the French made the most of their publicized indifference to the contest of the superpowers and their disdain for adversary politics. It was an approach that for many years, at least until late 1979, gave them a touch of added credibility among the elitist rulers they supported – even though some of those elitists, groomed as they were in the sophisticated salons of French power, were unlikely to be fooled for long. As James O. Goldsborough perceptively observed: 'French paratroopers jumping into Shaba are not the same as US paratroopers jumping into Shaba – even if the French are wearing US parachutes.'[7] And as a Gabonese spokesman, anticipating Dacko, remarked in July 1978, in the same Shaba context: 'Gabon is a small country. It is our sovereign right to ask our friends for help, Africans or not, if we are being threatened. Some countries have called in the Cubans. Why shouldn't we call in the French?'[7]

To the extent, then, that Cuban activism in Angola, Ethiopia and elsewhere in Africa served Soviet strategic purposes, so did France, too, in Shaba and certain other francophone situations, perform the kind of tasks that the Americans would have wanted to be done. In the same way that Castro claimed he had acted independently, without Moscow's request, so Giscard, too, would make that claim in relation to the Americans. If there was coordination or collaboration, it presumably was the coordination or collaboration of like-minded allies. The Cubans could argue plausibly that they were as much the surrogates of the Soviet Union as France was the proxy of the United States.

The Political Goal

In the political context, France's approach to Africa was simplistic and neutral. Neutral in the sense that the French did not care much about the nature of the regime they were prepared to support and generously aid, provided only that it was pro-French.

The deposition of Bokassa might have been widely welcomed in France, Africa and beyond. But the manner of its execution aroused controversy. Previously most French economic, military and political activity in Africa had been shrouded in secrecy, even when major operations took place. The practice of secrecy dated back to the years of the Nazi occupation of France during the Second World War, when security silence was maintained during de Gaulle's struggle to regain France from his North African platform. The black-out of information was, if anything, intensified during the anguished Algerian war years when a grand total of 300,000 French servicemen were employed to try to preserve the skeleton of France's imperial system.[8]

Even when Paris lured its NATO partners into a treaty obligation to help defend part of the North African littoral few ordinary French citizens were aware that nearly half US military aid to Europe was being diverted into the reconstruction of the French military power. It was a factor that became engraved more on Algerian than on French memories and one result was to throw some Algerian leaders into the outstretched arms of the socialist world.

The cosmetics of the French–African association have always been on proud display. Giscard, during his presidency from 1974 to May 1981, had made fifteen well-publicized official visits to various French-speaking countries, not counting several private journeys to rest, shoot game and perhaps to resolve undisclosed difficulties. But when French bombers, coordinating with Chad government forces, located and attacked a rebel concentration and killed an estimated 280 guerrillas on 31 May 1978, few investigative accounts emerged in the French press simply because no coverage of the campaign was allowed.

Giscard determined to use the continent to extend French influence through the outside world. The Convention of Lomé, Togo, was the first of a series of five-yearly arrangements binding developing countries economically to the European Community. It was also, in a sense, a base for the start of the north–south dialogue which, by the end of the decade, had still to establish fairer arrangements between the wealthier nations of the industrialized northern hemisphere and the needier countries of the southern.

International disquiet nevertheless persisted over the emphasis Giscard tended to give to French, rather than to western, initiatives in the search for an improved world economic order. Those complaints were augmented by doubts about the wisdom of French associations with and support for extreme right-wing regimes in Africa, from Bokassa through the 1970s to that of South Africa. To men like former Ambassador Andrew Young in America and to Belgians suspicious of Giscard's aims in Zaire, it all had the whiff of neo-colonialism. In defence, an Elysée official commented to the author once, as if he was repeating a slogan, 'Andy Young is not a policy.' As for the Belgians he remarked: 'After what they did in the Congo they shouldn't talk. In transferring power they created chaos. In the chaos they tried but failed to keep the best bit of the country, Katanga, to themselves.' France takes the condition of Africa 'as we find it and we do our best, politically and economically, to keep the regimes we deal with in place against sudden or radical change'. Africa, he continued, needed development and peace and France remained resolved to help where help was welcome.

It was a rationale that did little to still the resentments of French socialists in the National Assembly or the more radical member-nations of the OAU.

Alliance of Autocrats

In the 1960s de Gaulle, in urging the unity of *francophonie*, deliberately dissociated France from NATO and the west generally. But after the deepening energy crisis of the 1970s and the challenges posed by the communist powers in Africa and the Middle East, French policy under Giscard gradually and subtly changed. There was greater cooperation on certain levels with other western countries. Paris began taking a more holistic view of the continent with French ministers seeking, where they could, to penetrate the once-exclusive preserves of Britain's former colonies; Zaire where the Belgians used to be the masters; even Portugal's old territories. Nigeria in the late 1970s had become France's most important trading partner in sub-Saharan Africa. Zaire's Mobutu tended to look more to Paris than to Brussels and entered the exclusive club of French-speaking African states. Also, despite the French military and mercenaries having interceded covertly, like the Americans, against Neto in the Angolan civil war, France was the first of the European Community countries to recognize the Luanda government in 1976, breaking an accord with its partners to act together.

Giscard, like de Gaulle, was seeking to retrieve France's old glory and a world role but by other methods. He did not hit upon the notion of an evolving European–Islamic–African partnership in a moment of absent-mindedness. It was no mere chance that Raymond Barre became his prime minister after playing a key role in David Rockefeller's trilateral commission. The trilateral approach appealed to him in national and international terms.

The French president's carefully calculated policy later emerged as a mirror-image of the Rockefeller commission's ninety-five-page analysis – elements of which were embodied, at least for a while, in the Carter administration's international policies. This study accepted that the superpower status of the Soviet Union was a fact of life and would be managed best if Washington, and the Europeans, were together to place greater emphasis on relations with Japan; more attention to the north–south dialogue; higher priorities on the issue of human rights.

Giscard had for some time been distancing himself from the confining principles of Gaullism. He was receptive to the ideas of the commission and wanted, discreetly, to move French policy closer to the Americans. It was easy for him to recognize that when Washington spoke of a closer relationship with the European allies it meant, essentially, West Germany, which possessed the strongest armed forces and the most powerful economy in allied Europe. The entire US business and military orientation for years had been towards the Germans. Britain was too weak, Italy was floundering and the French had left NATO's military system.

Giscard knew he could not lead France back into NATO without losing the support of the Gaullists and to lose that support would be to imperil his presidency. In the context of his relationship with the Carter team, therefore, it was essential for France to recognize the reality of West German supremacy in allied Europe. A German–American understanding, if not an alliance, was in the making. It was essential also for Giscard to seek new outlets for French leadership and Africa provided a ready setting.

Conditions for a French initiative in Africa – and in the Middle East, too – therefore existed. France had the experience. It had a ready-made network in francophone Africa. There was an African need for a European connection. Britain, in deep trouble over Zimbabwe and preoccupied with troubles at home, could not compete. West Germany encouraged the idea when Chancellor Helmut Schmidt reflected at a summit meeting of the nine European Community states in Copenhagen, 7 April 1978: 'France, for historical reasons, has a large and precious experience [of the Third World] which should be saved and used in the interest of all Europe.'[9]

If a German–American understanding relating to Europe was forming, it seemed, too, as if a French–German understanding over Africa had emerged without fuss or fanfare. Like Bismarck, Schmidt was telling the French to get busy in Africa so that the Germans could go about the more serious task of managing allied Europe.

The arrangement, in a variety of ways, suited Giscard. He had an entrenched position in Europe and could speak for the Community. The prospects in Africa were promising in the sector of raw materials and minerals. Relations with the Arab oil producers had been nurtured assiduously, and the Arabs needed European friends. French activism in Africa suited Carter's hawks like Zbigniew Brzezinski even though Andy Young might protest. Tests came first in 1977, again in 1978, with France's interventions in Katanga, and Giscard found that the Americans, like most of the French themselves, were behind him.

Some of France's actions in Africa undoubtedly offended several African leaders, even within the francophone zone. There were grumbles, too, in Belgium, Britain and among the Scandinavian allies. But the Americans and Germans were supporting him.

Giscard's attempts to preserve the *status quo* in large parts of Africa initially appeared to succeed. But by 1980 that policy had begun to crumble. A year later Giscard had lost the presidency.

Among the few francophone states to have registered successes in the 1970s were Cameroon, the Ivory Coast, Senegal and Djibouti which seemed like oases in the general context of African development. In other companion states of the system the outlook ranged from restless to dismal. The surface calm of some was belied by stirrings of opposition as new generations of politicians emerged with few of the elitist advantages that had attended their predecessors; Benin, the Congo, and Guinea were among them. Others were beset by internal strife or by war. Giscard chose to support King Hassan of Morocco in his quarrel over the Sahara with Algeria, the country to which the French were still devoting most aid. Mauritania and the Central African Republic became settings for French military intervention. Giscard withdrew from Chad seven months before that unhappy land fell to Libyan-led forces using Soviet and, ironically, French weapons, a withdrawal that was followed by a new oil-exploration agreement between Tripoli and a state-owned French oil group. In the controversy that ensued Giscard's government, despite denials, stood accused of sacrificing, for the sake of a few barrels of oil, a country France had created.

This was not all. In subcontinental Africa the French were not directly involved in the problems attending the black struggle for majority rule which was, for most African nations of whatever complexion, politically the all-important issue of their times. France had supported successive UN resolutions imposing sanctions on the then white-ruled Rhodesia and banning arms sales to South Africa. But a French company, Total, was first to break those sanctions with supplies of oil to the Rhodesians (and British firms were quick to follow). At the same time French arms kept finding their way to South Africa, leading Paris three times to declare separate, yet ineffective, embargoes designed to stop that traffic. Perhaps those ghostly embargoes had a secondary purpose, which could have been to distract attention from the $1,000-million sale of a nuclear-reactor complex to South Africa.

Militant black African states by 1980 were assailing Giscard's policies on a variety of grounds – notably over the Kolwezi airlift, France's support for an African security force in Shaba, and the abandonment of Chad. A more important development for Giscard personally was the rising tempo of controversy within France over the entire content of his Africa policy. François Mitterrand's socialists had denounced it consistently for years and so, too, had George Marchais's communists. But the most significant criticism came from Jacques Chirac, the Gaullist leader, who was scathing over Giscard's role in the progressive deterioration of relations with Algeria.

These were among other misgivings about Valéry Giscard d'Estaing's presidency of the Fifth Republic - misgivings that led to his humiliating electoral defeat on 10 May 1981 by the socialist Mitterrand. As if to emphasize the popular mood of disenchantment a French crowd, assembled outside the gates of the Elysée Palace on 21 May, greeted Giscard with shouts of 'Give us back our diamonds!' It was an expression of the widespread belief that France's former leader had not passed to the state all the gifts the tyrant dictator Bokassa claimed he had presented. Giscard stared stonily ahead as his limousine swept by. He had just, with customary haughtiness, surrendered his office to Mitterrand.

It was not accidental that two senior Socialists lost little time in the first full fine flush of victory to pledge publicly that Mitterrand's administration would give diplomatic and political support to all engaged in struggling for democratic rights and fighting racism. Party Secretary-General Lionel Jospin told a conference convened by the United Nations on 20 May that France's Socialist Party would support the imposition of economic sanctions against South Africa as one means of ending the *apartheid* system. His party, he said, also favoured direct aid for South Africa's militant black nationalists. Five days later Claude Cheysson, newly appointed foreign minister, plainly conscious of his new responsibilities, was more discreet. He spoke of France's backing for all 'denied their rights, . . . cast out by society, . . . harassed and sometimes condemned because they are different from those who govern them'.

Savouring these first tastes of the likely content of a new French foreign policy, Africans attending the 100-country conference in Paris (which the Americans, British and West Germans boycotted) confessed to feeling a surge of hope. But one veteran southern Africa liberation-movement leader added cautiously: 'After what we've been through in the past . . . seeing is believing . . .'

9. Britain

Britain's imperial mission in Africa ended on 18 April 1980, when the Union Jack was hauled down in Salisbury, Zimbabwe, 174 years after the British had established themselves in the Cape of Good Hope, at the tip of the subcontinent.[1] The long, slow struggle by the blacks of Zimbabwe for liberation was, in its outcome, both an epilogue and a prologue: an epilogue to the downfall of Portugal's empire in Africa and a prologue to the coming struggle for power in the Republic of South Africa. In between, there would be the Namibian chapter, itself emerging as a contest with an east–west dimension imposed upon an escalating conflict between a black majority striving to free the country and their white rulers. Situations throughout the region were inter-related: what happened in one territory shaped events in others.

The withdrawal of the Portuguese; Zimbabwe's emergence as a black-ruled republic; intensifying guerrilla warfare within and along Namibia's frontiers with Angola; and the ever-developing sophisticated resistance activities of the liberation movement inside the Republic; these had the combined effect in 1980 of compelling the Pretoria government to place South Africa on a war footing, with a well-oiled military machine engaging itself in overt and covert operations against its northern neighbours. In the twenty years from 1960 to 1980 the country's military spending had soared 550 per cent to approximately $3 thousand million yearly, according to published versions of the Republic's defence budgets.

There were rumblings of thunder in the south.

Gold, greed and an empire-builder's lust lured Cecil Rhodes to the land of Lobengula, king of the Ndebele, in 1888. He trekked north from the Cape to foil a Portuguese plan to seize all territory between Angola and Mozambique and so realize Lisbon's old dream of a transcontinental belt linking the Atlantic and Indian Oceans. By deceit and duplicity, Rhodes and his agents acquired what they portrayed as 'rights' to Lobengula's domain. They were a trickster's 'rights' which Britain subsequently inherited, then lost to the country's rebellious whites, and finally recovered, belatedly, in order to surrender sovereignty to the black majority.[2]

The process of surrendering sovereignty was prolonged, perhaps understandably after fourteen years of white rebellion, half the time taken up in meeting, yet not beating, the challenge of black guerrillas. A frail settlement reached after months of controversial negotiations in London, in late 1979, yielded a new constitution, a ceasefire, a tortuous process of transition and Zimbabwe's first election of an internationally recognized black majority government. For the sake of a precarious peace all the parties retreated from long-held positions of principle hoping, with more faith than conviction, that the compromise would hold. Repeatedly Britain's foreign secretary, Lord Carrington, urged the contenders to 'trust us'. But that trust in British even-handedness evaporated temporarily in the hot Salisbury summer almost as soon as Lord Soames, Britain's governor, set out to implement the settlement. Soon accusations began to fly that some of the guerrillas loyal to Robert Mugabe, a self-proclaimed socialist, were intimidating their opponents and breaching the truce. An estimated 6,000–7,000 of Mugabe's Zimbabwe African National Liberation Army (ZANLA) were on the loose. Little was said in answer to counter-charges that Bishop Abel Muzorewa's private army (renamed Auxiliaries, under white command and numbering more than 20,000) were themselves harassing if not frightening Muzorewa's opponents. To ZANLA and some Commonwealth, Asian, European and even American observers, it looked as if an informal, collusive alliance of whites and cooperative blacks had been formed, with British and South African backing, with the object of ensuring Mugabe's defeat. It was an open secret that the code guiding Soames's entourage – indeed Carrington's team, too, in London – was 'A–B–M', an acronym for 'Anybody–but–Mugabe'. Even if that was not the calculation it certainly was the widely-held suspicion among blacks and it served only to guarantee the stunning, landslide victory Mugabe achieved that made him an unchallengeable victor and premier. Thus he became the symbol of popular black protest – and hope – against continued white-managed domination of the country, whatever its form and whoever might agree to give it expression.

Once again, as in the Portuguese context, the world's major powers, with all their computerized logic, had failed to recognize the dynamics of revolutionary change. The British and South African governments, along with most white Rhodesians, were stunned by the size of Mugabe's victory; winning, as he did, nearly two-thirds of a 94 per cent turnout. The Soviet Union had long been counting on Joshua Nkomo's emergence as the leader of a coalition government; not least because of Mugabe's supposed orientation towards Peking. The United States, influenced by British forecasts, had expected an alliance between Nkomo and Bishop Abel Muzorewa that would have kept Mugabe in opposition. Even Tanzanian President Julius Nyerere, alarmed by what he took to be signs of British bias, had assumed that the governor, Lord Soames, under Carrington's direction, would so arrange the political gerrymandering that Mugabe would be denied leadership.

'The British cannot use us in the Commonwealth cynically, dishonestly, perfidiously,' Nyerere told journalists two days before voting began on 27 February. 'We cannot accept the government in Rhodesia which has been concocted for the purpose of satisfying a bunch of racists in Rhodesia, South Africa and Britain.' The Tanzanian leader was as premature in prejudging the outcome as he insisted the British were in attempting to influence it.[3] Four days later, on 4 March, when Mugabe's victory was complete, Nyerere acknowledged that he had been mistaken. 'This is not the first time I have been proved wrong,' he said. 'This is not the first time I am very pleased I was wrong.'

It was yet another classic example of the way the logic of white outsiders was shown to have little relevance to African experience, and not least because few whites possessed either the capacity to identify or the ability to communicate with the blacks. A striking contrast in perception was evident nevertheless in the attitude of an eleven-nation Commonwealth observer team, on site to check the fairness and freedom of the electoral process. The group arrived less than three weeks before the ballot. Within four days of their arrival a key member telephoned Commonwealth Secretary-General Shridath Ramphal in London with an initial assessment: 'It's going to be a Mugabe landslide.'

Patently a 'Stop-Mugabe' strategy was under way. James MacManus of the *Guardian* reported after the election on 5 March: 'What the British, Rhodesians and South Africans privately agreed [in conjunction with several countries] was the need to cut Mr Mugabe out of power if possible ... The idea of Mr Mugabe in power thus became equated with a white exodus, civil conflict and possible South African intervention. Therefore when Lord Soames arrived in Rhodesia on 12 December, the villain of the piece had been clearly identified to all but Mr Mugabe's close backers in Tanzania and Mozambique.' The Tanzanians had put it officially on record before the election, despite British dismissals of their charges as 'outrageous'. Tanzanian complaints, in a 24 February document, circulated to Commonwealth governments, noted:

1. Rhodesian forces, augmented by Muzorewa's Auxiliaries, were being allowed to roam the country on the pretext of preserving law and order, restoring public services and, as Rhodesian authorities put it, 'countering the socialist ideology of the guerrillas'. This contravened

the London agreement which required all forces to remain in their garrisons.

2. South African army units and regular soldiers had been allowed to stay on in the country after the ceasefire, again in breach of the London agreements. The Republic's units guarding the northern approaches to the Beitbridge were asked to leave after a while but an unquantifiable number remained integrated in Rhodesia's security forces.[4]

3. At least two attempts on Mugabe's life were made. Both failed. One was by members of the Selous Scouts, an élite tracker group whose members often posed as ZANLA guerrillas. Rhodesian authorities acknowledged that two army men died while attempting to destroy a church in outer Salisbury, in an evident attempt to discredit Mugabe's followers.

In the aftermath of the election, these incidents were widely seen as white scare tactics. The fact that they proved counter-productive underlined the political awareness of Rhodesia's black voters. Each attempt on Mugabe's life probably earned him 100,000 votes. Each British charge that his own forces, rather than the Auxiliaries, were intimidating their political foes strengthened his position. Failure of British, South African, white Rhodesian and other observers to recognize this merely confirmed their ignorance of the sensitivities of the Africans.

Yet out of that failure, new opportunities and new hope of conciliation arose. If Mugabe had emerged as the victor without an overall majority, there would have been scope for Soames, as Prime Minister Margaret Thatcher had plainly indicated, to assign the premiership to someone else, probably to Nkomo. If that had happened, as Mugabe himself forewarned, the struggle for power would have been resumed in battle, with results that could hardly be estimated. The help of outsiders – most probably the communist countries – might well have been invoked. There would have been the danger, in such a contingency, of South African intervention, as high officials of the Republic had suggested to journalists before the election.

Mugabe, with his victory and subsequent commitment to a go-slow fulfilment of his manifesto, transformed the elements of tragedy into the promise of triumph – taking the form of a brave new experiment in multiracialism. If fulfilled, it could offer a model for the resolution of conflict looming over Zimbabwe's neighbour to the south.

The Luck of Lord Soames

Soames, though, seemed to see it all as a gamble for peace which, if it had failed, could have meant war for southern Africa with dangers of

Soviet-backed intervention. As he told it to the author, in a 27 May 1980 interview, the way he presided over Rhodesia's transition to the Republic of Zimbabwe suggested that political brinkmanship, threats and elements of bluff contributed to an outcome that surprised a sceptical international community. The former governor of Britain's last African colony disclosed that he had devised a strategy designed: to defuse an explosive situation; to reduce the level of intimidation he said was being used by Mugabe's followers in the countryside during the truce and electoral period; to allay the suspicions of nervous whites and security forces that they would be left to the mercy of the bush fighters; and to ensure that all contestants and a watching world would respect the result.

He disclosed that he had assumed emergency powers enabling him to ban Mugabe's party from the election – but never intended using them. He delayed telling Mugabe so, until the eve of the balloting. And he did so in a fateful man-to-man encounter that transformed confrontation into cooperation, tension into trust, after weeks of angry argument. His threat of a ban, he claimed, succeeded in reducing intimidation.

'It was the first time we'd met alone,' Soames recalled, in speaking of his 26 February session with Mugabe. 'We were having some pretty confrontational meetings in the previous four weeks because there was a lot of intimidation going on, most laid at the door of his people in the countryside. I couldn't see him too long before the election because what I was going to say was that I wasn't going to proscribe his party. I couldn't tell him too soon because he was a bit fearful of this.' If the threatened use of those powers had been lifted prematurely, he added, the intimidation might have increased. 'We had a very good talk and it was then that I saw clearly the general direction he would go as prime minister.'

Soames nevertheless acknowledged that if Mugabe had emerged winner with less than fifty seats – meaning without an overall margin in the hundred-member parliament – it would have been possible for Nkomo and Muzorewa to form a coalition government with the support of the bloc of twenty whites whose seats had been reserved for them. Such a result was what white Rhodesians and South Africans, the Soviet Union and the British themselves would have preferred at that time.

Zimbabwe's assumption of statehood was something to celebrate by a world gloomily witnessing revolution in Iran, a Soviet invasion of Afghanistan, heightening east–west tensions and deepening international recession. Predictably, concerned powers rationalized the significance of the event to conform with their own interests. The British, who presided over the settlement, viewed it as an overdue assertion of their long-latent diplomatic skills. The Americans claimed credit for contributing, at crucial moments, to the evolution of the ultimate compromise although assistant secretary for African Affairs, Richard M. Moose Jr, could not resist interpreting the development as the Soviet Union's 'greatest reverse in Africa for years'. This was a far cry from President Carter's definition of policy towards the continent in 1977 when he said that the US aim was to help build 'a strong, prosperous Africa at peace with itself ... not to gain some advantage over the Soviets, Cubans or any other power'. The Russians drew at least lukewarm comfort from the victory of Patriotic Front guerrillas, despite the fact that they had counted on Nkomo, not Mugabe, emerging as prime minister. South Africans were plainly stunned, in spite of reports that they had expected the result. They remained in a state of political shock for months, while adjusting to the failure of their own overt and covert efforts to promote a victory for Muzorewa and his white allies. As for Africans themselves, Mugabe's total triumph was held from the Cape to Cairo to vindicate the proposition that recourse to arms was justifiable for a subject people fighting for freedom.

Britain's retreat from Africa was seen in the long term to have been more graceful than glorious, after the fourteen years of real or imagined impotence over Rhodesia. It was a retreat that contrasted with an otherwise reasoned, if rushed, record of decolonization. The rebellion, the war, and the pain and anger of the final exit could have been avoided. The British, after all, had led in the process of dismantling war-bruised Europe's great African empires. Belgium and France, Spain and Portugal, found themselves compelled sooner or later to follow that lead. Why, in fact, was it Britain which had set the pace? Some suggested it was a recognition of necessity. Others considered that factors of self-interest prevailed among the policy-makers, who believed that it would be ultimately more rewarding to retire gracefully than to withdraw in enforced disarray. The truth may have embodied both factors. Britain, once the supreme imperial power, had been so drained and exhausted by world war, by economic tribulations and by the trauma of failure at Suez that it no longer possessed the resources, energy or will to contend with the rising forces of African nationalism, especially in territories with a dubious economic, strategic or political value. At a time, too, of shrinking global commitments, it became a strategic luxury to maintain footholds in Africa that offended indigenous sensitivities.

Thus within roughly a decade, beginning with Ghana (then the Gold Coast) in 1957, independence was conferred upon fifteen African countries, sprawling over three million square miles and taking in nearly 140 million subjects of Queen Elizabeth II.

However, in the early 1960s, when it came to the matter of Zimbabwe's future, successive British governments ducked the issue of how and to whom power should be transferred. Since 1923 the self-governing colony had been under the rule of fewer than a quarter-million whites, outnumbered more than twenty to one by blacks. In an age of anti-colonialism, in a continent of rising nationalism, the British could hardly repeat the monumental blunder that they had committed over South Africa after the Anglo-Boer war, at the turn of the century. Then they had simply transferred sovereignty to a white minority dedicated to perpetuating racism. But if Conservative and Labour leaders alike were unable in good conscience to vest power in Zimbabwe's whites, they found it equally impossible to pluck up the courage to bequeath sovereignty to the black majority; or even to insist upon and implement transitional constitutional arrangements based upon genuine racial equality and partnership.

London's decision, therefore, was to take no decision, effectively leaving it to Zimbabweans themselves to work out or fight out their own destiny. This is precisely is what did happen, with the prime ministers of the two countries, Sir Harold Wilson and Ian Smith, playing into each other's hands and creating the conditions for the warfare that would follow. For months Smith had been advertising his intention to seize independence illegally if it was not given to him formally. Wilson went through all the motions of attempting to dissuade Smith from embarking upon what later would be denounced as the course of 'treason' and 'rebellion'. Yet, at a critical point in the late summer of 1965, Wilson announced publicly that his administration would not consider using force if Smith were to issue his long-threatened Unilateral Declaration of Independence (UDI). The Rhodesian leader, once a Royal Air Force fighter pilot, recognized a green light when he saw one. Symbolically Smith chose Armistice Day, 11 November 1965, to proclaim his UDI. It was an Armistice Day that marked the beginning of a new war, rather than the end of an old one.

What followed is history: the structure of a reinforced white supremacist system, modelled on *apartheid* principles; paramilitary intervention by South Africa to sustain Smith in office; mandatory sanctions, including an oil embargo, which major British oil companies were quick to circumvent, with the knowledge of key British Labour government ministers and without ever being prosecuted; the build-up of black guerrilla armies, helped by the Soviet Union, China and other communist powers. It was a cruel and vicious war that ground on for years, with white Rhodesians launching devastating air-raids against neighbouring black states – Zambia, Mozambique, Angola – that provided sanctuary for refugees and bush fighters.

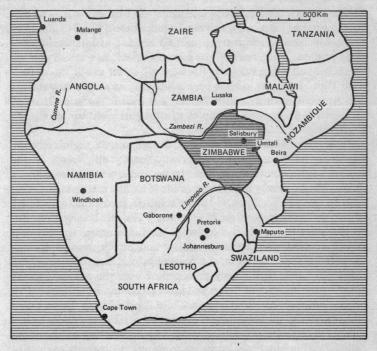

Fig. 12: Zimbabwe's key position in southern Africa
SOURCE: *The New York Times*, 18 April 1980.

This then was the unnecessary war, the war that did not have to happen but for Britain's protestations of impotence, its miscalculations, and its tacit collaboration with Smith and with those Wilson called his band of 'small and frightened' men.[5] The cost in men, money and arms plus the loss of Britain's credibility around the world will almost certainly never be known. At the start of the 1980s, even as Mugabe's duly-elected government was struggling with a spate of inherited and current difficulties, the bills were still coming in.[6] And Zimbabwe's burdens were by no means all; its Zambian and Mozambican neighbours had been economically devastated, too, besides having sustained a toll of military and civilian casualties running into tens of thousands.

Strategy of the Widening Laager

The emergence of Zimbabwe as a black-ruled state, immediately neighbouring the Republic, hardly simplified the nature of the crisis extending throughout Southern Africa.[7] There was still a Soviet–

Cuban–East German presence in Angola and Mozambique. The disputed future of Namibia, involving Angola where SWAPO guerrillas could still count on sanctuary, possessed international dimensions because of the UN interest and the investments of the western powers. On the ground SWAPO guerrillas were still on the attack, more effectively than in the past, despite huge South African air and land thrusts into Angolan territory, ostensibly in 'hot pursuit' of guerrillas and their bases. An explosive complex of problems piled up testing the governments of east and west alike.

At the centre of that wider complex, though, was the regime of white supremacy in South Africa. Internally, nearly all aspects of the country's existence were dominated by the unresolved relationship of a restless black majority living in servitude to a white master race. Going into the 1980s P. W. Botha, the prime minister, proclaimed a readiness to give the unacceptable face of *apartheid* a less provocative look. But no cosmetics seemed likely to change the fundamental features of a system evolved over centuries of law and practice which institutionalized discrimination on the basis of colour. Internationally, the country's rulers were chiefly preoccupied with the assumed threat posed by the advance of Soviet and general communist influence. In a preface to South Africa's Defence White Paper of 1979, Botha called attention to the 'imperialism and expansion' of unnamed major *powers* (plural) in the subcontinental bastion. The interlocking nature of the national and international problems menacing the security of the Republic was underlined in the prognosis offered by Botha's Defence Department. It predicted mounting Soviet support for guerrillas operating throughout southern Africa; introduction of East German combat units into Angola and Mozambique; and the consequent need for a regional defence system under Pretoria's leadership which would take in an 'independent' Namibia, Botswana, Lesotho, Zimbabwe and the black 'homelands' being created within the confines of the Republic.

Botha's rationale for a Fortress Southern Africa strategy presupposed ultimate unwillingness by the western powers to become identified, or as Third World countries might see it, tainted with any sort of overt association with South Africa. His concept was to evolve a subcontinental security system with lots of economic care packages to go with it, in a region embracing fifty–sixty million people endowed with vast mineral and other valued resources and able therefore to survive almost any challenge. It would be a security zone bounded initially by the Zambezi and Cunene Rivers but capable eventually of extension northwards to take in Zambia and Zaire. Since the prospect of success for so ambitious a scenario was very remote, Botha often spoke of a readiness to move towards a form of multiracialism

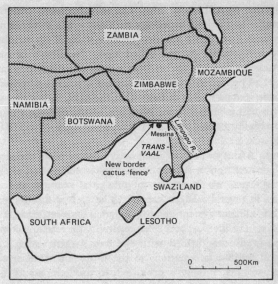

Fig. 13: South African border 'fence' against Zimbabwe

that would yet leave the essentials of white supremacy inviolate.

The pattern of Pretoria's politico-strategic thinking appeared to rest on several other assumptions, some of them obviously untenable. These assumptions were that:

1. Britain would manipulate the transference of power plainly to ensure the rise of a moderate and collaborative government in Zimbabwe. It would be one willing to live under the protective umbrella of the South Africans who, in turn, would help underwrite and develop its economic potential. If such a regime in Salisbury were to be disowned or assailed by radicals inside or outside Zimbabwe, the Republic would be ready to defend it, however the world might react.

2. Five key western powers negotiating with South Africa to settle the future of neighbouring Namibia would prefer the emergence of a tame, middle-of-the-road black regime to which the Republic also could safely yield the trappings of independence. Such a solution would eliminate what, for both South Africa and the west, could be the danger of a takeover by the radical SWAPO, which had long been recognized by the United Nations as the sole legitimate representative of the Namibian people. South Africa had advised the western powers – Britain, the USA, France, West Germany and Canada – that it was not prepared to surrender Namibia under any other conditions. As proof of its intentions, it had begun by 1980 to set up a Namibian

administration on multiracial lines. The self-appointed western 'Contact Group' – and Britain especially within it – was sorely tempted to go along with just such a solution because each of its members had extensive investments in and relied upon Namibia's considerable mineral riches. For years the territory's uranium, diamonds and other resources had poured into Europe's nuclear reactors and other industries. But it seemed highly dubious that the UN, in law the acknowledged trusteeship authority for Namibia, would endorse a transfer of power to a regime beholden to and reliant upon the goodwill of Pretoria for its existence.

3. South Africa's vision of itself at the centre of an economic and military constellation of subcontinental states committed to the anti-communist cause would appeal to influential political and defence authorities in several western capitals. The idea of a self-supporting black–white alliance system in a region laden with resources would, if it worked, relieve the west of the responsibility for resisting communist advances. It also conformed with the west's own search for non-violent and multiracial solutions to the problems of an area had it controlled so long. Finally it promised, in the latter's and in South Africa's analyses, to stabilize the Cape sea route by lessening the danger of internal upheavals, thereby contributing to the general security of the west.

There seemed to be some wishful thinking in the assumption that events in Africa would mark time while white South Africa set about deploying black millions, near and far, in a forward defence system to protect its modern laager. It could be seen as an extension of the master–servant relationship on which the ideology of *apartheid* rested. Fallacies vitiated the logic of Pretoria's concepts. The rise of Zimbabwean, Namibian and other black leaders playing the role of Uncle Tom would not guarantee an end of internal turbulence. The presence of the Russians, Cubans or East Germans could not be wished away. Nor was it likely that they would passively witness the destruction of a widely recognized national liberation movement. The vulnerability of the oil route around the Cape for a decade had been greatly exaggerated. The 1979 crisis in Iran demonstrated that the greater danger of disrupted oil supplies lay in a spontaneous, or induced, change of a single government or policy in oil-rich regions.

Storms of struggle gathering over the subcontinent pointed to the emergence of southern Africa as a flashpoint region, where the east–west contest might merge with a black–white confrontation. The situation possessed global implications, particularly for multiracial societies and not least for the USA. Outside Nigeria, the United States has the biggest black community in the world. It was a danger which most governments, statesmen and politicians of all colours and creeds found hard to face.

South Africa's leaders, long convinced that the sanctity of white supremacy was at stake, acted systematically to meet the dangers head-on. From 1960 to 1980 they built up their military power to meet any conceivable challenge by air, land or sea. Their capacity to manufacture nuclear weapons was unquestioned, even by sympathetic authorities in Washington and Paris.[8] The only issue in doubt was whether the Republic had, by 1980, begun building an actual nuclear arsenal.

It was inevitable, therefore, that those black states which considered themselves potential targets of attack would turn ultimately to one or other superpower either for means or for guarantees of protection. The case of Zambian President Kenneth Kaunda, in this context, illuminated the African dilemma. Kaunda was described even by antagonistic whites as a moderate, dedicated to what he himself called Christian humanism rather than to orthodox socialism. He led a country which had never known real peace since independence. From 1964, for a decade, the Portuguese rulers of Mozambique and Angola had constantly attacked his eastern and western provinces. From 1966 Rhodesian and South African white forces together, over a thirteen-year period, had thrust into his territory, as deeply as Lusaka, the capital, in search they said of guerrillas, and destroying bridges, roads, and refugee camps. Kaunda's appeals for defensive weapons met with unsatisfactory British and negative US responses. Ultimately Kaunda felt compelled to turn to the Soviet Union and he negotiated the purchase of about a dozen MIG-21 jet fighters, plus a range of other modern weapons, at an estimated cost of up to $150 million.[9]

Winds of Change and Changing Winds

Afrikaners of the ruling Nationalist Party stirred restlessly in the Cape Town parliament that summer's day in 1960 as Macmillan approached his solemn peroration. Dr Hendrik Verwoerd, the prime minister, stared stonily ahead.

'The great issue in the second half of the twentieth century is whether the uncommitted peoples of Asia and Africa will move to the East or the West,' the British leader said with prescience. 'Will they be drawn into the communist camp or will the great experiments in self-government that are now being made in Asia and Africa prove so successful and, by their example, so compelling that the balance will come down in favour of freedom and order and justice.'[10]

For South Africa's rulers the suggestion that black nationalism was a force to be reckoned with was anathema. To urge that it should be placated with such democratic nonsense as 'experiments in self-govern-ment' was worse. Sixteen months afterwards, Verwoerd led South Africa out of the Commonwealth rather than bow before the arguments of fellow-members that *apartheid* was inconsistent with their adopted principles of racial equality.

Nevertheless Macmillan's words were received in many lands and places as an essay in realism and in courage, too, considering the locale in which they were uttered. Oddly, in the debate that rumbled on for years, protagonists and antagonists alike were deafeningly silent on the moralities involved in the liberation process or in the desire to make amends in the future for the inequities endured by subject peoples in the past and present.

The wind of change became a tempest sooner, probably, than Mac-millan himself could have anticipated. It began at Sharpeville, along the Vaal River, just forty-six days after he spoke. A motley crowd of blacks, protesting peacefully against the country's hated pass laws, turned and fled when suddenly, panicky white police opened aimless fire. More than 150 fell dead and wounded before the fusillade; with official investigators reporting that most had bullets in their backs. In the years that followed thunder rumbled over the land; bringing, in 1976, a flash storm to Johannesburg's black, overcrowded dormitory city of Soweto.[11] There teenage and younger pupils walked out of schools in defiance of a government edict (later withdrawn) that they should be taught some subjects in Afrikaans, rather than all in the English lan-guage. So began a blood-letting that went on for months countrywide, claiming a toll estimated between 500 and 1,000 dead and more than 10,000 wounded. A state investigator reported in early 1980 that the tragedy of Soweto was attributable not to communist or other alien influences but to the failures of *apartheid* itself.

The road from Sharpeville to Soweto and beyond was littered with other nameless and numberless corpses. There were also those who, like black consciousness leader, Steve Biko, died in police custody. There were others slain in night vengeance raids on real or suspected informers, guerrillas, saboteurs and on those supposedly trying to escape.[12] Sharpeville and Soweto emerged, consequently, as political symbols remembered outside, as well as inside, the country for their connotations of a frightened white society at bay. Each event generated tensions which, in their own way and perhaps even only temporarily, shook the South African system to its foundations. Both alarmed foreign investors of the west who, confusing black protest against white oppression with imminent red revolution, with-drew their funds until stability returned. But South Africa's rulers

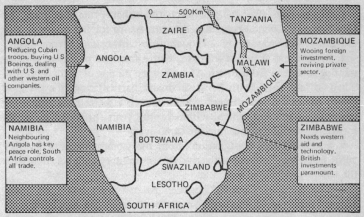

Fig. 14: Black states in southern Africa trading with the west
SOURCE: *Christian Science Monitor*, 25 April 1980.

permitted no threat to relax their hold on the levers of real power.

Pretoria instead went about applying its crude technique of beheading the leadership of just about every untamed black and white opposition organization in sight, from student societies to political and cultural groups. Through the 1960s and 1970s thousands were jailed either for specific or undefined offences, often under renewable ninety-day detention orders, without trial.

In time, internal and external confidence was restored, as Pretoria displayed a capacity to exert control. After a decent interval, when the killings were seen to have stopped, it was bonanza time again for a country that had drawn itself back from the brink. In a world made uncertain by other events – the Arab–Israeli wars, Vietnam, the 1973 fivefold increase in oil prices – gold, uranium and the whole range of South Africa's other much-needed stock of strategic metals and minerals took on a new significance and, coincidentally, record prices. Euphoria gripped the nation as foreign investors, governments and speculators scrambled out of money into commodities. Despite inflation at 14 per cent and two million out of twenty-four million blacks without jobs, the deputy governor of the South African Reserve Bank could, in early 1980, urge his countrymen: 'Prepare to meet thy boom!'[13]

Few Britons openly questioned the wisdom of Macmillan's call for a closer identification with the interests of black Africa. Yet, soon enough, a gap that ultimately became a gulf developed between the prime minister's solemn words and the deeds of his own and subsequent governments. This is the record:

1. Eleven days after the 21 March 1960 Sharpeville shootings, the UN Security Council condemned South Africa for the massacre and urged it to work towards racial equality. Britain abstained from voting.

2. Britain and America in 1950 jointly financed processes for extracting uranium from South Africa's huge dumps of spent gold ore. Then in late 1960, with West Germany participating, they helped South Africa's Atomic Energy Board launch a secret programme for uranium enrichment which, within twenty years, provided materials for use in manufacturing nuclear explosives.

3. South Africa's 'resignation' from the Commonwealth, in May 1961, in no way interrupted active British military collaboration with the newly-proclaimed Republic.

4. The Security Council, between August 1963 and June 1964, adopted three resolutions urging member-states to stop supplying arms to South Africa because *apartheid* policies were being intensified. Britain, France, West Germany and Italy excused themselves from observing the voluntary embargo, arguing that the weapons they were selling could not be used for internal repression. American corporations evaded the embargo, too.

5. Two months after UDI, Wilson averted a breakdown of the Commonwealth system with an assurance that an international ban on oil supplies would bring Smith's regime to its knees 'in a matter of weeks rather than months'. He had been warned by Washington before UDI that the oil embargo would not work. Shortly after his assurance, Wilson and his fellow-ministers learned that the embargo *was* being broken by way of South Africa and the Portuguese colonies. Later they discovered that two British-registered oil multinationals, Shell and the parastatal British Petroleum Company, were among the sanctions-busters. Neither company was ever prosecuted.[14]

6. Edward Heath, then Conservative prime minister, in January 1971, again almost broke the Commonwealth by announcing his intention to sell weapons of maritime defence to South Africa despite the UN embargo on arms sales. At one stormy private meeting with President Nyerere, who had come to plead for rejection of the proposed arms deal, an angry Heath warned in words like these: 'If you persist in your attitude, we [the British] will drop Africa, and you'll never be able to put it together again!' In another session at 10 Downing Street with Kaunda, who had come to make the same case as Nyerere, Heath's blank refusal caused the Zambian president to leave the dinner party in tears.[15]

There were other examples of how Macmillan's successors and officials manoeuvred and manipulated to transform his 'wind of change' into a 'change of wind'. British, along with other western, firms invested massively in key South African industries. Crucial sectors of the Republic's nuclear energy programme were funded despite Pretoria's refusal to adhere to the world-wide Nuclear Non-Proliferation Treaty. The attitudes of both Britain and South Africa towards the Rhodesian rebellion became increasingly more tolerant. British intelligence co-operation with the South Africans, Portuguese and white Rhodesians was never disrupted. Britain's voting pattern in the Security Council was consistently protective of the South Africans, Portuguese and even the Rhodesians. When African and Asian nations, usually with the support of the communist countries, sought to initiate punitive measures as a way of compelling the white minority regimes to ease or abandon their repressive policies against the blacks, invariably Britain and France, with occasionally the Americans, hurried to the rescue. One such situation developed in October 1974, when Britain, France and the United States joined in vetoing a Security Council resolution that called for South Africa's expulsion from the world body.[16] The decision of the western powers might have had some excuse in principle. In practice it placed them, at least in the perspective of Third World countries, on the side of the white supremacists.

How was it possible that a political premise laid down without apparent dispute by a British prime minister could have been rendered virtually meaningless in its fulfilment? Was it conceivable that Macmillan had indulged in an empty rhetorical exercise to project a contemporary, post-imperial image to impress the leaders of awakened Africa? If he said what he meant and meant what he said, did he not know how his subordinates were destroying his own and his country's credibility? Could it have been, as he humbly confessed to parliament after being confronted with the facts of the John Profumo affair, that 'nobody told me'?

Big issues of collective cabinet and individual ministerial accountability lay behind questions like these. They assumed an even more important dimension as a consequence of the state investigator's disclosures that Shell and BP evasions of Britain's sanction laws took place with the full knowledge of named government ministers, who then disavowed personal responsibility. The issues were given greater visibility still by a former Labour cabinet minister, Tony Benn, who claimed that his officials had failed to inform him of contractual arrangements for the purchase of uranium from Namibia, in contravention of UN General Assembly resolutions endorsed by the International Court of Justice at the Hague. The British Foreign Office reply to that has been that *no* General Assembly or Security Council decisions are binding on member-states except those taken under chapter seven of the Charter relating to threats to the peace.[17]

In Britain, prime ministers and their cabinet colleagues can enunciate the noblest of intentions, but, by the nature of the civil service system, they must leave fulfilment of policies to officialdom. After years of sophisticated, subtle practice, the British civil service has evolved a system vesting effective administrative power not in the domain of the elected political leadership but in the control of perhaps 100–150 well-placed, highly-intelligent permanent officials, who ensure the continuity of policy in what they consider to be the national interest. These officials head key ministries and offices, which include the Treasury, the Foreign and Commonwealth Office, the Defence Ministry, and, when their responsibilities are involved, the Home Office, the ministries of Technology, Trade, Energy and so on. The top people have their own network and standards. They are able to place their own emphasis on the implementation of a policy. Most rose to the higher echelons by virtue of their backgrounds, the schools and universities they attended, the values they share and their capacity to interpret Britain's interests in terms acceptable to the establishment.

The Option of Not Choosing

One of the most revealing interpretations of Britain's approach to Africa was offered in 1971 not by a British foreign secretary but by the serving British ambassador to Pretoria. Sir Arthur Snelling qualified his account by stressing that it was a personal view. But ambassadors present personal opinions at their own peril if they differ from official policy. He spoke before the collapse of the Portuguese empire, before Zimbabwean guerrillas had moved into top gear, before the Namibian situation had become acute. His starting point was to compare the importance to Britain economically of what was then black Africa and white Africa, and found that in trade and investment terms the balance was roughly equal. (Since then British trade with black Africa has easily outstripped business with southern Africa, partly because Nigeria has now replaced the Republic as Britain's biggest market.)

'The political inference to be drawn from this [roughly equal balance] is that, insofar as the British are a nation of shopkeepers, they must conduct their relations with Africa in such a way that they are not forced to choose between white and black Africa,' Snelling said. He estimated that Britain's economic transactions with all Africa at that time represented no more than one-tenth of its total global trading.

Turning then to security interests the ambassador rated Africa 'fairly low' in the list of east–west danger zones. (That rating has since changed.) The two greatest military perils lay in the possibilities of 'racial war between black and white Africa' and the 'maritime threat which is imposed by the growing Soviet naval power in the South Atlantic and Indian Oceans'. It was a paramount British interest to ward off the danger of racial warfare because of Britain's 'vast economic interests' in black and white Africa and because about 100,000 Britons in black Africa would become hostages in a war situation.

If, none the less, race war were to break out, Britain's resolve then was, and would remain, to be non-aligned, just as it had been in the Indian Pakistan, the Middle East and the Vietnam conflicts. On east–west issues, however, Britain could not be neutral. That explained Britain's concern over what he called the Russian 'maritime threat' in the region. The Russian navy had become second only to the United States' as 'a politico-military force on a global scale'. Much of Britain's ocean traffic passes the South African coast. Britain thus would become 'intolerably vulnerable' to any change in the balance of naval strength. That accounted for Britain's limited collaboration with South Africa in the past. It had been accepted as a political reality, nevertheless, that African member-states of the Commonwealth would see British supplies of defensive weapons to South Africa as 'symbolic support for *apartheid*' – and therefore it could have the effect of driving them into the arms of the communists. This made it imperative for Britain to avert the need to choose between black and white Africa.

'There is an area of common interest between Britain and South Africa in that both of us would be adversely affected by the spread of communist influence in Africa,' Snelling continued. 'But the question which the British government continually ask themselves over such problems as Rhodesia, or South-West Africa [Namibia], or arms for South Africa, or other issues affecting this part of the world, is whether Britain will alienate black African countries to such an extent that some of them will react against British interests and turn to the communists in desperation for support.' That seemed to echo Macmillan's thesis.

Ambassador Snelling, in summing up, defined two principal options pressed on Britain by those who favoured support either for black or white Africa.

First, because racialism was 'the greatest of all evils', transcending other forms of injustice, Britain on moral grounds should help those determined to bring about the downfall of South Africa's *apartheid* system, using financial, economic and military pressures, boycotts, sanctions and social and political ostracism.

Secondly, because communism was the greatest enemy facing both Britain and South Africa, and because some African countries already were under communist influence, Britain should, on grounds of morality and self-interest, accept the Republic as its only true and reliable friend on the continent.

The British government rejected the logic and prescribed conduct suggested in the first of those views. It considered the second approach to be 'a surefire way of converting all the uncommitted neutrals into enemies', and that would not have been in the British interest.

'Britain therefore picks her way through the African jungle conscious that down every path there are half-concealed tripwires,' Snelling concluded.[18]

A British policy of non-alignment in any confrontation between black and white Africa, as Snelling portrayed it, was held by each side to be not only mistaken but also immoral. It accounted, on the one hand, for the persistent pressures exerted by African (and Asian) member-states of the Commonwealth on successive British leaders for a more active commitment in the struggle to arraign South Africa, so as to compel a change in its racial practices. It explained, on the other hand, the erosion of Britain's influence and authority in white Africa, except at times when it became clear that in reality the British were defending white interests.

Yet to most black leaders it was not the professions of British non-alignment that were most provoking. The standards and self-interest even of a 'nation of shopkeepers', if loyally observed, might have commanded a certain respect. The complaint of the Africans was that Britain's posture of non-alignment in the continental setting was a sham; and that in virtually every crucial situation which arose between 1960 and 1980, the British effectively sided with the whites.

A fundamental principle binding the forty-four member-states of the Commonwealth together had long been that each respected the interests of others. Without diminishing any member's freedom of action, this principle implied that no one would deliberately undercut the interests of its partners. Another principle of the multiracial Commonwealth, spanning as it does six continents and embracing all racial groups, was total opposition to discrimination on grounds of colour or creed.

By virtue of history, relative economic strength and political influence, Britain was always looked upon by its partners as occupying a special position, with the obligation, as the first among equals, to set an example in fulfilment of shared values. It was in such a context that African countries, in particular, tended to examine Britain's relationship with white Africa; they learned, over the years, that British leaders needed no lectures about the injustices, degradations and humiliations imposed upon the blacks of South Africa by their white rulers. They came to expect, however, that the British in time would become sensitive to the fact that most Africans felt demeaned by the sufferings of their fellows whose colour they shared. That was what African nationalism, black consciousness, or the African identity was all about. This was also what lay behind the refusal of most black states to compromise with the South Africans and other white supremacists on the issue of racism. 'If anyone fails to understand the depths of Africa's feelings on this matter, then they do not understand *apartheid* or they do not understand the reaction of people who have suffered from racial discrimination,' Nyerere said in Singapore in 1971. 'It is in fact impossible for Africa to understand how anyone who really opposes racialism can fail to share Africa's hostility to the South African regime, even if they are not prepared to do anything against that regime.'[19]

Against that background, Africans scrutinized Britain's approach to Africa for its *realpolitik* content. They concluded that, on three priority issues in the subcontinent, London was in no way non-aligned but instead concerned more with preserving its own material investment and trading stake. These related to:

1. The stealthy build-up of South Africa's 'candidate' membership of the exclusive nuclear weapons club, with British and general western help.

2. The passivity displayed towards South Africa's illegal occupation of Namibia for reasons connected with the trust territory's uranium, diamond and other mineral resources.

3. Signs of connivance between the British, Zimbabwean whites and South Africans to keep the new state of Zimbabwe 'safe from communism', perhaps as a base of future action to reduce, if not to expel, the Soviet–Cuban presence in Angola and Mozambique.[20]

Three brief case histories which follow tell their own stories. They concern: a suspected detonation of a nuclear weapon deep in the South Atlantic in September 1979; preparations for what appeared to be a nuclear test-blast in the Kalahari Desert in August 1977; and the involvement of key western powers in building up the Republic's capabilities to develop its nuclear power resources and technology, among other reasons because of South Africa's access to assured supplies of uranium.

The Light in the Southern Sky

It could have been a streak of lightning that brightened the southern hemisphere sky on the night of 22 September 1979. But, after fading, the brilliant flash reappeared a second before vanishing.

The double-pulse of light south of the Cape of Good Hope resembled the signature of a low-yield nuclear explosion. It was detected by two sensors, or 'bangmeters', aboard a nine-year-old American Vela satellite in elliptical orbit from 5,400 to 69,000 miles above the earth, launched for the precise purpose of monitoring nuclear test-blasts. Looking down upon vast expanses of land and ocean, the satellite told little more than that the flash occurred at some place within a 4,500-square-mile area between Antarctica and southernmost Africa.

After a round-the-world check of all monitoring operations, the CIA advised congressional committees of two other pieces of evidence, which tended circumstantially to support the belief that South Africa may have detonated its first nuclear device. The first was that a task force of South African naval ships that night were engaged in a secret exercise, roughly in the same area as the suspected explosion. The other was that scientists at Areibo, Puerto Rico, sighted through the world's biggest radio telescope a ripple moving through the ionosphere a few hours after the double-flash had been detected. 'This ripple was consistent with the effects of a shock wave displacing electrons in a layer of the ionosphere,' according to a congressional aide who heard the account of the CIA specialists. 'It's the sort of thing that would happen after an atomic detonation in the atmosphere.'[21]

The Kalahari Incident

Two years earlier, on 8 August 1977, the official Soviet news agency Tass published pictures purporting to show that South Africa had built a nuclear test site in the Kalahari Desert, near Namibia. Brezhnev at once advised President Carter and British, French and West German leaders of the evidence gathered by a Soviet satellite. Using their own sky monitors, the Americans soon confirmed that a group of buildings and an instrumentation tower had appeared in the area, suggesting preparations for a test. The western powers called on Pretoria to desist, if indeed an atomic shot was being contemplated, on pain of undefined retribution. South Africa's Foreign Minister R. F. Botha branded the accusations as 'wholly and totally unfounded'.[22]

The southern flashes and the Kalahari tower focused world attention on South Africa's nuclear capabilities and, flowing from that, an evident readiness to defend its way of life by all means against all comers. Initially, US authorities seemed sceptical of Pretoria's vehement denials.

Studies by the White House Office of Science and Technology (which commissioned a panel of outside specialists to sift the evidence), the CIA, the Pentagon and the US Naval Research Laboratory left American scientists deeply divided over whether or not South Africa had in fact test-fired a nuclear device. The White House group after months of research concluded that the southern flash was, most likely, not a nuclear event. The C I A, Pentagon and Naval Laboratory researchers disputed that conclusion and produced various theories ranging from the possible test-blast of a neutron bomb to a joint South African–Israeli test-firing over the Antarctic land mass of some unspecified sort of nuclear device. The Pretoria and Jerusalem governments both vehemently dismissed the suggestion of nuclear weapons collaboration.

Neutron bombs have been designed for battlefield use. They produce small fireballs causing little physical destruction but a great excess of killer neutrons. The neutrons are lethal to people in the area of the explosion but do not travel long distances. Nor do they persist in the atmosphere as radioactive dust does. 'An explosion of a neutron weapon would certainly explain the low yield of that event,' one weapons scientist, versed in nuclear technology, told the *Washington Post*. 'It takes a complicated design process to build a neutron bomb but I wouldn't be shocked at the idea that somebody was smart enough to test one.'

Two senior African delegates who attended the Zimbabwe peace talks in London, late in 1979, offered their own interpretation of the event. They noted that the suspected test was publicized just as the peace talks began. Both said it was more than a possibility that the Mugabe and Nkomo wings of the Patriotic Front were being 'reminded' where real power resided in the continent; in other words that it would be a good idea for them to settle. Nevertheless the Zimbabwean leaders showed few signs of nervousness in the prolonged negotiations that followed. 'We've seen no smoking pistol, not even a mushroom cloud,' a spokesman for Nkomo remarked.[23]

Western Help for South Africa's Nuclear Development

South Africa advanced towards the status of a nuclear weapons power with American, British, French and West German help. The western powers argued that their policies of nuclear collaboration with the Republic held promise of precisely the opposite result. 'The United Kingdom and the United States will persist in active efforts to persuade South Africa to sign the [Nuclear] Non-Proliferation Treaty (NNPT) and accept international safeguards on all her nuclear facilities,' said former Labour foreign secretary David Owen in November 1978. 'This would be the best way for South Africa to allay suspicions about her nuclear intentions.'

South Africa was not, however, especially interested in allaying such suspicions. If anything, political pressures at home and clamour of critics abroad on a range of issues led South African officials to stress the strategic content of their nuclear programme. Five weeks after the Kalahari affair, Steve Biko died in police custody. On the same day, 12 September 1977, a British newspaper sympathetic to South Africa carried a dispatch from the Republic headlined, 'South Africa to tell the West: Back Us or We Make A-Bomb'.[24] Two days later Vorster urged his countrymen to join the 'war of survival', because South Africa had its 'back to the wall'.

If the export-hungry corporations and governments of the major western powers had consulted in trust, exchanged information relating to their dealings with the South Africans, and sought a consensus, they would have been in little doubt that their policies were enabling South Africa to create the nuclear Frankenstein in Africa which all professed to dread. The concept of an *apartheid* atomic bomb could have the effect only of compelling African states to look around for protectors other than those countries which had contributed to the build-up of the Republic's strike-power. If the situation were ultimately to assume an east–west dimension, the Americans, British, French and West Germans would have only themselves to blame.

The Republic in 1980 was operating two small research reactors, known as SAFARI 1 (American-designed) and SAFARI 2 (South African-designed),[25] both located at Pelindaba, about thirty miles north of Pretoria. They were supplemented by a plant producing uranium hexafluoride, or 'hex', which can be used to turn raw uranium into fuel for reactors or into material for nuclear explosives. In Valindaba, not far away, another plant had been set up for enriching uranium, again for use as a fuel or for explosives. Besides several other plants for the manufacture of uranium oxide (called yellowcake), two reactors were funded and supplied by a French consortium at Koeberg, near Cape Town, for power generation. Both were due to 'go critical' by 1982. It would be possible, eventually, for South Africa to set up a reprocessing plant at Koeberg, where the spent fuel rods from the civil reactors could be turned into plutonium – again, with a military application. Over and beyond these facilities, the South Africans were richly endowed with natural resources of uranium ore. Approximately one-fifth of the world's known reserves are in the Republic itself and in Namibia.

The Americans, British, French and West Germans all played parts in helping develop various aspects of South Africa's nuclear capability: the Americans with fuel that powered the SAFARI plants and with materials, equipment and financing; the British with techniques for transforming raw uranium into reactor fuel, with training facilities and with funding; the French with reactors and the West Germans with enrichment techniques. Since late 1976, however, the United States barred the export of enriched uranium needed to fuel South Africa's first full-scale nuclear power plant under construction near Cape Town for service in 1982. Pretoria's refusal to adhere to the NNPT lay behind the embargo which, in 1978, was reinforced by the US Nuclear Non-Proliferation Act. This law further limited US nuclear cooperation with countries like South Africa not prepared to accept full international supervision of their entire nuclear programme. If, for lack of fuel, the two French-built reactors were to be idle, it would cost the South Africans $1·3 million a day. But the Botha government showed few signs of concern around the end of 1980, despite having sought vainly for three years to change the situation in talks with the Americans. Pretoria was confident that an administration headed by Ronald Reagan would prove to be more accommodating.

Britain's contribution to the development of South Africa's nuclear programme was equally significant. With the Americans in 1950, the British joined the South Africans in a secret agreement setting up the Combined Development Agency that financed a multi-million dollar programme for extracting uranium oxide from the spent gold ore hidden in the mine dumps along the Witwatersrand. Plants were set up at twenty-seven mineheads with the Agency designated the sole customer for the entire output of nearly 7,000 tons.

On the basis of that arrangement, South Africa secretly set about building its own independent nuclear industry. But, on a variety of levels, it needed foreign help. Britain became the source for the Republic's enriched uranium supplies. The British also provided extensive training for South African scientists at top-secret establishments, and permitted their own senior experts to advise on the running of the South African programme. Several unannounced commercial agreements were negotiated.

In 1958, and then in 1967, South African teams asked, and were allowed, to watch and monitor US and French nuclear weapons tests in the South Atlantic and Pacific respectively. This deepend Pretoria's interest in the military applications of nuclear power and led the west to obvious conclusions.

Britain, in 1970, formally reached an agreement that gave South Africa techniques for conversion of uranium ore into 'hex'. This was a big step towards the development of the Republic's own enrichment facilities, thereby enhancing its ultimate independence.

British collaboration spilled over into the private sector, when the government authorized private funding of South African nuclear development. Barclays Bank, for instance, in the late 1970s, helped raise a loan of $1·2 thousand million to finance the Koeberg power-generating plants. Without that massive funding, South African nuclear-energy development could not have progressed.

Whether or not the South Africans actually had manufactured nuclear weapons by 1981 became secondary to the fact that western collaboration had *helped* the Republic's approach to nuclear-power status.

Furthermore, to the extent that South Africa felt able to extract concessions, secret or otherwise, from the west, in return for uranium, the lesson that counted with Pretoria was that it could exploit its uranium riches with other countries also, just as oil-producers used the oil weapon in pursuit of political objectives. Some Middle Eastern nations with nuclear ambitions (like the Shah's Iran before 1979) needed uranium, enriched and otherwise, which they could not always get from the Americans or Europeans. It was possible for South Africa to trade uranium for oil, in case oil and other sanctions were imposed against the Republic. Pretoria therefore won greater importance and negotiating power to withstand mounting international pressures. Economically and politically those considerations were highly important. But militarily they also created the impression that South Africa had more to rely upon than merely conventional power for either defence or offence. It had ways of delivering nuclear bombs. It presumably had targets in mind. It may well have believed that its bargaining power, and therefore its capacity for intransigence, had begun to soar with the price of gold and other commodities.

The Uranium Factor

Nominally, the western countries transgressed no international law, broke no rules, in assisting South Africa to achieve a form of nuclear independence. They had, indeed, shared a good deal of their know-how with, for example, India and Pakistan, overtly and covertly. None the less some authorities and governments argued that key allied nations had violated the spirit of arrangements reached when the controversial NNPT was concluded and the Nuclear Suppliers Club formulated its guidelines.[26] This supposed violation of the will of the world community emerged most clearly in October 1977, when Britain, the United States and France vetoed a Security Council resolution which called for an end to all forms of nuclear collaboration with South Africa. Two years later, on 12 December 1979, the General Assembly urged the Security Council once again to take mandatory action to stop the Republic 'from detonating, developing or acquiring nuclear weapons and to warn that the acquisition or testing of nuclear weapons by it would be met with [UN] enforcement action' under chapter seven of the Charter relating to threats to peace. The Assembly resolution also precisely called on France, West Germany, Britain and America, among all other states, to stop collaborating with Pretoria in the nuclear field, to cease buying any form of uranium from the South Africans, and to bar private corporations from collaboration in any form.

The factor of broken international obligations and of the law itself arose in clear-cut form when a British-based conglomerate, Rio Tinto-Zinc (RTZ), with British governmental support, won a leading role and financial stake in the Rossing mine project in Namibia. Rossing is the biggest uranium mine in the world. It functions under South African control, in defiance of international rulings as laid down by the International Court of Justice at the Hague (1971) and successive resolutions of the United Nations, revoking the Republic's mandate over Namibia. An international consortium of South African, British, French and West German corporations financed it, with RTZ actually in charge of production.[27] Until the Conservative government assumed office in 1979, Lord Carrington, Britain's foreign secretary, was a member of the RTZ directorate. But then the conglomerate had always maintained close links with successive British Conservative and Labour governments. Not surprisingly Britain emerged as the largest foreign beneficiary of Rossing's huge uranium output, with a contract, negotiated between the state-controlled British Nuclear Fuels Limited and RTZ, for the purchase of 7,500 tons of uranium oxide in the six years ending in 1982 and later extended to 1984.

Long before Europeans descended upon the people of Namibia – taking its name from *namib*, which is the Nama word for 'shelter' – the Hereros, Ovambos, Damaras and Namas lived in the serenity of their mountains and desert territory, over an area of some 300,000 square miles. Then, with the scramble for Africa, came the Germans, whose seizure of the land was formalized in Berlin a century ago. The formalities of the colonizing powers did not interest the Africans. They resolutely resisted the German occupation. It took an act of near genocide – the fully documented Herero War in which hundreds of thousands of blacks were killed – for the Germans to establish their mastery. But it was a mastery that did not last long. South Africa wrested the land from Kaiser Wilhelm's forces during the First World War and was awarded a mandate by the old League of Nations to manage it, pending ultimate statehood.

To understand how Britain and other western governments came to breach international obligations requires a little more history. South Africa's mandate over Namibia was revoked in 1966, and a UN Council was set up as the sole administering authority for the territory, albeit without power to assert itself. All UN member-states nevertheless were bound, from then on to recognize 'the illegality of South Africa's presence', a ruling endorsed by the Hague Court in 1971. From this and from the confirmatory ruling of the International Court, much else followed. It became illegal for governments, or corporations, to support, help or imply recognition of South Africa's presence in Namibia. Companies functioning in the territory under Pretoria's authority, therefore, were defying the judgement of the World Court. The UN Council for Namibia sought to give practical expression to the Hague Court's ruling by adopting, on 27 September 1974, its famous 'Decree No. 1 for the Protection of the Natural Resources of Namibia'. This declared that the country's natural resources could not be extracted or exported without the consent of the Council. 'Any animals, mineral or other natural resource produced in or emanating from the Territory of Namibia without the consent and written authority of the UN Council for Namibia,' the decree continued, 'may be seized and shall be forfeited to the benefit of . . . the people of Namibia.'

Long before Decree No. 1 was announced, the US government had begun officially discouraging investment in Namibia. Indeed, one year after the proclamation, in 1975, four important American oil companies (Standard, Phillips, Getty and Continental) abandoned options to explore granted by the South Africans. Britain, under Labour as well as Conservative governments, never recognized the UN Council for Namibia nor its Decree No. 1.

RTZ, with resources exceeding $4 thousand million and accordingly much greater than those of many African states, resolved to defy the decree. The conglomerate had moved into Namibia around the mid-1960s in search of uranium and had discovered the Rossing deposits shortly before the revocation of the South African mandate. To develop those deposits needed a lot of capital. Capital could be raised only if there were to be a guaranteed market for the output. To obtain those guarantees, RTZ and British authorities engaged in negotiations for a contractual arrangement that has yet fully to be explained. Tony Benn, secretary of state for Technology in the 1966–70 Labour government, has claimed that he – and associates in the cabinet – were misled by officials over the source of RTZ's uranium supplies. RTZ and the British Atomic Energy Authority have both insisted that the cabinet was told it was Namibia, not Canada, which would be the source.

Then James Callaghan, in his capacity as foreign secretary before becoming prime minister, told the Labour government that he had been assured by leaders of SWAPO, in January 1975, that they would not object to the Rossing deal if and when they assumed power. Its leaders later denied the Callaghan version. The implication was plain. If and when SWAPO took office, it would hold both RTZ and the British government responsible for any claims to damages and compensation that might in the future be made under the provisions of Decree No. 1.

Controversy which began with the RTZ–British government deal over the Rossing contract continued through the late 1970s with Foreign Secretary Lord Carrington asserting that Britain was under no 'international obligation' to end the arrangements. His statement contradicted not only UN General Assembly and Hague Court findings but also a specific Security Council resolution on the issue. The council, in October 1971, acknowledged the validity of the World Court's opinion that the South African presence in Namibia was illegal and declared that any contractual or other arrangements made with Pretoria would not be subject 'to protection or espousal by their states against claims of a future lawful government of Namibia'.[28]

Tortuously, successive British governments sought to distinguish between their own view of the South African occupation of Namibia and that of the World Court and UN bodies. Where the international organizations described the occupation as 'illegal', the Foreign Office labelled it 'unlawful'. Few were fooled by explanations seemingly designed to last just so long as Britain needed Rossing's uranium.

Another issue of principle was involved. Normal political and commercial practice in the west requires individuals, parties, or states with a vested interest in negotiating situations either to declare their interests or to recuse themselves. The fact that Britain, France, West Germany, the United States and Canada possessed in varying degree considerable investments in the territory meant that they were interested parties. Therefore they seemed likely to pursue an outcome that would best serve their own interests rather than those of the Namibians. On the face of it, and in the short term, their interests were not so far removed from those of the South Africans who were committed to resist radical change. Yet they attempted to disguise, instead of declaring, those interests, and conducted themselves as though they were indeed disinterested parties.

The Foreign Office itself provided a revealing insight into Britain's approach to the Namibian uranium deal when it distributed a brief prepared for Minister of State Richard Luce, who was being interviewed on a *World in Action* television programme. The text of the brief, in question-and-answer form and dated 3 January 1980, is as follows:

Q: Why do Her Majesty's Government [HMG] allow this illegal trade?

A: Nothing illegal about this trade. 'Decree No. 1' of the Council for Namibia, set up by the UN General Assembly (1967), purported to ban foreign 'exploitation' of Namibia's natural resources; but HMG does not recognize UN Council as Namibia's administering authority and the 'Decree' has no international legal force. General Assembly not empowered by UN Charter to impose binding obligations of this sort on member states.

Q: What about SWAPO, 'the sole legitimate representative of the Namibian people'?

A: HMG, like most other western countries, has never accepted UN General Assembly's exclusive recognition of SWAPO. People of Namibia must decide, in UN supervised elections, who represents them.

Q: Why is the [uranium] trade clandestine?

A: It is not. The companies concerned naturally take account of commercial considerations in deciding how much to say publicly about the details of these supplies. That is a matter for them.

Q: Links between RTZ and HMG?

A: No question of 'special treatment'.

Q: Effect of Uranium Contract on British policy towards Namibia?

A: HMG is working to bring Namibia to peaceful independence through free elections under UN supervision. Our Namibia policy is actively coordinated with the others of the Five [US, Canada, France, Germany], repeatedly endorsed by the UN Security Council and supported by the African Frontline States and other African countries. This hardly suggests that our motives are selfish or improper or that our only real concern is with our uranium supplies. HMG look forward to uranium and other mining exports contributing to prosperity of all the people of independent Namibia.

Q: Conditions at Rossing Mine?

A: Mine provides valuable training and employment. Management pursue enlightened labour policy. Questions of detail are for the company [Rossing], not for HMG.

Q: Importance of Namibian uranium to the UK nuclear programme?

A: Uranium from the Rossing mines makes an important contribution to UK civil uranium supplies at present. Total UK consumption of uranium is currently some 2,000 tonnes of uranium per annum. These supplies are made from long-term contracts with Rossing and Rio Algom of Canada, and from stocks, which include uranium recovered from reprocessing.

Q: The effect on the UK nuclear programme of a loss of uranium supplies?

A: Hypothetical.

Q: Details of Contract and Schedules of Delivery?

A: A matter of commercial confidentiality.

Q: Details of transport to Europe?

A: A matter for the companies concerned.

Q: Were ministers misled when they approved the original contract?

A: Approval was given by the previous [Labour] government, and it is not for me to comment.

Q: Will the UK cancel the contract if the UN plan is not implemented and if South Africa imposes an internal settlement which the rest of the world refuses to recognize?

A: Hypothetical. Our whole effort is devoted to ensuring that the UN plan will be implemented.

Q: Uranium supplies after independence?

A: Up to the elected government to decide its mineral export policy. But we would hope to continue and expand mutually beneficial trade links with Namibia after independence – overseas trade and investment on mutually agreed terms will have major role in promoting Namibian development. U K companies have shown themselves flexible and adaptable in agreeing on continued collaboration in other countries after independence; every confidence same will be true in Namibia.

Q: Uranium for civil or military use?

A: The contract in question is for civil energy purposes.

The Struggle for Zimbabwe

Battle lines for the black-white power struggle in the heartland of the continent were already being drawn in 1963, with the break-up of the Central African Federation. The federation was a failed British effort to unify what were then the colonial territories of Southern Rhodesia, Northern Rhodesia and Nyasaland. In winding up the short-lived experiment the British turned over just about all the powerful military forces and equipment of that self-ruling territory to a government in Salisbury committed to preserve white supremacy. The pooled defence resources of the three territories, including Canberra bombers, Hunter fighters and Alouette helicopters, made the restored colony of Southern Rhodesia one of the militarily most advanced countries in all Africa. Indeed, Salisbury found itself possessing more military hardware from the federal pool than it had had at the start. The British move aroused international concern. The Security Council on 13 September 1963 sought to block the transfer, suspecting that Southern Rhodesia would use its power not only to suppress its nationalist populace but also to threaten its neighbours. Britain vetoed the resolution, arguing that fears that the whites would misuse their power were simply 'irrelevant, untrue and the wildest flights of imagination', so long as London remained in control.[29]

London remained in control for exactly another twenty-five months. Then came Smith's U D I. The issue of the transfer of air and land weaponry came up at a summit conference of Commonwealth leaders in Lagos, in January 1966. Sir Harold Wilson, then U K prime minister, sought to rebut charges that Britain had increased the striking-power of the white Rhodesians by providing them with the armaments of the defunct Federation. He replied that this had been done with the assent of the Northern Rhodesian and Nyasaland governments. But he was quickly reminded that those countries had then still been colonies and so subject to London's directives. (By 1965 Northern Rhodesia and Nyasaland had become independent and been renamed respectively Zambia and Malawi.)

Vice-President Kamanga (deputizing for Kaunda) said: 'They [Zambia and Malawi] were informed by the British Government authorities that the arms, military aircraft and equipment were outdated and obsolescent and they were advised against accepting them since, by doing so, their countries would be incurring wasteful expenditure which they could ill afford . . .'

They were advised that they should, instead, request compensatory financial assistance for the purchase of new arms and equipment, and they were assured that such a request would be met. Since then his (Kamanga's) government had put in a request for aid, but Mr Wilson's government had refused to honour the commitment . . .[30]

In Zimbabwe it was a war without mercy. Wars are rarely won. The lesson of history is that one of the antagonists in a conflict usually loses more than the other and the extent to which losses become unacceptable is invariably the factor that decides the issue. Yet in Zimbabwe, if the outcome were to be judged by Ian Smith's memorable forecast in an election speech of December 1962, the black nationalists emerged as clear winners by something like 985 years. Tragically, it was only in the aftermath of the 1980 election that the man who led Rhodesian whites into rebellion and a regime of supremacy, which he said would last a thousand years, could bring himself to proclaim something he had never dreamt of saying: that he had detected in Mugabe 'the pragmatism' he had never before encountered in other Marxists.[31] There are few recorded occasions of Smith ever having met with Marxists of any kind.

In the fighting that began, sporadically at first, ferociously later, the Soviet Union armed and trained the guerrillas loyal to Joshua Nkomo's Zimbabwe People's Revolutionary Army (ZIPRA); while China did the same for Mugabe's ZANLA. Zambia provided sanctuaries for Nkomo's wing of the Patriotic Front. Mozambique was Mugabe's base of operations. As a steady flow of arms reached the guerrillas, Smith's Rhodesian security forces, with South African help, were building up their fire-power, too. Using loopholes in national laws, vague definitions of what constitutes military material, and foreign licensing procedures, the Americans, British, French, Italians and West Germans, among others, were involved in bolstering Rhodesia's resistance. International corporations and some of the governments concerned seemed oblivious, or indifferent, even when the Rhodesians used their weapons in trans-border operations.

One month before Kissinger undertook his safari through Africa in quest of a Rhodesian peace settlement in September 1976, Mozambican President Samora Machel summoned all the leaders of Zimbabwe's divided political factions to Maputo. Bishop Muzorewa, who attended, told the story in his autobiography. Machel greeted the group with the announcement that they were going to be shown the scene of the massacre at Nhazonia, a refugee camp sometimes used by bush fighters. A Rhodesian land and air assault had devastated the camp and its inmates. Fourteen graves were heaped with at least 675 Zimbabwean bodies. A stop-over at the nearby hospital in Chimoyo enabled the speechless politicians to see some of the survivors, women and children among them, burnt and bullet-ridden. Some of the walking survivors had begun constructing a new camp. 'Close to 8,000 people were there, men, women and children,' Muzorewa wrote. 'Everyone was busy. Some were cutting grass, others were felling trees, others were constructing new huts, while still others were preparing the evening meal. Most of the people were dressed in rags. The children looked underfed and sickly. Nevertheless, shouting, singing and laughing, these Zimbabweans went about the task of building a home away from home!' [32]

By 1979 Muzorewa was prime minister of Ian Smith's short-lived 'internal settlement' government and helping to direct the operations of the same Rhodesian forces against the same sort of target in Mozambique, Zambia, and within his own country. 'I believe it has been customary in the history of decolonization by the British government that the forces who were there before are taken by those who come to power,' the bishop later explained to a British television interviewer. [33]

The diminutive Muzorewa, wearing the purple of his ecclesiastical rank, projected a sense of godly moderation among southern Africa's whites and most British leaders, too. For the 1980 election, South Africans, in particular, flooded his campaign coffers with funds and his party machine with vehicles, banners, and advisers. He was permitted to deploy his private army to campaign across the country, using methods which few uncommitted witnesses considered to be orthodox. The results gave him and his backers little joy.

Curiously the Russians put their money on the wrong political horse in backing the cause of Nkomo. Some British authorities suspected that there may well have been a Machiavellian element in the policy of the Kremlin. If Nkomo had emerged as leader of an anti-Mugabe coalition, these British analysts argued, the insurrectionary situation in southern Africa would have been resumed, pitting Mugabe's ZANLA forces against the rest, and involving perhaps the South Africans, too. In such a situation of turbulence, Soviet opportunities and influence in the region might well have been extended. Moscow seldom works like that, however. For years, Soviet support for Nkomo had been consistent and generous. He visited Moscow frequently. The East Germans not only trained his cadres but also provided him with regular medical attention. ZIPRA maintained an office in Havana. The more plausible explanation of the Soviet miscalculation appeared to relate rather to Moscow's ideological feud with Peking. To the extent that he was ideologically committed, Mugabe, since he chose exile in the Mozambique bush in early 1975, had looked towards China. Significantly, Brezhnev's congratulations after the announcement of the election result were addressed both to Mugabe and Nkomo. Since 1979 the Russians had backed the programme of the Mugabe–Nkomo alliance within the Patriotic Front and seemed glad to observe formally Mugabe's reconstruction of that old alliance, when he invited Nkomo to join his government of national unity and reconciliation.

The Ascent of Robert Mugabe

Robert Mugabe took office, at the age of fifty-five, as the first internationally recognized prime minister of the new Zimbabwe with a proclaimed resolve to temper the revolutionary ideas attributed to him by a pragmatism designed to unify the disparate ethnic groups of the country. His programme had envisaged the nationalization of the country's chief resources, from land to mines, implying full-scale socialism. 'But we have inherited a capitalist economy,' he said in Salisbury on 4 March, 'and we have to build on that.' He pledged that Zimbabwe would follow a policy of non-alignment between east and west, associating with either bloc as it served the country's interests; would seek membership of the Commonwealth; and provide political, moral and diplomatic support for the opponents of South Africa's *apartheid* system – yet without involving Zimbabweans in armed struggle or confrontation with its powerful neighbour to the south.

A massive task faced his government when it took office after years of conflict. There were up to 400,000 refugees to repatriate and resettle from neighbouring lands – and, in that context, he had his eye on some of the rich, unused farms belonging to absentee white landlords. In rural trust territories whole villages, destroyed by the security forces, had to be rebuilt to shelter those displaced in the campaign and compelled to live in shanty towns and matchbox structures. Schools, hospitals, clinics, dams, roads, bridges and canals, damaged or destroyed or shut down during military operations, needed swiftly to be reopened. Dip tanks had to be restored to counter an explosion of cattle diseases which had already lost the country almost one million head, one-third of them owned by Africans. More than 1,600 primary and secondary schools had been closed because of the risks to children in operational areas. Rural health services had broken down, with about 200 hospitals and clinics shut and only two out of fifty doctors still working in the countryside.

Finally, the big problem of food had to be tackled quickly if mass hunger and starvation were to be avoided in a country that had often been described as a potential bread-basket for the entire region. Security forces had destroyed crops and food dumps stockpiled by black farmers to prevent the guerrillas from seizing them. White farmers had found it more profitable to export their products for hard currency than to sell them locally.

These social problems were challenging enough. But there were political problems also that would require action if Mugabe was not to lose credibility among those who endured the bush war and who had supported his electoral cause. He presided over the process of unifying Zimbabwe's three rival armies into a national force and for that purpose took two actions that aroused anxieties inside and outside the central committee of his party. He invited General Peter Walls, once his sworn enemy, to stay on as commander-in-chief to supervise the integration of the forces. And he accepted a British offer to provide a military mission to train the new Zimbabwean army and air force. Mugabe, it was clear, had not forgotten Soviet Russia's attempt to pressure him to step aside for Nkomo.

The scale of Zimbabwe's needed reconstruction opened up possibilities for another east–west tussle in a new setting. During electioneering in February 1980, a US aid mission had quietly busied itself in assessing the country's immediate needs. The day after Mugabe was proclaimed the victor, President Carter's administration announced its readiness to provide help. Britain's offer of military training was another signal. A third was the start of urgent consultations among western countries to put together a two-stage aid programme – initially for reconstruction, later for land development. Contributors would include the Americans; the British, French, West Germans and other members of the European Community; the Scandinavian countries; Australia, Canada and Japan. The underlying concept was to keep Zimbabwe tied, safely, to western institutions if possible. Mugabe was quietly advised that he would be welcome to adhere to the Lomé Convention, which gives Third World countries special trading advantages with the European Common Market; and to the (western-managed) International Monetary Fund and World Bank, from which he could count on getting development loans.

Both the Russians and the Chinese declined to join the rush for a while. Equally Mugabe kept his options open. He would be unwilling to accept aid from anyone if there were 'strings attached'.[34]

Mugabe had set off down a long, winding, perilous trail to complete the kind of revolution he had begun in early 1975, after escaping into the Mozambique bush. Reared in mission schools, he remained a devout Roman Catholic who always insisted that he had not abandoned his Christian principles. In a 1979 interview he proclaimed his belief that those principles could be equated with the socialist ethic in its commitment to social justice, racial equality and a fairer distribution of men's worldly goods. He displayed both amusement and irritation at the various labels of 'Marxist' and 'communist' attached to him by his white enemies, the media and even by some fellow blacks.

'It's rather as if I would regard a Russian as a racist merely because he is white,' he told the interviewer. 'If believing that certain Christian and socialist principles are compatible means that I am a "Marxist" or a "communist" then I suppose I am. But I see myself as a Zimbabwean first of all, engaged in a struggle to help free my captive people and to win for them the rights that they have never in a century been allowed to possess.'[35]

Eight years of schooling had won Mugabe a scholarship to the all-black university college of Fort Hare in South Africa where he took the first of his eventual seven degrees and where the beginnings of his political militancy took root. For he learned then and there that passivity and attempts to seek change 'within the system' would get African nationalists nowhere.

He then went on as a teacher to Ghana where the pan-Africanism and African-style socialism of the late President Kwame Nkrumah fired him. He met and married his wife Sally there and returned home in the early 1960s to throw himself into African politics. Soon he became Nkomo's publicity secretary but his leader's lack of militancy ultimately brought a parting of the ways. Mugabe moved into the Zimbabwe African National Union (ZANU).

Mugabe's preaching and teaching that white power in Zimbabwe could never be broken by persuasion or by constitutional means soon brought him into conflict with authority and in 1964 he was arrested. For ten years he endured detention until, as Muzorewa's autobiography has disclosed, he and his fellow prisoners were released in 1974 at a word from South Africa's B. J. Vorster who, at the time, was embarking upon his short-lived essay in white–black *détente*. Mugabe's only child, a four-year-old son, died while he was in captivity. The Smith government denied him permission to attend the funeral.

The ascent of Robert Mugabe was for southern Africa's whites more than a frightening reminder that their vision of a system of eternal supremacy was an illusion. It also showed that a black populace, however unsophisticated or untrained, was far more sensitive and perceptive than its own rulers. Smith and his followers had for fourteen years lived in the never-never land of hope, expediency and a blank refusal genuinely to compromise, even after the collapse of the Portuguese empire had transmitted its unmistakable warnings.

In March 1980 the rule of the gun was about to end – at least for a while – in the land renamed Zimbabwe. There were signs from the prime minister-designate that the country could – and should – become the setting for an honest experiment in black–white cooperation. Yet, as General Walls would later acknowledge, white Rhodesians were then, at the twenty-fourth hour, still unready and unwilling to recognize the Rubicon even though it was a small river to cross. Walls himself, army commander at the start of the war in 1972 and commander-in-chief since 1976, knew that Mugabe's ZANU–PF was surging to power. In an interview with Richard Lindley of the British Broadcasting Corporation's *Panorama* programme, he told how he picked up a three-month-old invitation from Prime Minister Margaret Thatcher to approach her directly any time he wished. He sent her a long signal repeating what he had been urging upon Lord Soames for several weeks: for the British government to proclaim the election null and void, as neither free nor fair because of the great degree of intimidation he claimed Mugabe's followers were exercising on the electors. Mrs Thatcher, knowing world attention was focused on the electoral process and heeding Soames's advice, declined to act and indeed did not deign even to answer the man Mugabe later was to ask to stay at his post. 'I won't forgive her for that,' Walls told Lindley. 'I would like at least to have had the courtesy of a reply.'[36]

Disappointed by Mugabe's refusal to promote him to the rank of full general, Walls made his disclosure to the BBC after tendering his resignation to the Zimbabwean government. He explained that he was retiring because he did not like the way things were going politically in the country with President Canaan Banana and other Mugabe ministers criticizing colleagues. For that and other unstated reasons he acknowledged, furthermore, that contingency plans had been prepared for his security forces to intervene if the post-electoral situation degenerated into violence. In the end he consigned those plans to the wastepaper basket, presumably because Britain would have no part in them. Plainly it was not fortuitous that the London government began hustling its 1,200 or so troops out of the country almost as soon as the election result was announced.

There was, nevertheless, irony in the spectacle of General Walls condescendingly criticizing Zimbabwean ministers and President Banana himself for their political manoeuvring, when he himself, a soldier with thirty-two years' service behind him, was preparing to attempt a *putsch* if the circumstances were right, meaning if there was a chance that it would succeed. In a land 'acquired' by tricks and sharp practices, conspiracies were commonplace. Two years before, for instance, Walls and some members of his high command had been plotting to oust Smith himself and return the rebel colony to British rule, according to a former British Foreign Office minister who was then in office. Ted Rowlands, then minister of state under Labour Foreign Secretary David Owen, told the BBC in a 2 September 1980 interview that it was not clear just what the plotters intended to do after their anti-Smith *coup*. Britain, at the time, would have been interested, he said, if there had been guarantees that the conspirators would be ready to move towards black majority rule and free, fair and supervised elections. No such guarantees were forthcoming. And so that conspiracy, like several others, withered on the vine.[37]

Around the Republic of South Africa, meanwhile, the ring had tightened. Zimbabwean independence could only raise expectations among blacks in the isolated southern laager. The country's rulers would still perhaps try to make *apartheid* move with the transformed times but only so as to secure the essential structure of white supremacy. To that end South Africa had turned itself into one of the world's most heavily armed states. Taking account of all reserve and civil-defence personnel, every second white male of military age had, by 1980, reached a stage of actual or potential mobilization. White women and blacks were being trained too. The country's massive military machine – the most powerful in Africa – had reached the capacity not only of preserving white domination against any combination of African challengers but also of attacking each and every state to the north as far as Zaire.

The power build-up by South Africa's rulers appeared to some outsiders as a substitute for thought. There was little evidence to suggest that they had picked up the message provided by Mugabe, the man no white Rhodesian leader had tried to get to know in the seventeen years he spent either in detention or in the bush. Within the Republic there was no attempt to initiate a dialogue with black nationalist leaders. And so the potential for explosions inside the country appeared greater than ever, especially if the night attacks on three oil-from-coal plants on 1 June 1980 were to be taken as a portent of the acquired talents of African National Congress guerrillas.

Part Four

Two Case Histories

10. Angola

It was like a dialogue of the deaf. In early 1976, Secretary of State Henry A. Kissinger and President Leonid Brezhnev were expounding, at long distance, the global implications of the Angolan war in super-power terms.

Kissinger spoke first in testimony before the US Senate Sub-committee on Africa, 29 January: 'The Soviet Union's massive and un-precedented intervention in the internal affairs of Africa – with nearly $200 million of arms, and its military technicians and advisers, with 11,000 Cuban combat troops and with substantial sea and airlift and naval cover in adjacent waters, is a matter . . . directly [affecting] global stability.'

Brezhnev, twenty-six days later, gave his reply to the twenty-fifth congress of the Communist Party of the Soviet Union (CPSU) in Moscow: 'The Soviet Union does not meddle in the internal affairs of other countries and peoples.'

Speaking of America's own aims, Kissinger insisted: 'The objectives which the US has sought in Angola have not been aimed at defending or acquiring intrinsic interests in that country. We are not opposing any particular faction. We could develop constructive relations with any Angolan government. We have never been involved militarily in Angola. We are not so involved now. We do not seek to be so involved in the future.'

Brezhnev, too, declared: 'The Soviet Union is not looking for any benefits for itself, is not hunting for concessions, is not trying to gain political supremacy and is not seeking any military bases.'

Kissinger pressed his argument: 'If a continent, such as Africa, re-cently freed from external oppression, can be made the arena for great power ambitions, if immense quantities of arms can affect far-off events, if large expeditionary forces can be transported at will to domi-nate virtually helpless peoples – then all we have hoped for in building a more stable and rational international order is in jeopardy.'

'We do not hide our views,' Brezhnev countered. 'In the developing countries, as everywhere, we are on the side of the forces of progress, democracy and national independence and we treat them as our friends and comrades-in-arms.'

'To the Soviet Union and Cuba,' Kissinger warned, 'the administration says we will . . . not tolerate wanton disregard for the interests of others and for the cause of world peace.'

'Our party is rendering and will render support to peoples who are fighting for their freedom,' an unmoved Brezhnev retorted. 'We are acting as our revolutionary conscience and our communist convictions permit us.'

'Let's make no mistake,' Kissinger said sombrely. 'The real culprits in the [Angolan] tragedy are the Soviet Union and Cuba.'

Knowing, as he spoke, that Kissinger's controversial Angola policy was crumbling around him, Brezhnev declared, low-key, that Moscow looked favourably upon the success of the struggle of the People's Republic of Angola to 'defend its independence' with the 'support of progressive forces throughout the world'.

Over the next few years a series of disclosures emerged suggesting that the portrayal of events in Angola by Kissinger, CIA Director William Colby and others lacked balance, had been less than accurate and verged on distortion. Some of the evidence came from officers of the National Security Council, State Department and the CIA itself. They were mainly officials who opposed clandestine US involvement in the troubles of the West African country as Portugal's empire in that continent was collapsing. A good deal of material came, too, from American academics who had, over the years, developed closer links with Angolan nationalists than had American officialdom.

The US Senate Committee on Intelligence examined the evidence and reported to President Carter on 27 May 1978 that the CIA and others had in fact misled Congress about what had been going on in secret during the 1975–6 crisis in Angola.

During the Brezhnev era, Soviet policies in the Third World on the whole had been controlled, cautious and concerned with the need to avoid confrontation. Angola changed all that. Moscow read sinister designs in Kissinger's actions and apparent intentions and, after careful appraisal, hastened by a Cuban decision to act independently if necessary, became uncompromising. To governments in the west, the Soviet attitude towards a situation thousands of miles from Russian territory denoted a new and more challenging approach to and involvement in the affairs of the Third World. Kissinger himself betrayed no sign that he accepted the view that Moscow might have been responding to his own activism. He became deeply anxious, particularly when massive

Cuban forces began flying and sailing to the troubled land. Ultimately those Cuban forces determined the outcome of Angola's internal struggle for power.

The view from the Kremlin was that Soviet–Cuban involvement in Angola in no way threatened the process of east–west *détente*. The journal *New Times* reflected exactly the thesis argued by one of the CPSU's leading theoreticians,[1] M. A. Suslov, when, in discussing Angola, it said editorially in January 1976:

No one seeks to deny that the Soviet Union and other socialist countries render moral and material assistance to the Angolan people and its vanguard, the MPLA. This assistance contributed to the successes of the Angolan patriots in their armed struggle against colonial rule and now helps them defend the sovereignty, independence and territorial integrity of their country. As for the contention voiced from time to time, even by responsible western government leaders, that this policy does not accord with the spirit of *détente*, it only testifies to a false understanding of the meaning of *détente* which never implied and cannot imply giving a free hand to aggression.

As the Americans saw it, Soviet provision of armaments guaranteed the success of Cuban intervention. The Cubans were believed to have brought in only light weapons. Moscow supplied the big tanks, the MIG-21 fighter-bombers, the 122-mm rocket launchers and other armaments with which the Cubans were already familiar. Thus, Washington argued, it was a carefully coordinated dual operation.

What, though, motivated the Russians to involve themselves so deeply in a faraway land at the risk of wrecking the Strategic Arms Limitation Talks (SALT) and other expressions of east–west *détente*? There seemed to be three generalized factors: political, economic and strategic.

The Political Factor

There was almost certainly growing awareness in Moscow that Chinese influence might well spread in Africa, unless checked. By backing the American-sponsored FNLA (Frente Nacionale de Libertação de Ângola), the Chinese intensified Soviet fears that their favourites, the MPLA, might lose out. To have permitted the Chinese free rein to 'win' would, for Moscow, have been a grave setback in the struggle for influence in the Third World. Kremlin leaders throughout the postwar period set great store on the political and ideological benefits of help for Third World countries in their 'anti-colonial struggles'. Angola offered the chance not only to reaffirm the commitment but also to establish a promising relationship with an independent state run by the MPLA.

The Economic Factor

Potentially Angola has always been deemed to be a land rich in scarce mineral resources and agriculturally fertile. Because of the Kremlin's own giant-sized economy, this could only have been a secondary or tertiary consideration in its involvement – but with one qualification. It had long been a suspected part of overall Soviet strategy to deny, or to raise the cost of, western access to the commodities of the Third World. Beyond this, however, there was little doubt that a friendly Angola would be able to contribute only marginally towards some of the Soviet Union's mineral and agricultural needs.

The Strategic Factor

Self-evidently, a left-leaning Angola could exercise a progressive influence on the affairs of southern and central Africa. In a regional sense, so long as Angola remained under threat of attack by its neighbours, the Russians or Cubans would be bound to maintain a strong military presence in the country. For this would give them a role, even a negative or counterbalancing role, in the area. Soviet access to Angolan air and sea ports, in global strategic terms, had extended the reach of Moscow's air and sea forces to the South Atlantic. MPLA government leaders insisted that Moscow had not asked for, and anyway would be unlikely to get, air and naval base rights in their country. But access to facilities was a different matter. Already Soviet and East European countries were routinely flying and sailing to and from Angola, facilitating their watch on western air and sea movements besides adding a new dimension to their already huge air- and sea-lift infrastructure throughout Africa.

The Soviet Union, then, seized and used the new opportunities made available to them by the miscalculations of US policymakers. If Kissinger could be – as he was – severely criticized for not trying to exercise a diplomatic rather than a military option in Angola through talks to prevent, or reduce, foreign intervention, it was open equally to Moscow to take the lead. However, the Russians, like the Cubans, accurately perceived a general American popular unwillingness, in the aftermath of Vietnam, to become deeply involved in a distant conflict where US national interests seemed slight. Moscow, too, was well aware of congressional opposition to Kissinger's covert programme in Angola.

To Henry Kissinger the struggle for Angola was unique in several respects and had a global significance that, for him, transcended its regional content. As he stated to the Senate Africa Sub-committee:

The effort of the Soviet Union and Cuba to take unilateral advantage of a turbulent local situation where they have never had any historical interests is a wilful, direct assault upon the recent constructive trends in U S–Soviet relations and our efforts to improve relations with Cuba. Military aggression, direct or indirect, has frequently been successfully dealt with but never in the absence of a local balance of forces. U S policy in Angola has sought to help friends achieve this balance. Angola represents the first time since the aftermath of World War II that the Soviets have moved militarily at long distance to impose a regime of their own choice. It is the first time the U S has failed to respond to Soviet military moves outside their immediate orbit . . .[2]

Kissinger's argument attempted to justify his eighteen-month covert programme of support for Angola's anti-communists, but it did not impress his congressional listeners, who knew that it was riddled with errors of fact, dates and interpretation; besides being, as he himself blandly confessed, 'biased'. It maximized the achievement of the 'side' he was backing and minimized those of the radically oriented movement he opposed.

The secretary claimed that Washington, since 1961, had wanted 'self-determination' for Portugal's African colonies. But even more than his predecessors, he had helped arm the Portuguese, knowing that such weapons were being used to crush the independence movements and therefore their chances of early 'self-determination'.

Kissinger knew, perhaps better than any of his listeners, that he could never activate his paper commitment to support 'self-determination' for Angolans or any other African peoples ruled by America's NATO allies. This flowed from the U S adherence to a NATO doctrine which barred Washington from taking any position in Africa that might imperil cooperation with those fellow members of the Alliance having interests and colonies in the continent. In practical terms this meant that the Americans had to avoid stepping on the toes of the Portuguese, Belgians, British and French until the decolonization process was completed. In reality, therefore, the Americans and other NATO nations were bound to go on supporting the Portuguese with arms and loans, despite their wars in Africa where some of those weapons were used against the resistance movements. With the Lisbon uprising, the NATO doctrine became not totally but largely irrelevant.

Soviet arms and Cuban troops began flooding into Angola *after* Zaire, China, South Africa and the Americans became involved. The value of Soviet aid, because much of it was secret, was impossible to quantify, but American and other western experts suggested that during 1975 Moscow pumped in equipment worth not much less than $200 million.

Kissinger's assertion that Moscow sought to 'take unilateral advantage' of local turbulence and US domestic troubles ignored the Soviet Union's bitter rivalries with China. Peking wielded some influence in Angola, Mozambique and Zaire until mid-1975. The Russians set out to supersede the Chinese and succeeded (although not in Zaire). China, in fact, began disengaging as soon as the South Africans entered the arena, presumably to avoid the dangers of guilt by association.

Among Kissinger's factual errors were his statements that Angolan leftists began their insurgency in the mid-1960s when, in fact, they became active in 1961; and that the anti-communist front backed by the Americans was set up in 1961, when he should have said 1962.

Some time after testifying to congressmen Kissinger conceded privately to associates that he had misjudged certain crucial aspects of the crisis. He considered that the goals he had set himself had been correctly perceived, but he acknowledged that the methods he had used to attain them were wrong. Details of his 'confession' were relayed to the author by US State Department authorities and these appear later in the chapter.

The Chronicles of Kissinger – and Corrections

The analysis that follows outlines a chronology of the main events in Angola as Kissinger related them to the Senate Sub-committee on Africa. Each version he presented is accompanied by examples to show that he told only those parts of the story which he seemed to feel would justify his failed policy.[3]

Autumn 1974: Moscow, 'convinced a revolutionary situation was developing in Angola', began shipping arms to the MPLA.

But Kissinger failed to report that Zaire, China and even communist Romania had, months before then, started training and equipping the forces of the MPLA's stronger rivals, the FNLA. Nor did he mention that the CIA had resumed funding the FNLA in July of that year without formal authority.[4] Help for the FNLA from other countries soon followed.

January 1975: Washington 'never opposed participation by the Soviet-backed MPLA' in an Angolan coalition government.

He omitted to say that a sub-group of the National Security Council, the four-member '40 Committee', on 22 January adopted a CIA plan to give the FNLA $300,000 for immediate political action, representing a thirtyfold increase in the stipend that the movement had already been getting annually. Kissinger and Colby were members of the '40 Committee' which also included the chairman of the joint chiefs of staff and the deputy defence secretary, then General George S. Brown and William Clement. One week *before* that decision, Angola's three feuding factions had signed the Alvor Accord with Portugal, providing for the formation of a coalition caretaker government to lead Angola to independence on 11 November. Nine days *after* the decision of the '40 Committee' that government was formally installed.

March 1975: It was 'no coincidence major violence broke out in March 1975, when large shipments of Soviet arms began to arrive . . . On 23 March, the first of repeated military clashes between the MPLA and FNLA occurred.'

What Kissinger did not point out was that on 23 March, the FNLA, helped by Zairean regular troops, attacked and took the town of Caxito with a force over 4,000 strong, massacring more than sixty MPLA supporters. For the MPLA leadership this marked the start of the civil war. And for John Stockwell, a former US marine who had become chief of the CIA Angola task force, 'the fate of Angola was then sealed in blood'.[5]

July 1975: 'All-out civil war began when the MPLA attacked the FNLA and UNITA (National Union for the Total Independence of Angola), driving both organizations out of Luanda, thereby ending the short-lived coalition government,' Kissinger testified. 'By mid-July the military situation radically favoured the MPLA.'

He overlooked the widely reported fact that since February 1975, the FNLA, with Zairean army help, had been trying to drive the MPLA out of the northern provinces and Luanda, the capital, too. Nor did he observe, as his assistant secretary of state for African affairs, Nathaniel Davis, subsequently did, that by March–April, 'it was clear the Alvor Accord was breaking down' because of factional fighting.[6] He chose to stay silent about a warning sent him by Davis on 1 May that UNITA was soliciting arms 'everywhere' and that South Africa was clearly interested in helping. Ten countries, by this time, were actively and liberally supporting the FNLA; China, however, recognizing perilous internal complexities, was beginning to withdraw. In late July, President Ford, on the recommendation of the '40 Committee', approved the start of a $31 million paramilitary programme of covert support for FNLA and UNITA against the MPLA. Kissinger did not mention this.[7]

August 1975: The CIA indicated 'the presence of Soviet and Cuban military advisers, trainers and troops, including the first Cuban combat troops'.

Approximately 100 Cubans had been aiding the MPLA in Angola since the early 1960s, just as others were helping the FNLA and UNITA. Kissinger did not point out, as Davis did, that the build-up of the Cuban mission to some 250 members had been proceeding for some time – and that the Cubans had had even larger teams for years in other African, Asian and Latin American countries. He might have forgotten something Davis remembered – that Zaire had already deployed a commando company, an armoured car squadron and two paratroop companies in Angola for combat. 'The Cuban decision to send combat troops to Angola was being made in Havana [that month],' Davis wrote.[8]

Apparently Kissinger considered it irrelevant to acknowledge (as Colby finally did, in a Columbia Broadcasting System television programme on 14 May 1978) that during August the CIA lied to Congress on the subject of US arms deliveries to Angola and the use of American advisers in Angola, so as to keep the overall covert operation secret.

September 1975: Notwithstanding the US arms-lift, 'the poorly-equipped UNITA forces turned in desperation to South Africa for assistance against the MPLA ... South Africa responded by sending in military equipment and some military personnel – without consultation with the United States.' Then UNITA counter-attacked and 'swept the MPLA out of the southern and most of the central part of Angola'.

Kissinger left a gap which Davis later was to fill when he wrote: 'South Africa was supporting the two factions fighting against the MPLA [in July]' and he added the South Africans might well have moved into Angola as early as June. Certainly, he said, they were occupying the Cunene Dam complex along the southern (Namibian) frontier during August. In disavowing government-to-government 'consultation' over South Africa's intervention, Kissinger chose not to mention that there had been constant liaison over Angola between officers of the CIA and Pretoria's Bureau of State Security (BOSS). The CIA was running the covert programme. If, then, Washington had no foreknowledge of South Africa's action, the CIA chief of station in Pretoria should have been fired and the US satellite-spy system should have been overhauled. The South African prime minister of the day, B. J. Vorster, made it clear to an interviewer, in May 1976, that the Republic had been given 'the green light' by Kissinger for an operation in Angola. And several of Vorster's ministers later insisted publicly that the invasion had taken place with 'the knowledge and encouragement' of Washington. Furthermore, in public statements they advertised that it was their leadership that had made the 'UNITA counter-offensive' so successful.

October 1975: 'Massive increases in Soviet and Cuban military assistance' began arriving. 'Cuba inaugurated its own airlift of troops in late October. And the MPLA declared itself the government of Angola in violation of the Alvor Accord.' To halt 'a dangerously escalating situation' Kissinger had made his 'first overtures' to Moscow, suggesting that the superpowers jointly seek to end foreign intervention. He described Soviet responses as 'evasive but not totally negative'.

Seemingly Kissinger did not consider the likelihood that the MPLA might have appealed for extra Cuban help *after* South Africa's August incursion, believing, rightly, that this incursion was the prelude to a bigger attack. About 480 Cuban instructors, newly arrived with their equipment by sea, were assigned to set up four training centres – in Delatando (Salazar), Benguela on the coast, Saurima (Henrique de Carvalho) and Cabinda.[9] The secretary failed to mention that the CIA, only a few weeks earlier, had discouraged Savimbi's UNITA from initiating conciliation talks with Neto's men and that the State Department had rebuffed an MPLA peace feeler. He was, furthermore, quite wrong in saying that the MPLA had proclaimed itself the government of Angola 'in violation of the Alvor Accord'. The Portuguese had declared the Alvor Accord invalid (on 29 August), dissolved the transitional government and advanced by some months the previously agreed date for their own troop withdrawal.

The real reason for Washington's belated approach to Moscow emerged late in October. Four South African columns (code-named 'Zulu', 'Foxbat', 'X-Ray' and 'Orange') supported by several hundred Portuguese, French and other white mercenaries, joined UNITA in a 500-mile drive northwards towards Luanda during October, evidently hoping to reach the capital by 11 November, Independence Day. In a coordinated action Roberto's FNLA forces, supported by a crack Zairean battalion and a few South African specialists, thrust southwards towards Luanda, too, despite Pretoria's advice that they consolidate their grip on the north. The capital was under threat of a well-timed pincer-assault, with South African and CIA officers, according to Stockwell, collaborating in the field. For the first time, it seemed, Kissinger had visions of a quick kill, and with it, 'the bargaining chips' he needed for negotiating with the Russians. 'We had them [the Russians] defeated in Angola,' the secretary told *Public Opinion* magazine late in 1978, 'and then we defeated ourselves.'[10]

'By Independence Day – 11 November – the MPLA controlled only the former colonial capital of Luanda and a narrow belt across north-central Angola.' That was the extent of Kissinger's record of events in Angola for the month that saw an end to those visions of victory he seems to have entertained.

He did not refer to the CIA shipment of a 1,000-man 'arms package' to support an FNLA–Zairean–mercenary attack that failed on the Cabinda oil enclave, long coveted by Mobutu, where Gulf Oil of America possessed a lucrative concession. To questioning, he denied US recruitment of mercenaries, when he should have known that the

CIA had contracted to engage French and Portuguese 'military advisers' at great cost and that the FNLA was hiring Britons and Americans with US funds.

Nor did he report that the beleaguered MPLA and Cuban defenders of Luanda, using Soviet-supplied *Katyusha* multiple rocket launchers, had routed the FNLA–Zairean–mercenary force from the north, on 12 November 1975, the day after Neto claimed governmental power. That force had begun its assault on the capital two days before, but when the screaming, fire-streaking *Katyushas* opened up, the attackers fled in panic, leaving tons of weaponry behind. In the south, meantime, UNITA and its South African associates had been delayed by a blown-up bridge across the River Queve, 300 miles short of Luanda. By this time Castro was rushing thousands of 'the men and weapons necessary to win the struggle', as he put it, in an almost daily airlift augmented by sea transports.[11] In the eyes of black Africa, Cuba's massive intervention had acquired respectable acceptance because of South Africa's now-open involvement in Angola.

December 1975: Five principles for a settlement, sent by President Ford to heads of the Soviet and thirty-two African governments, began by saying that 'Angola is an African problem and should be left to Africans to solve'. The fifth principle urged that 'Angola should be insulated from great power conflict'. In reporting this Kissinger noted that the Russians 'halted their airlift until December 24' from the day Ford's message went to them on 9 December. During the thirteen-day period, he added, 'the impact of our domestic debate overwhelmed the possibilities of diplomacy'. The Senate voted on 19 December to cut off all further secret aid for Angola. Then 'the Cubans more than doubled their forces and Soviet military aid was resumed on an even larger scale'.

Kissinger, though, was making a virtue out of necessity. He knew, but did not say, that the CIA had been asked *before* the president acted to examine other options for Angola – including options militarily to *defeat* the MPLA–Soviet–Cuban coalition and not merely to *contain* it. Various programmes for escalating the war were considered, with the most ambitious estimated to cost $100 million. Stockwell, whose disenchantment with CIA concepts began first in Indo-China, wrote that Americans would have involved themselves in 'another Vietnam' if any of these escalations had taken place. Among plans he said were discussed were those for the introduction of surface-to-air and anti-tank missiles, US air and army units, heavy artillery, a gunboat display near Luanda, and even 'an overt military feint at Cuba itself to force Castro to recall his troops' for home defence.[12] Kissinger testified too that the US had opposed South Africa's intervention. But it did not escape the attention of his congressional listeners that his first belated call for the withdrawal of South African troops had come on 23 December, or five months after they had appeared on the operational scene.

In the event, none of the new options formulated by the CIA was chosen. The agency itself had no more money to spend, the Pentagon declined to lend any of its funds, and Congress refused to play. By late January 12,000 Cubans were said to be in Angola. South Africa quit the battle zone. The FNLA and UNITA forces were crushed, at least for the time being.

If any one incident showed why Kissinger had been wrong to reject State Department advice for that of the CIA, it occurred when CIA Director Colby testified before the House Select Committee on Intelligence on 12 December 1975. Members questioned him about the differences between Angola's three contending factions and he replied: 'They are all independents. They are all for black Africa. They are all for some fuzzy kind of social system, you know, without really much articulation, but some sort of "let's not be exploited by the capitalist nations".'

In that case, the committee wanted to know, why did certain countries back one faction while other countries supported another? This exchange followed:

Congressman Les Aspin: And why are the Chinese backing the moderate group?
Colby: Because the Soviets are backing the MPLA is the simplest answer.
Aspin: It sounds like that is why we are doing it.
Colby: It is.[13]

Roots of Conflict

Portugal's 'group of captains', who led the Armed Forces Movement against the dictatorship of Prime Minister Marcelo Caetano on 25 April 1974, did not *cause* Lisbon's decision hurriedly to dismantle the 500-year-old Lusitanian empire in Africa. They prompted recognition that the long, grinding wars of independence, waged by the people of Mozambique, Angola, Portuguese Guinea, the Cape Verde Islands and São Tomé and Príncipe, could not be won. To most Portuguese, those wars had begun to seem endless. Nearly 12,000 had died, more than 40,000 had been wounded – sons and brothers, fathers and lovers – in the swamps, savanna and bushlands of East and West Africa. Losses of the African freedom fighters were never assessed. Ordinary Portuguese folk were more than ready for change.

The change, when it came, was sudden. The swiftness of the Lisbon *coup* caught Washington and Moscow alike by surprise. The failure of the CIA to anticipate and to alert the administration to the uprising called forth the scorn of the House Select Committee on Intelligence in January 1976. Kremlin reactions to the parallel performance of the KGB did not, apparently, become a subject for investigative reporting by Soviet journalists.

In Washington, the administration was still captive of a four-year-old appraisal that Portugal's wars in Africa would go on indefinitely. 'The rebels cannot oust the Portuguese and the Portuguese can contain but not eliminate the rebels,' said the ill-starred NSSM 39 which Kissinger had commissioned for President Nixon in 1969. To the end, the Caetano government was being armed by the United States.

In Moscow, Soviet leaders some months before the Lisbon *coup*, had suspended their supply of arms and funds to the MPLA, whom they had been backing since the early 1960s. The cut-off preceded a January 1974 report by an unofficial Soviet scout functioning as a journalist, Victor Louis, who suggested that personal and policy squabbles had hopelessly split the MPLA. The suspension was to last until the late autumn of 1974.

The presumption must be that neither great power expected major trouble. They had, between them, a long-secret understanding reached between the late President John F. Kennedy and Nikita Khrushchev after the 1962 Cuban missile crisis. Broadly, this was that the superpowers would not meddle militarily in the already-developing turmoil of Africa. After all, before the Cuba crisis, there had been near-confrontation in Zaire (then the Congo). Details of the unwritten, open-ended 'military moratorium' on Africa to this day remain the secret of the superpowers but the fact of its existence was disclosed to chosen confidantes by the late Adlai Stevenson when the former vice-president was ambassador to the United Nations.

Intervention, like truth, can mean different things to different people. The competitive provision of weapons, or military training, to established governments and even to resistance movements plainly was never regarded by Washington or Moscow as forbidden in the African context. It would be hard, also, to establish a consensus over where political support ends and military involvement begins. Furthermore, there could be indefinite argument on how to categorize the covert operations of CIA and KGB officers and their task forces in the field.

The practice of diplomacy often involves finding ways of evading compacts or treaty commitments without actually cheating or being caught out, especially when national interests overtake original or outdated agreements. Angola was a fine proving-ground for exercising that concept; a setting also for what the watching world took to be a proxy war waged on behalf of the superpowers.

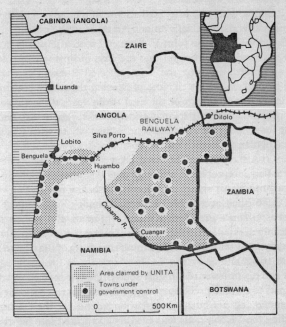

Fig. 15: Key points in Angola
SOURCE: *Los Angeles Times* map by Don Clement.

The roots of indigenous conflict run deep in Angola, a land of 481,000 square miles. Its artificial frontiers are drawn around a mosaic of ethnic, linguistic, cultural and often rival groups whose members total 6·3 million, sparsely scattered from Zaire in the north to Namibia in the south. Through centuries of control, the Portuguese had found it easy to exercise the classic imperial technique of divide and rule. Like fellow-subjects in Portugal's other African colonies, nearly all Angolans were united in a wish to wave their white masters goodbye. They shared aims, also, at land reform and the more equitable distribution of the country's natural resources by the people and for the people. But differences of personality, political philosophy, and ethnic and regional interests – all assiduously deepened by the Portuguese – fractured the independence movement into three main parts.

These parts reflected the aims and interests of the world's principal power centres, although periodically they shifted in their allegiances. Ironically, each, at one time or another, accepted aid from communist countries and sought the backing of the Americans and their friends.

Holden Roberto, born in 1925, led the FNLA with considerable elegance. He began his political career in 1959 with a visit to the

United States, where he projected a sense of moderate nationalism and won many friends, especially among American trade unionists. It was a well-timed visit because John F. Kennedy soon afterwards brought to the presidency the conviction that the days of Portuguese colonialism were numbered. In 1962 the CIA selected Roberto as a moderate worth cultivating for his chances of heading the future government of an independent Angola. For the next seven years Roberto was on the CIA pay-roll, with a personal stipend worth about $10,000 a year mainly for keeping the Americans 'informed' about what was going on in the Angolan resistance movements.[14]

The CIA's choice might have been sensible when it was made. Roberto had good contacts, although outside rather than inside Angola. His anti-imperialist stance and fleeting association with Patrice Lumumba established acceptable credentials among such radical African leaders as Ghana's President Kwame Nkrumah. But Roberto, always impeccably dressed, articulate, aware of his own dignity, involved himself increasingly with the cabal running the affairs of the Congo through the late 1960s and early 1970s. He married into President Mobutu's family and his soft-centred, highly social life-style seemed to onlooking diplomats to assume precedence over his role as a revolutionary leader. He commanded his bushfighters from behind for the thirteen years preceding the Lisbon *coup*; and even then ventured into fighting zones only occasionally, with a personal bodyguard trained in Israel. Jonas Savimbi, his 'foreign minister', who later became a power contender in his own right, asserted, after stalking out of Roberto's camp in mid-1964, that Roberto followed a 'flagrantly tribalist' line in building up the FNLA. It was true that Roberto's power-base rested mainly on the Bakongo people of Northern Angola, whose kinsfolk live as far away as Zaire, the Congo Republic and Gabon. About 500,000 Bakongo refugees from Northern Angola had settled in Zairean frontier regions, awaiting the liberation of their homeland.

Even while receiving his CIA stipend Roberto also turned to Peking and Moscow for help, initially to the consternation of the Zaireans and the Americans. The Chinese obliged. Roberto's astuteness as an entrepreneur was not limited to politics or diplomacy. In his spare time he attracted the fascinated attention of Kinshasa's diplomatic colony, who closely followed his investments in the city's real-estate market.

The late Dr *Agostinho Neto*'s MPLA was founded as a sort of Popular Front in 1957, seeking a broad, multiracial base like that first built by the outlawed Portuguese and Angolan communist parties. The MPLA sought to accommodate all tribal and ethnic elements ready to join the struggle for national liberation. Leftist radicalism laced its programme, attracting the black and mulatto intelligentsia, the workers and Mbundu peasantry of Luanda and its surrounds. Thus the MPLA had a multiracial, even a national look, that contrasted with the narrower tribal and black nationalist appeals of its rivals. For Neto, born in 1922, trained as a doctor, and a writer of poetry in his Mbundu language, this was a strength but also at times a weakness. The MPLA's wide appeal provided a political shelter not only for the mulattos but also for those Portuguese settlers who stayed on after independence. Some extremist Africans were resentful. They polarized around the person of Interior Minister Nino Alves, who acted as if he were an exponent of American-style black power. In 1977 he tried but failed to oust Neto and was killed in an abortive uprising.

The MPLA rose to power the hard way. In the late 1950s, its leaders, Neto among them, contended with the system of colour, class and social distinctions which the Portuguese evolved as a way of discouraging the development of a national consciousness. Whites lorded it over the mulattos. The mulattos were a class apart from the blacks. The blacks, apart from being tribally separated, were also subdivided between the *assimilados* and the ordinary folk. To become an *assimilado* a black had to read and write Portuguese; be able economically to raise a family on standards equivalent to whites; obey the law, possess an education and be 'approved' by the authorities; and finally stop speaking his native tongue and generally 'behave' like a white.

Neto returned from his medical training in Lisbon – punctuated by several terms in gaol because of political activity – to decide how best the MPLA could reach the people of Angola in these conditions. The MPLA began by setting up a number of cultural and other societies to cover its political work. The most effective of these proved to be the Angolan Nurses Movement, in which the leaders were men. It was a vocation that attracted the *assimilados* who, because of their education, were becoming more and more politically conscious. Most white settler families employed a male nurse. So began a clandestine political movement with access to the secrets and the activities of the ruling class. Neto, a doctor, soon assumed a central role in the communications system that spread through Angola's cities, towns, villages and farms.

The MPLA radicalism at the time did not differ vastly from that of Roberto's FNLA in its aims for an independent Angola. But the Soviet diplomatic mission in Kinshasa clearly observed, as did others, Roberto's commitment to the Americans. From the late 1950s Moscow displayed an active interest in the MPLA, expressed first in terms of political support and then materially. That backing began to wane somewhat in 1972, partly because of Neto's cautious pragmatism. He publicly disavowed any final dedication either to Marxism or Soviet communism. First the Portuguese, then some of his own MPLA colleagues, unconsciously provided testaments to his defiant Angola-first stance. In 1960 Portuguese security men flogged him in the presence of his family before consigning him yet again to gaol. In 1972, 1973 and then 1977, when he was already president, he escaped assassination attempts by men who considered his leadership too tame. Significantly, at two key moments, Neto explored the possibilities of working with the Americans – first in 1962 before turning eastwards, then again in 1974, before the fighting in his homeland reached flashpoint. The reception he got in Washington on his first visit, however, was as icy as his winter's journey.[15]

Neto died in a Moscow hospital of cancer on 10 September 1979, two months short of the fourth anniversary of his presidency. The poet-politician who wrote himself into the history of Africa was, to those who knew him, an unassuming leader and an improbable guerrilla. Yet his decisiveness, coupled with a single-minded awareness of his political goals, proved crucial when Angolans had to fight and struggle out of the cocoon of colonialism into the community of sovereign states. Those Americans, Europeans and Africans who in 1975 portrayed him as an instrument of a new-style Soviet–Cuban imperialism were confounded. His commitment to what he perceived to be Angola's true national interests led him into friendly relations with his once-hostile Zairean neighbours and once-supreme Portuguese masters. He sought friendship with Washington, only to be rebuffed, and began a process of cooperation with western powers, even inviting European capital investment into Angola and participating in the search for a Namibian settlement. Predictably, the South Africans let loose a new wave of air raids against Angolan territory one day after his death; as though to destabilize the country before a successor could be chosen. But if that was the intention the operation failed. Within fifteen days, the MPLA's central committee elected José Eduardo Dos Santos, a 37-year-old engineer, as president. Dos Santos combined widely acknowledged administrative talents with an allegiance to Neto's ideas and particularly to his commitment to non-alignment in the world-wide east–west power struggle.

Jonas Savimbi, leader of UNITA, broke with Roberto believing that he was better qualified to lead the Angolan people than the man with whom he had frequently quarrelled over a range of issues.

UNITA was last on the scene in the internal struggle for power and was, therefore, the weakest movement. But in himself Savimbi, born in 1934, turned out to be in some ways perhaps the most interesting of the three main contenders. In parting company with Roberto, he published a critique that read like a Leninist tract. In the mid-1960s he could count Ché Guevara among his supporters. He won arms aid from the Chinese as well as from the Americans and, at one point, with a dozen of his top lieutenants, went through a course outside Peking of intensive training in guerrilla strategy and techniques. He made various efforts to promote three-way political reconciliation with Neto and Roberto but when these failed he turned, risking political doom, to South Africa for help. MPLA and Portuguese leftists, who were in government after the 1974 *coup*, produced what they said was incontrovertible documentary evidence to show that from around 1970 Savimbi was in regular contact with the Portuguese military hierarchy, collaborating with them in the field against their shared MPLA foes.

Savimbi built UNITA on the strength of the two million Ovimbundu in the southern and eastern plateau region of Angola. The Ovimbundu form about 30 per cent of Angola's people, compared with Neto's 1,400,000 Mbundu and Roberto's 750,000 Bakongo. The loyalty of Angola's other two main tribes – the Luanda–Kioko–Tchokue and the Ganguela – were divided among the main protagonists.

Some US authorities have said that they thought Kissinger and the CIA miscalculated when they put American money on Roberto instead of Savimbi. Their view was that UNITA's leader had a more powerful base, more efficient support from the South African hinterland and, among the guerrillas, greater charisma as a fighting man's fighter than the elegant Roberto.

'I don't know whether it's true or not but I've been told that a $20 million stipend from the United States to the forces in the south could possibly have achieved an entirely different outcome,' General Haig reflected shortly before leaving his post in mid-1979 as SACEUR. 'The forces were there and if the arms had been provided it would have been decisive.'[16]

The FNLA, MPLA and UNITA were bitter rivals through the years of insurgency. The Portuguese industriously stoked the embers of ethnic and ideological hostility. The Salazar regime used iron-hard techniques to deal with its challengers: nationalist leaders were gaoled; sympathizers simply vanished; travel within Angola was perilous; police watched homes, confiscating uncensored literature. Members of resistance movements met in secret, worked in secret and developed their own systems of communication. Some chose exile. Angolans seeking independence became strangers to trust. The frontiers crackled with tension. Zaire, for instance, barred the use of its territory by Roberto's MPLA antagonists, fearing Neto's radicalism might prove infectious. Zambia expelled Savimbi's followers after attacks on the Benguela railroad that once carried Zambian copper to Atlantic ports. In 1980, years after the installation of the MPLA government, Savimbi with South African operational support could still claim that his writ extended throughout much of the south and that the Benguela route to the sea was still closed, its rails rusting.

Professor John Marcum wrote of the effects of the oppressive Portuguese techniques on the fragmented resistance movements, explaining that limitations on their range of action made it difficult for them to transcend ethnic, regional or class loyalties. 'Clandestinity left its mark too,' he said. 'Decimated by infiltrators and corroded by insecurities and tensions of underground politics, Angola's nationalists became obsessively distrustful of everyone, including each other.'[17]

A Byzantine quality characterized the unfolding struggle. Conspiracies bloomed like Luanda's mauve-flowered jacarandas. Intrigues among the contenders mirrored the geopolitical designs of the Americans and Russians. Alliances, contrived or fortuitously formed, found the Romanian, Chinese and North Korean communists arming the factions favoured by the Americans, French, West Germans, British, Belgians and Israelis. The states of the continent were split down the middle with white-ruled South Africa improbably linking up with black governments. Leading statesmen lost credibility when they were accused of lying or concealing the truth. Gunmen and bombers prevailed over the exercise of diplomacy, which came too late.

The political merry-go-round became dizzier still when foreign governments and entrepreneurs focused on Angola's extensive, yet underdeveloped, natural resources. These, apart from profitable oil and coffee production, included diamonds, uranium, phosphates, copper, iron ore, manganese, gypsum, bitumen, alabaster, silica, bauxite, gold, quartz and mica. A French oil company secretly asked Neto to oust Gulf Oil of America from the Cabinda enclave so that it could take over the exploitation of the fields on terms which, it said, would benefit Angola more. But, on Fidel Castro's advice, the project was rejected.

Roland 'Tiny' Rowland, chairman of a British multinational engaged in mineral development throughout Africa, funded the treasuries of both Soviet- and American-backed factions, hoping, presumably, to win special mining concessions whoever triumphed. And Stockwell reported that President Mobutu coolly pocketed $1,376,000 sent to him by the CIA for transfer to Roberto and Savimbi, so that they could settle certain debts incurred, with US sanction, during the fighting. There was little that the CIA could do about this, since it feared that Mobutu might make the whole original arrangement public and deeply embarrass the agency.[18]

Three Crucial Questions

On three issues crucial to the outcome of the struggle there was a conflict of evidence which persisted years after the Angolan war. Who
began the big arms build-up in defiance of a general international
embargo: Washington and its friends or Moscow? Did top members of
the Ford administration, or their subordinates, know in advance and
encourage South Africa's entry into the conflict? And was Cuba's intervention with combat troops the cause or effect of South Africa's involvement?

Who started the arms build-up?

Kissinger testified that the Russians began exploiting 'the revolutionary situation' in autumn 1974, through 'shipment of some arms and
equipment to the MPLA'. Then, he went on, 'large shipments began
to arrive' in March 1975, as major violence erupted.

It is known that the Russians in 1973 switched their support from
Neto to Daniel Chipenda, an Ovimbundu. This was Moscow's way of
mounting a challenge against Neto's political leadership. Chipenda,
possessor of a Lenin Centenary Medal and a frequent visitor to Eastern
Europe, organized what became known as the 'Eastern Revolt' faction
and, in consequence, was first suspended, then expelled, from the
MPLA. He thereupon led a 3,000-strong fighting force into alliance
with Roberto's FNLA. The switch by the Russians to Chipenda meant
a cut-off of help for Neto which lasted from late 1973 to the autumn of
1974. Then, learning of a Chipenda plot to assassinate Neto, Moscow
turned back to the MPLA, warned Neto and resumed the help it had
been providing.

Stockwell, however, claimed that 'in July, 1974, the CIA began
funding Roberto without "40 Committee" approval, small amounts at
first, but enough for word to get around that the CIA was dealing itself
into the race'.[19] This funding went on until January when the '40
Committee' authorized a $300,000 stipend to Roberto, nominally for
political action or, as Kissinger put it, to buy bicycles, paper clips and so
on. Some of the bicycles and paper clips, by the accounts of diplomats
on the spot, looked remarkably like military transports and guns. In
addition to CIA payments, from mid-1974 Roberto was also receiving
arms from Zairean stocks which Mobutu, his brother-in-law, knew
would in due course be replaced by the Americans.

Mobutu's commitment to the FNLA had Washington's blessing. It
enabled Kissinger to tell the Senate Sub-committee on Africa with his
metaphoric hand on his metaphoric heart: 'The United States received
requests for support from other Angolan elements at that same time
[autumn 1974] but turned them down.' But he was not telling the whole

story. He knew – because Peking announced it – that China had sent a 112-strong team of military instructors led by a general to train FNLA forces at their base near Kinshasa in May 1974, one month after the Lisbon *coup*. By the end of the summer a 450-ton consignment of Chinese weaponry had arrived. Peking's action, in the light of its embittered ideological dispute with Moscow throughout the Third World, had a bigger impact on the development of Soviet policy in Angola than the American authorities ever conceded publicly.

But Zairean, Chinese and American aid for Roberto still was not all. Communist Romania, in one of its many departures from Moscow's leadership, in August delivered a quantity of equipment, described by Zairean newspapers as large, to the FNLA. A variety of other material also began flowing into the FNLA arsenal from a curious assortment of near and distant supporters including France, South Africa, Israel and West Germany.

The initial secret payment of $300,000 by the '40 Committee' to Roberto in January did not, it seems, stay secret for long in Kinshasa, where the KGB was as active as the CIA. By July most of the money had been spent and, in response presumably to the big March–April increase in Soviet supplies, the CIA covert funding soared upwards. The programme, modestly valued by the CIA at $31 million, began with an air- and sea-lift of arms from US depots routed via Zaire and then transferred to Savimbi as well as to Roberto. There was no way of costing the total value of weaponry which reached the FNLA and UNITA. But, given the Senate Committee on Intelligence appraisal that US aid in reality exceeded $62 million, plus Chinese, West European and Zairean contributions, the grand total could not have been much less than the $200 million which Kissinger estimated had been supplied by Moscow.

There was yet another authoritative sign that Kissinger's portrayal of the initial causes of conflict in Angola was simply not believed by Congress. The House Select Committee on Intelligence, in a report to the White House on the CIA submitted on 19 January 1976, said at one point:

For reasons not altogether clear, and despite the opposition of senior government officials, the US has been heavily involved in the current civil war in Angola.

The CIA has informed the Committee that since January 1975, it had expended over $31 million in military hardware, transportation costs and cash payments by the end of 1975. The Committee has reason to believe that the actual US investment is much higher. *Information supplied to the Committee also suggests that the military intervention of the Soviet Union and Cuba is in large part a reaction to US efforts to break a political stalemate, in favour of its clients.*[20]

Circumstantially, then, the record suggests that CIA payments to Roberto directly, and arms supplied to the FNLA indirectly through Zaire, started while there was still a Soviet cut-off of material to Neto. The one certainty was that China and Romania were ahead of Moscow and Washington in their deliveries. Because those deliveries went to the FNLA, Moscow was angry, Washington pleased. That Chinese–Romanian factor, on top of the covert CIA programme, probably influenced the Kremlin to 'rediscover' Neto's MPLA, according to the House Committee report. But there were other vital considerations. They were the South African and Cuban connections. And, of course, in the wake of Vietnam and Watergate there was a manifest withdrawal syndrome among Americans, weary of becoming involved again in distant foreign entanglements.

Did Washington encourage South Africa's intrusion?

Kissinger firmly disavowed foreknowledge or encouragement of South Africa's invasion of Angola. 'Some charge that we have acted in collusion with South Africa,' he said before the Senate Africa Subcommittee. 'This is untrue. We had no foreknowledge of South Africa's intentions and in no way cooperated with it militarily.'[21] The assumption must be that he was referring to Pretoria's major attack which, the South Africans said officially, began building up from 24 September through to October, in consultation with Savimbi and Roberto.

Pieter Botha, the defence minister who in 1979 succeeded Vorster as prime minister, later told the Cape Town parliament with some bitterness that Washington, after encouraging South Africa to invade, then 'recklessly left us in the lurch'.[22] To back up his claim that there had been active military cooperation in the field he related how he and a cabinet colleague personally witnessed the transfer of US arms from US aeroplanes to South African transports at an Angolan airfield held by South African forces. He ordered his department to compile an official war document detailing his country's participation in the Angolan conflict 'from A to Z' in all its diplomatic as well as military aspects. The document in book form was due to appear by 1981. But it seemed possible that the South Africans would, after the election of Reagan as president, decide against releasing material likely to embarrass the administration.

South African intervention was, in the eyes of Africa, rightly or wrongly more sinister than Soviet–Cuban involvement. In fact, as most blacks saw it, communist involvement became justifiable if only because it ensured the defeat of the South Africans. The issue of Kissinger's whole credibility arose. It led the Washington correspondent of the *Guardian*, Jonathan Steele, to pose the question in a dispatch on the affair in these terms: 'Did Dr Kissinger lie to the Senate when he told them two years ago [1976] that the CIA had no military coordination with South Africa during the Angolan civil war?'[23]

Pretoria's official version put out at defence headquarters on 3 February 1977 was that both Savimbi and Roberto sought South African help for a phased pre-Independence Day campaign to reconquer South and Central Angola and to consolidate their hold in the east and north. Planning began on 24 September at Silva Porto, south-east of Luanda. The South Africans agreed to help. Overall the strategic aim seemed to be to drive the MPLA back into the isolated laager of Luanda. Indeed, Pretoria insisted that it had urged the FNLA to concentrate only on securing their position in the northern provinces and not to attempt an attack on the capital. In the event, Roberto had ignored that advice and the result, in Pretoria's statement, of 'a badly planned . . . careless' assault was 'total disaster'. In the south, centre and east of the country, the anti-communist 'allies' fulfilled their mission with ease, the South African authorities claimed.

If Pretoria's account was accurate it is hard to believe that Savimbi and Roberto had not simultaneously consulted with their CIA liaison officers, who would in turn have reported to headquarters at Langley, Virginia. It was always Kissinger's claim that he kept himself fully informed of what the much-assailed CIA was doing, learning and seeking to accomplish. If reports of South African planning and their subsequent field collaboration with the CIA failed to reach Kissinger, then someone somewhere was keeping things from him.

There was a lot more to it. The South Africans acknowledged that they had repeatedly crossed into Angola before their big invasion. One stated purpose was to protect the Cunene Dam and power complex along the two sides of the Namibian frontier. Another purpose was to pursue and destroy SWAPO guerrillas in their Angolan sanctuaries. Both missions gave them the chance to provide help for UNITA and FNLA forces. If Kissinger recognized the politically embarrassing implications of having the United States identified as a partner of the South Africans, it would have been easy to convey his disapproval to Vorster. He did not do so, South African diplomats told the author.

The reality, according to Stockwell, was that the CIA and BOSS coordinated at all levels their approaches to settling the Angola crisis in their preferred way. 'The South Africans escalated their involvement in step with our own,' he wrote. The CIA chief of station in Pretoria passed on most of his intelligence on Angola to BOSS. The then director of BOSS, General Hendrik van den Bergh, twice made secret visits to Washington for talks with CIA high-ups. After all, the CIA was running the covert activities in Angola. And van den Bergh had the ear of Vorster.[24]

'The allied FNLA–UNITA forces supported by South Africa could have conquered the whole of Angola,' boasted the Defence Department statement in Pretoria. Botha himself went further on one unpublicized occasion. In the aftermath of South Africa's enforced retreat he escorted a party of parliamentarians to the Namibian frontier in order to explain to them how the invasion had been organized. At a barbecue one night, where meat and drink were plentiful, he told his listeners in Afrikaans: 'I tell you, we could have gone all the way to Lagos!' (One legislator, who heard Botha, related the story to the author.)

The circumstances of South Africa's withdrawal were humiliating. It was not only that the Cuban–MPLA striking power grew too fast. Nor was it just the fact that intervention yielded the results it was intended to prevent. It was the dismal realization that the country's costly venture in cooperation had been – and probably would again be – disowned by even the most ardent members of the international anti-communist community.

Less than four months after Kissinger's formal denial to congressmen that Washington had known about and encouraged South Africa's entry into Angola, Vorster was interviewed by a senior editor of *Newsweek* magazine, Arnaud de Borchgrave. This exchange of 17 May 1976 was reported:

De Borchgrave: Would it be accurate to say that the US solicited South Africa's help to turn the tide against Russians and Cubans in Angola last fall?

Vorster: I do not want to comment on that. The US Government can speak for itself. I am sure you will appreciate that I cannot violate the confidentiality of government-to-government communications. But if you are making the statement I won't deny it.

De Borchgrave: Would it also be accurate to say that you received a green light from Kissinger for a military operation in Angola and that at least six moderate black African presidents had given you their blessings for the same operation?

Vorster: If you say that of your own accord, I will not call you a liar.

Later the former South African prime minister denied making that statement. De Borchgrave was told he could not ever re-enter South Africa. But the ban was subsequently cancelled.

In private conversation with a leading South African cabinet minister the author was told that Vorster had, in fact, been accurately reported but that he had immediately received a diplomatic reprimand from Washington protesting against the indiscretion. He had thereupon, on the advice of his Washington embassy, disowned the statement.

In diplomacy, as in human relations, there is always the possibility of honest misunderstandings and that may, of course, have happened between Pretoria and Washington. More significant, though, was the fact that South Africa was ready to be 'encouraged' to invade. No government needs to act against its will or better judgement. Its leaders are expected to weigh words of encouragement and discouragement in order to act in what they perceive to be in the best interests of their country. If that is so, the South Africans had no reason to complain if the decision they took ended in humiliation.

Was Cuba's intervention the cause or the effect of South Africa's invasion?

Kissinger's version, supported by the South Africans, was that the Cuban combatants had been first in the field. President Fidel Castro, not surprisingly backed by the MPLA and the Russians, insisted that Cuban intervention had been a response to what he called South Africa's 'aggression and invasion'.[25] On some key issues, though, the account that Kissinger presented to congressmen was contradicted both by the South Africans and Cubans. On 28 November 1975, for instance, the secretary was still telling journalists that 'to the best of my knowledge the South Africans are not engaged *officially*'. By that time, as Davis and Stockwell were later to reveal, both the State Department and CIA *knew* that the South Africans had been involved since July and P. W. Botha, as defence minister, officially acknowledged it in the Cape Town parliament four days before Kissinger testified on 29 January 1976.

The truth of the matter will doubtless have to await history's judgement. But in the meantime, on the basis of public statements and private disclosures by some of the key persons and governments concerned, it is possible to present three varying accounts – American, South African and Cuban – which indicate that South Africa went into action first.

Kissinger's Story to the Senate Sub-committee on Africa

'Intelligence reports' in August indicated 'the presence of the first Cuban combat troops'. And 'if statements by Cuban leaders are to be believed a large Cuban military training programme began in Angola in June and Cuban advisers probably were there before then'. Indeed, Castro's Cuba had been advising and training the MPLA for a decade, just as the Americans had been supporting Roberto and, of course, also arming Portugal since NATO was formed in 1949. Kissinger neither named the 'Cuban leaders' to whom he referred nor quoted their statements. The Cuban mission at UN headquarters in New York and its embassy in London, responding to a request by the author, checked the

Kissinger statement and reported that they could not trace anything to support it. Kissinger also told the Senate Sub-committee that Savimbi had been so 'desperate' in September that he appealed to Pretoria for aid, and that South Africa had then sent in military equipment and 'some military personnel'. Washington, he stressed, had not been consulted or informed.

The presumption must be, then, that Kissinger had not been consulted or informed previously when South African incursions had taken place. If that is a correct presumption it follows that Kissinger could not confidently claim to know who had entered the fighting first.[26]

South Africa's Story as Told by Botha, His Defence Department and Officials Who Asked Not to be Identified

'The allied FNLA–UNITA forces supported by South Africa could have conquered all Angola,' the Defence Department claimed.[27] But Savimbi insisted that he was only interested in controlling his traditional area because he was determined to reach a settlement with the MPLA to the advantage of the whole of Angola.

Pretoria's first official account of the country's six-month involvement in Angola claimed that under 2,000 troops and advisers had been used in a major offensive that had begun in September–October. It had got within reach of Luanda inside a few weeks. Exactly one year before, Botha had acknowledged to a *Washington Post* interviewer that 4,000–5,000 South African troops were then holding a fifty-mile-deep buffer zone on the Angolan side of the Namibian frontier. And on 23 January 1976, Botha told the Cape Town parliament: '. . . from 14 July 1975 to 23 January 1976, twenty-nine troops had been killed in action and fourteen in accidents'.

Even in private, South African authorities would not say just how frequently their forces had made forays into Angola, whether to root out SWAPO guerrillas, or to help out Savimbi and Chipenda. (Both had flown secretly, at various times, to coordinate plans with top South African commanders.) But the officials did say that South African fighter-bombers, transports, spotter aircraft and helicopters had often been in action from bases in Namibia and Zaire. One reconnaissance plane with a three-man crew had officially been reported lost.

South African authorities, and those of allied European countries, conceded privately that they had never expected so massive a Cuban commitment to ensure an MPLA victory. 'We saw it initially as a small war with a limited measure of internationalization,' a senior British politician said. 'Looking back, it may well be that the Russians were the surrogates of the Cubans and not the other way around, because the Cubans know a lot more about Africa than the Russians. We were surprised to have had no forewarning from Washington which professes to know more about Cuba than we do but even they seem to have had no inkling of Havana's intentions.'[28]

Through the second half of 1975, according to South African officials speaking privately, there was constant cooperation with the Americans in supporting the FNLA and UNITA; cooperation in distributing arms to both movements, in organizing helicopter-drops of food and supplies, in providing fuel for their transports, in servicing their vehicles. Pretoria's first official statement implied that the Cubans had been in the field before their own big push in September–October. In one hunt for SWAPO fighters, the statement claimed, a Cuban arms cache had been discovered, placing the security situation in Southern Angola, for Pretoria, 'in a completely different light'. But there were neither references to, nor explanations of, South Africa's entry into Angola in early August. And it was this large-scale intrusion which convinced Neto, and it seems the Cubans, too, that a major invasion ought to be expected. The South Africans appeared to dispute Kissinger's portrayal of Savimbi during September as a man in despair for want of arms. They described him, on the contrary, as fully confident that he could force Neto to form a national government, provided that UNITA could keep control of the southern provinces.[29]

Cuba's Story as told by Gabriel García Márquez, Checked with Havana through Cuban envoys in New York and London and Supplemented by Allied European Officials Who Had Served in Luanda Consulates

Neto first sounded out Cuba about arms and other aid in May 1975, without making specific requests. In July, a Cuban mission visited Luanda to establish his precise needs. His first priority was for a new complement of instructors to establish four military training centres where Angolans could learn how to use some of the modern weapons received from the Russians. Castro agreed, knowing that the FNLA was then being helped by the Zaireans, Americans, French and other sympathizers, as well as having received weapons from China and Romania. While a 480-strong contingent of specialist trainers was being assembled, South Africa entered Angola with considerable force in early August. This suggested to Neto and the Cubans that more help was needed urgently. As an initial measure, to supplement the group of instructors, a medical brigade, communications and transport units and other specialists were mobilized. Equipped, complete with their own fuel as well as weapons, they sailed to Angola in three ships – *Vietnam*

Heroico, Coral Island and *La Plata* – and reached Angola during the first eleven days of October.

By that time the South Africans, an assortment of mercenaries, UNITA and Chipenda's forces had begun rolling north. Meanwhile Roberto's FNLA, with Zaireans in battalion strength, were thrusting south towards Luanda. Within days of arrival at their four training establishments the Cuban contingent of 700–800 men found themselves hard-pressed and in action. 'The Cuban instructors had to break off their classes to lead their apprentice soldiers against the invaders, teaching them during lulls in battle,' Márquez wrote. In the first week of November, the MPLA was against the ropes. More help still was wanted – and fast. Luanda was under threat of encirclement. Neto sent an SOS to Havana, where Castro and the Politburo had to weigh the risks of counteraction by Washington if Cuba entered the war. Their analysis was that the Americans, at the crunch, would stay out, and Márquez offered this explanation:

> The US had just freed itself from the morass of Vietnam and the Watergate scandal. It had a President no one had elected. The CIA was under fire in Congress and rated low in public opinion. The US needed to avoid seeming – not only in the eyes of African countries but especially in the eyes of American blacks – to ally itself with racist South Africa. Besides all this it was in the midst of an election campaign in its Bicentennial year. Furthermore Cuba was sure it could count on the solidarity and material aid of the Soviet Union and other socialist countries although it was also aware of the implications its actions might hold for the policy of peaceful coexistence and international *détente*.

On 5 November, he continued, the Politburo decided that it had to intervene. 'Regardless of what was so often said, it was an independent and sovereign act of Cuba,' he added. 'Only after the decision was made, and not before, was the Soviet Union informed.'[30]

Hurriedly, according to Márquez, a 650-strong battalion of well-trained and politically educated 'warriors' set off across 6,000 miles of Atlantic waters and African jungle in ancient Bristol Britannia turboprop transports. He said that the thirteen-day airlift began on 7 November (although Castro in his anniversary speech gave the date as 5 November). The venture was code-named 'Operation Carlota' after a nineteenth-century woman slave who died leading a rebellion of sugar plantation workers. Wearing civilian clothes, the soldiers carried suitcases crammed with weapons and ammunition. They had no time to rest before being rushed into action to defend the threatened capital. Meanwhile, shiploads of further reinforcements were on the high seas, bound for Angola.

The time sequence as narrated by Márquez does not seem to square exactly with the pace of events. If the Politburo in Havana took its decision on 5 November, as he reported, it would have been hardly possible to assemble, equip and send off the special battalion within forty-eight hours. Perhaps contingency planning took place in advance of the Politburo meeting, in order to assemble the men, prepare the aircraft and send off shiploads of reinforcements. Castro's reference to the arrival of the first Cuban combat unit on 5 November suggests an earlier Politburo decision. Indeed such a decision was signalled on 8 October by Cuba's chief delegate to the United Nations. Ricardo Alarcón de Quesada told the General Assembly that in the face of intervention in Angola by what he called 'imperialists, colonialists and racists' it was Cuba's 'elementary duty to offer effective assistance' to the Angolan people for the achievement of their sovereign independence.

Four Conclusions

Four broad conclusions emerge from the American, South African and Cuban versions of what happened in Angola during the second half of 1975. They explain why the OAU recognized Agostinho Neto as the legitimate president of the People's Republic of Angola.

1. Henry Kissinger misinformed Congress in claiming that Cuban combat troops had arrived during August. In African eyes he also compromised himself politically by failing to mention the intervention of South Africa.

2. South Africa on its own admission entered the fighting from at least mid-July on the side of FNLA and UNITA, who were described as 'allies'.

3. The Cuban role had centred, at least until late September or early October, in training, instructing and advising MPLA forces. This was an extension of support which had been given since the early 1960s.

4. Havana's Politburo decided to commit an unlimited number of combat troops after developments, from August to October, seemed to threaten defeat for the MPLA. These developments included South Africa's first large-scale invasion of the country in early August, which was seen as the prelude to an all-out involvement; Portugal's cancellation of the Alvor Accord and attempted resumption of power; the combined Zairean–FNLA–mercenary attack on Cabinda; escalation of the American involvement with the start of the multi-million dollar programme of arms supplies to Roberto and Savimbi; and, perhaps most significant of all, the major new South African invasion in October which, for all that the MPLA knew, might have aimed at the conquest of the whole country.

Henry A. Kissinger's skills as a diplomatic negotiator were internationally acknowledged. To him the ends he sought generally justified the means he used. Thus he would feign fury, crack jokes, threaten, philosophize, behave haughtily and profess humility, calculate, cajole and contrive. Over the secret US wars in Laos and Cambodia he stood accused of misleading Congress. Some Israelis reckoned he deceived them during his intensive shuttle diplomacy when, by an apparent miracle, he brought about the disengagement of their forces from those of their hostile Arab neighbours.[31] He argued that the 'global interests' of the United States transcended the 'regional interests' of the West European allies, infuriating France and others for what they considered his arrogance.

Nobody ever accused Kissinger of being contrite. Rarely did he feel the need to apologize for the real or imagined failures of the foreign policies he pursued during his periods of office, first as National Security Affairs adviser, then as secretary of state, in the administrations of Presidents Nixon and Ford.

That was the public man whom former subordinates likened to a latter-day Metternich or Machiavelli. His style of diplomacy won this description from the Congressional Research Service of the Library of Congress: '... personal, secretive, manipulative, and some would say amoral ... more characteristic of the 19th century classical European diplomacy than that in the American democratic tradition . . .'[32]

Kissinger never yielded openly in public to fellow academics, politicians, diplomats or columnists who dissected the anatomy of his failed policies in Angola or southern Africa. Nevertheless he was hurt by those critics who, in chorus, described his handling of the crisis variously as 'a blunder', 'a tragedy', 'a story of stupidity'. The balloon of his infallibility had already been deflated over the role he had played in accepting an unworkable Vietnamese settlement and in launching secret military operations in Cambodia and Laos. He had now to defend himself anew and this he attempted to do by diverting attention to what he portrayed as the misdeeds of the communist powers.

Privately, though, Kissinger did concede to senior State Department officers that he would have handled Angola differently if he had known at the time what he had learned later. As evidence of his reassessment, these officials called attention to the efforts he made through 1976 to redeem US credibility in Africa. In April of that year he visited Zambia for the double purpose of affirming American backing for black majority rule throughout the region and of consolidating moderate black governments. In June he met Vorster to enlist his help in achieving an early settlement in Zimbabwe where guerrilla warfare was escalating – and to urge him also to modify South Africa's system of *apartheid*. In September he set out on his last safari in quest of a Zimbabwean solution but the outline agreement he thought he had reached in Pretoria with Ian Smith, then leading Rhodesia's all-white government, soon crumbled. A central reason was in the ambiguities embodied in his message to the Salisbury regime, setting forth what proved to be his mistaken understanding of what the black states of the area and the guerrilla leaders would accept. The dispatch to Smith was transmitted from his aircraft after he had conferred with Kaunda in Lusaka and Nyerere in Dar es Salaam.

To understand why the Americans 'lost' Angola and other parts of Portugal's African empire – at least temporarily – it is essential to examine how Kissinger's calculations made it relatively easy for the Russians to 'win' with Cuban help.

Kissinger's approach to the problems of southern and central Africa broadly embodied ideas set forth in the second of five policy options presented in N S S M 39. One starting-point for all these options was to question 'the depth and permanence of black resolve' militarily 'at any stage' to defeat the white rulers of the Portuguese territories, Rhodesia, and South Africa (which also controlled Namibia). The memorandum went on: 'The whites are here to stay and the only way constructive change can come about is through them. There is no hope for the blacks to gain the political rights they seek through violence which will only lead to chaos and increased opportunities for the communists.'

As a result, and in line with the recommendation offered in Option Two, Kissinger had adopted the policy of 'relaxing political isolation and economic restrictions on the white states' while continuing publicly to denounce oppression and discrimination practised on grounds of race and colour.[33]

The United States had also reaped the bitter harvest of Vietnam but without beginning to understand the dynamics of national revolutionary struggles. The contradiction was that a commitment to the concept of self-determination just could not be squared with the policy of arming and aiding the Portuguese to preserve their imperial system, thus deferring indefinitely prospects for the blacks to exercise self-determination. If anyone realized this contradiction, it was the Portuguese themselves, the white rulers of Zimbabwe and the South Africans. None were likely to be shifted by contrived expressions of support for black aspirations by Washington while it displayed its ambivalence by reducing the 'political isolation' of the white-ruled states.

From the time that N S S M 39 was presented to Nixon in 1970 through to 1974, Kissinger managed to ride the two horses of his African policy. He was using arms deliveries to sweeten the Portuguese, in a negotiation for continued U S base rights in the Azores. The administration fell in line with a congressional decision to breach the UN embargo on trade with Rhodesia by importing Rhodesian chrome. There was continuing cooperation with South Africa in satellite-tracking and in nuclear development.

Then came the *coup* of the captains in Lisbon. There was no longer validity in the bland assumption that white stamina and conviction were greater than 'the depth and permanence of black resolve'. Equally, Washington's evident unawareness of the factors that caused the Lisbon uprising, and the events in its trail, should have given a cautious secretary of state reason to wonder why he had not been forewarned about the state of Portuguese morale and the course the guerrilla wars had taken in Africa. Outsiders could have been forgiven for concluding that US policies had been based more on wishes or prejudices than on realities, and appeared to reflect the attitudes of white rulers in the region.

With hindsight, Kissinger acknowledged privately that the Africa Bureau of the State Department (at the time headed by Nathaniel Davis) had been right in pressing for abandonment of the covert activities programme in Angola. He told associates that he ought to have set about achieving his central objectives by different methods, although he did not spell them out. He remained sure, he insisted, that it had been essential to challenge the involvement of the Soviet Union; and in that view he felt reinforced by later events in Ethiopia, Afghanistan and South Yemen. But two admissions were surprising for someone who had had so many supposedly sound sources of information at his disposal.

First, it had been his analysis that the Lisbon revolt would not come as soon as it did. Perhaps because his gaze was fixed on Indo-China, or because of the preoccupations of Watergate, the early collapse of the Caetano regime did not cross his mind. If anything, US access to the Azores bases during the 1973 Arab–Israeli war had only strengthened his belief that it would be wrong to weaken Portugal for the sake of what he saw as vague African policy considerations. (Caetano, alone among the NATO leaders, had allowed US planes, rushing arms to Israel in 1973, to refuel in the Azores.) When revolutionary change did come to Portugal, Kissinger realized that the policies which flowed from his mistaken analysis were no longer valid. Yet he failed to adjust to the implications, and the focus of his attention then turned to thwarting the possibility of Portugal going communist.

Secondly, as the conflict on the ground developed in Angola, he did not recognize what the impact would be of any tacit, explicit or fortuitous American alliance or collaboration with the South Africans. In the event, the impact was so great that it let the Russians and Cubans intervene without exciting African fears or hostility. All his disavowals of collusion with the South Africans left key African nations un-impressed. To them the symbolism of South African involvement, beyond its borders, in African trouble-spots, outweighed any threats they were told would arise if Moscow were to establish a communist outpost in Angola, 6,000 miles from Soviet territory. It is an article of faith among OAU member-nations that Enemy Number One in con-tinental Africa is South Africa with its white supremacist policies.

'The Angolan war represents a tragedy of missed opportunities,' Professor Marcum told the Senate Sub-committee on Africa on 4 Feb-ruary 1976. He went on to pose a series of questions which went to the heart of the problems that Kissinger's policies had created for the Americans and Angolans alike:

When in March and April [1975] the Zaire-based and equipped troops of Holden Roberto's FNLA, which expelled all rivals from the northern districts of Angola, launched military operations against the Luanda-based MPLA, did the US government try to constrain its client? Or did the administration hope for the quick elimination of a movement that had been receiving Soviet support for fifteen years?

Did the American government think to advise the Soviets that it was prepared to guarantee that Neto's MPLA, and not a Zairean-sponsored rival faction, would remain part of the tripartite transitional government? Did it convey to Moscow and other interested parties strong American backing for an inclusive coalition, in preference to the imposition of any movement by force? As Soviet arms began appearing in Luanda in April–May, did the Secretary of State sense the dangers of playing a 'cover game of soldiers' and alert Moscow about his concerns? [34]

The Road from Caxito

The professor's questions were largely rhetorical. The truth was that Kissinger missed several chances to defuse a crisis that he never ex-pected to explode in his face. The armed forces revolt, for instance, offered Washington a golden chance to disengage from the politically embarrassing embrace of the old regime in Portugal.

The United States then could have done what the Portuguese them-selves were doing – abandoning the African policies of Salazar and Caetano and identifying instead with the aspirations of the key indepen-dence movements throughout Portuguese Africa and especially in Angola, where the factional struggle had been building up for years. Kissinger missed the moment. Within three months, presumably with his sanction, the CIA had begun funding Roberto's FNLA, in the mistaken belief that it was going to prove strong enough to keep Neto – and maybe Savimbi, too – out of the Luanda power structure.

There was a second missed chance when Kissinger could have revised his perceptions and switched his search from a military to a political solution. Such an occasion arose with the events of 23 March 1975.

The place was Caxito, a strategic coastal town thirty-five miles north-east of Luanda and on the route southwards from Zaire. It was a town that would change hands many times. FNLA forces, reinforced by an estimated 4,000 Zairean troops, were driving south to establish links with their units in Luanda. They took Caxito and then set out to round up all MPLA followers.

The soberly edited *Financial Times* in London described on 29 March what happened then: 'Eyewitness reports of the massacre by FNLA soldiers of civilians and others suggest beyond a reasonable doubt that what has occurred is a first terrifying attempt by FNLA to kill substantial numbers of MPLA soldiers and supporters and instil a climate of fear in the country such as it did in 1961 on the Zairean border.'[35]

More than sixty MPLA supporters were killed and mutilated in the action by Roberto's men. Neto proclaimed the event as the formal start of the civil war. Clashes between the two movements had frequently occurred before but few were as serious as this, against the background of attempted conciliation enshrined in the Alvor Accord.

Implicitly Kissinger acknowledged the importance of the event, but in reporting to the Africa Sub-committee he put his own gloss on it: 'It is no coincidence that major violence broke out in March 1975, when large shipments of Soviet arms began to arrive – thousands of infantry weapons, machine guns, bazookas and rockets. On March 23, the first of repeated military clashes between the MPLA and FNLA occurred.' However the secretary failed to point out what independent US and other investigators established. It was that the FNLA initiated the Caxito battle; that the MPLA suffered most; that American-armed Zairean troops participated; that the arrival of 'large shipments of Soviet arms' could hardly have reached untrained MPLA cadres miles away from MPLA headquarters.

Given the long history of factional rivalries, it was plain that the killings at Caxito represented the point of no return for the Angolan contenders and their foreign champions, on at least two levels:

1. Domestically, it had the effect of escalating the conflict between them, so eliminating any lingering possibility of forming a three-party coalition.

2. Internationally, it had the effect of transforming a regional African conflict into what Kissinger himself described as a 'geopolitical event of considerable importance'.

Perhaps the final chance for Kissinger to have abandoned attempts for a military solution and to switch instead to negotiation came by way of private signals from the Chinese. Peking sent word to Washington that it was pulling out, partly because it did not want to be seen associating with the South Africans, partly because it recognized that the struggle was degenerating into a naked superpower tussle in the context of a national civil war. China has long maintained that it has no wish to be involved in the internal affairs and feuds of foreign countries, however friendly.

The Chinese reading of the situation and China's consequent withdrawal had no visible effect on Kissinger's resolve to fight to the finish. The finish for Kissinger, for all his resilience, must have been hard to take.

Unapologetic in public after Carter assumed the presidency, Kissinger later invoked Soviet–Cuban actions in Ethiopia to argue, in terms of *realpolitik*, that he had been right in his efforts to thwart the communist intervention.

Yet what he could not conceal from himself, according to the accounts of insiders which have reached the author, were these acknowledged consequences of his policy:

1. The presence of up to 20,000 Cubans, a mix of Havana-style Peace Corps workers and troops, enabled the communist countries to rally swiftly to the aid of Ethiopia's tottering radical regime in 1977–8.

2. With the help of his defenders, Neto was able to beat off continuing challenges to his regime by internal rivals and external assailants, including the white Rhodesians and South Africans.

3. The evolution of Neto's policies showed that he was not the Marxist extremist he had been painted but a pragmatic leader more than ready to work with the west in Angolan national interests. Thus he proved helpful in the international search for a Namibian solution; he responded to West European diplomatic recognition by offering positive working links with the member-nations of the European Common Market; he developed good relations with U S firms operating in the country, while serving notice that Angolan non-alignment would not permit countries like the Soviet Union to establish military bases in his territory; and he persisted in efforts to broaden an Angolan national awareness of its identity opposed by extremist supporters of black power, who resented the influence of mulattos and some whites in the administration.

4. Through the Carter years, the hostility generated by Kissinger's policy lingered on in Washington despite the endeavours of Ambassadors Andrew Young and Don McHenry for normalized rela-

tions. In June 1979 Young told the author that US recognition of the Luanda government was *very* near. But clearly he had not reckoned on the ability of Zbigniew Brzezinski to persuade the president that total Cuban withdrawal had to be a precondition for a diplomatic relationship. By the time Reagan was elected, the administration was under pressure by key US oil companies to bury the past and to establish formal links with Luanda. Gulf Oil and Exploration, with a 49 per cent stake in the Cabinda enclave, maintained that they had always had good relations with the Angolans and the Cuban military authorities guarding the area. The Texaco company signed an agreement with the Angolans permitting the development, along with other international oil firms, of fuel reserves in offshore seabeds and at the mouth of the Zaire River.

Too late, then, Kissinger came to learn that Neto, his successor José Dos Santos and their fellow-leaders were not red ogres but committed African nationalists resolved to fulfil the Angolan people's long-dreamt aspirations for unity, peace and the better, more prosperous days their resources promised.

Ronald Reagan began his presidency with a campaign commitment to arm Savimbi's UNITA guerrillas; with a National Security Council adviser, Richard Allen, who before 1974 had lobbied on behalf of Portuguese interests; and with a proclaimed resolve to stand by South Africa, a valued 'wartime ally' possessing essential minerals and of strategic importance. Alongside came Reagan's denunciation of the Russians as 'liars and cheats' in their international relationships. Not surprisingly, this initial hardline posture was taken in Europe and Africa to foreshadow serious new superpower tensions.

Specifically, in African capitals, there was concern that conservatives dominating the US Senate would overturn a 1976 law barring American intervention in Angola, intervention aiming at driving Luanda's socialist government, with its Cuban, Soviet and East German defenders, from power. Angola, like Mozambique, had been contributing crucially to the search for settlements in Zimbabwe and Namibia and had displayed readiness to trade and talk with the west. The country's leaders had stressed, moreover, that a Namibian peace with an end to ceaseless South African cross-border attacks on them would make it possible for Cuban forces to withdraw.

It was clear, conversely, that active American support for Savimbi would harm those prospects for a Namibian peace, increase Angolan (and Mozambican) dependence on East-bloc protection and range most of black Africa against the United States.

11. The Horn of Africa

Soldiers of the Dergue drove to the Imperial Palace in Addis Ababa late on 12 September 1974 – twenty weeks after the *coup* of the captains in Lisbon – and told Haile Selassie that he was no longer emperor of Ethiopia.

They read an indictment charging that he had 'abused the authority, dignity and honour of his office for personal benefit and interest'.

The durable monarch, who had ruled for half a century, disdainfully replied: 'We have always done what is good for Ethiopia. If this is for the good of the nation, so be it.'[1]

Only when they led him away did the diminutive, 82-year-old Lion of Judah betray signs of unease. That was when he was ushered into the sort of small police car which in less troubled times would escort his shining limousine on ceremonial occasions. Erect in the back seat, staring straight ahead, he endured the scornful yells of demonstrators as he passed through the palace gates for the last time on his way to a detention that would end with his death a year later – in circumstances still to be explained.

So ended a dynasty founded by the first Menelik, who was said to have been the son of King Solomon and the Queen of Sheba. So began a soldiers' regime committed to a brand of revolutionary 'socialism' heralding heightened turbulence in the already tempestuous condition of the Horn of Africa.

Karl Marx and Vladimir Lenin would not easily have recognized the purportedly 'socialist' factor in the confused ideological orientation which the new soldier-rulers offered the disparate ethnic groups of the Ethiopian empire. Nor, indeed, did the radical intelligentsia, the students, teachers, taxi-men, public servants, village priests, workers and peasantry who had joined the country-wide movement that ousted the old regime. At least initially, the Dergue had no coherent programme beyond a series of sometimes disconnected socio-economic reforms designed to modernize the society, eliminate corruption and dispense social justice. Equally, there was no sustained effort to broaden the base of the regime by sharing power with those one-time allied civilian elements working for the establishment of a 'people's government'.

Even before the deposition of the emperor, the Dergue (Amharic for 'committee' of the armed forces) had begun alienating their civilian fellow rebels who had led the fight for a new Ethiopian order. The Dergue's first draft constitution, for instance, preserved the monarchy and the throne for Haile Selassie's descendants. Mikael Imru, a liberal-minded aristocrat related to the emperor, was named prime minister. The motto of the junta was 'Ethiopia First' which prompted *Democracia*, the mimeographed weekly voice of the left-wing radicals, to ask rhetorically: 'Which Ethiopia is to be first? We say the broad masses of Ethiopia first!'

Disenchantment deepened when the Dergue set out to eliminate all opposition by gaoling or executing its critics whether they were soldiers or civilians. Old promises of civil and political rights were withdrawn. Public demonstrations were banned. A once-popular general, Aman Andom, was propelled out of obscurity into the chairmanship of the Dergue and command of the Defence Ministry and government in what was interpreted by opponents as a move towards outright dictatorship. 'Democracy is not the immediate need of the Ethiopian people,' proclaimed the *Ethiopian Herald*, organ of the new establishment, ten days after Haile Selassie left the scene.

By October leaders of the Dergue themselves were deeply divided along lines reflecting the social composition of the armed forces. Soldiers, airmen and specialists below senior officers' rank tended towards radicalism, while those above field officers' rank predictably preferred a moderate, reformist, even conciliatory approach to the country's problems. Aman soon displayed his dislike for the summary procedures used by his more junior colleagues in dispensing 'justice' to those who had served the old regime and for their refusal to share power with civilians. But the real crunch came over relations with the secessionists of Eritrea, who had been fighting for their independence since 1961. Eritrean-born himself, Aman favoured political compromise, an amnesty and a truce, and twice visited the embattled region on missions of peace. But he returned empty-handed on both occasions: the Dergue found it impossible to concede the precondition set by the Eritreans, which was that their right to independence had to be recognized. In the arguments that followed, Aman was unyielding on most counts, and it seemed to the hardliners that he had played out his role as a figurehead who could command national and international respect for the regime.

Haughtily Aman retired to his home in suburban Addis Ababa and refused to attend working sessions. On the night of 23 November the Dergue sent a contingent of troops to demand his appearance at a special meeting where he would be called upon to explain himself. The general remained defiant and, threatened with arrest, he called in his own guards. In the shooting that followed he was killed. The same night, fifty-nine political prisoners were massacred in circumstances still unknown. Among them were two former prime ministers, several of the emperor's former courtiers and a number of army leaders.[2]

The Dergue's own slogan of 'Change without Bloodshed' was now bloodstained itself. The revolution had entered a stage of prolonged repression with far-reaching international consequences.

The downfall of a dynasty anywhere in today's world of ideological rivalries would pose dangers of internal bids for power. But Ethiopia's upheaval brought with it the greater threat of a gladiatorial contest between the Soviet Union and the United States who, for years, had been contending for dominance in the Horn of Africa. Because of its geography and resources, indigenous and imported animosities had endowed the region over the past century with all the elements needed for exercises in *realpolitik*. Long before access to oil and energy became the preoccupation of states, the Horn had become geopolitically important to Europe as well as to Africa and the Middle East and Moscow and Washington inherited the roles played by Egypt, Britain, France and Italy in the past.[3]

'The Horn' is a metaphor. It describes 700,000 square miles of north-eastern African bushland and desert, forbidding mountains, volcanic plateaux and rivers that roll down to the Indian Ocean, the Red Sea and the Mediterranean. Construction of the Suez Canal in 1869 led the imperial powers to defend the routes that linked Europe with West and East Asia. They set up their separate bastions for the defence of their shipping at such crucial choke points as Suez itself, the Bab el Mandeb Strait at the southern tip of the Red Sea and along the coast of the protruding Horn. Intermittent closures of the Canal resulting from the Arab–Israeli conflict made it essential, in the oil age, for most powers to ensure the freedom of the Red Sea for use by giant tankers carrying Middle Eastern oil to North America, Japan, Israel and Western Europe.

Three sovereign nations at the start of the 1980s were scratching out a bare existence in the Horn. Their destinies were inexorably interlinked if only because religious, ethnic and political differences rendered life more precarious still in Ethiopia, the Somali Democratic Republic and Djibouti, the former French-ruled Territory of the Afars and Issas.

For 1,500 years imperial Ethiopia was a Christian island washed by the encroaching tides of Islam and other foreign adversaries. Religion was not the only important element. The Blue Nile rises in the west of the country and meanders northwards through the Sudan and Egypt,

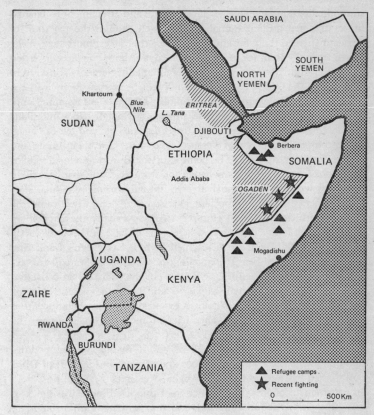

Fig. 16: Strategic position of countries in the Horn of Africa

supplying four-fifths of the Nile River's own waters which now cool,
feed and light the lives of millions along its slow journey to the sea.
Khartoum and Cairo had long feared that a hostile Ethiopia would, if
driven, tear up early-twentieth-century treaties and shut the iron gates
in a deep and narrow gorge not far from Lake Tana, cutting the flow of
water to the Sudanese and Egyptians. That explained why, in advance
of those treaties, Egypt four times between 1867 and 1875 vainly set
out to conquer the hardy Ethiopians. Christians and Moslems are
about equal in number in present-day Ethiopia, making up some 80 per
cent of a thirty-million population, five million of whom are animist.

If the affairs of the Ethiopians, given their traditional isolation,
seemed tangled to most outsiders, they were not nearly so complex as
those which attended the emergence of modern Somalia. A cultural

commonality – in language, social structure and attachment to Islam – unites the five million Somali people even though the partition of Africa dispersed them far and wide across the easternmost slice of the Horn, from the Red Sea to Northern Kenya. About 70 per cent settled in the Republic itself, 20 per cent were nomadic elements scattered in and around the Ogaden region of Ethiopia, 5 per cent were in northern Kenya and the rest were living in and near Djibouti and its hinterland.

Before the colonial era, a loose alliance of Somali tribes and clans wandered sometimes freely, other times defiantly, in and out of Christian Ethiopia, in search of pastures and water for their herds and quarry for their hunters. The coming of the Europeans in the 1880s and 1890s began a process of change and frontier-fixing that has still to be completed. First the British arrived, initially to ensure regular supplies of beef for their important garrison at Aden. Then came the Italians with dreams of an empire in Africa. Finally the French set themselves up with a coaling station and major base in Djibouti, partly because their old British rivals denied them use of Aden's bunkering and victualling facilities. In parcelling out chunks of Somaliland territory between them, neither the British nor the Italians ever consulted the Ethiopians or the Somalis and it became inevitable that the bargains struck by the Europeans – usually as extensions of their policies within Europe – would ultimately cause friction and even war between the affected African peoples.

The Territory of the Afars and Issas and its mainly Moslem population of about 80,000 was small, poor and obscure but its port of Djibouti, linked by railroad to Addis Ababa, ever since 1916 has possessed an enormous economic importance for Ethiopia. France was quick to recognize that Djibouti could serve as the main trading thoroughfare into Ethiopia if Addis Ababa ever lost control – as periodically it did – of its only other access to the sea, through Eritrea. And with Eritrean separatists limiting Ethiopia's free use of the Red Sea ports, Djibouti's first-rate harbour and rail link during the 1970s carried more than half Ethiopia's incoming and outgoing goods at lush freight and handling charges. The Ethiopians attributed their defeat by fascist Italy in the 1930s to France's unlawful closure of Djibouti. Another closure, if Somalia were to seize the Territory, would not find the Ethiopians passive, as leaders of the Dergue bluntly warned.

The East–West Contest Deepens

East–west rivalries in the Horn long preceded Ethiopia's upheaval. They fed on local animosities. And they threatened the security of regional states including Sudan and Kenya in Africa, Israel, Saudi

Arabia and North Yemen in the Arabian Peninsula, and Iran and its neighbours in the Gulf. Among these countries there was a shared fear that the Red Sea one day would be transformed into a Red Lake.

Soviet–American competition in the Horn, of course, was just one reflection of their global contest, which neither knew quite how to lessen. The competition began in the early 1960s when the Russians befriended the fledgeling Somalian Republic and became next-door neighbours to the Americans who had established themselves in Ethiopia in 1953. Each superpower had its own geopolitical reason for being where it was. Both met the military rather than the economic needs of their clients, acting not for the sake of the Africans but in their own national interests.

Through the 1970s, as American influence in the Middle East increased, the Russians paid more and more attention to the opportunities presented by the growing turmoil in Africa. They made full use of the confusion which followed the collapse of Portugal's empire. It was an event they had long anticipated by arming and funding radically oriented liberation movements which ultimately were to become governments. In the same way they foresaw that an era of change lay ahead for the peoples of the Horn. Somalia promised to be a staging-point for the Russians on their way to Ethiopia, a black and truly African land with a storied past, the seat of the OAU. Politically and strategically, the temptation of an Ethiopian connection was overwhelming.

In practising their 'arms diplomacy' in countries carefully selected for their revolutionary potential, the Russians were accused of opportunism or worse. They remained unapologetic. Humanitarianism, by their criteria, lay in the process of freeing nations from what they described as the exploitative grip of the capitalist–imperialist world system. They disavowed any wish or compulsion to join with the west in combating the poverty, disease and hunger that blighted the lives of millions in parts of the Third World. That was the heritage of colonialism, a debt that the former imperial powers were duty-bound to redeem. Thus it was that, in the twenty years ending in 1974, Soviet military aid to Somalia totalled $115 million; in the twenty years ending in 1976, economic aid totalled $154 million; in 1975, the year after Ethiopia's revolution, Soviet credit extensions to Somalia exceeded $60 million; and in the same year a major new weapons agreement was signed that gave Somalia one of the biggest arsenals in black Africa.[4]

Beyond these factors the Russians did not attempt to conceal their awareness of the strategic considerations involved in future dominance of the region. Their authoritative journal *New Times* observed, early in 1978, that the Red Sea basin 'has been allotted an exceptionally important place in the imperialist strategic plans because of its geographical location at the junction of two continents, Asia and Africa, its first-class ports in the Gulf of Aden and [access to] the Indian Ocean and, above all, its proximity to key sea-lanes linking oil-producing countries with America and Europe'. The article went on: 'Some 70 per cent of the oil and other raw materials imported by Western Europe is carried over these sea routes.'[5] In the west there were many who wondered whose 'imperialist strategic plans' *New Times* was talking about.

The rationale of the Americans derived from what former Defense Secretary Donald H. Rumsfeld called 'the central objective' of US foreign policy: '. . . to maintain an international order that assures the physical security of the United States, its economic well-being and the preservation of its institutions and values'. Because Moscow had set out to change the existing 'international order', Rumsfeld said, the 'Soviet Union is and will remain for the foreseeable future the major threat to the United States and the international system on which we depend'. From this it followed that it was a vital American interest to safeguard its political, strategic and economic links with Third World countries because they formed part of the 'international order' that the Russians would want to transform.[6]

In geopolitical terms the United States has always had to trade in order to survive. In order to trade, the freedom of the seas needed to be preserved. To ensure this, the US navy assumed for itself a global mission: to defend and control all sea-lanes used by merchant-men fetching and carrying goods and raw materials essential to the nation. Rumsfeld put it thus: 'We must be vitally interested in the freedom of the seas and the narrow waters that connect them.' These 'narrow waters', straits, or choke points, are mostly in and around Third World territories. Hence the importance, for example, of the Red Sea.[6]

An added dimension to the concept of freedom of navigation emerged in the 1960s and 1970s with the advent of the space age. Increasingly, free access to space for strategic and military purposes became essential. This in turn required the development of a world-wide infrastructure to permit satellite tracking, monitoring, control and corrective missions. Many Third World countries, including Ethiopia, provided the facilities for the build-up of that infrastructure. In return the Americans shared the benefits of their space programme with helpful Third World nations. To be deprived of access to those facilities nowadays would be as serious, virtually, as to lose rights of free navigation in some seas.

Taken together, these factors demonstrated the depth of American interest in regions like the Horn and in countering Moscow's strategy of denial. They also underlined Washington's need more precisely to define American interests in the Third World. President Carter's administration attempted for a while to do just that. But while that attempt was being made, Carter's men shelved the Kissingerian perception of the role of the Third World. At the time of the Ethiopian revolution, Kissinger was secretary of state. As he saw the challenge of the 1970s, the Americans faced the central geostrategic task of trying to cope with the rise of the Soviet Union to superpower status. He argued that that task would be managed best by setting off 'Soviet power around the world through a combination of political, military and economic means'.[7] To him, Third World countries were there to be used as a way of maintaining regional power balances so that the overall global balance could be preserved.

If regional balances were disturbed, as he claimed had happened in Angola because of Cuban–Soviet intervention, then Moscow's challenge ought to be countered or be made unacceptably costly. Congress rejected that thesis essentially because Kissinger's attempted justification for the covert operations he had authorized simply was not believed. After the Angolan civil-war crisis, during the troubles in the Horn, the Carter administration attempted to learn from Kissinger's mistakes, assuming a stance of neutrality principally because, in international law, the Russians were on the right side of the line. They were helping a regime, worthy or not, to defend itself against an attacker who had violated a basic tenet of the UN Charter *and* of the OAU – that international frontiers are sacrosanct and to cross them is to threaten peace. It was an argument reminiscent of the justification that the Americans themselves offered for their own involvement in the Vietnam war. It was also an argument Moscow would advance and 104 member states of the United Nations would reject in 1980 when Russian forces invaded Afghanistan.

In the real world little is static, least of all the striving of people and powers to advance their own interests. Since the Second World War the people of the Horn had been haunted by the problems of poverty, hunger, disease and social injustice. Frontiers within the region were either disputed or insecure. Resurgent Islam was on the move. Foreign powers were disgorging arms, men, money and destabilizing propaganda into the area.

Three dynamic processes emerged, each with indigenous origins, all aggravated by imperial and post-imperial factors. The effects further destabilized the lives of millions and led the superpowers to assume positions from which they could, in certain situations, intervene when opportunities presented themselves. The three processes related to:

1. The deteriorating condition of the Ethiopian people under the

government of Prime Minister Aklilu Habte Wold, who had been in office since 1930.

2. The expansionism of Somalia which, years *before* achieving statehood in 1960, had been encouraged by Britain to contemplate a Greater Somaliland made up of part of Kenya and Ethiopia (the Ogaden), Eritrea and all of the former British, Italian and French Somalilands.

3. The secessionist struggle of an autonomous Eritrea illegally annexed at gunpoint by Haile Selassie in 1962.

By the time that the Dergue seized power in 1974 these situations had become not only interactive but also possessed of their own momentum and, with that momentum, their own logic. The imminence of profound change was recognized internationally. The 2,000-year-old Ethiopian dynasty had disintegrated. Survival of the Ethiopian state seemed in doubt. No one could be sure what and who would fill the vacuum.

Somalia, in July 1977, invaded a crippled Ethiopia. Within eight months its forces retreated, bruised and battered by the Ethiopians with Cuban and Soviet help. A variety of historical, ethnic and international complexities contributed to that climactic event. To understand those complexities, it is necessary to consider the situation in the Horn as it was in mid-1977, immediately before the Somalis moved in, and to assess the implications for the superpowers after the Somalis moved out.

Ethiopia

Ethiopia, in mid-1977, was gripped by revolutionary turmoil which persisted long after the emperor's deposition. The military government of Colonel Mengistu Haile Mariam, still claiming a socialist orientation, commanded little popular support. It had executed an untold number of politicians identified with the old regime. In most towns it sought relentlessly to crush civilian and military opponents who once had been revolutionary allies but who had since accused the new regime of betraying the Marxist–Leninist principles it professed. In the countryside peasants were up in arms against aspects of the land-reform programme. Banks, private enterprises and foreign firms had been nationalized but the economy was sagging. Independence-seeking insurgents controlled most of Eritrea, after inflicting major defeats on the armies of the Dergue. But separatism extended far beyond Eritrea, from Tigre in the north to Bale in the south of the empire, from the Begemdir mountains near Sudan in the west to the lowlands of Afars in the east.

The Americans had shut down their communication base at Kagnew, outside Asmara, and cut off military aid begun in 1953. The Russians started moving in with limited weapons deals in December 1976 and March 1977, but the small arms they supplied were used more for internal security than for national defence purposes. Overall, then, Mengistu was in deep trouble, unable to preserve order outside the big cities and witnessing the infiltration of thousands of Somali reinforcements into the Ogaden in preparation for what seemed certain to be a major new insurgency. Ethiopia looked to be in danger of dismemberment.[8]

Somalia

Somalia, in mid-1977, in contrast seemed to be riding high. The Soviet Union was well installed as an ally of the military government of President Mohammed Siad Barre. Siad Barre, just like Mengistu, professed Marxist aspirations and in 1974 had formalized military, political and economic relations with the Soviet Union in a friendship treaty. Moscow by 1977 had invested up to $450 million of military and economic aid in Somalia, providing the country with supersonic MIG-21s, surface-to-air missiles, T35 tanks, coastal patrol craft and nearly 3,000 military trainers. In return, Siad had made available Somali naval, airfield and missile-handling facilities to the Soviet Union; permitted close cooperation between the two countries' security services; and sent more than 2,500 Somali officers and men to the USSR for sophisticated military instruction. Somalia had for some years, too, been backing Soviet-held positions in international affairs. The Angola crisis provided a classic illustration. The government of the late President Neto was recognized by Siad on 11 November 1975, the day that it claimed power in Luanda. Soviet–Cuban help for Neto's MPLA was fully backed – a precedent which Siad reckoned might yet have to be invoked should Somalia ever find itself in need of foreign, non-African support. For the Somali leader would later insist that the insurgency of the Western Somali Liberation Front (WSLF) was no invasion. He called it an attempt by a national liberation movement to achieve the right of self-determination against the opposition of Ethiopian 'colonizers' who, he argued, were no different from Portuguese 'colonizers'. American influence in Somalia, around this time, was virtually non-existent, confined to a small-scale embassy without even a sharp-eyed military attaché. US naval ships had no access to Somali port facilities. American aid for the country had ended in 1971 when Somali-flag vessels began trading with North Vietnam.

Eritrea

Eritrea, in mid-1977, was a bloodsoaked land in the sixteenth year of a struggle for independence from Ethiopian rule. Outside the Moslem and communist spheres, it was largely a 'forgotten war', certainly over-shadowed by the Ethiopian conflict against Somalia, with its overtones of superpower involvement. Yet for Addis Ababa, the outcome would be more significant because the viability of the Ethiopian state and the survival of Mengistu's regime were at stake. Eritrea was not simply a reminder of Italy's once-grand imperial hopes. It provided Ethiopians with their only outlet to the Red Sea, indeed to any sea.

The country's three million Moslems, Christians and other smaller ethnic groups had, over the past century, endured six changings of the (foreign) guards. But the status imposed on them by the emperor in 1962, as the fourteenth province of his empire, became intolerable. The annexation defied the ruling of the United Nations which, a decade earlier, had accorded autonomy to Eritrea within a special federal rela-tionship under Ethiopian sovereignty. The tough, self-reliant people, linked with the Tigrinia-speaking Christians of northern Ethiopia and the Arabic-speaking Moslems along the Red Sea littorals, buried their own old internecine feuding in order to fight for the independence known by their forebears from the tenth century until the colonial scramble.

The removal of Haile Selassie initially raised hopes that the Dergue, with its progressive pretensions, would look kindly upon a political settlement. Instead, its hard-liners chose to perpetuate the emperor's policy and, accordingly, intensified the struggle with bigger guns, better warplanes and greatly reinforced armies. Plainly, Mengistu's regime misunderstood the nature and depth of Eritrean resistance which, by 1977, also possessed a leadership with a radical orientation. Eritrean calls for self-determination were ignored. Mengistu posed a stark choice for all 'Ethiopians': 'Unity or Death!' So death it was for tens of thousands of Eritrean civilians and Ethiopian peasant soldiers in the relentless insurrection that knew no formal battle lines. Ethiopian garrisons were beleaguered in key cities. Eritrean guerrillas for a while commanded up to 90 per cent of the countryside. There were super-power dimensions to the conflict as well. Mengistu's forces, trained by the Americans, and using American arms, were up against Eritrean fighters using techniques of warfare provided by Cuban instructors and using Soviet weapons bought with Arab petro-dollars.

The Horn saw the first 'war of the socialisms in Africa'. The second, between the professed revolutionary regimes of Mengistu and Siad, was imminent.

To Siad, the Ogaden seemed, on the face of things, like a plum ripe for the picking. Euphoria may have clouded his vision. But there were certain realities. Bitter disaffection divided Ethiopian civilians from their military masters. Eritrea had bogged down 40,000 Ethiopian troops and seemed to be approaching its goal of achieving an independent destiny. The Dergue had thrown away its American military umbrella and turned virulently anti-western in the process. Although the Russians were attempting to do the splits between Addis Ababa and Mogadishu, they were still sending in arms under a major 1976 agreement. To cap everything else, President Carter and four key West European powers had promised to provide Somalia with 'defensive' weaponry, presumably in the belief that Siad might yet break his bonds with the Russians.

It became a matter of active speculation whether Siad would take this western response to his plea for help as sanctioning Somalia's long-cherished dream of occupying the Ogaden. If so, it was only one of several misinterpretations of events that had been taking place to transform the power equation. There were other events which, at the time, were not fully understood.

In April, Washington suspended all military aid to Ethiopia, while Mengistu expelled a variety of American military and civilian agencies from the country. Washington, in an *ex post facto* rationalization, cited violations of human rights going back twenty-nine months as a justification for the cut-off. Almost immediately the Dergue proclaimed itself a Marxist regime.

In May, Somali regulars began infiltrating into the Ogaden, to reinforce the already-active WSLF. Soviet specialists moved into the places vacated by the Americans expelled from Ethiopia.

In June, Siad formally asked Washington, London, Paris, Bonn and Rome for weapons. He was told that they agreed 'in principle' but would provide 'defensive' arms only. At the time he was still getting military help from Moscow.

In July, Siad ordered the bulk of his 20,000-strong, well-trained regular army into the Ogaden to help the WSLF in its proclaimed attempt to win rights of self-determination. He was compelling the Russians to choose between Ethiopia and Somalia.

In August, two developments sent Siad hurrying to Moscow with a final appeal (in Marxist–Leninist terms) to back Somalia's fight to achieve self-determination for the Ogadeni people. The positive development was that units of his army and WSLF forces had chalked up several spectacular successes against the Ethiopians and were thrusting into the Ethiopian highlands. The negative development was that the Americans, British, French, West Germans and Italians, aware of the sanctity of African frontiers in OAU eyes, had decided against arming an evident aggressor. Siad's reception in the Kremlin was icy. He was told to pull his troops out of Ethiopian territory.

In September and October, the conflict dragged on with both sides sustaining undisclosed losses.

In November, finally, Siad knew for certain that the Soviet Union would not budge. He denounced the 1974 treaty of friendship, expelling Soviet personnel and cancelling all facilities. Within thirteen days, the Soviet Union launched a huge air- and sea-lift of arms into Ethiopia at the invitation of Mengistu's government. At the same time, the first of thousands of Cuban combat troops began flying in, from Angola and Havana. Armour, guns, clothing and transportation for an entire division arrived from bases in the southern republics of the Soviet Union, in more than 200 plane-loads. The bulk came by sea. Ranking Soviet and Cuban military officers helped the Ethiopians chart a counter-offensive.[9] By March it was all over. A defeated Somali army drifted homewards preceded by more than 600,000 refugees. The exodus from the Ogaden went on, and an official Somali estimate in March 1980 put the refugee total at 1·5 million.

When the rush of events subsided, western analysts attempted to clarify certain obscurities relating to the logic and motives of the principal players. Their main preoccupation centred on why the Russians had switched alliances, jumping from their entrenched, prized positions in Somalia into the darkness of a turbulent Ethiopia, still racked by the Eritrean insurrection.

There was general agreement that Moscow had reacted more swiftly and decisively than Washington when opportunities arose. No government suggested Moscow had contrived, as part of some 'grand design', to create the situation it exploited. (Privately Kissinger offered a different premise, reflecting his own Machiavellian thinking – that Kremlin leaders indeed had coolly engineered the entire conflict situation in the area.) There was, again, general agreement that the huge Soviet–Cuban intervention had injected a serious new imperial content into Soviet global policies which left the Americans and their friends baffled, defensive, groping for an effective counter-strategy.

The Favoured American Theory

In 1977 the Russians were attempting to make maximum political use of their arms diplomacy in Ethiopia and also to preserve their position in Somalia by keeping Siad's expansionism in check. That would explain Fidel Castro's peace mission (outlined in Chapter 5). Its failure foreshadowed the probability of a Somali invasion. An invasion would inevitably compel Moscow to choose between supporting an aggressor or his victim. Given that Moscow aspired to develop a symbiotic relationship with Third World countries and that Africans regarded their frontiers as sacrosanct, it became inevitable that Russians would hurry to the aid of Ethiopia. Furthermore, in Kremlin forward planning, ideology usually took precedence over strategy, if only for a while. Siad was, after all, not immortal. Somalia could wait. The future might bring chances for a resumed partnership, and a revival of the Castro plan for a socialist confederation stretching from the Sudanese frontiers to the Gulf of Aden and taking in all of the Horn.

From that stance it was possible for the Russians to rationalize their own and Cuba's intervention. They argued through their media that Siad's adventurism had been curbed from 1969 to 1977 (without reference to the deterrent factor of US arms supplies to Ethiopia). They claimed, not without justice, that Somalian territorial expansionism had precipitated the crisis which they said they had tried hard to contain. They stressed their altruism in surrendering a huge economic and military investment (without detailing its concomitant strategic benefits) in Somalia, for the sake of defending hapless, helpless Ethiopia. Also, in private exchanges with Third World governments, they pointed with pride at the swift, efficient, and effective conduct of their operation.[10]

Thrown out of Somalia, invited in by Ethiopia, the Russians then committed themselves totally to rescuing Mengistu's regime despite its disordered Marxist ramblings. In terms of international law and politics, the western powers soon recognized that the Russians and Cubans could not be easily assailed, except possibly for the massive scale of their intervention so far from their shores. Washington could only hammer the need for 'African solutions to African problems' even while acknowledging that its own 'wait-and-see' posture might give an impression of political paralysis. The US posture indeed drew criticisms from some allied and most conservative Islamic authorities. Africanists in the State Department argued, nevertheless, that the Soviet leap into Ethiopia could yet turn out to be a wild gamble. Moscow had to be prepared to sink thousands of millions of roubles into the economy of a torn and impoverished land whose people were yearning to share the material benefits of twentieth-century civilization. In fact a huge Soviet economic aid programme, backed by most East European communist countries, was launched. Initial estimates suggested that its cost ran to some $2 thousand million.

The Alternative American Theory

For nearly two years ideologues and military leaders in the Kremlin hierarchy had argued long and deeply over whether or not to abandon Somalia for Ethiopia. Naval strategists, in particular, had been strongly opposed to leaving Somalia. They preferred access to the port, docking and repair facilities of a harbour like Berbera, facing the wide, open Indian Ocean where the grand total of western infrastructural arrangements along the littorals far exceeded those of the Soviet Union. Just as western naval men did, they disliked the prospect of trading an open oceanic position for the option of being bottled up in the Red Sea.

The ideologues, for their part, professed to detect several striking similarities between pre-revolutionary Ethiopia and the pre-1917 Russia of Peter the Great. Both countries had highly centralized monarchical systems, with attendant, privileged, supine aristocracies and a supportive, nationalist-minded church. Both had officer classes in the armed forces quite detached from a disgruntled yet spirited rank-and-file drawn from the peasantry and the middle and lower classes of the towns. The downtrodden peasantry of each country, serfs of absentee landlords, were hungry and restless, captives of a stagnant feudalism with little heart for fighting internal 'foes' whose aspirations they shared.

In the view of the ideologues Ethiopia, then, was the one African state where objective conditions existed for the kind of 'genuine' revolution that conformed with the Soviet experience. Time and again Russians, Cubans and Eastern Europeans stressed in public what they called the 'genuineness' of Ethiopia's revolution. In doing so they aroused the disgust of the country's civilian communist movement. It did not take the incoming Russians long to impress upon Mengistu the need to introduce civilian Marxist advisers into his entourage, as a preliminary to broadening the base of his regime by organizing a country-wide communist party. It was intended as the first stage towards installing civilian rule to replace the junta.[11]

There was, patently, one glaring difference between the Russian and Ethiopian revolutions. The Dergue did not have a Lenin to provide them with a political or philosophical framework for their actions, their needs, and their directions. Ethiopia's new leaders had to borrow, to improvise, and to learn as they went along.

The Kissinger Scenario

The former secretary of state's thesis reflected the thinking of right-wing Republicans, like-minded politicians in Western Europe and the monarchical rulers of the Middle East. Here, in his own words, is how Kissinger explained events in the Horn in an address to the International Radio and Television Society, New York, in mid-1978:

The move into Ethiopia cannot be analysed in terms of the quarrels between Somalia and Ethiopia. Nor is the issue primarily who crossed the border first. The first thing to notice is that Soviet equipment went first to Somalia, a country that had put forward claims on the territory of all its neighbouring states; Soviet equipment was thus guaranteed to be used in an expansionist way. And then when that equipment was used for the precise purpose that Somalia had always asked for it, the Soviet Union switched sides and became the defender of that territory which its own equipment had initially threatened. And 17,000 Cuban troops and a billion dollars' worth of Soviet equipment went into Ethiopia.

It is too cynical to be asked to accept the proposition that what is involved here is the unselfish Soviet desire to respond to the appeal of a sovereign country. The Soviet purpose is geopolitical; to outflank the Middle East, to demonstrate that the US cannot protect its friends, to raise doubts in Saudi Arabia right across the Red Sea, in Egypt, in the Sudan and in Iran.

Kissinger was in office for the first two years of the Ethiopian revolution. During that period, American arms deliveries to the revolutionary regime hit new peaks. Ethiopia had for years been the biggest single recipient of American military aid in black Africa.

There were many who rejected the Kissinger analysis. In particular two analysts – one British, one American – seemed concerned more with the ineffectiveness of US diplomacy than with the proposition that the Russians had somehow violated the norms of international behaviour.

'Except on one issue, the violation of third-country airspace, it was difficult to accuse the Russians of any specific impropriety in the Horn,' James Mayall, a senior lecturer in international relations at the London School of Economics, wrote in September 1978. 'It is true that in Ethiopia they had elected to prop up what is by all accounts an exceptionally unsavoury regime, but not only were they there by invitation but also during the years of their alliance with Somalia, when the United States supported Haile Selassie's regime, there is no firm evidence that the Soviet Union ever encouraged the Somali government to pursue its irredentist ambitions.' [12]

'Of course, Moscow is not responsible for the territorial ambitions of Siad Barre and his associates,' Dimitri K. Simes argued in a special supplement of the *Washington Review* devoted to the Horn of Africa in May 1978. 'Neither is it responsible for the revolution and subsequent civil war which provided a pretext for a dramatic reduction of Addis Ababa's ties with the United States and their replacement by a client relationship with the USSR. All these developments were not of

Soviet making.' Simes, director of Soviet studies at the Georgetown University's Center for Strategic and International Studies, Washington DC, added that Soviet involvement first with Somalia, then with Ethiopia, determined the forms which the confrontation took with the Americans. 'Moscow in effect established the parameters of the conflict and then assured an outcome considered favourable to Soviet interests.'[13]

Any rational solution for the people of the Horn, if ever they were going to live in peace, demanded the evolution, somehow, of a functional unity on the basis of their shared economic and political destiny. For the Horn itself is a natural economic unit despite the diversity of its inhabitants.

No such unity was allowed, or encouraged, during the colonial era. In fact, the reverse – division, enmities, competition – resulted from the intervention of Europeans. Those frontiers that they drew were arbitrary. But they left several undefined. Disputes were bound to follow.

Decline and Fall of the Lion of Judah

If ever there was a monument to the cynicism of states, it was on display in the Horn. A survey of the conditions which contributed to the crises of the 1970s in Ethiopia, Eritrea and Somalia shows why the happy hunting-ground of the European colonizers of yesterday became the testing-ground of the superpowers of today.

In Ethiopia nearly two decades of rising disillusionment with the feudal rule of the emperor reached its highest point in the year before his fall. If the autocrat, who had wielded absolute power longer than any other contemporary ruler, read the signs he showed no evidence of it. Through the 1960s poverty and hunger stalked the empire. Ethiopia had a 5 per cent literacy rate. There was one doctor for every quarter of a million people. The numbers of landless peasants ran into millions. No one could know how many, because there was no census. From 1970 on, warnings reached the imperial court from the ancient provinces of Wollo and Tigre that drought conditions, similar to those which ravaged the Sahel across the continent, were now threatening the northern region with starvation. Emergency aid was essential. In 1972 the Food and Agriculture Organization of the United Nations drummed out the same message and spelt out the amounts of grain needed to head off a disastrous famine.

Nothing was done. Indeed the government then possessed adequate reserves of grain but chose to export some in 1973. In January of that year ragged-trousered peasants trudged into the capital pleading for help. Police turned them away. In the stricken provinces, a few hours drive from Addis Ababa itself, people died along the roadside, more than 70 per cent of the crops were lost, 90 per cent of the cattle perished. The long-predicted famine had arrived. Still, the government did not act. Instead it sheltered behind an official cover-up. Unwilling to intervene for fear of shaking the emperor's now-wobbling throne, a variety of international relief agencies and foreign embassies became parties to the conspiracy of silence.

'From April to November 1973, Haile Selassie's government persistently denied that any widespread starvation was taking place in Ethiopia,' wrote one reporter in 1975. 'Publicly there was no famine. The government would not be embarrassed. By May 1973, when the OAU met in splendour for its tenth anniversary celebrations in Addis Ababa, officials in every international agency and embassy in the capital knew what was happening to Ethiopia's people. Some agencies, including the United Nations, had documented it and US embassy cables to Washington were detailing the famine graphically . . . Yet not one agency or nation – no one – spoke out.'[14]

Students demonstrated in protest against the government's inaction when they learned of what was going on. Violent street clashes followed. By mid-1973, according to Markakis and Ayele, about 100,000 people had died. The ultimate death toll, the authors estimated, was at least 200,000.[15]

Sixteen days before Haile Selassie's dethronement, an Ethiopian commission of inquiry unanimously indicted his whole government for the way it had handled the drought, the hunger and the problem of relief. It accused Habte Wold's cabinet of covering up the calamity; ordered him and thirty-four subordinates to stand trial; and blamed Haile Selassie with some of his courtiers for failing to heed the warnings they had received four years earlier. There was little doubt that the affair contributed largely to the collapse of the dynasty.

The silence of both superpowers in circumstances loaded with tragedy seemed more eloquent than a thousand protestations of concern for Ethiopians. On the face of things, it should have been in their interests to have urged Haile Selassie, publicly if necessary, to accept emergency help for his starving subjects. Moscow and Washington blew no whistles. They proceeded, instead, to consider just how much more military hardware they might be called upon to provide in the region so as to preserve their positions.

By August 1974, the emperor had lost his clothes, and his throne was tottering. But legend still gilded the 226th descendant of King Menelik I, and the legend had to be destroyed. The denunciations of the Dergue, therefore, droned on. Posters plastered the capital showing pictures of Haile Selassie feeding his dogs with juicy cuts of meat – alongside shots of staring, starving victims of the famine. The financial dens of the Lion of Judah were exposed to justify state seizure of his assets. Those ranged from ownership of breweries and public-transport companies to urban and rural real-estate holdings across the land. And for a rainy day, perhaps, they included all the gold produced by Ethiopia's only mine, safely stored in the vaults of a Swiss bank.[16]

Still silent, the Russians and Americans looked on as humiliations were heaped upon the monarch and his court. Nobody wanted to be identified with the crumbled regime of a discredited ruler. Everybody needed to assess the political stance of his successors.

As early as 1973 Washington, reading the signs, had ignored the emperor's pleas for more military supplies to meet the rising threats he foresaw in Eritrea and the Ogaden. The Americans were all too aware of the odium they would incur if they were to pour into a famine-stricken land more guns than bread. From early 1974, for more than a year, they kept their ambassador out of Addis Ababa. Yet significantly, the level of US military aid – in grants and sales – soared during 1975, the first year of Dergue rule. From $11 to $13 millions annually through the 1960s, American assistance in fiscal year 1975 rose to between $22·3 and $30 million in grants and cash sales – augmented by an approved supply of weapons worth $53 million over a two-year term.

The Soviet ambassador, in contrast, stayed at his post during the transition. He and his subordinates kept their heads down but their eyes open. Where they could, they made cautious contact with key members of the new regime. They noted that, at least initially, their Chinese rivals were making most of the running with the military government. Their appraisal was that Peking was coordinating with Washington. That belief was shared by several other embassies including those of France, Britain and India, diplomats reported.

According to the envoys of several countries who were serving in Addis Ababa and Khartoum at the time, the Kremlin initiated discreet exchanges with the Dergue through diplomatic and military channels that passed mainly through the Sudanese capital. It was there, away from the gunfire, killings and counter-killings taking place nightly in Addis Ababa, that the foundations of the Ethiopian–Soviet alliance were laid.

Insurrection in Eritrea

Eritrea's Christians and Moslems, whose numbers were about equal, fought through the 1970s not only to free themselves from Ethiopian rule but also against each other. Successive attempts by the Dergue, since 1978 with Soviet help, to reassert Addis Ababa's authority over the region served only to drive the culturally separate communities into political and military unity. The Sudan helped promote that alliance. That alliance offered evidence of something more than a people's resolve to regain the distinctive independence that they had lost a century before. It was also a unique demonstration in the African–Arab and Christian–Moslem context that new causes can transcend old rivalries.

The Italians first colonized the country in 1882, joining the British and French in the territorial encirclement of Ethiopia. All three European powers gazed greedily towards the well-watered plateaux of the Ethiopian highlands. Then, in 1896, the Italians tried but failed on their own to conquer the country and had to sue for peace after a crushing defeat at Adowa. That victory secured the territorial integrity of Ethiopia, to the extent that it was defined, for nearly forty years.

The inter-war years brought Benito Mussolini to power and he revived Italy's design for a thriving empire in Africa. By then Adolf Hitler was in full cry. 'The need of keeping fascist Italy from joining Nazi Germany led Britain and France at the Conference of Stresa in 1934 to abandon all rivalry for Ethiopia and to allow Italy a free hand there,' American expert John H. Spencer testified before the Senate Sub-committee on Africa in 1976. 'Before that year was out Italy had attacked Ethiopia in the Ogaden.'[17]

Italy's occupation of Ethiopia and Eritrea was brief. British and South African forces reconquered the countries in 1941–2 during the Second World War. The British treated all of Ethiopia, Eritrea and the Italian and (Vichy) French Somalilands as liberated enemy territories and Haile Selassie was restored only on condition that his authority remained subject to London's overriding control. That control took many forms, from supervising the emperor's correspondence to moving traffic on the roads from right to left.

The fate of Eritrea was at the centre of the post-war negotiations between the big powers and later at the United Nations for an Italian peace treaty. For a while the Soviet Union sought trusteeship of Libya, also a former Italian colony. Britain had the idea of restoring Eritrea to Italian control minus its western province, which would then be attached to the British–Egyptian condominium of Sudan, and so extend the influence of London. Ultimately the Americans came up with the plan for a federal solution, a self-ruling Eritrea under Ethiopian sovereignty. The compromise was adopted and implemented in 1952.

Washington's scheme was not altogether altruistic. Haile Selassie had been forewarned that the Americans wanted the big wartime communications base outside Asmara (named Kagnew after the contingent that a grateful Ethiopia sent to fight in Korea). Kagnew was needed for its special qualities as a link in the world-wide US network of military communications. The base was in a zone where seasonal variations and magnetic storms would reduce the need for frequency changes in the signals network that ran through the Philippines, Ethiopia, and Morocco to Arlington, Virginia. It was especially valuable to NATO's communication system in Europe.[18]

Ethiopia was glad to take back Eritrea but far less glad that it should enjoy self-rule. Autonomy could be infectious in an imperial system scarred with wounds of bygone separatist struggles – from the Oromos in the south to the Afars in the east. With their own elected parliament, their own flag and their own conviction that, historically, they had never formed part of Ethiopia, the Eritreans could endanger the unity of the empire. In an age of decolonization, Eritreans considered themselves victims of Africa's partition just as much as the people of any other colonial entity. The country had been part of the Ottoman empire since the sixteenth century, until the Italians arrived to take over Assab Bay in 1882.

Haile Selassie, bearing the aura of a heroic past like a badge, seemed incapable of facing contemporary realities. He set out at once to undermine the 1952 settlement. He stirred Moslem resentment by eliminating Arabic from schools and by relegating non-Christians to inferior status. Working-class Christians lapsed into sullen hostility when he disbanded their labour movement. Threats, pay-offs and punitive expeditions failed to prevent nationalist sentiment from taking active forms in 1961. Ten years after the gallery of the nations had produced its formula for a promising federal alliance, the defiant emperor delivered its death-blow. A rigged vote by the Eritrean legislature, in a session held under the machine-guns of Ethiopian troops, came out for full union with Ethiopia. Addis Ababa hailed the decision and proclaimed Eritrea the fourteenth province of the empire.

There was a certain sadness in the spectacle. When Mussolini's fascists conquered Ethiopia, the monarch had aroused world-wide sympathy with his appeal to the old League of Nations, on 30 June 1936, to honour '. . . the value of promises made to small states that their integrity and their independence shall be respected and assured'. Now Haile Selassie was reneging on the same pledge.

The hijack of a people was complete. Like the League, the United Nations was inert, its key members silent. But insurrection, already a possibility, was assured.

Russia's road into Ethiopia ran through Somalia and it was mapped for Moscow by the obliging political cartographers of the west. Britain, liberator of the Horn, began the process in 1943 by developing the concept of a Greater Somaliland. As Spencer described it in his testimony to the Senate Africa Sub-committee it would comprise 'parts of Kenya, Ethiopia [the Ogaden], all of Italian, British and French Somalilands and Eritrea'. As part of this process the British sponsored the formation of the Somali Youth League which became the forerunner of the Western Somali Liberation Front in the Ogaden, then still occupied. 'Thus was launched a project that has continuously, since that time, lain at the heart of the crisis in the Horn of Africa and which has become the tool of the Russians for the advancement of their aims in that vast area,' Spencer argued before the sub-committee. Twice the British sought U S backing for that scheme, along with a second proposal that they should assume trusteeship over all Ethiopia. Twice, somewhat coldly, the State Department rejected the ideas.

In the post-war negotiations for an Italian peace treaty, something resembling a minor scramble developed among the big powers over the component territories of Italy's empire in Africa. Moscow staked a claim to trusteeship over Libya but this was blocked by the Americans, British and French. The Russians sided with the Americans and French in resisting Britain's Greater Somaliland scheme. France favoured a return to the *status quo ante* which would permit the restoration of Djibouti to French control. The United States adopted a wait-and-see attitude until 1948 when new political factors entered the confused situation.

President Harry S. Truman was facing an election in which the Italian ethnic vote in America could be crucial. Italy, too, was approaching a national ballot with prospects of a communist victory rated high and therefore worrying to the western powers. Truman came out for restoring Somaliland to Rome. So, too, did Moscow, seeking to promote the electoral chances of the Italian communists. In the event, Truman won his presidential election and the communists lost out in Italy.

In a changing situation the peace-making process became more complex because of economic as well as political and strategic rivalries among the big powers. There was, for instance, a sniff of oil in the air suggesting that more was at stake than the claims of the Somalis to graze and water their herds in the disputed region. American firms had obtained rights to explore for fuel deposits believed to be in the area of the unresolved frontier. Later, indeed, the Tenneco group would discover commercially interesting reserves of natural gas. There were, however, few if any explicit references to this kind of consideration by the peacemakers.

The British after 1948 hoped for a bargain with Haile Selassie – his surrender of the Ogaden for their support of the restoration of most of Eritrea to Ethiopia. The Americans opposed detaching the Ogaden from Ethiopia for the enlargement of Britain's Somaliland Protectorate. They produced instead a plan that would permit Italy's return to Eritrea and allow only token Ethiopian access to the Red Sea. 'A corridor for camels!' Ethiopia's ambassador to Britain exclaimed disdainfully at the time, in talking with the author. By 1950 Washington had switched again – this time to the federation formula ultimately adopted.

The Democratic Republic of Somalia came to independent life on 26 June 1960, with a five-pointed star on its national flag, symbolizing a constitutional requirement to unify the fragmented elements of the Somali nation. As outlined in the Manifesto of Mogadishu the year before, the envisioned union would combine the British, Italian and French Somalilands and their hinterlands with the Ogaden and the northern frontier district of (then British) Kenya. Such a Somali state would have incorporated about 40 per cent of Ethiopia (including parts of Eritrea) within its borders making it bigger, even, than the Greater Somaliland that Britain had once contemplated.

Five days after British Somaliland assumed statehood, the Italian Trusteeship Territory of Somalia became independent, too, and merged with its neighbour. The merger had been carefully prepared with the backing of London and Washington. For Haile Selassie and his government, the development revived memories of the pre-war Italian conquest and suspicions that the British and Americans were plotting the dismemberment of their empire. The monarch hustled off to Moscow for help. He came away with a $100-million line of credit.

The British and Americans now were in deep trouble. They knew that the infant Somali Republic could not survive without outside aid. But they also knew that any economic and arms support they might provide would further anger the Ethiopians and even jeopardize the important Kagnew base. As though this were not enough, the new Somalia in the first, full flush of independence began practising the expansionism it had preached. In the Ogaden, fighting flared between Somali clansmen and Ethiopian troops. In Kenya's northern frontier province, Somalis launched what turned out to be a four-year guerrilla campaign which would ultimately lead the pro-western Kenyans into an improbable, albeit temporary, alliance with the pro-eastern leaders of the Dergue.

Waiting and watching from afar, the Russians swiftly moved into the opening presented to them by British–American misjudgements and Ethiopian–Somali hostility. In 1962, 1966 and 1974 Moscow negotiated substantial military and economic aid agreements with Somalia. In the process and for the first time they won for themselves a privileged strategic position in the Horn. Facilities for their naval and air forces in time exceeded those established by the Americans in Ethiopia. They gained, in addition, a leverage which enabled them to restrain the Somali forces from venturing deeply into the Ogaden, so long as the Americans were arming the Ethiopians.

Developments in the Horn through the 1960s served only to consolidate the Soviet position. In 1969 General Siad Barre seized power from a corrupt civilian administration, suspended the constitution, set up a military regime and adopted a programme of action based on what he called 'scientific socialism'. Tremendous tasks faced him in his avowed aim of raising the standards of life in a country of over 240,000 square miles listed among the world's twenty-five neediest nations. He mobilized the people to fight illiteracy, construct public works, reform the feudal farming system, build roads and bridges, schools and houses, and increase food and cotton production. He called this programme of self-help a revolution.

The 1960s also had seen the build-up of a 10,000-strong Somali military force, complete with air and sea elements and equipped with modern Soviet weapons. After Siad Barre took over in 1969, the size of that force at least doubled, its striking power enhanced by perhaps three or four times with even more sophisticated arms from the Russians. By the time the Dergue appeared on the scene five years after his own *coup*, Siad felt more than a match for his troubled, divided neighbours.

So it was, then, that the general moved into the Ogaden where up to about five million Somali nomads and farmers have over generations scratched out a living. In doing so, in July 1977, Siad ignored the threats of the Soviet Union that his arms supply would be cut off. Eight months later his beaten army came home, destroyed by the combined power of the Ethiopians and Cubans fighting under the military direction of Soviet generals. The Somali leader survived the attempts of rivals to unseat him. He had also to swallow hard words of advice from King Khaled of Saudi Arabia, by then his principal paymaster: advice that Somalia must abandon its old socialist pretensions, curb its expansionist ambitions and adjust its policies to those of its neighbours committed to resist new communist encroachments. For Khaled, by the accounts of his diplomats in private conversation, was convinced Moscow and Havana had not by any means forgotten the central concept of the Castro plan for a socialist federation of states throughout the Horn and reaching across the Red Sea into the Arabian Peninsula. Such a grouping would be like a bayonet pointing at the Saudi Arabian belly.

Khaled's initiative did not end in Mogadishu. He had his lines open to the Moslem leaders of the Eritrean resistance movement, too, even though the radicalism of some of its leaders was, for him, distasteful. Together with other conservative and even revolutionary-minded

Middle Eastern states and movements – including the Egyptians, Iraqis, Sudanese, Syrians and the Palestine Liberation Organization – he funnelled help through to the secessionists of Eritrea. The common interest of the supporters of Eritrea was their resolve to extend the frontiers of Islam and simultaneously to block the advance of Soviet influence. Up to a point these objectives had the unspoken blessing of the Americans and other western powers, who were less concerned with Islamic ambitions than they were with the encirclement of an Ethiopia professing adherence to a Kremlin-sponsored socialist destiny.

The Game of Nations

The aftermath of Siad's defeat saw the start of a new era of shifting alignments within, and among, the countries of the region and those adjoining it. Under Khaled's promptings, for instance, Siad Barre came together in Saudi Arabia with President Arap Moi of Kenya, both by this time qualifying for a gradual increase of U S military supplies. To counter, if not to supplant, Kenya's collaboration with Ethiopia, which flowed from a shared experience of Somali expansionism, Siad and Moi set the basis for a *rapprochement*. Siad offered a modification of the Somali constitution so that it would support the liberation of 'Somali territories' by 'peaceful and legal means' only.

That was by no means all. Egyptian backing was enlisted and was given by Sadat in the knowledge that his peace settlement with Israel had brought with it the stabilization of his eastern salient. By 1980 the Egyptians and Ethiopians seemed to be heading towards confrontation, with each accusing the other of conspiring to divert the life-giving waters of the Nile. Ethiopia accused Sadat of diverting Nile waters to Israel across the Sinai peninsula. Sadat countered with a warning to senior army officers in Ismailia to be alert to thwart any Ethiopian attempt to cut off Nile waters from Egypt. He emphasized any such move would mean war and, at the same time, he called for speedier deliveries of American arms because of what he called the 'new situation' that had developed.

The complex interplay of rivalries was reflected in still more manoeuvrings. Gadafi's Libya, sharing a confluence of interests although not of ideology with the Russians, intensified its old feud against Egypt by constructing a line of modern fortifications along their common border. The purpose, Gadafi's men insisted, was purely defensive. But Cairo saw them as a launching ground for an ultimate offensive against Egypt.

Eritrean resistance leaders, for their part, professed to detect sinister implications in an unannounced meeting, on 27 May 1980, between Mengistu and Sudanese President Numeiry. The highly secret session in Khartoum was assumed to have focused on the difficulties caused by the constant influx of Eritrean refugees across the Sudanese border where up to 500,000 had fled. The Khartoum government had reached a point of being unable to bear the huge costs of sustaining them. For his part, Mengistu plainly wanted Numeiry to close his frontier with Eritrea, effectively so as to block all the clandestine routes used by Eritrea's arms, food and other suppliers. Numeiry had for long been trying to promote a political settlement between the Ethiopians and Eritreans based on such concepts as 'federation', or 'regional autonomy' for the Eritreans or even some form of 'confederation'. None of these ideas, however, appealed much to hard-line Eritrean resistance leaders who vowed that they would settle for nothing less than the right of self-determination meaning, in effect, total independence.

The Russians and Cubans, who once had been among the suppliers and trainers of the radicals within Eritrea's liberation movement, were in favour of a negotiated settlement. They had been embarrassed when the turnabout in Ethiopian affairs led them to change sides but always insisted they had played no part in the military operations against the Eritreans. Mengistu had been embarrassed, too, by the inability of his forces to subdue the resistance of the Eritreans and passed word more than once to western governments that a peaceful settlement was at the centre of his objectives. There was little evidence to suggest his regime had tried very hard to achieve one, judging by the succession of air and land offensives the forces of the Dergue had launched against Eritrean guerrilla hide-outs and bases in the plateaux, ravines and mountains of Ethiopia's 'fourteenth province'. Yet, with warnings of the catastrophic effects of another drought on five million Ethiopians and nearly half their livestock, coupled with continuing turmoil in the Ogaden, there was no reason to disbelieve him.

For the United States, meantime, the continued presence of Soviet–Cuban military forces in Ethiopia (and just across the Gulf in South Yemen) remained a cause for anxiety, politically as well as strategically. 'They are particularly disturbing elements [for us] after the Soviet invasion of Afghanistan, an event which manifests a Soviet willingness to use force in the Third World,' Franklin D. Kramer, deputy assistant secretary of defence, told the House Foreign Affairs Sub-committee on Africa in early 1980.

Kramer continued: 'Our efforts in the region are designed to maintain the satisfactory condition of our friends while enhancing our ability to protect our own broader interests in the entire Indian Ocean area. These efforts must be carefully designed and orchestrated; our policy of seeking access, within a broader relationship of security cooperation with Kenya and Somalia, is intended to be a measured and careful response for a long term.'

The Defense Department official stressed that no base rights, only access to port and airfield facilities, were being requested. What he did not report was that Siad was making an agreement conditional on a multi-million dollar weapons deal to help re-equip his defeated army which had left most of its arms behind when it retreated in 1978.

'We are aware of dangers posed by this new framework,' Kramer told congressmen. 'In particular President Mohamed Siad Barre understands the depth of our concern that his support for Somali populations beyond the borders of Somalia [should] not provoke his neighbours.' [19]

Dangerous or not, the United States on 22 August 1980 came to formal terms with Somalia for the use of the Russian-built naval and air base at Berbera and other facilities in return for aid (mainly military) and credits over two years worth $45 million. The American presence in Berbera, 117 miles from the Ethiopian frontier, was designed as Kramer had explained for a dual purpose: to cover the oil route from the Afghan and Iraq–Iran fighting zones and to contain an Ethiopia radicalized with Soviet and Cuban help. Parallel accords had been negotiated with Kenya, Oman and Egypt to accommodate a rapid-deployment force which Washington hoped would deter any threat to the Middle Eastern oilfields and routes. A sum of $132 million also was allocated in fiscal year 1980–81 for the relief of 1·5 million refugees sheltering in Somalia. Unknown numbers of those refugees were families of W S L F guerrillas, campaigning in the Ogaden, plus the very young and very old members of nomadic Somali clans. These clans had, for centuries, been wandering back and forth from the interior with the rains, heedless of ill-marked and anyway disputed borders.

Uneasy members of the Africa Sub-committee of the House Foreign Affairs Committee, fearing Americans could become embroiled in an African war or, worse, confrontation with the Russians, stipulated that the administration had to ensure in advance that all Somali regulars were withdrawn from the Ogaden. Four days after the American–Somali agreement was signed, Assistant Secretary of State Moose told the group that Siad had provided 'oral and written assurances' to that effect. On the same day the CIA reported to the sub-committee that elements of three Somali battalions were still in Ethiopia.

The concern of some congressmen reflected the alarmed reactions of countries in and near the region including Ethiopia itself, Kenya and Iraq. Ethiopians saw the deal as the internationalization of their ancient conflict with the Somalis. Kenyans, while supporting American global policies, nevertheless warned Washington that the Somalis, who previously had 'sold' themselves to the Russians, could not be trusted. Iraq asserted that the development would intensify big-power tensions in the Horn and was an act of hostility towards the Arab nation. Within two months President Siad proclaimed a state of emergency in his land, citing 'the continuing invasion' by Ethiopians, Russians and Cubans. It was an 'invasion' nobody ever confirmed and some of his neighbours suggested that Siad had attempted, theatrically, to speed the flow of American arms which he then would use in the Ogaden.

The name of the game the powers were playing in and around the Horn was cynicism unlimited. And the sadness was that regional states, because of the sins of long-forgotten fathers of empire, dealt themselves in, dreaming, doubtless, of reclaiming or safeguarding lost or disputed heritages. The falsity of frontiers, the poverty of people and rivalry of religions all contributed to local conflicts which the superpowers were only too ready to exploit if they saw any prospect of advancing their strategic aims. In the Horn that process of exploitation took place, in the superpower context, years before Siad's failed invasion. Moscow moved into Somalia, with sophisticated weapons, well aware of the country's constitutional commitment to expand. The process gathered pace even before the remnants of Siad's defeated army straggled home. Carter's security adviser, Zbigniew Brzezinski, early in 1978 invoked the analogy of the Fashoda incident which in 1899 took Britain and France to the brink of war. Brzezinski told journalists that Fashoda presaged the kind of clashes he anticipated between American and Soviet forces in the Horn. 'Sporadic violence,' he said, could have 'a suction effect on US and Soviet intervention forces' resulting in some 'unprecedented confrontations'.

All these developments, seen together, heralded a new phase of dangerous adversary politics in the Horn of Africa through the 1980s, with the superpowers lining up clients from the Mediterranean to the Mountains of the Moon in Uganda and Kilimanjaro in Kenya.

References and Sources

Chapter 1. Overview

1. Harold Macmillan, speech to the two houses of the South African parliament in Cape Town, 3 February 1960.

2. *The Soviet Union and the Third World: A Watershed in Great Power Policy?*, a report to the Committee on International Relations, US House of Representatives, by the Senior Specialists' Division of the Congressional Research Service, 8 May 1977, p. 156.

3. The celebrated Fashoda incident nearly touched off a British–French war in 1899. Paris envied London's designs on the Sudan. A French column, led by a Colonel Marchand, moved along the Nile and hoisted the tricolour at Fashoda, near Khartoum. Intense British political pressure on the French forced the reckless, although gallant, colonel to withdraw.

4. For detailed studies on US and West European reliance on raw materials from abroad see Lester Brown's *World Without Borders*, Random House, New York, 1972; and the final report of the US National Commission on Materials Policy entitled *Material Needs and the Environment Today and Tomorrow*, 1973, Washington DC.

5. V. I. Lenin, *Imperialism, the Highest Stage of Capitalism*, first published as a pamphlet in Petrograd, 1917, and taken from *Lenin: Selected Works*, vol. 1, part two, issued by Foreign Languages Publishing House, Moscow, 1952, pp. 562–8. Also published in Lenin's *Collected Works*, vol. 22, Lawrence & Wishart, 1969.

6. Extracted from 1979 reports of the UN High Commissioner for Refugees and the World Health Organization.

7. Congressman Charles C. Diggs advised the Sub-committee on Africa of the Committee on Foreign Affairs of the US House of Representatives that: (a) the pooling of African efforts to aid the Sahelians contrasted with 'the fragmentation of authority that is a major problem in post-colonial Africa, divided up arbitrarily by the European imperial powers'; (b) the international relief effort found Soviet aircraft transporting American grain to stricken areas; (c) some Africans resented France's portrayal of relief as 'charity' and a demonstration of African weakness, making it seem like a continuing reliance on the 'paternalism and condescension' of the rich countries.

See Congressman Diggs's 'Factsheet on the African Drought Emergency', June 1973, published by the Foreign Affairs Committee of the US House of Representatives under the title, *The Drought Crisis in the African Sahel*, appendix 15, pp. 125–8.

8. For an authoritative account of the Ethiopian drought and its effects see *The Politics of Starvation*, by Jack Shepherd, published by the Carnegie Foundation for International Peace, Washington D C, 1975.

9. E C A report to a conference in Kinshasa, Zaire, February–March 1977, quoted by E. C. Chibwe in *Afro-Arab Relations in the New World Order*, Julian Friedmann Publishers, 1977, pp. 53–6. Chibwe, a Zambian banker-turned-diplomat, was at the centre of African efforts to attract Arab investment in sub-Saharan Africa.

10. See Chester A. Crocker's 'The African Setting', in a May 1978 special supplement entitled *The Horn of Africa*, published by the *Washington Review of Strategic and International Studies*, editor Michael A. Samuels.

11. A mid-1979 breakdown, compiled by Britain's Foreign and Commonwealth Office, categorized the political systems in fifty-two African territories as follows:

Plural-party countries: Afars and Issas, Botswana, Comoros, Egypt, The Gambia, Lesotho, Malagasy Republic, Mauritius, Morocco, Namibia (awaiting independence), Nigeria, Senegal, South Africa, Upper Volta, Zimbabwe.

De jure *one-party states:* Angola, Central African Republic, Equatorial Guinea, Guinea, Guinea-Bissau, Malawi, Mozambique, Sierra Leone, Swaziland, Tanzania, Tunisia, Uganda (multi-party elections, after Idi Amin's downfall, were held in early 1981), Zambia.

Civilianized military regimes with one-party system: Algeria, Benin, Burundi, Congo (Brazzaville), Mali, Rwanda, Somalia, Sudan, Togo, Zaire.

De facto *one-party states:* Cameroon, Cape Verde, Gabon, Ivory Coast, Kenya, Liberia, São Tomé and Príncipe, Seychelles.

States under military rule: Chad, Ethiopia, Ghana (where a return to multi-party civilian rule failed to take place in July 1979), Libya, Mauritania, Niger.

The foregoing groupings should be regarded as subjective and based on differing standards recognized in each country. Therefore the classifications ought by no means to be seen as rigid.

12. See *World Military and Social Expenditure, 1978*, edited by Ruth Leger Sivard, W M S E Publications, Leesburg, Va, p. 5.

13. John Foster Dulles, on 3 April 1956, characterized Nasser as a patriot seeking 'the genuine independence' of the Middle East from residual British–French dominance. A year later, on 2 April 1957, Dulles, seeking to justify the withdrawal of U S support for the Aswan project, compared Nasser's neutralism with blackmail. He was also to tell an Iowa audience on 9 June 1957 that neutralism in the western sphere of interest 'is an immoral and shortsighted conception'. On 13 June, just four days later, he was urging the U S Senate Appropriation Committee to approve aid for neutralist Yugoslavia which had broken loose from the Soviet bloc and was displaying 'passionate dedication' to preservation of its independence. To Dulles, then, neutralism in the western sphere was 'immoral', in the eastern sphere it was commendable and warranted support.

14. *The New York Times*, 17 August 1976.

15. Colin Legum, *Congo Disaster*, Penguin Books, 1961, p. 85.

Chapter 2. Realities

1. Raymond Scheyven, report of the Inter-Departmental Working Group on Sahelian Problems, submitted to FAO Director-General A. Boerma, 23 June 1973.

2. Hal Sheets and Roger Morris, *Disaster in the Desert: Failures of International Relief in the West African Drought*, published by the Carnegie Endowment for International Peace, New York, 1974.

3. Scheyven reported that out of the fifty-one aircraft appealed for, only twenty-one actually were provided by the nations of the world.

4. The comments of the Soviet official were made in a private conversation with the author in Brussels during December 1974.

5. The authoritative French business weekly, *Marchés Tropicaux et Méditerranéens*, on 20 July 1973, p. 2252, reported that the European Community had requested NATO's aid for a massive airlift desperately needed to fly food and other supplies into the region. The response of the Alliance was negative on grounds that such a mission was beyond its scope and, anyway, individual member-nations already were involved in mercy flights. In the third of a series of articles entitled: 'The Drought in West Africa: The Logistics of Relief Operations', Victor D. Du Bois raised the question 'Where was NATO?', although he might also have asked: 'And where was the Warsaw Pact?' Du Bois commented: 'NATO was a logical source of such assistance since it has under its command thousands of aircraft ... The crisis in the Sahel has afforded NATO a rare opportunity to demonstrate that its vast armada can be used for peaceful and constructive purposes. The failure of NATO authorities to take an initiative has not gone unnoticed in Africa. The fact that NATO facilities *were* so quickly mobilized just a few months later for another crisis of quite a different sort – the transport of munitions to Israel to be used against fellow Africans – compromised whatever small credit NATO still had in the eyes of some African leaders.' Du Bois's article was reprinted as an appendix to a report by the Africa Sub-committee of the US House of Representatives, which held hearings on 'The Crisis of the African Drought' in Washington DC, 19 November 1974. Du Bois was wrong in suggesting that NATO airlifted arms to Israel in the October 1973 war. Key European member-nations including Britain, France and West Germany refused to do so. The Americans, however, did airlift supplies using Portugal's Azores bases as a staging-point. Another factor was that de Gaulle almost certainly would not have wanted to see the NATO he was jousting with play a leading role in rushing to the aid of those francophone lands for which Paris claimed first responsibility.

6. Before Sir Harold Wilson visited Moscow in 1964 the author, in an informal talk, suggested to Britain's former Labour prime minister that he might propose to Brezhnev and Khrushchev an experiment in east–west cooperation in some part of then newly independent Africa. The idea was that the two sides, with the assent of the local authorities, should work together on one or more model projects designed to help Africans help themselves. The projects would be undertaken in an area where political factors either did not exist or could be

totally subordinated to the work in hand. Wilson said he liked the idea. On his return he reported he had put it to Kremlin leaders. Their response, as he relayed it, was to say in effect: 'No way.' They had indicated complete uninterest in identifying the Soviet Union with any of the former colonial powers, or with the west generally, in Africa of all places. That, it seemed, was that.

7. Henry Kamm, *The New York Times*, 10 November 1974, dispatch from Dakar, Senegal.

8. Jean-Pierre N'Diaye, *Jeune Afrique*, 19 May 1973.

9. Nicholas Wade, *Science*, 19 July 1974, 'Sahelian Drought: No Victory for Western Aid'.

10. See H. Lhote, *Fresques du Tassili*, Paris, quoted by René Dumont in *False Start in Africa*, André Deutsch, 1969.

11. Paul Bohannan, *African Outline*, Penguin African Library, AP 17, 1964, p. 16.

12. ibid., pp. 103–4.

13. Charlotte and Denis Plimmer, *The British Empire: Black Ivory – Britain's Infamous Slave Trade*, Orbis Publishing, 1979, pp. 85–112.

14. H. Bismuth and C. Menage in a report to the *Haut Comité d'Étude et d'Information sur l'Alcoolisme – Dans les États Francophones d'Afrique Occidentale*, Paris, 1960.

15. General H. Meynier, in *L'Afrique Noire*, Paris, 1911.

16. Walter Rodney, *How Europe Underdeveloped Africa*, Bogle l'Ouverture Publications, 1978. A data sheet on world population prepared by Thomas T. Kane for the Population Reference Bureau, Inc., Washington DC, estimated that in mid-1979 there were then 457 million Africans with a forty-six per thousand birth-rate compared with a seventeen per thousand death rate. By the year AD 2000 Africans should number around 831 million.

17. *History of Parliament*, vol. XXIII, 17 June 1783.

18. Dr Eric Williams, *Capitalism and Slavery*, André Deutsch, 1964.

19. The London-based Anti-Slavery Society, formed in 1839, in 1978 accused Morocco of using children from the age of five to work in Moroccan carpet factories; it asserted that forced labour is still going on in Equatorial Guinea; and it charged that vestiges of slaving have been found in Algeria and the neighbouring Sahara Desert. See the society's publications including: *Child Labour in Morocco's Carpet Industry* and *Equatorial Guinea: The Forgotten Dictatorship*, by Suzanne Cronje; *Western Sahara*, by John Gretton; and the *Annual Report* for 1978. See also *Africa's Slaves Today*, by Jonathan Derrick, Allen & Unwin, 1975.

20 Sir Philip Mitchell, *Land and Population in East Africa*, HMSO, 1952.

21. Senior British defence authorities warned relatives in Kampala, by telephone hours before the *coup*, to keep their heads down. It was never foreseen then that the British-trained Amin would turn sour towards the British themselves.

22. For a detailed exposé of the excesses of the Macías regime see Suzanne Cronje's *Equatorial Guinea: The Forgotten Dictatorship*, Research Report No. 2 of the Anti-Slavery Society, London, 1976.

Chapter 3. The Arms Race

1. Andrew Young, in a talk with the author in New York, 19 January 1979.

2. Lt-Gen. Olusegun Obasanjo, former Nigerian chief of state, quoted in the *Los Angeles Times*, 31 December 1978. See also Claude Ake's *Revolutionary Pressures in Africa*, where he maintains: 'The African bourgeoisie is as much a mechanism of imperialism as international capital; it is itself a social manifestation of imperialist penetration of Africa; it is in every sense a creation of this penetration and an integral part of the structure of dependence' (Zed Press, 1978). Implied confirmation of this viewpoint came also from a European Economic Community document, issued in Brussels under the title *The European Community and the Third World*, which said: 'The Third World is, however, subject to the western economic order, either through the influence of colonization by the western powers or because it has too little real influence in the bodies where decisions on international relations are taken . . . Seen through the eyes of industrialized countries, the Third World remains what it was during preceding decades – a supplier of raw materials such as mineral ores and agricultural produce.'

3. Data on arms expenditure supplied by the Stockholm International Peace Research Institute (SIPRI).

4. Henry Kissinger, *The White House Years*, Weidenfeld & Nicolson and Michael Joseph, 1979, p. 427.

5. All the foregoing statistical information was derived from or based on material contained in *World Military and Social Expenditure, 1978*, edited by Ruth Leger Sivard, WMSE Publications, Leesburg, Va; and from the 1979 annual report of the World Bank, Washington DC.

6. Frank Barnaby, director of SIPRI, writing in the *Guardian*, London, 18 June 1979, under the title: 'Africa's Endless Strife.'

7. *Communist Aid to Less Developed Countries of the Free World 1977*, a CIA research paper prepared at the National Foreign Assessment Center, Washington DC, November 1978.

8. *International Herald Tribune*, 31 October 1979, 'US Report sees Hassan's Power in Peril', p. 1.

9. US Senate Select Committee to Study Government Operations with Respect to Intelligence Activities, *Alleged Assassination Plots Involving Foreign Leaders: Interim Report*, ninety-fourth congress, first session, 20 November 1975, pp. 14–16, 55.

10. ibid., pp. 48–9.

11. All the foregoing information was provided in answer to the author's questions by Britain's Defence Ministry after Minister of State for Foreign Affairs David Ennals told parliament on 31 March 1976 that Cuban regulars were being employed in Equatorial Guinea in 'advisory and training roles'.

12. For a fuller account of the Ethiopian revolution and subsequent developments see Chapter 11, 'The Horn of Africa'.

13. Soviet, East European and Ethiopian diplomats volunteered this interpretation of American-sponsored counter-strategy to the author during background discussions in London, New York and Brussels in 1979.

14. The US arms build-up in Kenya, which included 2,100 anti-tank guided weapons and thirty-two Hughes helicopters, was augmented also by Britain and West Germany. Although numbers, costs, delivery dates and other details of the European armaments remained secret, agreements in 1978 and 1979 with Kenya were known to have provided for Rapier surface-to-air missiles, Hawk trainer aircraft, tank transporters and medium tanks.

15. Foreign Assistance Legislation for Fiscal Year 1980–81, part 6, Hearings and Mark-up before the Sub-committee on Africa of the Foreign Affairs Committee, House of Representatives, ninety-sixth congress, 13 February–12 March 1979, Washington DC.

16. ibid., pp. 272, 296.

17. An appraisal of the coming struggle for power in southern Africa appears in Chapter 9.

18. *Arms Across the Sea*, by Philip J. Farley, Stephen S. Kaplan, and William H. Lewis, published by the Brookings Institution, Washington DC, March 1978, p. 14.

19. *The Arms Trade and the Third World*, published by SIPRI and Penguin Books, 1975, pp. 224, 231.

20. Richard Moose, assistant secretary of state for African affairs, in testimony before the Africa Sub-committee of the US House of Representatives; hearings on 'Economic and Military Assistance Programmes in Africa, 1980–1981', 14 February 1979.

21. *The Military Balance: 1979–1980*, published by the International Institute for Strategic Studies, London.

22. All the information in the preceding four paragraphs is extracted from the SIPRI Yearbook for 1979, *World Armaments and Disarmament*.

23. Ten US corporations, most involved in arms exports, gathered about one-third of the total sales in 1976, the last year of the Ford–Kissinger administration. Their share amounted to about $4 thousand million. These firms promoted foreign sales of their weapons systems and services through agents, specially trained lobbyists, and contact men. The Lockheed and Northrop corporations also used bribes and dubious commissions as a means of picking up contracts. When their methods were exposed in congressional hearings, foreign politicians, and even governments, trembled.

24. For penetrating, although subjective, accounts of the crises in the Congo and Nigeria see Conor Cruise O'Brien's *To Katanga and Back* and *The Biafra Story*, by Frederick Forsyth, published, respectively, by Hutchinson and Penguin Books, in 1962 and 1969.

25. Moose testimony, op. cit., p. 80. The late Adlai Stevenson, then chief US delegate to the United Nations, had pledged on 2 August 1963 that his government expected 'to bring an end to the sale of all military equipment to the government of South Africa by the end of this calendar year'. He added the qualification that Washington reserved the right to interpret its policy 'in the light of requirements for assuring the maintenance of international peace and security'.

26. The Indian deal evidently was private enterprise in action, resulting from a lack of official vigilance. Government spokesmen said it was 'utterly unthink-

able that India could be party to the supply of material' to South Africa or Zimbabwe. But inquiries by the author established that the aged tanks had been advertised for sale as scrap, bought by an entrepreneur, shipped to Abu Dhabi, then transferred for delivery to South Africa.

27. President Julius Nyerere, in a special message to foreign governments, delivered through their envoys in Dar es Salaam, 8 June 1978.

Chapter 4. The Soviet Union

1. Kennet Love, *Suez: The Twice-Fought War*, Longman, 1970, p. 90.

2. This account of the Dulles–Hussein meeting was reconstructed by Egyptian and American participants in subsequent talks with the author, and by the former US assistant secretary of state for Near East, South Asian and African affairs, whose version was quoted by Love, op. cit., p. 315.

3. The duration of the Soviet–Egyptian relationship proved shortlived in the light of the communist-bloc investment. In the twenty-five-year period ending in 1978, total economic aid was $2·2 thousand million, according to a British Foreign Office assessment dated May 1979. Total military aid could not be quantified by outsiders but almost certainly exceeded that figure. Sadat expelled nearly 20,000 Soviet military and technical advisers exactly sixteen years after Moscow picked up the Aswan commitment and sixteen months after signing a friendship treaty with the USSR. Cairo–Moscow relations had been worsening for months with Washington discreetly stirring the pot of simmering suspicions, whenever possible.

4. Quoted in an analysis by Roger E. Kanet on 'The Colonial Question' published in *The Soviet Union and the Developing Countries: Policy or Policies?*, edited by Kanet and Donna Bahry, after the first International Slavic Conference, Banff, Alberta, Canada, 1974.

5. Morton Schwartz, quoted in *The USSR and the Leftist Regimes in Less Developed Countries*, a survey, vol. 19, 1973, p. 211.

6. Prime Minister James Callaghan, interview with the author, London, 20 June 1978.

7. Frantz Fanon, *Toward the African Revolution*, Penguin Books, 1964, from the French *Pour la Révolution Africaine*, Maspéro, 1964.

8. US State Department authorities in Washington, London and other European capitals privately related to the author that this had been the gist of informal utterances, conveyed to Washington by Soviet envoys, after President Kennedy and Nikita Khrushchev negotiated, through their governments, terms for the Soviet withdrawal from Cuba.

9. Guy Arnold argues, in a penetrating study of the international aid business, that 'eastern bloc countries push the idea of interdependence more genuinely than do western powers'. Their approach, he says, is to ensure that 'the donor must also get something out of any aid deal'. Arnold suggests that 'the west – the old colonial powers – is winning a battle to keep the Third World in economic vassalage'. See *Aid in Africa*, Kogan Page, 1979.

10. Statistics extracted from American CIA and British Foreign Office papers show that total communist economic credits and grants, extended to developing

countries from 1954 to 1977, amounted to $27·5 thousand million, while, in 1975 alone, western resources made available to the developing countries added up to $38 thousand million. Aid nevertheless lies in the eye of the beholder and statistics can lie. There were no direct country-by-country comparisons shown. The western flow of resources included private investments and project money which yielded, presumably, comforting profits. If the figures disclose anything it is that the vastly greater proportion of western money injections into African, Asian and other regions have done little to resolve the fundamental problems of the needy nations and, if anything, heightened their dependence on outsiders. See *Least Developed Countries: Economic Characteristics and Stake in North–South Issues*, a CIA research paper published in May 1978, Washington DC; and *Soviet and East European Aid to Africa*, a British Foreign Office analysis issued in June 1979.

11. Daniel P. Moynihan in his own critique of Third World policies entitled 'The United States in Opposition', published in *Commentary*, March 1975, p. 34. Moynihan argued that the political traditions of the French, Belgians, Dutch, and Portuguese hardly varied from those of the British. Consequently their former colonies, on achieving statehood, were 'ideologically uniform having fashioned their politics in terms derived from the general corpus of British socialist opinion as it developed in the period roughly 1890–1950'.

12. According to British and US authorities, Aeroflot concluded air services agreements with Algeria, Angola, Benin, Burundi, Cape Verde Islands, Central African Republic, Chad, Congo (Brazzaville), Egypt, Equatorial Guinea, Ethiopia, Ghana, Guinea-Bissau, Libya, Madagascar, Mali, Mauritania, Mauritius, Morocco, Mozambique, Nigeria, Rwanda, Senegal, Somalia, Tanzania, Tunisia, Uganda, Zaire and Zambia by the end of the 1970s. Other accords for regularly scheduled commercial flights were under negotiation.

13. This statement was made to the author by a senior British defence authority with access to the west's pooled intelligence information on the event.

14. The Russians negotiated agreements on fishing with at least twenty-three out of Africa's thirty-five littoral states by the 1980s. The accords were with Algeria, Angola, Benin, Congo (Brazzaville), Egypt, Equatorial Guinea, Ethiopia, Gambia, Guinea-Bissau, Ghana, Kenya, Libya, Mauritania, Mauritius, Morocco, Mozambique, Senegal, Seychelles, Sierra Leone, Somalia, Sudan, Tanzania and Tunisia. Anchorage, storage, victualling and other facilities were part of the arrangements which also provided for the delivery of part of the Soviet catch to the host country.

Chapter 5. Cuba

1. President Castro's address at the congress of the Cuban communist party, 22 December 1975. The Spanish conquest of Cuba began in 1511, nineteen years after Columbus discovered the island. Slaves from the coastal lands of West Africa, including Angola, were imported from 1517 and the traffic continued until about a century ago. Millions of Africans were brought in over the cen-

turies, according to the Cuban national poet, Nicolás Guillén, and the historian, Fernando Ortiz, whose *Los Negros Esclavos*, published in Paris in 1971, is widely considered a classic study of the subject.

2. Castro's speech at the opening ceremony of the International Conference of Solidarity with the Struggle of the African and Arab Peoples against Imperialism and Reaction, held in the Africa Hall, Addis Ababa, 14 September 1978.

3. President Castro claimed at the summit conference of the world's non-aligned movement in Havana in September 1979 that: 'Cuba has twice as many doctors serving abroad as does the World Health Organization, WHO.' He gave no figures. Nor later did WHO itself which classifies all its field workers as 'professionals'. These include administrative and technical officers.

4. Castro on 5 December 1977 told US Democratic congressmen Frederick W. Richmond and Richard Nolan (of Brooklyn and Minnesota) that about 60 per cent of Cuban troops had been withdrawn from Angola by the spring. The Katangan invasion of Shaba was perceived by Neto, Castro told the Americans, as a provocation designed to touch off new attacks on Angola and he therefore appealed for the return of some of the Cuban troops. Around April–May, too, a build-up of South African forces along the southern frontier was detected and Castro maintained that there would have been new Zairean–South African invasions if Cuban troops had not been sent back.

5. Reuter dispatch from Havana published in the *Guardian*, 8 February 1980.

6. President Carter, press conference, Washington DC, 14 June 1978.

7. Ambassador Leslie Harriman, interview with the *Nairobi Times* quoted in the *Miami Herald*, 10 July 1978.

8. President Carter, news conference with Hispanic media, Washington DC, 12 May 1978.

9. President Castro, interview with Barbara Walters of the American Broadcasting Company, Havana, 18 June 1978. See also John Stockwell's assertion that the CIA learned after the Angolan affair that the Cuban decision to intervene was taken independently (*In Search of Enemies: A CIA Story*, W. W. Norton, New York, 1978, p. 172. British edition published by André Deutsch, 1978).

10. Dr Gordon Adams, assistant professor of political science, Rutgers University, Newark, in a paper presented at the twenty-first annual meeting of the African Studies Association, Baltimore, Md, 1 November 1978.

11. Gerald R. Ford, *Business Week* special advertising supplement relating to South Africa, 9 October 1978.

12. President Carter, news conference, Washington DC, 13 May 1978.

13. Andrew Young, interview with CBS TV, 26 January 1977.

14. Andrew Young, interview with the author, New York, 19 January 1979.

15. Fidel Castro, speech after the seventeenth anniversary of the Bay of Pigs, 26 April 1978, reported in *Granma*.

16. R. Roa-Kouri, interview with the author, 18 January 1979.

17. Details of these exchanges, hitherto secret, were among documents de-

classified in mid-1978 at the Johnson library in Austin, Texas. They have received scant public attention.

18. Professor Jorge I. Domínguez, Center for International Affairs, Harvard University, in an article on 'Cuba's Foreign Policy' in the autumn 1978 issue of *Foreign Affairs*, New York. Domínguez also cited Cuban–Soviet difficulties over (a) Havana's public criticism of Moscow's trade and cooperation policies with Cuba's Latin American antagonists, (b) Havana's attacks on Soviet-oriented communist parties in Latin America for apparently abandoning their revolutionary commitments, (c) defiance of Moscow's wishes by active Cuban aid for revolutionary movements in Latin America during the 1960s when the Russians were in formal state relations with the governments concerned.

Problems arose in the economic sector, too, as Cuba began trading more heavily with Franco's Spain than with East European communist countries. Domínguez recalled that Cuba took advantage of rising world sugar prices in 1963–4 by switching exports from socialist to more lucrative capitalist markets.

19. Herbert Walker, Jamaican delegate to the UN Conference on Trade and Development, Nairobi, Kenya, June 1976, reported in *New Times*, Moscow, under the title 'The Conference is Over, the Struggle Continues', p. 24.

Chapter 6. China

1. New China News Agency report from Mogadishu, Somalia, 3 February 1964. Countries visited by Chou in 1963–4 were Egypt, Tunisia, Morocco, Algeria, Ghana, Mali, Guinea, Sudan, Ethiopia and Somalia.

2. General Alexander M. Haig in a talk with the author on 11 May 1979, at SHAPE headquarters, near Brussels, before Haig retired as SACEUR.

3. There have been many versions purporting to explain the actual causes of the Peking–Moscow split, with all its implications for the contemporary east–west contest in Africa. The foregoing account has been based on the author's conversations with Chinese, Soviet and American authorities in Peking, Moscow, Washington and elsewhere.

4. George Ivan Smith in a talk with the author.

5. *The Great Uhuru Railway: China's Showpiece in Africa*, by Richard Hall and Hugh Peyman, Victor Gollancz, 1976. Some detail was also provided by George Ivan Smith, former personal representative in East Africa of the late UN Secretary-General U Thant, in personal conversation with the author.

6. *Communist Aid to Less Developed Countries of the Free World 1977*, a CIA research paper prepared at the National Foreign Assessment Center, Washington DC, November 1978, pp. 10, 16.

7. Lin Piao in an article headed 'Long Live the People's Republic!', US State Department daily report monitored 3 September 1965.

8. *Peking Review*, 6 January 1978.

9. A Chinese diplomat, who asked not to be identified, in a talk with the author.

Chapter 7. The United States

1. The 'senior US official', throughout Kissinger's many shuttles, always declined to be named. The correspondent who asked the question was the author.

2. Roger Morris, *Uncertain Greatness: Henry Kissinger and American Foreign Policy*, Quartet Books, 1977, pp. 117, 118.

3. Richard Crossman, *The Diaries of a Cabinet Minister*, Hamish Hamilton and Jonathan Cape, 1975, vol. 1, p. 418. In personal talks with the author at the time, Crossman detailed some of the Wilson–Johnson exchanges as he understood them but asked, as he had done on other occasions, that there should be no immediate publication, presumably wanting to keep ultimate disclosure for his own purposes. 'Harold,' Crossman remarked to the author at the time, 'now has become Johnson's poodle over Vietnam and most things.'

4. Baron Selwyn-Lloyd, *Suez 1956: A Personal Account*, Jonathan Cape, 1978, p. 200.

5. ibid., p. 258. Pineau recounted in his memoirs *1956 Suez*, published in 1976, that Dulles in a private chat had remarked: '*A Suez, nous nous sommes trompés. C'est vous qui aviez raison*' ('We were wrong about Suez. You were the ones who were right').

6. ibid., p. 219.

7. Sir Winston Churchill, speech at the Mansion House, London, 10 November 1942.

8. Cordell Hull, 23 July 1942, *Documents on American Foreign Relations*, Boston, Mass., 1944, vol. 5, p. 6.

9. Ambassador Robert Murphy in *A Diplomat Among Warriors* related how in 1942 he came to pledge, in the name of the US government, unqualified support for the restoration of French sovereignty in all the pre-war colonies despite the pronouncements of the president (Doubleday, New York, 1964).

10. Henry Byroade, assistant secretary of state in charge of Near Eastern, South Asian and African affairs, 30 October 1953, quoted in Professor E. Vernon McKay's *Africa in World Politics*, Harper & Row, New York, 1963, p. 321.

11. George V. Allen, Byroade's successor in the State Department, 21 April 1956.

12. Vice-President Richard M. Nixon, election campaign speech, 2 November 1956, in Hershey, Pennsylvania. Britain's Selwyn-Lloyd later described Nixon's remarks as 'a blatant piece of electioneering'. Waldemar A. Nielsen, in his perceptive book *The Great Powers and Africa*, published for the Council on Foreign Relations in 1969, revealed that Dulles had written that portion of Nixon's text.

13. For fuller accounts of the complexities involved in the crisis of the Congo, see *Congo Disaster*, by Colin Legum, Penguin Books, 1961; *The Congo Since Independence*, by Catherine Hoskyns, Oxford University Press, 1965; *The Last Days of Dag Hammarskjold*, by Arthur Gavshon, Barrie & Rockliff, 1963.

14. Henry Kissinger, summary of a speech delivered secretly to a London meeting of US ambassadors in December 1975, published in *The New York Times*, 7 April 1976, p. 2.

15. Andrew Young, in a talk with the author, 19 January 1979; later in an interview with *Encore American and Worldwide News*, 2 July 1979.

16. Argument went on for months over whether Kissinger misled Smith or Smith twisted the truth, as he had been accused of doing in previous negotia-

tions. Homeward-bound Kissinger had sent Smith a signal from Dar es Salaam, seen by the author and Bernard Gwertzman of *The New York Times*, on 21 September 1976. It said in effect that on the basis of his talks with Presidents Kaunda and Nyerere he felt that the placing of responsibility for law, order and security in white hands could be included in the package agreement. Smith had agreed in principle to announce publicly that he would be accepting black majority rule within two years. The message, in fact, did not say all this in precise terms. It was ambiguously worded leaving an impression shared both by Salisbury and Pretoria that the black presidents would go along with the proposal. Later Smith suggested Kissinger had misled him or that the presidents had changed their minds. On the basis of the Kissinger cable, there is little doubt that Kissinger was not about to let such a 'detail' stop Smith from making his central commitment from which he could never easily disengage. Kissinger may have won that round but he lost the fight because the entire package disintegrated in due course with the law, order and security issue a main cause.

17. Andrew Young, interview with Jonathan Power, *Observer*, 9 September 1979.

18. For more detail see Chapter 5, 'Cuba', pages 114–15.

19. Donald H. Rumsfeld, Defense Secretary, annual 'posture statement' in the *Report of the Department of Defense for Fiscal Year 1977*, Washington, p. 22.

20. *Survey of Current Business*, U S Department of Commerce, August 1979.

Chapter 8. France

1. Bokassa's attack on Journiac was made known to the author on 15 September 1979 by French authorities who declined to be identified. The monthly journal *Africa*, in its November issue, printed a similar version under the heading: '"Operation Barracuda" rules in CAR.'

2. *The New York Times*, 4 October 1979.

3. *Time* magazine, 8 October 1979.

4. Claude Bourdet, distinguished French socialist writer, in 1978 compared France's policies in Africa to Metternich's nineteenth-century attempt to create a Holy Alliance of autocrats. That alliance was intended to preserve Europe's monarchical system and for a time it worked. But, Bourdet asked, was it not 'a bit late for Metternich in Africa or elsewhere?'. *New Statesman*, 21 July 1978.

5. Alain Peyrefitte, information minister, 26 February 1964.

6. These included 5,000 soldiers, sailors and airmen in Djibouti; 4,500 soldiers, sailors, airmen and fifteen warships in the Mayotte and Réunion Island colonies off the East African coast; 1,700 troops in Senegal supported by airmen operating a Jaguar squadron; more than 2,600 troops in Chad with an air force maintenance and operational depot in Fort Lamy (although they were under notice to leave); 600 troops in the Ivory Coast; 500 soldiers in Gabon and about 500 troops in Mauritania with air support. France also maintained air and naval bases, with supporting personnel, on the islands of Les Glorieuses, Tromelin, Juan de Nova Europa and Bassas da India. Finally, in the (quickly renamed) Central African Republic, up to 1,000 troops with air cover were in place to

preserve order after the departure of Bokassa and two bases were under construction.

7. See James O. Goldsborough, 'Dateline Paris: Africa's Policeman', *Foreign Policy*, winter 1978-9, pp. 174-90.

8. At the height of their war against the independence movements of Angola, Mozambique and other African colonies, Portugal's expeditionary forces exceeded 200,000, according to official Lisbon accounts.

9. Schmidt, courteously, omitted any reference to the French 'experience' in Indo-China and Algeria.

Chapter 9. Britain

1. When Dr Daniel Malan led South Africa's Afrikaner nationalists to victory over General J. C. Smuts in 1948, he exclaimed: 'Today South Africa belongs to us once more. For the first time since Union [1910], South Africa is our own. May God grant that it will always remain our own.' *The Economist*, 31 May 1955.

2. For detailed accounts of the early conflict between the intruding British and settled blacks of Zimbabwe see *Origins of Rhodesia*, by Sam Kange, Heinemann, 1968; and *The Afrikaners*, by John Fisher, Cassell, 1969.

3. President Julius Nyerere, news conference in Dar es Salaam, 25 February 1980, reported by the Tanzania News Agency.

4. Sir Anthony Duff, the deputy governor, acknowledged privately that it had been 'a mistake' to permit the South African army to guard Beitbridge. No protests had been foreseen, he explained.

5. Prime Minister Wilson, statement in the House of Commons, 11 November 1965.

6. Estimates of white Rhodesian security forces suggested that by the end of 1979 more than 25,000, mainly black Zimbabweans, had been killed. This figure left out of account thousands in Zambia, Mozambique and Angola who died in air and land attacks. The number of wounded was said easily to exceed 150,000. Hundreds of farmsteads and homes were destroyed. Thousands of cattle perished. Entire African villages in the trust territories were razed.

7. 'Southern Africa' and 'subcontinent', in the present context, relate to territories south of Zaire and Tanzania, covering nearly two million square miles. Events in Angola are dealt with in Chapter 10.

8. US State Department and CIA officials were widely quoted, in February 1977, as saying South Africa could develop nuclear weapons by 1981 if a decision to do so were taken; Raymond Barre, then French premier, in the same month told the National Assembly that the Republic already possessed a military nuclear capacity.

9. *Times of Zambia*, 4 February 1980; *Christian Science Monitor* and other US and British newspapers, 5 February 1980.

10. Macmillan, op. cit.

11. Soweto, short for South Western Townships, with more than 1·6 million legal and illegal residents, emerged as one of Africa's largest black cities. The riots which flared on 16 June 1976 began eight months of violence throughout

South Africa. Judge Petrus Cillie, sitting as a one-man commission of inquiry, reported on 29 February 1980 that the government's race laws, official bungling and police unreadiness were to blame for the uprising. Specifically the judge cited the 'bitterness and frustration among blacks' over racial laws which included influx control, segregation rules and social injustice (*International Herald Tribune*, 1 March 1980).

12. South African police shot dead 163 people during 1979 alone, the minister in charge of police affairs told the Cape Town parliament on 20 February 1980. Most were 'prisoners attempting to escape from custody', Louis Le Grange said, adding that 495 others also had been wounded by police bullets in the same circumstances. The *Guardian*, quoting a Reuter dispatch, 21 February 1980.

13. Dr Gerhard De Kock, deputy governor of the South African Reserve Bank quoted in the *Sunday Telegraph*, 24 February 1980.

14. For a detailed account of the oil sanctions-busting scandal see Martin Bailey's *Oilgate*, published by Coronet Books, 1979. Bailey, with Bernard Rivers, followed the sanctions trail for years in a brilliant, sustained example of investigative journalism at its best.

15. Accounts of Heath's encounters with Nyerere and Kaunda over the arms-for-South Africa affair came from top-level Tanzanian and Zambian personalities who declined to be identified.

16. R. W. Johnson, *How Long Will South Africa Survive?*, Macmillan, London, 1977, p. 122.

17. On the issue of Shell and BP culpability, and British ministerial knowledge of it, see the *Report on the Supply of Petrol and Petroleum Products to Rhodesia* by Thomas H. Bingham, QC, and S. M. Gray, FCA, September 1978, released by the Foreign and Commonwealth Office. On Benn's charges against officials of the Department of Energy see *The Rossing File*, by Alun Roberts, published by the Anti-Apartheid Movement, February 1980. Benn's initial charges were made in a letter to the *Guardian* on 13 September 1973, when he was an opposition Labour member of parliament. The Labour Party leadership, under rank-and-file pressure, agreed to cancel the Rossing contract when it regained office. The pledge was, nevertheless, broken.

18. Sir Arthur Snelling, KCMG, KCVO, British ambassador to South Africa, presenting 'A Personal View of Africa' to the South African Institute of International Affairs in Natal, 26 August 1971.

19. Julius Nyerere, 'South Africa and the Commonwealth', a paper circulated at the Commonwealth summit conference in Singapore, January 1971.

20. President Nyerere, chairman of the heads of government of the five front-line states with a special interest in Zimbabwe, told foreign envoys in the week before the Zimbabwean election: 'At the time of UDI Britain did nothing to stop Ian Smith. But now it's worse. Britain is actively siding with the whites.' Besides Tanzania, the other front-line states are Mozambique, Zambia, Botswana and Angola.

21. *Washington Post*, 30 January 1980.

22. The Tass report was amplified in press releases issued by various Soviet embassies in western capitals. Botha's statement came after Washington confirmed the Soviet disclosure.

23. These Patriotic Front reactions were expressed in discussion with the author.

24. *Daily Telegraph*, 12, 14 September 1977.

25. SAFARI stands for South African Fundamental Atomic Research reactor.

26. The Nuclear Suppliers Club banded together governments of east and west committed to respect the provisions of the world treaty which aimed at checking the spread of nuclear weapons. To that end, they agreed to prohibit the export of a wide range of machinery, equipment and materials likely to help those non-nuclear nations still nursing pretensions of developing atomic weapons.

27. Composition of the Rossing Consortium: the state-owned South African Industrial Development Corporation – 25 per cent; General Mining of South Africa – 25 per cent; RTZ and its Canadian subsidiary Rio Algom – 25 per cent; the West German Urangesellschaft which included state-run firms – 10–15 per cent; Minatome, a French consortium including state-owned firms – 10 per cent.

28. Security Council resolution 301, 20 October 1971.

29. Elaine Windrich, *Britain and the Politics of Rhodesian Independence*, Croom Helm, 1978, pp. 15, 16.

30. Extract from the official minutes of the Commonwealth prime ministers' conference, Lagos, January 1966.

31. Associated Press, London-dated dispatch, 4 March 1980.

32. *Rise Up and Walk*, Bishop Abel Muzorewa's autobiography, published by Evans, 1978.

33. Bishop Muzorewa, interviewed on an Independent Television News 'Meet the Press' programme, 5 August 1978.

34. Robert Mugabe, in an interview with the author in Geneva, December 1976.

35. Mugabe, in a talk with the author in London, December 1979.

36. Lt-Gen. Peter Walls, in an interview with BBC correspondent Richard Lindley, broadcast in the *Panorama* programme, 11 August 1980.

37. Ted Rowlands, former Labour minister of state at the Foreign and Commonwealth Office, in an interview with the BBC, broadcast 2 September 1980.

Chapter 10. Angola

1. Extract from M. A. Suslov's article in the *Kommunist* of 11 September 1975, entitled 'The Communist Movement in the Vanguard of the Struggle for Peace and Social and International Liberation'.

2. Hearings before the US Senate African Affairs Sub-committee, 29 January 1976, p. 15.

3. All statements attributed to Kissinger are in a chronology extracted from his testimony to the US Senate African Affairs Sub-committee, 29 January 1976, pp. 14–21.

4. John Stockwell, *In Search of Enemies: A CIA Story*, W. W. Norton, New York, 1978, pp. 67, 258. (British edition published by André Deutsch, 1978.)

5. ibid., p. 68.

6. Nathaniel Davis, 'The Angola Decision of 1975: A Personal Memoir', *Foreign Affairs*, autumn issue, New York, pp. 109–24.

7. The House Select Committee on Intelligence reported to the White House on 19 January 1976 that the CIA valuation of 1975 Angolan aid was inaccurate and the $31 million ordnance figure 'should at least be doubled'. It cited examples of ·45 calibre automatic weapons being costed at $5 each and ·30 calibre semi-automatic carbines at $7·55.

8. Davis, op. cit., p. 121.

9. Gabriel García Márquez, *Operation Carlota: Cuba's Role in Angola's Victory*, published as a pamphlet by the Center of Cuban Studies, New York, April 1977.

10. Quoted by Bender, *New York Review of Books*, 21 December 1978.

11. Castro's speech, Havana, 19 April 1976, marking the fifteenth anniversary of the failed US-sponsored plan to land an invasion force in the Bay of Pigs.

12. Stockwell, op. cit., p. 216.

13. Extracted from the report on the CIA by the House Select Committee on Intelligence, 19 January 1976, published without authority by former CBS correspondent Dan Schorr in the *Village Voice*, New York, 16 February 1976, p. 85.

14. Leslie H. Gelb, *The New York Times*, 25 September 1975.

15. Bishop Ralph E. Dodge, testimony before the US Senate African Affairs Sub-committee, 6 February 1976, pp. 202–9.

16. General Alexander M. Haig in a talk with the author on 11 May 1979, at SHAPE headquarters, near Brussels, before Haig retired as SACEUR.

17. Professor John A. Marcum, 'Southern Africa after the Collapse of Portuguese Rule', in *From Mystery to Maze*, ed. Helen Kitchen, published by Lexington Books for the Commission on Critical Choices for the Americas, Lexington, Va, 1976.

18. Stockwell, op. cit., p. 246.

19. ibid., p. 67.

20. Schorr, op. cit., p. 85 (emphasis added).

21. Testimony before the US Senate African Affairs Sub-committee, 29 January 1976, p. 20.

22. P. W. Botha's statement to the House of Assembly, Cape Town, 18 April 1978, according to documentary reports supplied by the South African embassy, London.

23. Jonathan Steele, *Guardian*, 11 May 1978.

24. Stockwell, op. cit., pp. 187–8.

25. Fidel Castro, Jamaica, 17 October 1977.

26. In September 1976, when Kissinger flew to southern Africa and launched his Rhodesian peace initiative, the author asked 'a high American official' aboard the secretary's plane if, by then, it had become clear whether the South Africans or the Cubans had sent in troops first. The reply was: 'All I know is that Radio Havana broadcast a report that Cuban soldiers were among the casualties sustained when the South Africans were advancing to the north, in support of the UNITA forces. Therefore they must have been there ahead of the South Africans.'

27. South African Defence Department, 3 February 1977.

28. Stockwell (op. cit., p. 170) reported that he had warned the US inter-departmental working group dealing with Angola to 'think in terms of ten to fifteen thousand Cuban soldiers, a squadron of MIGs and a hundred or so tanks', after what he called the first introduction of Cuban regular army units in early October. But, he said, the concept appeared to be too big for the group to accept and discussions were resumed on ways to deal with a mini-scale conflict.

29. Pretoria put out an official version of its role in the war one month after Castro authorized the well-known Colombian author, Gabriel García Márquez, to publish an account of Cuba's role in the MPLA victory.

30. Some Washington authorities, including Kissinger, held this to be a tidy *ex post facto* rationalization. They hammered the theme that the Cubans, deeply indebted economically and politically to the Russians, had acted as Moscow's 'surrogates'. But this interpretation was challenged long before the appearance of Márquez's account. The *Washington Post*, on 18 February 1976, quoted high American officials as saying they did not believe 'the Cubans were pressured by Moscow into furnishing men for the Angolan battlefields'. Castro, on the fifteenth anniversary of the Bay of Pigs affair of 19 April 1961, insisted that Moscow 'never requested' the dispatch of Cuban soldiers. Stockwell (op. cit., p. 172) reported that 'after the war we [the CIA] learned that Cuba had not been ordered into action by the Soviet Union'.

31. Matti Golan, *The Secret Conversation of Henry Kissinger*, published by Bantam Books in association with *The New York Times*, 1976.

32. *The Soviet Union and the Third World: A Watershed in Great Power Policy?*, a report to the Committee on International Relations, US House of Representatives, by the Senior Specialists' Division of the Congressional Research Service, 8 May 1977.

33. National Security Study Memorandum 39 (1969) was commissioned by Henry Kissinger when the Nixon administration assumed office and was compiled as an examination of relations between the United States and southern Africa. It set forth a series of policy options intended to shape the Republican administration's approach. While its accuracy was never disavowed, controversy arose over whether any of the options it presented actually were adopted by Nixon and Kissinger. In fact the nature of subsequent US actions tended to confirm what many congressmen believed which was that Option Two had been accepted as the basis for US policy. The text and an accompanying analysis of its contents are contained in *The Kissinger Study of Southern Africa*, edited and introduced by Mohamed A. El-Khawas and Barry Cohen, Lawrence Hill & Company, Westport, Connecticut, 1976.

34. Marcum's testimony to the US Senate African Affairs Sub-committee, 4 February 1976, p. 126.

35. This was a reference to the 1961 uprising of the Union of Angolan People (UPA), Roberto's group, which in 1962 merged into the newly formed FNLA. In an attempt to match the MPLA's first essay in insurgency, one month earlier, tribal bands loyal to Roberto set forth in the northern districts, with machetes and swords, on a wild attack against Portuguese settler families, the African wives of Portuguese, mulattos and *assimilados*. The Portuguese an-

nounced that 267 'mainly Europeans' had been murdered and seventy-two were missing. The reprisals that followed within six weeks were, by all accounts, horrendous. Portuguese paratroopers and commandos from Portugal joined local forces and between 10,000 and 20,000 blacks were said to have been slain. Around 600,000 Bakongo fled to Zaire.

Chapter 11. The Horn of Africa

1. John Markakis and Nega Ayele, *Class and Revolution in Ethiopia*, published by Spokesman for *The Review of African Political Economy*, Nottingham, 1978, p. 114.

2. This version of the event was told to the author by Ethiopian diplomats and others, representing non-aligned nations, serving in Addis Ababa.

3. Even tsarist Russia in the late nineteenth century had a finger in the Ethiopian pie. But the pie was too hot and, in 1889, a Russian military expedition, attacked by the French at Sagallo, soon returned home. The region nevertheless remained tempting enough for leaders like Khrushchev and Brezhnev to keep their gaze fixed on it and to remain ready to reach out again when there would be less risk of being burned.

4. Sources: military aid, 1955–74, US Department of State report on *Communist Aid to Less Developed Countries in 1974*; economic aid, from *Communist Aid to Less Developed Countries of the Free World 1977*, a CIA research paper prepared at the National Foreign Assessment Center, Washington DC, November 1978, pp. 19–20.

5. *New Times*, no. 7, 1978, p. 4.

6. Donald H. Rumsfeld, *Annual Report of the Defense Department, Fiscal Year 1978*, Washington DC, 1977, p. 22.

7. Extracted from a State Department summary of Kissinger's speech to US ambassadors in London, December 1975.

8. Amnesty International, the world-wide movement professing to be independent, non-ideological and apolitical, reported in November 1978 that 'a consistent pattern of gross violations of fundamental human rights' had developed since the Dergue took office. It drew a picture of 'large-scale killings of civilians in areas of armed conflict', 'thousands of deaths' of political opponents in what it called a campaign of 'red terror' and of torture and repression. In response the Addis Ababa regime accused Amnesty International of conspiring with 'the enemies of the Ethiopian revolution' to spread venomous propaganda.

9. One key Soviet general advising, if not commanding, the Ethiopians was Vasily I. Petrov, first deputy commander-in-chief of Soviet ground forces. Raúl Castro, brother of Cuba's president, was Havana's ranking representative.

10. The air- and sea-lift of equipment for an entire division began from southern Soviet bases thirteen days after Somalia expelled 2,500 Russian specialists, advisers and technicians. Almost certainly advance planning had taken place. Allied intelligence authorities, as well as Third World governments, were impressed by the Soviet logistic performance. 'It was a brilliant operation,' one western intelligence officer told the author. 'It had to be coordinated with the

arrival of thousands of Cubans from different directions.' The CIA estimated arms and materials worth $1,000 million were supplied – but Moscow never disclosed details of its investment.

11. Mengistu, on the fifth anniversary of Haile Selassie's overthrow, announced the formation of a commission to draw up a party structure for the organization of the country's workers. The chief of government himself would preside over the commission. The promise to phase out the rule of the Dergue was made by Mengistu on 13 September 1979, with the late Soviet Prime Minister Alexei Kosygin at his elbow.

12. James Mayall, *The World Today*, September 1978, in an article entitled 'The Battle for the Horn: Somali Irredentism and International Diplomacy'.

13. Dimitri K. Simes, *Washington Review*, May 1978, in an article entitled 'Imperial Globalism in the Making', published by the CSIS, Georgetown University, Washington DC.

14. Jack Shepherd, *The Politics of Starvation*, Carnegie Endowment for International Peace, 1975.

15. Markakis and Ayele, op. cit.

16. ibid., pp. 112, 113.

17. John H. Spencer was chief adviser to the Ethiopian Foreign Ministry before the war. Hearings before the US Senate African Affairs Sub-committee, 4 August 1976, pp. 17–21; Sir Anthony Eden (Lord Avon), *Facing the Dictators*, Cassell, 1962.

18. John Spencer testified: 'The base at Asmara had little to do with either Ethiopia or Africa.' A twenty-five-year leasing arrangement reached in 1953 provided Ethiopia with rental, the spending power of an eventual 2,500 US specialists and annual military aid and economic packages. In the twenty-one years ending in 1974 this aid, excluding cash weapon purchases, exceeded $400 million.

19. 'The Horn of Africa: An Assessment of the Regional Military Balance', report delivered by US deputy assistant secretary of defence, Franklin D. Kramer, in testimony before the Africa Sub-committee of the US House of Representatives, 25 February 1980.

Index

Addis Ababa, 46, 73–4, 75, 303n8; Afro-Arab conference, 105, 108, 294n2; link with Djibouti, 262; and Eritrean independence, 268

Adowa, Italian defeat, 277

Aeroflot, USSR national airline, 102, 293n12

Afars and Issas, French Territory of the, 260, 262, 266; *see also* Djibouti

Afghanistan, 75, 163; USSR invasion, 74, 162, 253, 283, 284; world reaction, 92, 125; UN and, 265

Africa, 15; arena of competing power interests, 16f, 28–32, 36, 40, 68, 71; colonial legacy, 16, 27, 35f, 148, 290n2; Africa for the Africans solution, 16, 86f, 159; evolution of one-party political system, 18, 36, 287n11; black-ruled nations, 28 (Fig. 4); civil and trans-border strife, 28–9, 35, 64; possession of strategic raw materials, 32f, 56, 96, 117, 134, 163–4, 176; 1968–74 drought, 34; imposition of sophisticated political systems, 36f; experience of colonial governments, 36–7; major part of Third World, 38f; struggle for total independence, 39, 60, 64; geographical features, 49–51; variation in ethnic groups, 51; earlier civilizations, 51; fifteenth-century explorations, 53; demographic factors, 55, 289n19; havoc due to excesses of dictators, 63; post-independence violence and foreign domination, 64–5; rate of militarization, 67, 78; Soviet discovery of, 87–9 (*see also* Soviet Union); anchorages and refuelling stations, 95, 100, 102, 163; industrialization, 96; past and present recipients of Soviet military aid, 103 (Fig. 9); de-colonization process, 150, 189; struggle to end white-minority rule, 170; north-south dialogue, 179; French activism, 173–83; and racism, 203

'African Economic Community', 16

African National Congress (ANC), 97, 220

Africans: standard of living, 18; and UK attitude to *apartheid*, 19; ravages of war,

famine and disease, 27, 33–4, 45, 48, 49; impact of slave traffic, 30, 53, 55, 57; black refugees and displaced people, 33–4; life expectancy, 33–4, 46; irrelevance of ideological concepts, 37; socio-economic–agricultural needs, 37, 45, 67; and Great Uhuru Railway, 40–41; effects of *oncho*, 44; unrecorded migrations, 50; tribalism, 52; attitude to religion, 52–3; system of sacrifice, 52–3; human foes, 53–6; kinship status, 53; contribution to US and Caribbean output, 55; treatment by Leopold II, 57–8; illiteracy at de-colonization, 58; average annual cash earnings, 59; areas of employment, 59; inappropriate white political systems, 59–60; leaders' excesses at independence, 60–61, 72; areas of refuge after overthrow, 62 (Fig. 7); characterization of post-independence leaders, 64–5; hatred of *apartheid*, 66; need for Soviet understanding, 93–4, 98; concern with anti-colonialism, 94; assumed incapable of government, 118; Cuban identification, 119; Chinese demand for low-cost labour, 135; and communist seducers, 149, 201; US civil-rights movement, 155, 159; and Mugabe's victory, 189; creation of bourgeoisie, 290n2

Afro-Asian conference, Bandung 1955, 130

Agnew, Spiro T., 144

agriculture, 45, 56, 58; cattle deaths in the Sahel, 34, 286n7; agrarian reform movement, 48–9

air force; French, 69, 173f, 297n6; in francophone Africa, 175; anti-guerrilla campaign, 1978, 179

air force, Soviet, 100

Ake, Claude, on African bourgeoisie, 290n2

Algeria, 35, 99; and Morocco, 29, 37, 69, 109; Soviet aid, 70; expenditure on arms, 79; USSR/China and liberation struggle, 130; France and, 147, 148, 152; US and, 152, 179; vestiges of slavery, 289n19